The Other Judaisms of Late Antiquity

LEC

Library *of* Early Christology

Larry W. Hurtado
David B. Capes
April D. DeConick
Editors

SERIES INTRODUCTION

Forty years ago, Larry Hurtado set out on a quest to undo the pervasive influence of Bousset's *Kyrios Christos* in "history of religions" discussions regarding early Christian belief, specifically its Christology. Over the course of his career, he drew various compatriots to the cause and so formed a "new history of religions school." This series is a collaborative effort between Carey Newman, April DeConick, David Capes, and Larry Hurtado to bring together representative works of that "school," with a focus on the study of early Christology and its historic, Judaic antecedents. Most of these are titles originally published by other publishers as part of limited-run series. Baylor University Press has reached out to friends at Mohr Siebeck, Brill, and Fortress to secure North American print rights, and so bring these works to a new and wider audience. This series will be offered as an "essential reading" set with special appeal to seminary/religion students. We look forward to adding additional volumes to this library in the years ahead.

Available from the Library of Early Christology Series

Bousset, Wilhelm. *Kyrios Christos: A History of the Belief in Christ from the Beginnings of Christianity to Irenaeus*

Capes, David B. *Old Testament Yahweh Texts in Paul's Christology*

DeConick, April D. *Seek to See Him: Ascent and Vision Mysticism in the Gospel of Thomas*

Fossum, Jarl E. *The Name of God and the Angel of the Lord: Samaritan and Jewish Concepts of Intermediation and the Origin of Gnosticism*

Gieschen, Charles A.. *Angelomorphic Christology: Antecedents and Early Evidence*

Hengel, Martin. *Between Jesus and Paul: Studies in the Earliest History of Christianity*

Hurtado, Larry W. *Ancient Jewish Monotheism and Early Christian Jesus-Devotion: The Context and Character of Christological Faith*

Juel, Donald H. *Messianic Exegesis: Christological Interpretation of the Old Testament in Early Christianity*

Newman, Carey C. *Paul's Glory-Christology: Tradition and Rhetoric*

Newman, Carey C., James R. Davila, and Gladys S. Lewis, editors. *The Jewish Roots of Christological Monotheism: Papers from the St Andrews Conference on the Historical Origins of the Worship of Jesus*

Segal, Alan F. *The Other Judaisms of Late Antiquity: Second Edition*

Segal, Alan F. *Two Powers in Heaven: Early Rabbinic Reports about Christianity and Gnosticism*

Stuckenbruck, Loren T. *Angel Veneration and Christology. A Study in Early Judaism and in the Christology of the Apocalypse of John*

The Other Judaisms of Late Antiquity

Second Edition

Now includes
"Heavenly Ascent in Hellenistic Judaism, Early Christianity, and Their Environment"

Alan F. Segal

BAYLOR UNIVERSITY PRESS

The Other Judaisms of Late Antiquity published in 1987 by Scholars Press.

Cover Design by Nicole Holmes
Cover image: From a floor mosaic in the ancient synagogue at Beit Alpha, Israel.

Library of Congress Cataloging-in-Publication Data for the original Scholars Press edition:

Segal, Alan F. 1945–2011.
The other Judaisms of late antiquity / by Alan F. Segal
p. cm. — (Brown Judaic studies; no. 127)
Includes bibliographical references and index.
ISBN 1-555-40178-3 (alk. paper)
1. Judaism—History—Post-exilic period, 586 B.C.–210 A.D.
2. Judaism—History—Talmudic period, 10–425. 3. Judaism—
Doctrines. I. Title. II. Series.
BM176.S44 1987
296/.09/015—dc19

The Baylor University Press ISBN is 978-1-4813-0759-8.

Printed in the United States of America on acid-free paper with a minimum of 30 percent post-consumer waste recycled content.

CONTENTS

ABBREVIATIONS

1 Apol.	Justin Martyr, *1 Apology*
1QapGen ar	Genesis Apocryphon
1QH	Thanksgiving Scroll
1QS	Community Rule
1/2 Clem.	1/2 Clement
1/2/3 En.	1/2/3 Enoch
2/3/4 Bar.	2/3/4 Baruch
Abr.	Philo, *On the Life of Abraham*
Acts Paul	Acts of Paul
Acts Pil.	Acts of Pilate
ANRW	*Aufstieg und Niedergang der römischen Welt: Geschichte und Kultur Rom sim Spiegel der neueren Forschung.* Part 2: *Principat.* Edited by Hildegard Temporini and Wolfgang Haase. Berlin: de Gruyter, 1972–
Ant.	Josephus, *Jewish Antiquities*
Ap. John	Apocryphon of John
Apoc. Ab.	Apocalypse of Abraham
Apoc. Mos.	Apocalypse of Moses
Apol.	Justin Martyr, *Apology*
An.	Tertullian, *The Soul*
AR	*Archiv für Religionswissenschaft*
As. Mos.	Assumption of Moses
Ascen. Isa.	Ascension of Isaiah
b. B. Bat.	Babylonian Talmud Tractate Baba Batra
b. Ber.	Babylonian Talmud Tractate Berakhot
b. Hag.	Babylonian Talmud Tractate Hagigah
b. Hul.	Babylonian Talmud Tractate Hullin
b. Sanh.	Babylonian Talmud Tractate Sanhedrin

b. Shabb.	Babylonian Talmud Tractate Shabbat
b. Sukk.	Babylonian Talmud Tractate Sukkot
b. Yebam.	Babylonian Talmud Tractate Yebamot
BG	Berlin Gnostic Codex
BZNW	Beihefte zur Zeitschrift für die neutestamentliche Wissenschaft
C. Gal	Julian, *Against the Galileans*
CBQ	*Catholic Bible Quarterly*
Cels.	Origen, *Against Celsus*
Cher.	Philo, *On the Cherubim*
CIL	*Corpus Inscriptionum Latinarum.* Berlin, 1862–
CIS	*Corpus Inscriptionum Semiticarum.* Paris, 1881–
Comm. Jo.	Origen, *Commentary on the Gospel of John*
Corp. herm.	Corpus hermeticum
CPJ	*Corpus Papyrorum Judaicarum.* Edited by Victor A. Tcherikover. 3 vols. Cambridge, Mass.: Harvard University Press, 1957–1964.
Dial.	Justin Martyr, *Dialogue with Trypho*
Dial.	Origen, *Dialogue with Heraclides*
De Decal.	Philo, *On the Decalogue*
De Trin.	Novation, *On the Trinity*
Deus	Philo, *That God Is Unchangeable*
Eccles. Rab.	Ecclesiastes Rabbah
Ecl.	Vergil, *Eclogues*
Eph.	Ignatius, *To the Ephesians*
Epid.	Irenaeus, *Demonstrations of the Apostolic Preaching*
EPRO	Études Préliminaires aux Religions Orientales dans l'Empire Romain
Eqev	Parashat Eqev (Deuteronomy 7:12–11:25)
Exod. Rab.	Exodus Rabbah
FRLANT	Forschungen zur Religion und Literatur des Alten und Neuen Testaments
FG	Fourth Gospel
Fug.	Philo, *On Flight and Finding*
GCS	Die griechsischen christlichen Schriftsteller der ersten [drei] Jahrhunderte
Gen. Rab.	Genesis Rabbah
Gos. Eg.	Gospel of the Egyptians

Haer.	Hippolytus, *Refutation of All Heresies*
Haer.	Irenaeus, *Against Heresies*
Hist.	Livy, *History of Rome*
Hist. Eccl.	Eusebius, *Ecclesiastical History*
HTR	*Harvard Theological Review*
Hyp. Arch.	Hypostasis of the Archons
IG	*Inscriptiones Graecae. Editio Minor.* Berlin: de Gruyter, 1924–
Il.	Homer, *Iliad*
Int	*Interpretation*
J.W.	Josephus, *Jewish War*
JANES	*Journal of the Ancient Near Eastern Society of Columbia University*
JB	Jerusalem Bible
JJS	*Journal of Jewish Studies*
Jos.	Philo, *On the Life of Joseph*
Jos. Asen.	Joseph and Aseneth
JQR	*Jewish Quarterly Review*
JSJ	*Journal for the Study of Judaism in the Persian, Hellenistic, and Roman Periods*
JTS	*Journal of Theological Studies*
Jub.	Jubilees
LCL	Loeb Classical Library
Leg.	Philo, *Allegorical Interpretation*
Legat.	Philo, *On the Embassy to Gaius*
m. Naz.	Mishnah Tractate Nazir
m. Ned.	Mishnah Tractate Nedarim
m. Shav.	Mishnah Tractate Shavuot
m. Tamid	Mishnah Tractate Tamid
Mek. Exod.	Mekhilta Exodus
Metam.	Ovid, *Metamorphoses*
Midr. Rab.	Midrash Rabbah
Migr.	Philo, *On the Migration of Abraham*
Mor.	Plutarch, *Moralia*
Mos.	Philo, *On the Life of Moses*
MRI	Mekhilta R. Ishmael
MRSbY	Mekhilta R. Simeon
Mut.	Philo, *On the Change of Names*

Nat.	Pliny, *Natural History*
NAWG	Nachrichten (von) der Akademie der Wissenschaften in Göttingen
NedTT	*Nederlands theologisch tijdschrift*
NHC	Nag Hammadi Codex
NovTSup	Supplements to Novum Testamentum
NTD	Das Neue Testament Deutsch
NTS	*New Testament Studies*
Num. Rab.	Numbers Rabbah
OCD	*Oxford Classical Dictionary*
Opif.	Philo, *On the Creation of the World*
Or.	Origen, *On Prayer*
Orig. World	On the Origin of the World
PAAJR	*Proceedings of the American Academy of Jewish Research*
Pan.	Epiphanius, *Refutation of All Heresies*
PGM	*Papyri Graecae Magicae: Die griechischen Zauberpapyri.* Edited by K. Preisendanz et al. 2 vols. Dresden: Teubner, 1928–1931. 2nd revised edition edited by A. Henrichs. Stuttgart: Teubner, 1973–1974.
PR	Pesikta Rabbati
Praem.	Philo, *On Rewards and Punishments*
PRK	Pesikta R. Kahana
Praep. ev.	Eusebius, *Preparation for the Gospel*
Princ.	Origen, *On First Principles*
Prot.	Clement of Alexandria, *Exhortation to the Greeks*
Ps. Rab.	Psalms Rabbah
PW	*Paulys Real-Encyclopadie der classicshen Altertumswissenschaft.* New edition by Georg Wissowa and Wilhelm Kroll. 50 vols. in 84 parts. Stuttgart: Metzler and Druckenmüller, 1894–1980.
QE 1/2	Philo, *Questions and Answers on Exodus* 1/2
QG	Philo, *Questions in Genesis*
RB	*Revue biblique*
Recog.	Ps.-Clement, *Recognitions*
Rep.	Cicero, *Republic*
Rep.	Plato, *Republic*
RivB	*Rivista biblica italiana*
Rom. Hist.	Cassius Dio, *Roman History*

Sat.	Juvenal, *Satires*
SANT	Studien zum Alten und Neuen Testaments
SBLDS	SBL Dissertation Series
SBT	Studies in Biblical Theology
Sib. Or.	Sibylline Oracles
Scorp.	Tertullian, *Antidote for the Scorpion's Sting*
SLJA	Studies in Judaism in Late Antiquity
SNTSMS	Society for New Testament Studies Monograph Series
Somn.	Philo, *On Dreams*
SPAW	Sitzungsberichte der preussischen Akademie der Wissenschaften
Spec. Leg.	Philo, *On the Special Laws*
ST	*Studia Theologica*
Strom.	Clement of Alexandria, *Stromateis*
SUNT	Studien zum Neuen Testament
SwJT	*Southwestern Journal of Theology*
T. Ab.	Testament of Abraham
T. Benj.	Testament of Benjamin
T. Job	Testament of Job
T. Jud.	Testament of Judah
T. Levi	Testament of Levi
Tanh. Noah	Tanhumah Noah
TDNT	*Theological Dictionary of the New Testament.* Edited by Gerhard Kittel and Gerhard Friedrich. Translated by Geoffrey W. Bromiley. 10 vols. Grand Rapids: Eerdmans, 1964–1976.
Theol. Plat.	Proclus, *Platonic Theology*
TUGAL	Texte und Untersuchungen zur Geschichte der altchristlichen Literatur
TWNT	*Theologische Wörterbuch zum Neuen Testament.* Edited by Gerhard Kittel and Gerhard Friedrich. Stuttgart: Kohlhammer, 1932–1979.
VC	*Vigiliae Christianae*
Vit. Apoll.	Philostratus, *Life of Apollonius*
Vit. Pyth.	Iamblichus, *Life of Pythagoras*
Wis. Jes. Chr.	Wisdom of Jesus Christ
WMANT	Wissenschaftliche Monographien zum Atlen und Neuen Testament

WUNT	Wissenschaftliche Untersuchungen zum Neuen Testament
y. Ber.	Jerusalem Talmud Tractate Berakhot
y. Ta'an.	Jerusalem Talmud Tractate Ta'anit
ZNW	*Zeitschrift für die neutestamentliche Wissenschaft und die Kunde der älteren Kirche*

PART ONE

THE OTHER JUDAISMS OF LATE ANTIQUITY

INTRODUCTION TO THE FIRST EDITION

The Other Judaisms of Late Antiquity is an unexpected surprise and pleasure, for the impetus came from Jacob Neusner, the editor of the Brown Judaica Series, not from me. I am particularly grateful to him for his suggestion in 1985 that my essays be published together in one place. Although I am not Professor Neusner's student, he has been a sympathetic reader. The delay in publication has been due to a number of other tasks I have had to undertake and to the difficulties associated with transferring articles from one computer to another. I am especially glad to get the book out at this time. These chapters follow my academic wanderings. After graduate school at Yale and several years of teaching at Princeton, my academic career took me abroad, first to Israel on a Guggenheim grant, where I researched ascension texts, and then to Toronto for two years, before joining the Religion Departments of Barnard and Columbia. So my published work has been scattered widely. In Canada especially I began work with colleagues that continued after I changed teaching assignments. Some of the work in these volumes derives from research done in Toronto and for papers prepared for seminars of the Canadian Society for Biblical Studies—first, the Christian Anti-Judaism seminar and, second, the Torah-Nomos seminar, chaired by G. Peter Richardson and Stephen Wilson conjointly.

This volume gives me an opportunity to publish my work in the United States and also to get some new material out for scholarly scrutiny. It also gives me the opportunity to reflect, edit, correct, and revalue some of my earlier work. I have altered texts where needed and where the original could not be reproduced easily. I have also rethought many arguments. Consequently, some essays have been changed substantially.

The title should not mislead anyone into thinking that I consider only non-rabbinic Judaism in the book. Although each chapter partly focuses on non-rabbinic Judaism of the first few centuries, I consider each community in relationship to rabbinic Judaism. My purpose throughout has been to portray rabbinic Judaism and Christianity as deeply related Jewish movements of the first few centuries. During this critical period of their separation, they are often more aptly described as two kinds of Judaism than two different religions, for some varieties of Christianity and Judaism were more like the opposing religion than their ostensible siblings. To help define the relationships, underline the differences and avoid obvious prejudices, I have always relied heavily on methods developed in the social sciences. These chapters exemplify the issues and the methods.

The chapter, "Dualism in Judaism, Christianity, and Gnosticism," summarizes some of the research done in my book, *Two Powers in Heaven*. I try to show that in back of the rabbinic traditions about "two powers in heaven" was a halakic, exegetical, sociological, and theological issue about the status of angelic mediators in first-century Judaism. The book grew out of courses at Yale with Judah Goldin, Wayne Meeks, and N. A. Dahl. It began as an historical addendum to a passage in Parashat Shirata in the Mekhilta, given a literary analysis by my adviser and teacher Judah Goldin in his book *The Song at the Sea*.[1] The biggest impetus for new insights came from the research, encouragement, suggestions, as well as the very perspicacious comments and hunches of Professor N. A. Dahl.[2] Sid Z. Leiman read the manuscript and offered many important comments and corrections. With such good help, I was able to outline a relationship between rabbinic literature and early Christianity which was never clearly seen before. Though the halakic and exegetical issues were novel in themselves, the real surprise was that these issues concealed some of the sociological causes of the split between Judaism and Christianity.

[1] *The Song at the Sea: Being a Commentary on a Commentary in Two Parts* (New Haven, Conn.: Yale University Press, 1971); see also idem, "Not by Means of an Angel and Not by Means of a Messenger," in *Religions in Antiquity: Essays in Memory of Erwin Ramsdell Goodenough*, ed. J. Neusner (Leiden: Brill, 1968), 412–24.

[2] See "The Johannine Church and History," in *Current Issues in New Testament Interpretation*, ed. W. Klassen and G. F. Snyder (New York: Harper & Row, 1962), 124–42; *The Crucified Messiah and Other Essays* (Minneapolis: Augsburg, 1974); and *Das Volk Gottes: Eine Untersuchung zum Kirchenbewusstsein des Urchristentums* (Darmstadt: Wissenschaftliche Buchgesellschaft, 1963).

Two Powers in Heaven had implications for the study of Philo, rabbinic Judaism, early Christianity, and Gnosticism. Professor Dahl and I first followed up a hunch about how Philo's exegeses relate to rabbinic ones, in "Philo and the Rabbis on the Names of God."[3] Thereafter I wrote a piece contrasting the social position of the Johannine community with that of the rabbis, based upon their traditions of the "Lord of the World."[4] In it I tried to underline one historical relationship between Judaism, Johannine Christianity, and the rise of Gnosticism. The work was suggested by reading and discussing some issues of early Christianity with Mary Douglas. More recently, this work has been followed up by Jerome Neyrey.[5]

Not surprisingly, *Two Powers in Heaven* has received most attention from scholars interested in the rise of Gnosticism. I am especially proud to have made a contribution there. Foremost among those encouraging the work has been Gilles Quispel.[6] I would not claim that "two

[3] See "Philo and the Rabbis on the Name of God," *JSJ* 10 (1979): 1–28, not reprinted here.

[4] "Ruler of this World: Attitudes about Mediator Figures and the Importance of Sociology for Self-Definition," in *Jewish and Christian Self-Definition*, vol. 2, *Aspects of Judaism in the Greco-Roman Period*, ed. E. P. Sanders with A. I. Baumgarten and Alan Mendelson (Philadelphia: Fortress, 1981), 245–68, 403–13, reprinted with permission.

[5] Jerome Neyrey, "'My Lord and My God': The Divinity of Jesus in John's Gospel," in *Society of Biblical Literature 1986 Seminar Papers*, ed. David J. Lull, SBLSP 25 (Atlanta: Scholars Press, 1986), 152–82.

[6] See Gilles Quispel, "The Demiurge in the Apocryphon of John," in *Nag Hammadi and Gnosis*, ed. R. Mc. L. Wilson (Leiden: Brill, 1978), 1–33, esp. 24–27; I. P. Culianu, "The Angels of the Nations and the Origins of Gnostic Dualism," in *Studies in Gnosticism and Hellenistic Religions: Presented to Gilles Quispel on the Occasion of his Sixty-Fifth Birthday*, ed. R. van den Broek and M. J. Vermaseren (Leiden: Brill, 1981)—hereafter cited as *Studies in Gnosticism*; I. Gruenwald, "The Problem of Anti-Gnostic Polemic in Rabbinic Literature," in *Studies in Gnosticism*, 171–89; idem, "Jewish Sources for the Gnostic Texts from Nag Hammadi?" in *Proceedings of the Sixth World Congress of Jewish Studies* (Jerusalem: World Congress of Jewish Studies, 1977), 45–56; idem, "Aspects of the Jewish-Gnostic Controversy," in *The Rediscovery of Gnosticism: Proceedings of the International Conference in Gnosticism at Yale University March 28–31, 1978*, 2 vols., ed. B. Layton (Leiden: Brill, 1981), 2:713–23—hereafter cited as *The Rediscovery of Gnosticism*; E. M. Yamauchi, "Jewish Gnosticism? The Prologue of John, Mandaean Parallels, and the Trimorphic Protennoia," in *Studies in Gnosticism*, 467–97, esp. 489–97; N. A. Dahl, "The Arrogant Archon and the Lewd Sophia: Jewish Traditions in Gnostic Revolt," in *The Rediscovery of Gnosticism*, 2:689–712, esp. 689–706; R. van den Broek, "The Present State of Gnostic Studies," *VC* 37 (1983): 41–71, esp. 56–62; Gilles Quispel, "Gnosis," *Die orientalischen Religionen im Roemerreich*, ed. M. J. Vermaseren (Leiden: Brill, 1981), 413–35; Jarl E. Fossum, "The

powers heresy" was the only way to understand Gnosticism. Gnosticism is a wide and varied phenomenon, partly a convenient invention of twentieth-century intellectual history. Furthermore, some gnostic groups had nothing to do with Judaism. But the relationship between "two powers in heaven" heresies in rabbinic Judaism and Gnosticism is representative of a wider process of polemic within the ancient world. Gnosticism seems to have translated the opposition of many communities into their mythology. In gnostic eyes, the God of the Jews became an evil demiurge. Elaine Pagels' book, *The Gnostic Gospels*,[7] pointed out a different but similar polemical projection of earthly opposition into cosmology, since the gnostics' description of orthodox bishops corresponds to their descriptions of the evil archons. Though the two polemics are linguistically unrelated, the method and dynamic underlying them is similar. Both reflect gnostic responses to criticism by projection of the opposition into supernaturally evil opponents. Although the consensus built on our two independent studies does not yield a complete picture of the nature of gnostic exegesis, we have isolated in our different ways, an important characteristic of Gnosticism.[8]

Ten years have passed since *Two Powers in Heaven* was published. During that time, the book has also played a role in a number of other discussions—notably in midrashic studies and primitive Christology, Samaritanism, and early Jewish mysticism.[9] Various concepts of intermediation, especially the mediation of angelic figures, were noted by early rabbinic literature and clearly have some bearing on defining apocalypticism and unraveling the earliest Christologies.[10] Several new

---

Origin of the Gnostic Concept of the Demiurge," *Ephemerides Theologicae Lovanienses* 61 (1985): 142–52, esp. 144; and idem, "Gen. 1,26 and 2,7 in Judaism, Samaritanism and Gnosticism," *JSJ* 16, no. 2 (1985): 202–39, esp. 207–17, 224–29, 236–39.

[7] Elaine Pagels, *The Gnostic Gospels* (New York: Random House, 1979).

[8] See also the very important book by Klaus Koschorke, *Die Polemik der Gnostiker gegen das kirchliche Christentum* (Leiden: Brill, 1978). He stresses the inner Christian polemic.

[9] See I. Gruenwald, "Anti-Gnostic Polemic"; P. W. van der Horst, "De joodse toneelschrijver Ezechiel," *Nederlands Theologisch Tijdschrift* 36, no. 2 (1982): 97–112; Baruch M. Bokser, "Recent Developments in the Study of Judaism, 70–200 C.E.," *The Second Century: A Journal of Early Christian Studies* 3 (1983): 1–69, esp. 32–36; Christopher Rowland, *The Open Heaven: A Study of Apocalyptic in Judaism and Early Christianity* (London: SPCK, 1982), 462, 468–73, 496.

[10] See esp. Jarl E. Fossum, *The Name of God and the Angel of the Lord: Samaritan and Jewish Concepts of Intermediation and the Origin of Gnosticism*, WUNT (Tübingen: Mohr Siebeck, 1985), 17, 197, 227 29, 310, 319–21; also see idem, "Kyrios Jesus as the Angel of the

studies of "two powers" in Philonic Judaism, Qumran, and Christianity are underway in the United States, Canada and Europe. Professor Larry W. Hurtado, for instance, suggests that the worship of the second power was a decisive, and characteristically Christian innovation, which became determinative of Christian heresy so far as rabbinic Judaism was concerned.[11] Professor D. Juel shows that the traditions of the second power in heaven were discussed in exegetical fragments and not part of a packaged formulation of the return of a preexistent well-defined heavenly figure.[12]

All this interest suggests that much more can be said on the subject of "two powers in heaven," so I cannot claim to have been comprehensive. But I can claim that my findings were an impetus to a number of other scholars working in different fields. My book was one of the first to see the importance of the problem "two powers" for the history of religion, though it was primarily a study of midrash. If I were to mention the areas in which considerably more work could still be done, I would mention midrash,[13] but also the philosophical background of the problem of the *deuteros theos*, which is now becoming evident,[14] and the relationship between "two powers" and stories of creation. This issue has come into new focus from the Nag Hammadi material and the new and very complete treatment by Jarl Fossum[15] of the problem generally and the Samaritan context for the debate. Fossum shows that the link

---

Lord in Jude 5-7," *NTS* 33 (1987): 226–43. See also the debate engendered by J. D. G. Dunn's work, esp. *Christology in the Making: A New Testament Inquiry into the Origins of the Doctrine of the Incarnation* (Philadelphia: Westminster, 1980). Some of the debate has been well captured in *Christology and Exegesis*, ed. Robert Jewett (Chico, Calif.: Scholars, 1985) and partly deals with the problem of Hellenistic Jewish intermediation—esp. J. D. G. Dunn, "Some Clarifications on Issues of Method: A Reply to Holladay and Segal," 97–105; L. W. Hurtado, "New Testament Christology: Retrospect and Prospect," 15–29; Robert Jewett, "New Testament Christology: The Current Dialogue between Systematic Theologians and Biblical Scholars," 3–14; Donald Juel, "Incarnation and Redemption: A Response to Reginald H. Fuller," 117–21, esp. 118; Alan F. Segal, "Pre-Existence and Incarnation: A Response to Dunn and Holladay," 83–97.

[11] L. W. Hurtado, *One God, One Lord* (Philadelphia: Fortress, 1988).

[12] Donald Juel, *Messianic Exegesis* (Philadelphia: Fortress, 1987).

[13] See, e.g., the interesting start made by Rosalie Gershenzon and Elieser Slomovic, "A Second-Century Jewish-Gnostic Debate: Rabbi Jose ben Halafta and the Matrona," *JSJ* 16 (1985): 1–41.

[14] Gilles Quispel, "Review of J. Frickel, *Hellenistische Erloesung in christlicher Deutung*," *VC* 39 (1985): 186–88.

[15] Fossum, *Name of God and the Angel of the Lord*.

between the cooperating powers in Hellenistic Judaism and Christianity and the antagonistic creator God of Gnosticism may be found in Samaritanism, where there are uniquely positive notions of angelic participation in the creation.

After *Two Powers in Heaven*, I became interested in the social description of first-century Judaism. I was able to indulge my sociological and anthropological inquiries with the data I compiled for *Two Powers in Heaven* in "Ruler of the World," written for the McMaster Conference in Normative Self-Definition, as mentioned above. Much of this work developed in dialogue with Professor Wayne Meeks in classes at Yale as well as with Professors John Gager and Mary Douglas as colleagues at Princeton.

Thereafter, I wrote several pieces which attacked difficult problems in Hellenistic religion by resorting to structural theory. In "Heavenly Ascent in Hellenistic Judaism," I tried to use the structural study of myth to understand the so-called pre-Christian myth of the redeemed redeemer.[16] That article is not included here because it is too long, over one hundred pages of typescript, even without the bibliography at the end. In it, I set the groundwork for a larger study on ascension in the Hellenistic world, to which I hope to return soon. But meanwhile, many other scholars have concerned themselves with the problem.[17]

I applied structural theory of mythology and the anthropology of religion to the problems in defining Hellenistic magic.[18] In that study I attempted to show that social context affected the definition of magic in the ancient world in a way that suggested that religion and magic were a continuum, open to constant reinterpretation by the social actors.

[16] Alan F. Segal, "Heavenly Ascent in Hellenistic Judaism, Early Christianity and their Environments," *ANRW* 23.2:1333–94 (repr. as Part Two in this volume).

[17] The most complete work is I. P. Culianu, *Psychanodia I: A Survey of the Evidence Concerning the Ascension of the Soul and its Relevance* (Leiden: Brill, 1983), also a longer French work, *L'expériences de l'extase* (Paris: Payot, 1984). See also Martha Himmelfarb, "From Prophecy to Apocalypse: The *Book of the Watchers* and Tours of Heaven," in *Jewish Spirituality: From the Bible Through the Middle Ages*, ed. Arthur Green (New York: Crossroads, 1986), 145–65; idem, *Tours of Hell: The Development and Transmission of an Apocalyptic Form in Jewish and Christian Literature* (Philadelphia: University of Pennsylvania Press, 1983); Mary Dean-Otting, *Heavenly Journeys: A Study of the Motif in Hellenistic Jewish Literature* (New York: Peter Lang, 1984).

[18] "Hellenistic Magic: Some Questions of Definition," in *Studies in Gnosticism*, 349–75, reprinted with permission.

Another methodological foray took me into literary theory. The reason for looking in that direction was to solve an historical problem in the development of the Akedah tradition. I tried to show that a literary appreciation of the style of midrash helps us understand the historical development of the Akedah legends.[19]

The last chapters come from the Torah-Nomos seminar of the CSBS and were published in the Canadian journal for religious studies, *Studies in Religion/Sciences Religieuses*. Besides attempting to clarify aspects of the previous study of covenant, I also tried to show how social psychology and sociology help clarify these issues. These enterprises are more fully explored in my two books, *Rebecca's Children*,[20] a work for a general intellectual audience, and *Paul the Convert*,[21] its companion volume.

Rabbinic Judaism has always been studied by New Testament scholars, even if it was necessarily an incomplete study. One interesting and unanticipated corollary of these chapters, when they are read together for the first time, is their emphasis on using Christian texts for the reconstruction of first-century Judaism. Since the Mishnah is a late second-century document and, as Jacob Neusner has shown, often displays the attitudes of its latest redactors, it is not the best possible witness for first-century Judaism. The New Testament, although it is an unfriendly witness, for the most part contains an unmediated first-century report of Judaism, including the birth of the rabbinic movement. Hence, the traditional use of rabbinic sources for the exploration of Christianity is exactly backwards methodologically. The New Testament is one of the finest sources we have for the study of Judaism, in spite of its various biases. It needs to be read far more carefully and seriously by scholars equipped to read Jewish history and, of course, without falling victim to ancient polemics. The irony is that, although Judaism and Christianity have split to become two separate religious, the witness of each is necessary to understand the history of the other.

[19] Alan F. Segal, "'He Who Did Not Spare His Only Son . . .': Jesus, Paul and the Sacrifice of Isaac," in *From Jesus to Paul: Studies in Honour of F. W. Beare*, ed. Peter Richardson and John C. Hurd (Waterloo, Ontario: Wilfrid Laurier, 1984), 169–84, reprinted with permission.

[20] Alan F. Segal, *Rebecca's Children: Judaism and Christianity in the Roman World* (Cambridge, Mass.: Harvard University Press, 1986).

[21] Alan F. Segal, *Paul the Convert: The Apostolate and Apostasy of Saul the Pharisee* (New Haven, Conn.: Yale University Press, 1990).

I am grateful to Barnard College, which supported the word-processing of these articles and to Sue Zayac of the Columbia University Computer Center for trying to help me overcome some of the still insuperable technical problems of printing Hebrew and Greek. Thomas Boslooper and Avent Beck both helped input the data and prepared the indices. Professor Ogden Goelet took time out from his Egyptology to confer on setting up the laser printer and to help print the book. David Eaton and Rob Crutchfield at Mark of the Unicorn were very helpful in suggesting how to adapt *The Final Word II* to process older EMACS, MINCE, and FW files and to print the Hebrew and Greek. In the end, we had to give up trying to get pointed Hebrew or accented Greek. Consequently, I have used these foreign typefaces sparingly, for the purposes of clearing up possible confusions. Longer citations have been translated. The remaining problems will certainly be cleared up in time for the next manuscript. Thanks, too, to Tedd Byfield and Sandy Chiu for proofreading the manuscript with me. I am also grateful to Barnard College and the National Endowment for the Humanities, which shared in underwriting my sabbatical, when work for this book was begun. I am deeply appreciative of the support and financial assistance of Joan and Stanley Hart, fellow workers towards the common goal of Jewish-Christian understanding.

ONE

DUALISM IN JUDAISM, CHRISTIANITY, AND GNOSTICISM
A Definitive Issue

"Two Powers in Heaven"

Those rather rare heretics who believed in "two powers in heaven" (שתי רשויות בשמים) present a promising start for uncovering the vexed relationship between Judaism, Christianity, and Gnosticism. Some kind of dualistic doctrine seems inherent in the rabbinic designation and several scholars have seen a relationship between "two powers" and Christianity.[1] However, the rabbinic texts define "two powers in heaven" from a confusing variety of perspectives. Furthermore, the texts were written over a long period of time, probably referring to a variety of different phenomena, so only an outline of the complete problem can be presented here.[2]

[1] The study of rabbinic heretics (the *minim*) has had several distinguished forebears. See, e.g., M. Joël, *Blicke in die Religionsgeschichte zu Anfang des zweiten christlichen Jahrhunderts* (Breslau: Schottlaender, 1883), 2:711; I. Elbogen, *Der jüdische Gottesdients in seiner geschichtlichen Entwicklung* (Hildesheim: 1962), 36; M. Simon, *Verus Israel: Étude sur les relations entre Chrétiens et Juifs dans L'Empire Romain (135–425)* (Paris: de Boccard, 1964), 217f; R. Travers Herford, *Christianity in Talmud and Midrash* (London: Williams & Norgate, 1903), 1:362f; S. M. Wagner, "Religious Nonconformity in Ancient Jewish Life" (Ph.D. diss., Yeshiva University, 1964); A. Marmorstein, *Religionsgeschichtliche Studien: Die Bezeichnungen für Christen und Gnostischen im Talmud und Midras* (Schotschau: Selbst Verlag des Verfasser, 1910), 1:66–81; A. Büchler, "The Minim of Sepphoris and Tiberius in the Second and Third Centuries," in *Studies in Jewish History*, ed. I. Brodie and J. Rabinowitz (Oxford: Oxford University Press, 1956), 245–74. See also the works of Lieberman and Urbach.

[2] For further detail, see my book *Two Powers in Heaven: Early Rabbinic Reports about Christianity and Gnosticism* (Leiden: Brill, 1977). This chapter condenses several arguments from the book and has been used with permission.

The Mekhiltas

The best way to begin is to turn to some characteristic occurrences of the designation and try to outline the history of the heresy. The most significant passage may be found in several places in midrashic literature and is alluded to in many more. The tradition occurs often in different versions in the Mekhiltas. A simple form of the tradition occurs in the Mekhilta of Rabbi Simeon bar Yohai (hereafter cited as MRSbY). In the Mekhilta of Rabbi Ishmael (hereafter cited as MRI) the passage occurs in two places (Bahodesh 5 and Shirta 4) in virtually identical form. In Bahodesh alone, a closely related tradition, adduced in the name of R. Nathan, was added because of its obvious relevance. Finally, the tradition was known and discussed in Pesikta Rabbati (hereafter cited as PR), but there it has undergone considerable development.[3]

[3] "(Another comment: *Face after face*) R. Levi said: God faced them in many guises. To one He appeared standing, and to one seated; (see Gen 28:13 and Isa 6:1) to one as a young man, and to one as an old man. How so? At the time the Holy One, Blessed Be He, appeared on the Red Sea to wage war for His children and to requite the Egyptians, he faced them as a young man, since war is waged best by a young man, as it is said: *The Lord is a man of war, the Lord is His name* (Exod 15:3). And when the Holy One, Blessed Be He, appeared on Mount Sinai to give the Torah to Israel, He faced them as an old man, for Torah is at its best when it comes from the mouth of an old man. What is the proof! The verse: *With aged men is wisdom and understanding in length of days* (Job 12:12); and therefore Daniel said: I beheld till thrones were placed, and one that was Ancient of days did sit (Daniel 7:9)." In regard to God's guises R. Hiyya bar Abba said, "If a whoreson should say to you, 'They are two gods' quote God as saying in reply: I am the One of the Sea and I am the One of Sinai. (Another comment) R. Levi taught that at Sinai the Holy One, blessed be He, appeared to them with many faces, with a threatening face, with a severe face, with an angry face, with a joyous face, with a laughing face, with a friendly face. How so? . . . In regard to God's many faces, R. Hiyya bar Abba taught: Should a whoreson say to you, 'They are two gods,' reply to him, Scripture does not say 'The Gods have spoken . . . face after face' but *The Lord has spoken with you face after face*" (see PR I Piska 21 100b, in *Pesikta Rabbati: Discourses for Feasts, Fasts, and Special Sabbaths*, trans. W. Braude [New Haven, Conn.: Yale University Press, 1968], 421f.).

MRSbY	MRI
Bashalah 15, p. 81	Bahodesh 5; Shirta 4
Another interpretation: *YHWH is a man of war, YHWH is His name.*	
	I am YHWH your God: Why is this said?
Because, when the Holy One Blessed be He was revealed at the sea He appeared to them as a young man making war.	Because when He was revealed at the sea, He appeared to them as a young man making war. As it is said, *YHWH is a man of war.*
YHWH is His name.	
He appeared to them at Sinai like an old man, full of mercy:	He appeared at Sinai like an old man, full of mercy, as it is said: *and they saw the God of Israel* (Exod 24:10). And of the time after they had been redeemed what does it say? *And the like of the very heaven for clearness* (Exod 24:10).
	Again, it says,
I beheld 'til thrones were set down (Dan 7:9).	*I beheld 'til thrones were set down* (Dan 7:9). And it also says *A fiery stream issued and came forth from Him.*
So as not to give an opportunity to say "There are two powers in heaven." Rather	Scripture would not give an opportunity to the nations of the world to say "There are two powers" but declares:
YHWH is a man of war (Exod 15:3).	
	I am YHWH your God (Exod 20:2).
Another interpretation: YHWH is *a man of War.* YHWH fought in Egypt. YHWH fought at the Sea. And He is at the Jordan, He is at the Arnon streams.	I was in Egypt. I was at the Sea.
And He is in this world. And He is the world to come. He is in the past and He is in the future.	I was in the past, I will be in the future. I am in this world. I will be in the world to come.
As it is said: *Behold now, I, even I, am He,* etc. (Deut 32:39)	As it is said: *Behold now, that I, even I, am He,* etc. (Deut 32:39). *Even unto old age I am the same* (Isa 46:4).
Thus says YHWH the king of Israel, etc. *I am YHWH, the first and the last,* etc. (Isa 44:6).	*Thus YHWH the king of Israel and his redeemer, the Lord of Hosts, I am the first and the last* (Isa 44:6). And it says: *Who has wrought and done it? He that called the generations from the beginning. I, the Lord who am the first, and to the end I am He* (Isa 41:4).

In MRSbY the subject is introduced as an exegetical comment on the two statements made about YHWH in Exodus 15:3. The exegesis notes the repetition of the name YHWH in Exodus 15:3 and explains its significance. "YHWH is a man of war" is to be interpreted as a literal description, referring to God's manifestation as a young warrior when He destroyed the Egyptians at the Red Sea. "YHWH is His name" is necessary because at Sinai, He will reveal Himself as an old man, showing mercy. Hence, it is important for the Israelites to realize that the same God is speaking in both places, though the manifestations look different.[4]

The text in MRI is even more complex and is obviously the result of a long history of redaction. First, the issue is no longer merely the repetition of the divine name YHWH, because the biblical verse differs slightly. In this case, the dangerous doctrine is the idea that there are two different manifestations of God—one, a just, young man, appearing at the sea; the other, a merciful, old man, appearing at Sinai.[5] Neither MRI nor MRSbY can itself be the most ancient tradition. However, both are variations of it. The most ancient layer, which will later appear to be Tannaitic, must be carefully uncovered in comparing them and then comparing the rabbinic evidence with the Christian material, which can be accurately dated to the first century.

The common tradition must have been an exegesis of the meaning of the divine names, and probably also centered around the Sinai theophany. Daniel 7:9f. is a common proof text against the heresy. However, it is also likely to be the locus of a heretical argument since the passage describes two different figures in heaven in Daniel's night vision. Of course, the rabbis objected to such an idea, saying that the repetition

[4] See J. Lauterbach, "Some Clarifications of the Mekhilta," in *Sefer Klausner: A Collection of Science and Belle-lettres Gathered for Professor Klausner on His Sixtieth Birthday Celebration*, ed. Torchyner, Tcherikover, Kubeck, Shortrnan (Tel Aviv: 1937), 181–88, esp. 184–88. See also Judah Goldin, *The Song at the Sea* (New Haven, Conn.: Yale University Press, 1971), 126f.

[5] Space does not allow a complete discussion of the passage. But it should be noted that the rabbinic doctrine of the two middot or "measures" of God is implicit in this discussion in MRI. This aspect was missing in the version occurring in MRSbY. MRI has developed a special tradition about the discussion of God's attributes of justice and mercy, though the actual technical terms do not appear. The theme of God's justice and mercy is very important for dating the whole rabbinic tradition. We shall see that Philo and the midrash both record similar traditions about God's justice and mercy. For more detail on this aspect of the passage, see N. A. Dahl and Alan F. Segal, "Philo and the Rabbis on the Names of God," *JSJ* 9 (1978): 1f.

of divine names and the change in divine appearances were planned by God. From the rabbinic perspective, repetition of the divine name did not identify "two powers," but rather emphasized that the Israelites would have to recognize God in different forms throughout their history. In attempting to identify the heresy we should look for a doctrine which did associate "two powers" with the different names of God.

Other interesting details emerge from this passage. It is clear that the heretical doctrine in this particular case involves believing in two corresponding or cooperating deities. This means that the heretics who provoked this response from the rabbis are not dualists. Nor can they have been Marcionite Christians or extreme gnostics. Rather we have to look among the sects contemporary with the early rabbis for theologies with two complementary figures in heaven to find candidates for the heresy. This would include several of the apocalyptic systems where a central figure, like Michael, Melchizedek, or even a "son of man" were important partners of God in bringing redemption. No doubt, many varieties of Christians were also included, for Christianity was exceptionally interested in the interpretation of Daniel 7:9f. and Christianity is foremost most among those sects declaring a second divine hypostasis to share in the coming kingdom. Though Christianity's theology is trinitarian, it may not have appeared so in its original context. For one thing, Christian mention of the "Holy Spirit" would neither have been considered unique nor heretical by the rabbis. For another thing, Christianity of the period was much more concerned with the relationship between the Father and the Son. The concept of the "Holy Spirit" was not a source for the same kind of speculation.[6]

The rabbinic response to the heresy is clear. The rabbis appeal to Scripture to show that God is unitary. Deuteronomy 6, Isaiah 44–47, and Exodus 20 are used by the rabbis to show that God is unique. These verses are probably being employed against heretical interpretations of Daniel 7:9f; they are certainly being used against the idea that the names of God denote different divinities. This pattern of Scripture is characteristic both of the heresy and the defense against it. It will be especially important for reconstructing the history of the heresy and for understanding the radicalization of Gnosticism.

[6] See Jaroslav Pelikan, *The Christian Tradition: A History of the Development of Doctrine*, vol. 1, *The Emergence of the Catholic Tradition (100–600)* (Chicago: University of Chicago Press, 1971), 172–25.

However, the other aspects of the heresy are more mysterious. Determining the identity of the groups of heresy in question remains a serious question. MRI describes those professing belief in the doctrine as "gentiles." PR calls a person with such beliefs either a "whoreson" or a "son of heresy" depending upon the translation. So there can be no definite identification of the heresy from the terminology in the rabbinic writings. There is some evidence connecting this argument with a rabbinic polemic against Christianity. Elsewhere, PR 22 comments on "My God, my God, why hast thou forsaken me?" which in Aramaic is supposed to have been Jesus' last words (Matt 27:46). The rabbis say that the first "my God" refers to the sea while the second "my God" refers to Sinai. Since no other heretical group found this verse relevant for their doctrine, one may suppose that Christianity was identified as a "two powers heresy"; but the rabbinic charge of "two powers" may not have been originally or exclusively used against it. The many descriptions of the heresy in the different versions of the tradition suggest that the charge was used against several groups of heretics in different times and places. This logical conclusion can be demonstrated more soundly later, as more evidence is revealed.

In these passages, one becomes aware of the development of a single tradition in many different ways and probably over considerable periods of time. Traditions with so many layers present immense dating problems. Approximations alone can be made for the date of each layer. Although these texts occur in the "Tannaitic" midrashim, recent scholarship has shown that the traditional attributions should not be accepted without question.[7] The traditions may go back as far as the first century but the texts are not equally ancient. Even so, parts of the early layers of the tradition may be isolated.[8]

[7] For more information about the new attempt to date rabbinical traditions see, e.g., Jacob Neusner, "The Rabbinic Traditions about the Pharisees Before 70 CE: The Problem of Oral Transmission," *JJS* 22 (1971): 1–18. Also see some of his longer works, such as *From Politics to Piety: The Emergence of Pharisaic Judaism* (Englewood Cliffs, N.J.: Prentice Hall, 1973); *The Rabbinic Traditions about the Pharisees Before 70* (Leiden: Brill, 1971); *Eliezer ben Hyrcanus: The Man and the Legend* (Leiden: Brill, 1973).

[8] The criticism of S. Cohen (*AJS Review* 10, no. 1 [1985]: 114–17) that the exegesis of Exod 15:3 is entirely theoretical and bears no relationship to actual heretics has been shown mistaken by J. Fossum in *The Name of God and the Angel of the Lord: Samaritan and Jewish Concepts of Intermediation and the Origin of Gnosticism*, WUNT 36 (Tübingen: Mohr Siebeck, 1985), 228f. There we see that the Samaritan Malef 3:5 contains real traditions

Philo

With external evidence like Christianity, it is possible to push the origin of this tradition back much further than the rabbinic tradition would itself allow. Philo, too, attests to the pervasiveness and antiquity of the problem of God's appearances as well as His different aspects. His doctrine of the λόγος commands our attention first because Philo explicitly calls the λόγος a second God (δεύτερος θεός) in several places:

> Yet there can be no cowering fear for the man who relies on the hope of the divine comradeship, to whom are addressed the words "I am the God who appeared to thee in place of God" (Gen 31:31). Surely a right noble cause of vaunting it is, for a soul that God deigns to show himself to and converse with it. And do not fail to mark the language used, but carefully inquire whether there are two Gods; for we read "I am the God that appeared to thee," not "in my place" but "in the place of God," as though it were another's. What then are we to say? He that is truly God is one, but those that are improperly so-called are more than one. Accordingly, the holy word in the present instance has indicated Him who truly is God by means of the articles, saying, "I am the God," while it omits the article when mentioning him who is improperly so called, saying "who appeared to thee in the place" not "of the God" but simply "of God." (*Somn.* 1.227–229 [Colson, LCL])

> Why does (Scripture) say, as if (speaking) of another God, "In the image of God He made man" and not "in His own image?" Most excellently and veraciously this oracle was given by God. For nothing mortal can be made in the likeness of the Most High One and father of the universe but (only) in that of the second God, who is His λόγος. For it was right that the rational part of the human soul should be formed as an impression of the divine λόγος, since the pre-λόγος God is superior to every rational nature. But He who is above the λόγος exists in the best and in a special form—what thing that comes into being can rightly bear His likeness? Moreover, Scripture wishes to show that God most justly avenges the virtuous and decent men because they have certain kinship

---

of mediation attached to Exod 15:3: "The Glory too seemed to be saying: 'O congregation, keep yourself from me, for is there not before me a mighty deed? I slew, I oppressed, I destroyed, I made alive; and, with you, I did all this when I was at the sea and showed you every wonder and made you cross with great marvels by the mighty power of God.'" There is no guarantee that this is an old tradition, but it is certainly an actual heretical one. The Samaritans, of course, did not canonize the book of Daniel, which was so important to the Christian interpretation.

> with His λόγος, of which the human mind is a likeness and image. (*QG* 2.62 [Marcus, LCL])

He believes that "second God" is an appropriate and fitting title but criticizes those who cannot distinguish between the original god and the angelic copy:

> Here it gives the title of "God" to His chief Word, not from any superstitious nicety in applying names, but with one aim before him, to use words to express facts. Thus, in another place, when he had inquired whether He that is has any proper name, he came to know full well that He has no proper name [the reference is to Exod 6:3] and that whatever name anyone may use for Him he will use by license of language; for it is not the nature of Him that is to be spoken of, but simply to be. Testimony to this is afforded also by the divine response made to Moses' question whether He has a name, even "I am He that is (Exod 3:14)." It is given in order that, since there are not in God things which man can comprehend, man may recognize His substance. To the souls indeed which are incorporeal and are occupied in His worship it is likely that He should reveal himself as He is, conversing with them as friend with friends; but to souls which are still in a body, giving Himself the likeness of angels, not altering His own nature, for He is unchangeable, but conveying to those which receive the impression of His presence a semblance in a different form, such that they take the image to be not a copy but that original form itself. (*Somn.* 1.230–235 [Colson, LCL])

Here, the issue for Philo is the meaning of scriptural anthropomorphisms. This is a theme which runs throughout Philo's discussion of the "second god."[9] At the same time, Philo stresses that there is no God besides God the Most High and uses Deuteronomy 4:39, as the rabbis do, to deny that any other figure can be considered a God:

> But let Melchizedek instead of water offer wine, and give to souls strong drink, that they may be seized by a divine intoxication, more sober than sobriety itself. For he is a priest, even Reason, having as his portion Him that is, and all his thoughts of God are high and vast and sublime: for he is the priest of the Most High (Gen 14:18), not that there is any other not Most High—for God being One "is in heaven above and on earth beneath and there is none beside Him" (Deut 4:39)—but to conceive of God not in low earthbound ways but in lofty terms, such as transcend all

[9] See also *Migr.* 86–93, where Philo speaks of extreme allegorizers. The issue in that place, however, is loyalty to the commandments.

> other greatness and all else that is free from matter, calls up in us a picture of the Most High. (*Leg.* 3.81)

In this particular case, Philo denies that any other being can be God's agent, for there is only one God. It is interesting that Philo picks the allegory of Melchizedek as λόγος to discuss this issue, since elsewhere he allows that the λόγος can be considered as a "second god" and divine mediator. It appears as though Philo is opposed to some concepts of mediation, even while he maintains the agency of the λόγος.[10]

Philo also knows that the names of God connote His aspects of mercy and justice, just as the rabbis do. But Philo identifies the divine names, κύριος and θεός (= YHWH and Elohim) with the aspects of God in exactly the opposite ways that the rabbis do. Generally Philo equates YHWH with the attribute of strict justice and Elohim with the attribute of mercy, the exact opposite of the standard rabbinic doctrine. Philo's system is, however, the same configuration of terms that underlies the MRI passage.[11]

That Philo knows the issue of a "second god" and the themes of justice and mercy suggests a possible origin well before the birth of Jesus. But Philo's writings suggest more than a continuous issue. He employs very similar Scripture, indicating the existence of a widespread scriptural tradition, since the rabbis, a century later, know nothing of him directly and are not indebted to him for their exegesis. In fact, Philo elsewhere credits some of his exegetical information to traditions that he has learned from the elders (*Mos.*, beginning). This provides a second unambiguous first-century location for this dispute, which is present but not datable in midrash. Again, extra-rabbinic evidence helps establish the antiquity of certain issues within early rabbinic Judaism, the reverse of the more standard methodological procedure. Preliminary indications are, therefore, that many parts of the Jewish community in various

[10] Melchizedek was a heavenly figure of note in Qumran. See Fred L. Horton Jr., *The Melchizedek Tradition: A Critical Examination of the Sources to the Fifth Century A.D. and in the Epistle to the Hebrews* (Cambridge: Cambridge University Press, 1976); M. Friedländer, *Der vorchristliche jüdische Gnosticismus* (Göttingen: Vandenhoek & Ruprecht, 1898), 30–33; see also Birger Pearson, "Friedlaender Revisited: Alexandrian Judaism and Gnosticism," *Studia Philonica* 2 (1973): 26 for a discussion of this important text.

[11] See *Cher.* 9.27–28; *Fug.* 18.95; 19.100; see also H. Wolfson, *Philo: Foundations of Religious Philosophy in Judaism, Christianity, and Islam*, 2 vols. (Cambridge: Cambridge University Press, 1947), 1:223.

places and periods used the traditions which the rabbis claim is a heretical conception of the deity. This is certainly in line with our previous discovery that Christianity must have been accused of believing in "two powers in heaven." Christianity was vitally concerned with the concept of the λόγος, though, unlike Philo, Christians associated a definite personality with the mediating figure. Furthermore, the Jews of the Gospel of John are represented as opposing Jesus because he claims to be equal with God (John 5:18-21; 8:58-59; 10). λόγος theology also interested many church fathers, as we shall see.

More on MRI Bahodesh 5

A passage in the Mekhilta, immediately after the first one we have studied, reveals some interesting information about Gnosticism.

> Rabbi Nathan says: From this one can cite a refutation of the heretics who say: "There are two powers." For when the Holy One Blessed be He, stood up and exclaimed: "I am the Lord thy God," was there any one who stood up to protest against Him? If you should say that it was done in Secret—but has it not been said: "I have not spoken in secret," etc. (Isa. 45:19)? "I said not unto the seed of Jacob" (Isa 45:19), that is, to these alone will I give it. "They sought me in the desert" (Isa 45:19). Did I not give it in broad daylight? And thus it says: "I the Lord speak righteousness, I declare things that are right (Isa 45:19). (MRI Bahodesh 5)[12]

R. Nathan's argument follows immediately after the first passage that we studied. Indeed, it assumes an exegesis of Exod 20:2, for it is a further comment on the idea that one God gave the law. At the giving of the Ten Commandments, he argues, no other deity contradicted YHWH's statement that He is Israel's God. Since He made this statement openly and was not contradicted, there could be no other deity. R. Nathan used another quotation from Isaiah (45:19) to show that the statement in Exodus 20:2 was spoken publicly and openly. This is a theme mentioned elsewhere in the Mekhilta as well,[13] not far beyond R. Nathan's comment. The rabbis often emphasize that the law was given to all; the stubborn alone have refused to hear it. So R. Nathan's remark may merely be targeted for those who say the law was parochial.

[12] *Mekilta de-Rabbi Ishmael*, ed. and trans. J. Lauterbach (Philadelphia: Jewish Publication Society, 1961).

[13] See, e.g., MRI Bahodesh 5, trans. Lauterbach, 2:234.

But here the argument by the critics of the law may be stronger still. From R. Nathan's defense one can infer that the criticism on the part of those who believe in "two powers in heaven" was that the God who gave the law acted secretly or deviously. It becomes necessary to posit an opponent for R. Nathan who believed that the God of Israel did something in secret. The context of the Isaiah passage is creation, so the rabbis appear to want to emphasize creation as well as giving the law. This further suggests that the heretical group believed in other deities above the God of Israel. It seems apparent, then, that the God of Israel has been denigrated to the role of a demiurge for the heretics. Among those whom the rabbis had constantly opposed for believing that the law was not a universal gift, there seem to have been some, here called "two powers in heaven" heretics, who denigrated the God of Israel as a demiurge alone. The most likely group to have been opposed by the rabbis in this fashion is an extreme gnostic group. R. Nathan's remark *may* oppose extreme gnostic sectarians, that is, dualists rather than the corresponding "binitarians" of the earlier passage but, if so, it is not possible to define whether they are of a Christian or a non-Christian variety.

R. Nathan directs his remarks against the *minim* or sectarians, who are obviously viewed as heretics by the rabbis. However, some gnostic Jews or Jewish-Christians might still be included under the rubric of "sectarian" or "heretic" (as opposed to "gentile") during R. Nathan's time at the end of the second century. It is unlikely that they would have been so considered in the third or fourth centuries. Since we know from previous passages that "two powers" referred to Christians and moderate gnostics, but not to radical gnostics, we have to conclude that "two powers" was a catchall term for many different groups—including Christians, gnostics and Jews. The strategy of the rabbis in using this term was quite sophisticated. First, there is a sense in which the designation is apt. Christians and gnostics did posit a second divine hypostasis. Second, the rabbis subsumed many different groups under one category. This policy implies that the rabbis wanted to view various sectarians not as different groups but as one group sharing a single, basic misunderstanding. Putting all these heretics into one category and dismissing them is an effective way of dealing with opposition. One did not have to delve too deeply into the heresy. Thirdly, although the designation is apt from the rabbinic perspective, it is also exaggerated from the Christian one. In fact, neither the apocalyptic, mystical nor Christianized Judaism affirmed two separate deities. They understood themselves to be monotheistic, giving special emphasis to one divine hypostasis or manifestation.[14] Only radical Gnosticism posited two different and opposing deities. In effect, the rabbis were classifying the other groups together with extreme Gnosticism and treating them all alike. This tactic was effective because it was based not only on a plausible description but also on one which was a heinous charge from both the rabbinic and Christian perspective. In calling the sectarians "those who say there are two powers in heaven," the rabbis were stating that the sectarians violated the most basic tenet of Israelite faith, the unity of God. This ought to make clear that there were times when the rabbis were interested in defining Jewish theology quite carefully.[15]

Some further information can be gained by looking at this material. Of all the groups opposed by the rabbis with the term "two powers in heaven," only one, extreme Gnosticism, designed an opposing configuration of divinities. Within the rabbinic reports there is some helpful information about how Gnosticism became radicalized and how the second figure in the pantheon, the demiurge in this case, came to be denigrated. One has to pay very careful attention to the structure of the scriptural defenses against this heresy in order to see the clue. The rabbis fight all of the various heresies with the Scriptures which emphasize God's unity and uniqueness. They rely heavily on Exodus 20:2, the first of the Ten Commandments; Deuteronomy 6:4, the Shema; and Isaiah 44–47, to mention only the first few. We know that these Scriptures were used quite early in the battle.

The Opposition to Rabbinic Judaism

The relevance of rabbinic texts for the development of Christianity has been pointed out in the course of the chapter. Though the rabbis did not

[14] There is an interesting use of the term "ditheism" within the church fathers. Hippolytus (*Haer.* 9.7) notes that one of the charges made against him by Callistus was that he was a ditheist. It is a logical charge for Patripassionists and modalists to make against the "orthodox." So too Julian accuses Christians of having given up monotheism (*C. Gal.* 2133). On the other hand, Origen, in his *Dial.* 2, 3 agrees that Christianity can be said to believe in a second God, though only in a special way. It is quite clear then that the rabbis were not alone in debating Christianity's adherence to monotheism with the terms "second God" and "two powers."

[15] Of course, the rabbis were not alone in doing so. Monarchians and modalists used the same arguments in their battles with Christianity. See J. N. D. Kelly, *Early Christian Doctrines* (New York: Harper & Row, 1958), 109–26. See n. 14 above.

enter into detail about their Christian opponents, they certainly seized upon a principal point of the kerygma of the primitive church; Jesus had ascended to the Father and received the title "Lord," one of the titles reserved for God in rabbinic tradition. Every document in the New Testament agrees that this ascension took place as part of Jesus' exaltation, though Paul, in Philippians, probably states it most succinctly:

> Therefore God has highly exalted him and bestowed upon him the name which is above every name, that at the name of Jesus every knee should bow, in heaven and on earth and under the earth, and every tongue confess that Jesus Christ is Lord, to the glory of God the Father. (Phil 2:9-11)

It seems unlikely, however, that the rabbis invented the argument to counter Christianity. The notions of a split in the Godhead existed in Philo and there is little specifically anti-Christian in the rabbinic exegesis. Rather the rabbis and Philo appear both to reflect an exegetical issue which has taken on primal importance in the development of Jewish Hellenistic thought, although they each witness to the issue at a different stage of development and in a different social context. But the issue at the core seems to be the same: the names of God are not to be understood as separate hypostases of God. This argument was then put to use by the rabbis to counter Christian claims about the meaning of Jesus' divine name.

Justin, the gentile Christian, is the one church father whose relationship to the "two powers controversy" has been noted previously by several scholars. Justin Martyr was born at the beginning of the second century in Shechem, then called Flavia Neapolis, in Samaria. He called himself a Samaritan, which meant only that he was descended from people living in that part of the country and not part of that religious sect (*Dial.* 120), because he stated that he was uncircumcised (*Dial.* 29). Nevertheless, the details of Justin's life and his familiarity with a variety of exotic Jewish doctrines add evidence for the relationship we have already suspected between the Samaritans and early gentile Christianity. Justin's *Dialogue with Trypho* also evinces real polemical use of almost all the scriptural exegesis which the rabbis thought dangerous.

The setting for the *Dialogue* was Ephesus, whence Justin had migrated in his Christian mission. The date for the *Dialogue* must have corresponded closely with the Bar Kokhba Revolt, for Justin mentions it often (e.g., *Dial.* 108; *1 Apol.* 1.31) and Trypho is described as a Jewish fugitive who escaped from the turmoil.

Justin's use of midrashic traditions has sometimes been taken as evidence that the *Dialogue* is fictional, serving as a purely literary framework for presenting Justin's views.[16] Yet it certainly reflects one side of the debate between Judaism and Christianity in the early and mid-second century, whether the immediate incident be wholly fact, embellished incident, or pure fiction. By means of Genesis 19:24, Justin proceeds to show that a second divine figure, Christ, is responsible for carrying out divine commands on earth:

> "The previously quoted Scriptural passages will make this evident to you," I replied. "Here are the words: 'The sun was risen upon the earth, and Lot entered into Segor. And the Lord rained upon Sodom brimstone and fire from the Lord out of Heaven. And He destroyed these cities and all the country round about.' "
>
> Then the fourth of the companions who remained with Trypho spoke up: "It must therefore be admitted that one of the two angels who went down to Sodom, and whom Moses in the Scriptures calls Lord, is different from Him who is also God, and appeared to Abraham."
>
> "Not only because of that quotation," I said, "must we certainly admit that, besides the creator of the universe, another was called Lord by the Holy Spirit. For this was attested to not only by Moses, but also by David, when he said: 'The Lord said to my Lord: Sit Thou at My right hand, until I make Thy enemies Thy footstool,' and in other words: 'Thy throne, O God is forever and ever; the scepter of Thy kingdom is a scepter of uprightness. Thou hast loved justice, and hated iniquity; therefore God, Thy God hath anointed Thee with the oil of gladness above Thy fellows' (Ps 45:7-8)." (*Dial.* 56)

It is a Jew, not Justin, who admits that another divine being, "The Lord," was present at the destruction of Sodom and Gomorrah, and that this divine being was different from God. Genesis 19:24 is actually mentioned by the rabbis as the source of heresy (b. Sanh. 38b), where the defense against heresy is attributed to the Tanna R. Ishmael b. Yosi (170–200 C.E.). From our previous discussion, there is no reason to doubt that such heterodox Jews existed as early as Philo. Justin only endeavored to prove that this second divinity is the Christ. It is significant that the angelic figure is accepted by the Jew, only his messianic status is questioned. This is another piece of evidence that Christianity was the first

[16] E.g., C. Weizsäcker, "Die Theologie des Märtyrers Justinus," *Jahrbücher für deutsche Theologie* 13 (1867): 63.

to connect the messiah and the principal angel. In this place he relies primarily on the various descriptions of vindication and enthronement found in the Psalm texts.

Like Philo Justin calls the λόγος another God (ἕτερος θεός), distinct in number, if not in essence (*Dial.* 56). The sharply drawn personality of this manifestation, together with the doctrine of the incarnation, is the element which most distinguishes Justin's concept of λόγος from Philo's. But, as Goodenough has persuasively argued, both Justin and Philo should be understood to express variants of the same Hellenistic Jewish traditions.[17] Like Philo, Justin believes the λόγος is an angel in that it is a power (δύναμις) radiating from God. Like the angels it has freedom of choice, but unlike the angels, Justin's λόγος has self-direction (*Dial.* 88). Therefore, although Justin implies that the λόγος is the same as an angel, he prefers to emphasize its distinctiveness in ways that never occurred to Philo.

As further evidence that these traditions had a background in Hellenistic Judaism before they were put to Christian use, Goodenough shows that most of the titles applied to the λόγος by Justin are the same as those used by Philo and other Hellenistic Jewish writers: θεός, κύριος, ἄγγελος, δύναμις, ἀνατολή, λίθος, πέτρα, ἀρχή, ἡμέρα, φώς, σοφία, ἀνήρ, ἄνθρωπος, Ἰσραελ, Ιακοβ, etc.[18]

As Justin says:

> "So my friends," I said, "I shall show from Scripture that the God has begotten of Himself a certain rational power as a beginning before all other creatures. The Holy Spirit indicates this power by various titles, sometimes the Glory of the Lord, at other times, Son or Wisdom or Angel or God or Lord or Word. He even called himself the commander-in-chief when he appeared in human guise to Josue, the son of Nun." (*Dial.* 61)

One of the most significant titles is "the Glory of the Lord," which links the figure with the λόγος of the FG and also the human figure on the throne which Ezekiel saw. To substantiate the claim of the λόγος's primacy in the divine economy, Justin points to the grammatical plural referring to God in Genesis 1:26 and Genesis 3:22 (*Dial.* 62). After this he adduces passages to support the incarnation from the virgin birth to the

[17] E. R. Goodenough, *The Theology of Justin Martyr: An Investigation into the Conceptions of the Earliest Christian Literature and its Hellenistic and Judaistic Influences* (Jena: 1923), 147f.

[18] Goodenough, *Theology of Justin Martyr*, 168–72.

ascension (*Dial.* 63–65). Of course, the argument is not well received by his Jewish opponents, even those who admit the existence of the second power, so Justin goes over the same Scripture from a variety of different perspectives. At one point he goes into a rather fanciful exegesis to show that the name of God, which the angel in Exodus 23:21 carried, is "Jesus," a motif which cannot be original to the name of God tradition:

> Now from the book of Exodus we know that Moses cryptically indicated that the name of God himself (which He says was not revealed to Abraham or to Jacob) was also Jesus. For it is written: "And the Lord said to Moses, say to this people: Behold, I send my angel before thy face, to keep thee in thy journey, and bring thee into the place that I have prepared for thee. Take notice of him, and obey his voice; do not disobey him, for he will not pardon thee, because My name is in him." Consider well who it was that led your fathers into the promised land, namely he who was at first named Auses (Osee), but later renamed Jesus (Josue). If you keep this in mind, you will also realize that the name of him who said to Moses, "My name is in him," was Jesus. Indeed he was also called Israel, and he similarly bestowed this name upon Jacob. (*Dial.* 75)[19]

While it is clear that Justin is using "two powers" traditions to describe Jesus as λόγος and Christ, the traditions could have hardly originated with the identification of Jesus as the angel in Exodus. The attempt to see Jesus (Joshua) as the angel's name is secondary. Rather, Justin is taking over a previous exegetical, possibly mystical tradition, applying the name of his particular savior, and defending his belief against the other candidates for the office of angelic mediator. The tradition itself, without the Christian coloring, can be seen as early as Philo.

The Growth of Gnostic Exegesis

There are further clues about the relationship between Judaism, Gnosticism, and Christianity in the Scriptures they use. Gnosticism is an extremely widespread phenomenon in the late Hellenism occurring in many different communities—Jewish, Christian, and pagan—so no history of traditions in any one community can account for the whole development definitively. Nor can any single argument be viewed as absolute in such a complex situation. Nevertheless, one significant aspect of the development of Gnosticism in the Jewish and Christian communities

[19] Probably another form of the traditions evinced in the Prayer of Jacob lies behind this argument.

is highlighted by the scriptural traditions which we have been tracing, when seen together with the gnostic texts found in the church fathers and those from Nag Hammadi. The change from binitarian to dualistic and gnostic systems seems more closely related to polemical exaggerations between groups than to the earlier sectarian dualisms (like Qumran, for example).

I will explain further by investigating several systems leading to Gnosticism. The Poimandres is one of the earliest examples of these traditions. C. H. Dodd dates it just prior to the time of Valentinus (130–140 C.E.) but remarks that its exact date cannot yet be fixed.[20] Many scholars are willing to place it a century earlier. As Dodd shows, the work is an amalgam of the creation story based on the Bible and various conceptions current in Stoic and Platonic thought. At the base of the cosmos there is only a primal God, Νοῦς or Mind, who is manifested to the seer as the figure Poimandres. Creation is carried out by the primary manifestation of the highest being, the λόγος or Word. This λόγος is personified as the Son of God in ways similar to those in Philo and the Wisdom of Solomon (18:15-16).[21] It is clear then, whatever else may be of interest in the document, it would be considered "two powers in heaven" by the rabbis. We can see that those powers are complementary.

Among the Greek philosophers, just as among the theosophists who produced the hermetic literature, the concept of "second god" appears to have achieved some limited use, partially based on Plato's idea of the demiurge in the Timaeus and partially based on the application of the idea to the λόγος by Philo. Numenius of Apamea, for instance, though his work survives only in fragments, is known to have been influenced by Jewish Scriptures.[22] Origen, in the *Contra Celsum*, remarks that Numenius was familiar with the Scriptures of the Hebrews, which he endeavored to synthesize with Greek philosophy by means of allegory (*Cels.* 4.52). Numenius calls the first divinity "The Good" or "Reason" or "Thought" (frr. 16–17), even "the Standing God" (fr. 15).[23] But because Nume-

[20] C. H. Dodd, *The Bible and the Greeks* (London: Hodder & Stoughton, 1935), 209.

[21] Dodd, *Bible and the Greeks*, 117–19.

[22] For the history of scholarship on Numenius, see the new edition of the *Fragments*, edited by Édouard des Places (Paris: Les Belles Lettres, 1973). The numbering of the fragments will be according to Des Places' system, not according to the numbering of Leemans.

[23] Notice the affinities with Philo's discussion of God, based on the LXX phrase, "place where God stands." In fact, since the study of K. S. Guthrie, *Numenius of Apamea:*

nius also distinguishes radically between God and matter, he finds it necessary to assume a "second god" who mediates the chasm while participating both in divinity and matter. With this cosmology, Numenius has appeared to many scholars as a gnostic.[24] However, he can hardly be a radical gnostic, for the soul, while divine in origin, is distributed in sentient beings through the rational agency of the second god (fr. 13).[25] Thus, Numenius' second god is not the evil demiurge of the radical gnostics. However, when seen together with the hermetic literature[26] and possibly even the Chaldaean Oracles, Numenius' writing suggests that there was an occasional interest in Jewish thought among the pagan mystics and incipient neo-Platonists of the second century.[27] Perhaps some philosophers like Numenius, as successors to Philo, together with gentile Christians were included among the "nations of the world" identified by the rabbis as believing in "two powers in heaven." This philosophical usage of the term "second god" in the successors of Philo may be the basis of the use of the term in rabbinic literature and the christological controversies of the second and third centuries.

Some of the documents called "gnostic" by church fathers seem to play an intermediary role in the development towards radical dualism. Hippolytus gives us several instances of gnostic writings which have interesting conceptions of a second power in heaven together with the now familiar, concomitant, scriptural passages. In the Naasene Preaching (*Haer.* 5.6.3–5.11.1) considerable Adam speculation is combined with the idea of a primal creature on the one hand and the savior on the other. The primal man is the bisexual Adamas. He makes everything but is not identical with anything he makes. Apparently he is the primal helper of the highest principle, the preexistent, also known as the λόγος or as Hermes, the guide of souls. Evil comes not from him, but from another power who creates this material world without the knowledge and consent of Adamas. The object of mankind is to recognize

The Father of Neo-Platonism (London: George Bell & Sons, 1917), some relationship between Philo and Numenius has been generally assumed.

[24] See, e.g., the study of Beutler in PW Supplement 7 (1950).

[25] In this fragment Numenius uses the metaphor of a planter of a vineyard for God, as is common in Philo and Jewish tradition in general.

[26] *Deuteros theos* appears in Corp. herm. 8.5(16).

[27] For a more detailed study of this question, see R. P. Festugière, *La révélation d'Hermès Trismégiste*, 4 vols. (Paris: Gabalda, 1950–1953), esp. vols. 3 and 4.

the divine aspect within and, with this knowledge, seek to return to the purely divine realm through the mediation of the second figure.

In the *Apophasis Megale*, Hippolytus describes a gnostic system ascribed to Simon Magos of Gitta (*Haer*. 6.9.14–6.18.7). The highest power of God is again called the λόγος, which is in charge of creation of heaven and earth. He is described as he "that stands, took his stand, and will stand," (6.12.3) using terms for immutability reminiscent of the LXX and Samaritan traditions to describe the vision of the elders—namely, "the place where God stands," (LXX: Exod 24:10) which we have seen before in Hellenistic Judaism. The document uses "place of the Lord" to describe a divine presence (6.17.7). It is obvious that the document, like many other gnostic works, is a theological reworking of the biblical creation story together with angelophany scenes. So far, all stories posit a principal power of God who functions as His complementary (not antagonistic) helper because the highest God cannot enter into materiality.

Among the Samaritans, as J. Fossum has pointed out,[28] there is evidence that the figure of the angel of the Lord developed into a demiurge. For the Samaritans, the Glory mediates between God and Moses, as Exodus 23:21 allows. In *Memar Marqah*, a fourth-century Samaritan work, the Glory claims that it contains the "Great Name" and also applies to himself the basic scriptural passages describing the angel of the Lord. In *Memar Marqah* 3.5 the Glory—that is, the angel of the Lord—is credited with the annihilation of the Egyptian army at the sea. This shows that the passages which the rabbis specifically discuss as "two powers heresy" in the Mekhiltas are indeed real sources of heresy, in this case Samaritan ones.

The Glory's demiurge functions become even clearer in discussions of creation. In the Malef, a considerably later work, which may yet contain very ancient material, the angel of the Lord is credited with the creation of Adam from the dust of the earth, while the Name breathed life into him. Such concepts of angelic mediation at creation and thereafter are strictly forbidden by rabbinic authority but even in this heterodox environment the demiurge figure has not yet become an evil or ignorant figure. However, if Fossum is right, one critical step, namely the principal angel's role in creation, is taken in the Samaritan community.

[28] Fossum, *Name of God and the Angel of the Lord*, 227–28. See also idem, "Kyrios Jesus as the Angel of the Lord in Jude 5-7," *NTS* 33 (1987): 226–43.

The mediating figures in the *Book of Baruch* (Hippolytus, *Haer*. 5.26.1–5.27.5) are especially interesting. Since the Good cannot enter the evil world, according to the gnostic Justin, He is confined to His realm of light. In order to carry out His orders in the material world, He employs two other primal powers, the consorts Elohim and Edem, who are lovers. They sometimes appear to have the characteristics of earth and heaven divinities for they create and rule the earth and heaven respectively with their progeny of angels. Elohim and Edem therefore together function as demiurge. This is a first example of the Hebrew God represented as the demiurge alone, while a higher divinity rules the entire universe. However, Elohim is not yet the ignorant, arrogant god of later Gnosticism. In the process of creating the heavens, Elohim recognizes that a luminary, greater than any he created, can be seen at the limits of the heavens (5.26.15). He alone enters this highest abode through a gate and is enthroned next to the Good (Ps 110:1).[29] Thereupon, he contemplates destroying the imperfect world he has made, but he is dissuaded by the Good. Meanwhile, down below, Edem at first adorns herself to attract her consort but, when she realizes that she is abandoned, sets out to punish the spirit of Elohim in men. Thus, suffering comes into the world through the jealous female consort of Elohim, while he, the principal demiurge, remains an admirable creature. In any event, we can see a logical progression in the concept of the second power in heaven. Now the Hebrew God designates only the principal angel while there is a high god who is his master. Still, the Hebrew God is not yet evil; nor is he exclusively defined as YHWH.

Radical Gnosticism

Some of the more recently found gnostic documents illustrate the next (though not inevitable) step in the development from the earlier "two powers" heresy to radical Gnosticism. It is clear that the Chenoboskion library found at modern day Nag Hammadi contains many different

[29] See R. A. Bullard, *The Hypostasis of the Archons: The Coptic Text with Translation and Commentary*, with a contribution by Martin Krause (Berlin: de Gruyter, 1970), 134:27–135:4. Also A. Böhlig and P. Labib, *Die Koptisch-gnostische Schrift ohne Titel aus Codex II von Nag Hammadi im koptischen Museum zu Alt-Kairo* (Berlin: Akademie, 1962), 152:31–153:16. See also J. Doresse, *The Secret Book of the Egyptian Gnostics* (New York: Viking, 1960), 167; and Bentley Layton, "The Hypostasis of the Archons," *HTR* 67 (1974): 351–25 and 69 (1976): 31–101.

documents with varying characteristics. Some treatises seem hardly gnostic, others hardly Christian. Some show significant and considerable influence by Jewish mystical sectarianism.

In the midst of this gnostic library we often find traditions that associate the name of God with "place" and make the divine name both a manifestation of God and an independent hypostasis which mediates revelation. All of this strongly suggests that some gnostic ideas ultimately go back to Jewish heterodox traditions. The opposing configuration of deities insures that at least two (perhaps many) independent deities were present. Therefore it seems clear that the rabbis would have considered it heretical. When the powers are complementary—as they seem to be in the apocalyptic literature of the first century, in some of the "gnostic" and much of the Christian literature—the independence of the second power is a moot question. It is often possible that the later traditions in heretical literature are survivals of heterodox but not necessarily heretical Jewish or Christian exegesis, brought into a new context.

For instance, in the untitled document from Codex II, often called On the Origin of the World, and in The Hypostasis of the Archons there are long descriptions of the heavenly throne which depend to a great degree on the traditions we have been discussing from Exodus and from the beginning of Ezekiel. In both documents, as in those described by the church fathers, proto-*merkabah* or apocalyptic traditions abound. We see that the chariot is used as a throne surrounded by a glorious palace inhabited by a plethora of angels. The major cherubim have four faces—that of a lion, a bull, an eagle, and a man, as adduced from Ezekiel 1, the most important *merkabah* text. Similar chariots are also employed by the seventy-two gods who give man the seventy-two languages of the world.

Sabaoth, in the untitled work (Origin of the World), has many of the characteristics of the second figure in heaven. His name is evidently derived from the Hebrew ה' צבאות, Lord of Hosts or Powers, therefore he may be said to carry the name of God. In Origin of the World 152.10, he is said to be "over all the forces (*dynameis*) of Chaos." He also shares some of the characteristics given to Jesus in various traditions. Like Christ in the *Sophia Jesu Christi* (Wisdom of Jesus Christ), he is said to have created the angels.[30] Yet the parallel between the documents is not complete, since Jesus is himself one of the created angels, seated

[30] See Bullard, *The Hypostasis of the Archons*, 110; also Wis. Jes. Chr. 99.18–100.3.

at the right of Sabaoth in the untitled work (Orig. World 153.25–29), whereas in the Hypostasis of the Archons, it is Zoe who sits on the right of Sabaoth. Apparently, only the figure of the primary angel is consistent in the documents, not his name or identity. In cases of this type, it is the mythical structure, not any single version of the story, which carries the full meaning of the story.

In Origin of the World, Sabaoth is the son of Ialdabaoth, the demiurge. As in Valentinian thought, Sabaoth is to function as a savior. He has learned that what his father told him—namely, that his father is Lord of all—is untrue. Upon realizing this, he is taken to the seventh heaven and enthroned. Some of the "two powers" traditions have been applied to the gnostic savior and the reason is clear. Sabaoth functions as the role model for the ideal believer, who is to move beyond Judaism (and "orthodox" Christianity) to true gnostic belief.

Other parts of these esoteric Jewish traditions have been applied to the demiurge. This development points out a transformation characteristic of gnostic interpretation of these traditions. Throughout the document we are informed that Ialdabaoth, the demiurge whose name (like Sabaoth) is an obvious pun on YHWH Sabaoth (the proper name of the Hebrew God)[31] had exclaimed at his creation: "There is no other God but me," paraphrasing the same verses in Exodus, Deuteronomy, and Isaiah, which the rabbis had used to defend their God. In the gnostic text, the claim of the demiurge is patently false, because he is ignorant of the higher, good deity above him.

The pattern is far from unique. It occurs many times in the Nag Hammadi corpus. In every case, the ignorant demiurge (often Ialdabaoth) boasts that he is the only god, quoting or paraphrasing Deuteronomy 32:29; Isaiah 44:6 or 46:4. In every case the boast is ironic because the reader knows that there is a god higher than he.[32]

[31] See G. Scholem's explanation of this title, in "Jaldabaoth Reconsidered," in *Mélanges d'Histoire Religions*: *Festschrift H-Ch. Peuch* (Paris: Presses Universitaires, 1974), 405–21.

[32] According to the more recent numbering of the Nag Hammadi corpus the vain claim of the demiurge can be found in clear form also in Ap. John (NHC II 1) 14.18–21; 13.5–13 (with parallels to BG 44.9–17); Gos. Egyptians (NHC III 2) 58.23–59.4 and elsewhere. My thanks to Anne Maguire and N. A. Dahl for providing further references for the Nag Hammadi section of the 1976 SBL meeting in St. Louis. See N. A. Dahl's contribution to the International Conference on Gnosticism held at Yale, 1978: "The Arrogant Archon and the Lewd Sophia: Jewish Traditions in Gnostic Revolt," in *The*

From these texts, it is possible to abstract a pattern which is common to all the versions, even though only the untitled work (On the Origin of the World) contains all the elements.

(1) *Setting*: creation story, dependent upon a gnostic reading of the Genesis account.
(2) *Introduction*: often containing comments of the blindness, arrogance or ignorance of the demiurge—for example, Hyp. Arch. 86.23–30: "Their chief is blind, because of his power and his ignorance and arrogance, he said. . . ." (See Ap. John BG 44.9–13: "He looked at creation that was with him and the multitude of angels . . . and said to them. . . ." See also Hyp. Arch. 94.19–21; Orig. World 103.8–10; Ap. John BG 112.18–19; 135–138; Gos. Eg. 58.23–24; Irenaeus, *Haer.* 1.29.4; 1.30.6.)
(3) *The vain claim* in words derived from Isaiah 44–46—for example, Hyp. Arch. 86.30–31, "It is I who am God; there is none apart from me." (Hyp. Arch. 94.21f. [95:5]; Orig. World 103.11–13 [107.30f.; 112.28f.]; Apoc. John NHC II 11.20f.; Irenaeus, *Haer.* 1.30.6; Ap. John BG 44.14f.: "I am a jealous God; apart from me there is none" [Exod 20:5; Isa 46:9, or sim.]; cf. NHC II 13.8f.; Gos. Eg. 58.25f.; Irenaeus, *Haer.* 1.29.4.)
(4) *Comment*: "When he said this, he sinned against the Entirety." (Other comments: Apoc. John NHC II 11.21f.; Gos. Eg. 58.26–59.1; Ap. John BG 44.15ff.: "Already showing the angels with him that another god existed," etc.; cf. NHC II 13.9–13; Hyp. Arch. 86.31f.; 94.22f.)
(5) *Rebuke* by a voice from above (from Incorruptibility, from the Mother or another similar character). (Hyp. Arch. 86.32-37: "You are mistaken, Samael"; cf. Hyp. Arch. 94.24–26; 95.5–7; Orig. World 103.15–18; Irenaeus, *Haer.* 1.30.6: "Do not lie, Yaldabaoth.")
(6) *Disclosure*, combined with the rebuke or as an alternative to it. (Ap. John BG 47.15–18; NHC II 14.13–15: "The Man exists

---

Rediscovery of Gnosticism: Proceedings of the International Conference in Gnosticism at Yale University March 28–31, 1978, 2 vols., ed. B. Layton (Leiden: Brill, 1981), 2:689–712, esp. 689–706. See also H. M. Schenke, *Der Gott "Mensch" in der Gnosis: Ein religionsgeschichtlicher Beitrag zur Diskussion über die paulinische Anschauung von der Kirche als Lieb Christ* (Göttingen: Vandenhoeck & Ruprecht, 1962), 87f. Note the similarity to Rabbi Nathan's exegesis, above pp. 20–21.

and the son of Man"; cf. Gos. Eg. 59.1–3; Irenaeus, *Haer.* 1.30.6; Orig. World 103.19–28: "An enlightened, immortal man [or: an immortal Light-Man] exists before you . . .")

(7) *Challenge*: the Archon calls for a revelation. (Hyp. Arch. 94.27f.: "If any other thing exists before me, let it become visible to me!"; Orig. World 107.6–108.2: "If someone exists before me, let him appear so that we may see his light.")

(8) *Appearance of an image* (in the water and/or of light). (Hyp. Arch. 87.11–16: "As Incorruptibility looked down into the region of the Waters, her Image appeared in the Waters," etc.; cf. Orig. World 103.28–31; 107.18f. [Gen 1:2b?]; Hyp. Arch. 94.28–31: "And immediately Sophia stretched forth her finger and introduced Light into Matter"; cf. Orig. World 108.2–14; 111.29–31; 112.25f. [Gen 1:3]; Ap. John BG 48.1–9; NHC II 14.18–34; Gos. Eg. 59.4–9 [Gen 1:2b-3?]).

(9) *Proposal to create man*, made by the Archon or his Powers (Gen 1:26). (Hyp. Arch. 87.23–26; Orig. World 112.32–113.4; Ap. John NHC II 15.1–4; BG 48.10–14; Irenaeus, *Haer.* 1.30.6.)

(10) *Formation of man from the earth* (Gen 1:27–2:7). (Hyp. Arch. 87.27ff.; Orig. World 113.9ff.; Ap. John BG 48.14ff.; NHC II 15.5ff.; Gos. Eg. 59.9; Irenaeus, *Haer.* 1.30.6; 5.18.)

These several points must be seen as a summary, for no document reproduces all the items in this order. Rather, it appears that the myth of the arrogance of the demiurge was created to make gnostic sense of particular scriptural references, especially those from Genesis. But the gnostic interpretation appears to have been transmitted in elements, as a structure or pattern, rather than as a single exegetical or narrative interpretation.

It is also worth noting that while Christian tradition is evident in most places in the documents, there is nothing specifically Christian about this key scene—no speculation about the λόγος or messiah, for instance. It seems rather to depend on Jewish exegesis of Genesis. This points primarily to a Jewish sectarian origin for the polemic as it entered gnostic thought, even if the Jewish context was occasionally affected by Christianity as well.

In fact, there are a number of mythical precedents within biblical literature which help explain the development of the legend. In Scripture the King of Babylon (Isa 14) and the prince of Tyre (Ezek 28) both are said to have declared themselves "god" and have been punished for their impudence. It would not have been strange or unusual for Jews to have applied the same exegesis where the sin of arrogant claims of divinity was suspected. Certainly Nebuchadnezzar in Judith (3:8; 6:12); Antiochus Epiphanes in Daniel (11:36f.); Pompey in Psalms of Solomon (2:28f.); Caligula in Philo (*Legat.* 22, 74–80, 93–97, 118, 162); and Nero in the Sibylline Oracles (5:33–35, 137–154, 214–221) and the Ascension of Isaiah (4:6–8) are condemned in light of these biblical patterns. In 2 Thessalonians 2:4 the man of lawlessness is said to proclaim himself to be god (see also Rev 13:1, 5-6) and thus the arrogant claim becomes part of the anti-Christ tradition. Isaiah 14 is also used in the Christian polemic against Simon Magus and in the Jewish polemic against Jesus. Although the arrogant archon is not satanic, he may yet be a reinterpretation of the biblical precedent used against those who criticized Christians and others who impugned the uniqueness of the single god.

The gnostics made a different use of the traditions. They cast the creator of the world in the role of the arrogant ruler who claims that he is God. The polemic of the gnostic was that the arrogant ruler who falsely claims to be the sole God was the creator himself. The polemic logically is against the Jews in the first instance, but, in the second instance against those who value the Scripture of the Old Testament too highly, namely, "orthodox" Christianity. Therefore, gnostic interpretation also took over the claims of uniqueness of Israel's God, but applied them to a demiurge. Apparently gnostic exegesis split the tradition we find opposed by the rabbis into two parts. The traditions about a second figure were transmuted into the gnostic savior, while the scripture characteristic of the rabbinic polemic against "two powers" was associated with the evil demiurge who is still the God of Israel, but not the high god.

Polemic or Natural Evolution?

Of course, it is conceivable that "negative value" Judaism developed independently, not in response to orthodox disapproval in Judaism and Christianity. The books of Genesis and Deuteronomy and Isaiah and Ezekiel had been available for many centuries. But several considerations make it more probable that the specifically gnostic arguments date from a period considerably later, when several aspects of the rabbinic polemic against "two powers" had already been developed. First of all, even a quick reading of gnostic texts reveals that the scriptural focus of the gnostic mind was on the first few chapters of Genesis rather than on Deuteronomy, Exodus, or 2 Isaiah. The rabbis were the first sure witnesses to the use of Deuteronomy passages together with the principal angel passages. Since they brought them in for decidedly polemical purposes, there is little possibility that gnostics could have brought in the same traditions for any purposes other than polemical ones. It makes good sense to see these distorted claims about the ignorance of Israel's God as a polemical answer to the rabbinic polemic against "two powers" which relied heavily on Deuteronomy 32. Our problem is that we are used to seeing polemics carried on in well argued treatises. The rabbis, however, wrote down their arguments in abbreviated exegetical comments, while the gnostics fashioned a cosmogony to function polemically.

The beginning of the polemic can be seen in the New Testament—even in the Gospel of John. There, the Jews are represented as opposing Christianity to the point of excluding those who confess Jesus as Messiah (9:22). But according to the Gospel writer, the crime of Jesus in the eyes of Judaism is not just that he considers himself the Messiah but that he seeks to make himself equal with God:

> We stone you for no good work but for blasphemy; because you, being a man, make yourself a god. (John 10:33)
>
> For this reason, the Jews sought all the more to kill him—not only was he breaking the Sabbath; worse still he was speaking of God as his own father, thus making himself God's equal. (John 5:18)[33]

The penalty for this wrong view in the eyes of the Christian community is that the Jews have given up their role as Israel and become children of the devil:

> "If God were your Father, you would love me, for God is the source of my being. . . . Your father is the devil and you choose to carry out your father's desires. (John 8:42f.)[34]

[33] Translation from R. E. Brown, *The Gospel according to St. John*, AB 29–29A (New York: Doubleday, 1966)

[34] When the Gospel of Truth was published, Gilles Quispel recognized that theology of the name goes back to Jewish sectarianism. See "Jung Codex and its Significance," in *The Jung Codex: A Newly Recovered Gnostic Papyrus*, ed. H. C. Puech, G. Quispel, and W. C. van Unnik, trans. F. L. Cross (London: A. R. Mowbray, 1955), 72. See G. Quispel, "The Origins of the Gnostic Demiurge," in *Kyriakon: Festschrift for Johannes Quasten*, 2 vols. (Leiden: Brill, 1970), 1:271–76; and H. A. Wolfson, "The Pre-existent Angel of the Magharians and Al-Nahawandi," *JQR* 11 (1960): 89–106 for exceedingly cogent

Because they do not recognize the divinity present in Jesus and because they oppose the Christian message, the "Jews" give up their historic role and become demonic. The Johannine community uses the gentilic "Jew" in many places where the synoptic gospels would have used the name of a particular Jewish sect. This change appears to underline a border-passing for the Johannine community. The Johannine community has passed over the boundary between being Jewish and Christian, which was not yet passed for the synoptics. That would mean that the FG was written by a group that excluded itself or felt excluded from the Jewish community in ways that were not clear to the communities which produced the synoptics. Furthermore, the alternative title for Satan in the Gospel of John is the "Lord of this World."

In other words, the Johannine community has projected a dualistic and incipiently gnostic interpretation upon the Jewish community because it feels itself persecuted by it. It is not yet full-blown Gnosticism because the Johannine community values the term "Israel," still claims to worship the Hebrew God, and has not turned over to the Lord of the World the sole responsibility for creation. But the reasons for such a move by later groups within Christianity and Judaism should be obvious.

Some striking ramifications of the evidence in the Nag Hammadi library already seem to be clear. The hypothesis that the Jewish sectarian milieu was a crucial ingredient in gnostic origins as postulated by Quispel, Wolfson, and Scholem seems confirmed.[35] For instance, two documents from the library, which give primary importance to Shem or Seth as revealers, clarify an essentially Jewish sectarian setting for many of the gnostic documents by showing Christian influence to be secondary.

---

discussions of gnostic roots in Jewish sectarianism. See G. Scholem, *Jewish Gnosticism, Merkabah Mysticism, and Talmudic Tradition* (New York: Jewish Theological Seminary of America, 1965); idem, "Über eine Formel in den koptischgnostischen Schriften," *ZNW* 111 (1931): 176. Based on this evidence, Quispel suspects the presence of a related doctrine of heavenly journey by which the adapt's cosmic twin, the self, journeys to behold the angel of the name who is equivalent to "the Face of God" because he is the visible manifestation of God (see "The Birth of the Child," in *Gnostic Studies* [Istanbul: Nederlands Historisch-Archaeologisch Instituut te Istanbul, 1974], 1:221–39, here 223). If so, there would be a continuity in thought between early heretical mysticism, Jewish Christianity, Gnosticism, and Manichaeanism.

[35] See W. Förster, *Gnosis: A Selection of Gnostic Texts*, vol. 2, *Coptic and Mandaean Sources*, trans. R. M. Wilson (Oxford: Oxford University Press, 1972), 13–23.

In the Apocalypse of Adam,[36] Seth functions as the prophet to whom gnosis is given after creation, paralleled by Shem after the flood. Adam is quite important in this treatise. He helps in creation and is higher in rank than the god who created him and Eve. The demiurge attempts to stamp out gnosis by causing a deep sleep of forgetfulness to come over Adam but gnosis later triumphs. Adam is emphasized throughout the text, but he is not the redeemer, only an angelic carrier of the gnosis. Several other figures, including an "illuminator," function as redeemer. Persian themes are present in the birth of the illuminator, like Mithras, from a rock. Yet there is not a single myth of a redeemed redeemer or *anthropos*, because Adam and the redeemer remain separate figures. If any Christian material relating the redeemer to Adam is present at all, it is well disguised. We are therefore justified in describing this document as a non-Christian, heterodox, Jewish-gnostic document, though there is no reason to assume it is pre-Christian in origin.

The same evidence seems to be emerging in reports about the Paraphrase of Shem.[37] In this case as well, we have evidence for a primarily Jewish sectarian document in the Nag Hammadi library. Almost no Christian influence can be seen. On the other hand, the dependence on the Hebrew Bible is obvious. Not only are Sodom and the Sodomites mentioned in a favorable sense, but the flood and the tower of Babel also play a role. All of these contain primary places where the doctrine of "two powers" could be derived. In this case, the major character is called Derdekeas and functions primarily as a redeemer. He is also supposed to be the creator of heaven and earth, rather like Poimandres, except that the atmosphere is not anti-Jewish (Hippolytus, *Haer.* 5.19–22).

Instead of evidence of de-Christianization, we have some evidence that the tractate was Christianized. Hippolytus seems to use a form of the Paraphrase of Shem as his main source for the doctrine of the Sethians. He calls it the Paraphrase of Seth, but the document is essentially the same. In Hippolytus' version, however, several christological

[36] See F. Wisse, "The Redeemer Figure in the Paraphrase of Shem," *NovT* 12 (1970): 130–40.

[37] Fred Wisse finds that the notion of a pre-Christian savior myth is confirmed in this material, even though the document is not pre-Christian. It seems to me more warranted to say that many of the aspects of what is called "the gnostic salvation myth" are present, but the late date makes it impossible to decide when or how all the themes—helper in creation, Adam, angelic mediation, and redemption—came together.

interpretations have been added (5.19, 20). Since Sethians identified Seth with Christ, this indicates a peculiar relationship of Shem and Seth. We must also remember that Shem and Melchizedek are firmly connected with Samaritanism by Ps.-Eupolemos. Shem and Melchizedek are also equated by the rabbis. In the Sethian documents of the Nag Hammadi corpus, the vain claim of the demiurge appears often. In The Second Logos of the Great Seth (NHC VII 2), for instance, the cosmocrator says to the angels, "I am God" but is scorned. The savior in this case has the Hebrew theophoric name "Adonaios" and gnostics ridicule orthodox Christians for believing in "two lords, even a multitude." Preliminary study seems to be showing that this document is an example of non-Christian, Jewish sectarian gnostic work which was later Christianized. Like the *Poimandres* it makes use of material from the Hebrew Bible but in this case it is radically transformed into a "negative value" Judaism for polemical purposes.

It is now possible to speak of the history of the dualist polemic in Judaism and its repercussions in Christianity and Gnosticism. Just as the rabbis were passionately trying to preserve their faith, so too the various "two powers" sectarians were passionately trying to preserve theirs. They refuted the forceful rabbinic charge against binitarianism and dualism, based on Deuteronomy 32, by revaluing the biblical creation to make their God or hero come out on top. The heretics must have reasoned that Israel's God and Christian orthodoxy's God who claimed to be unique as recorded in monotheistic statements of Exodus, Deuteronomy, and Isaiah, was only an ignorant god. He did not know about the gnostic god, who was going to save only those who recognized him—that is, only the "two powers" heretics who were also "gnostic." The church offered a possible haven from the battle because some varieties of Christianity maintained Christologies which were very close to the gnostic idea of the redeemer, and Christianity shared the experience of expulsion from the synagogue for violating the doctrine of monotheism. But both church and synagogue reacted antagonistically to "gnostic" interpretation. Thus we actually have a three-cornered battle. Extreme anti-Jewish Gnosticism can be seen to arise in circumstances where groups holding "two powers" traditions run headlong into the polemics against "two powers" and "many powers" which developed in the rabbinic academies, but which were used by church fathers as well. In a real sense then, both Jewish and Christian orthodoxies and heresies were trying to manipulate scripture in order to demonstrate the veracity of their own beliefs and the authority of their own clergy. The rabbis attempted to use highly rationalized methods of exegesis to show that the stories of the heretics were completely faulty. Their method, midrash, was derived from the discussions of the academies and the sermons of the synagogues. The extreme gnostics countered by developing a massively polemical mythology.[38] The church fathers used both methods against both sides.

More recently, Klaus Koschorke[39] has pointed out that the description of the antagonism between the Jewish God and the Christ in the Testament of Truth and the Apocalypse of Peter parallels the antagonism between the "orthodox" and the "gnostic" in Christianity. The former brings sin into the world and smites with blindness; the latter forgives sin and heals the blind. In radical Gnosticism, the symbolism developed in the Jewish-Christian polemic is being put to a new use. This should not be entirely surprising because the issue of the use of the Old Testament (Marcion) and the term "second god"[40] had been controversial in the formulation of church doctrine as well. The church fathers even made use of the same scriptural passages as the rabbis did when they needed to. Koschorke's argument generally supports the observation of Elaine Pagels[41] that there is a parallel between the gnostic description of the demonic archons and the gnostic description of earthly "orthodox" bishops. It is difficult to know whether Jews were ever in a position to

[38] The whole issue of polemical mythology deserves more serious study, both phenomenologically within history of religions circles and exegetically among scholars of this particular period. In this case, for instance, Deut 32:39 occurs as the boast of the demiurge in such a variety of gnostic systems that one cannot escape the conclusion that the claim itself antedates any mythological setting. Probably many artificial myths were created in order to explain how the claim of the demiurge (that he was the only God) was to be treated. For an analogy, see A. Kragerud, *Die Hymnen der Pistis Sophia* (Oslo: Universitetsforlagets, 1967), esp. 159–220. In that case, the myths about Sophia were created to provide a setting for the Psalms and Odes of Solomon texts which the sect wanted to clarify and interpret. Elaine Pagels reports in "The Demiurge and his Archons—Gnostic Views on the Bishop and Presbyters?" *HTR* 69 (1976): 301f., that a similar battle can be seen between Christian and gnostic bishops.

[39] K. Koschorke, *Die Polemik der Gnostiker gegen das kirchliche Christentum* (Leiden: Brill, 1978), esp. 148–51. He also implies that "Gnosticism" existed more in the minds of the heresiologists than as a unified social movement. Certainly the role of the bishops in labeling a disparate group of phenomena as a single heresy has to be more adequately appraised.

[40] Novation, *De Trin.* 30; Hippolytus, *Haer.* 9.11, 12; Origen, *Cels.* 5.39; 6.61; 7.51; *Or.* 15.1; *Comm. Jo.* 2.2; 10.37 (21).

[41] Pagels, "The Demiurge and His Archons."

discipline and persecute the gnostics, as orthodox Christians were. All that can be said for sure is that the church would have agreed with the rabbis in calling Gnosticism a kind of dualistic heresy (though the rabbis would also have opposed the church on the same issues).

The transformation of values seen in Nag Hammadi is not limited to the third century, when Gnosticism was already full grown. The story of the arrogance of the demiurge was known to the early church fathers. It is reported in Irenaeus (*Haer.* 1.5.2–4 and 1.30.1–6), Hippolytus (*Haer.* 6.33 and 7.25.3), and Epiphanius (*Pan.* 26.2), indicating that the process of transvaluing Judaism to create an evil demiurge in contrast to the saving grace of the gnostic redeemer was already underway by the middle of the second century.

Within the Palestinian community, with its many sects, polemics for monotheism were used in a variety of ways. Paul seems to use anti-"two powers" polemic against Jews whom he charged with venerating angels, while he himself could have been charged with the identical crime by rabbinic Jews (Gal 3).

Once the debate is reconstructed, we are able to understand some of the historical issues affecting the exegesis. By the time of the consolidation of rabbinic authority at Yavneh and the attempt at a new Jewish orthodoxy, mediation traditions were seen as a clear and present danger within rabbinic Judaism. No doubt the rabbis' concern was linked to the political events which immediately preceded. The war had stimulated a terrible crisis of faith. Furthermore, Christians and others had taken the fall of Jerusalem as proof of the end of the Jewish dispensation. Such ideas were heinous to the majority of the Jewish community. A new set of standards was necessary to insure survival. In asserting further control over the synagogue, the rabbis excluded any sectarian who compromised monotheism from participating in the service. This meant that Christians, among others, were excluded from Jewish life. The growing emphasis on strict monotheism characterizes the rabbinic movement and sets it off from the other sects of its time.

The earliest reports about "two powers" in the rabbinic texts were associated with gentiles. This may further indicate that proto-gnostic interpretations of angelic mediation originated in a thoroughly Hellenized kind of Judaism or among gentiles attracted to synagogue services. Apparently, along with the Jewish sectarians, gentiles, who had been drawn to the synagogue to hear the Bible proclaimed, were attracted to biblical monotheism in a form that distinguished between the supreme

God and a divine agent, possibly in a more extreme form than the system that Philo had described. But "two powers" heresy has a clear Jewish sectarian setting as well. All such doctrines, whether in apocalypticism, Christianity, or philosophical speculations, were probably condemned by the rabbis as early as the end of the first century and the beginning of the second. But the gentiles opposed as Jewish heretics would have continued to hear the Christian message.

The response of the excluded groups varied. Orthodox Christianity claimed both that the legal aspects of the Torah were void and that the Jews stubbornly refused to hear the message of the fulfillment of their own Scriptures. A few Christians relied on the teachings of men like Marcion and Cerdo, who argued that the God of salvation was unknown to the Jews. But that was atypical. Others claimed that the god of the official synagogue, in whose name they had been excluded from worship, was not the high god. By his own intransigence he proved he was an ignorant and vain god. For these gnostics, a higher god was envisioned, one who was the author of salvation. These arguments might be phenomenologically similar to Marcion's, but they differed in their use of Jewish Scripture. Unlike Marcion, gnostics used familiar Old Testament verses to help prove their contention of the arrogance of the creator and prophesies the coming savior. Condemned by the standards of strict monotheism, some of the "gnostics" transformed the distinction between the transcendent God and His agent manifestation on earth into a contrast between the high god and the vain demiurge god of the Jews.

The gnostics drew mainly upon the early chapters of Genesis to prove their point. They inherited many ancient traditions congenial to their perspective. But they also created new interpretations: they elaborated cosmogonic myths in order to provide a setting for their claim that Israel's god is ignorant. They also found ways to turn the insults hurled at them into compliments. However, their knowledge and use of other parts of Scripture was more limited. The gnostic use of the Isaiah and Deuteronomy passages seems to have arisen as a defense against the previous Jewish and Christian use of those Scriptures against them.

There is further evidence that some who cherished moderate "two powers" traditions did not adopt anti-Jewish arguments. Jews who had a closer connection to the legal traditions of the community and were not part of the fierce polemic were able to give the traditions a limited form of acceptability in *merkabah* mysticism.

Most others, having been linked together with the Christians by the rabbis, found refuge in the church and incorporated Christian elements into their systems. However, Christianity immediately found itself faced with the same problem that the rabbis were facing. Using the same traditions, Christians began to define orthodoxy and heresy along much more complicated lines. Tertullian claimed that Marcionites, who postulated a second god, were antichrists like Jews. Monarchians and modalists claimed that "orthodoxy," like the gnostics and Marcionites, had compromised Christianity's monotheistic center. Therefore they used "two gods" as a term of approbation against "orthodox" Christianity, just as the rabbis did.

Obviously such a complex picture presents many possibilities for interaction, therefore it cannot be the single authoritative reconstruction of actual events. But it seems to be a credible account of the complete evidence. Besides a general chronological scheme, a new hypothesis is assumed: namely, that the radicalization of Gnosticism was partly a product of the battle between the rabbis, the Christians, and various other "two powers" sectarians who inhabited the outskirts of Judaism and Christianity. The battle was recorded as a debate over the meaning of several scriptural passages, among which were all the angelic or theophany texts of the Old Testament, followed closely by the plurals used by or about God in Scripture. Of course, it took many sides to make this argument. The rabbis' polemical statements were justified from their perspective by sectarian readiness to dilute strict monotheism in order to support traditions which applied to their ancestors, heroes and saviors. From the other perspectives, the attempt to establish a "normative" Judaism was seen as exclusivist and caused the radicalization of the sectarian community. Therefore, it is possible to say that Gnosticism arose in Judaism by social polarization initiated by the issue of God's primary angel.

One advantage of this new hypothesis for describing the gnostic debate is that it not only accounts for the large quantity of Jewish material in Gnosticism and the phenomenological similarity between various protognostic groups, but it also accounts for the anti-Jewish bias of extreme Gnosticism. Phenomenologically and historically, the gnostic demiurge is the second deity of the earlier "two powers" theology. Usually he has appropriated half of the traditions about the second power, yielding the honorable traditions to the gnostic savior. The agent manifestation of God was therefore identified with the limited god of the Jews while the high god, unknown to Jews or Christians, was reserved only for the gnostics.

This theory, of course, does not address the history of gnostic and anti-gnostic speculation within pagan philosophy. Many of the concepts employed by the heretics were also developed in Neoplatonism, for example. It is better suited for Sethian than Valentinian evidence. But the theory does give a good account of the history of the phenomenon as it existed within its Jewish context. One ramification of this hypothesis lies in the area of New Testament scholarship. This history of traditions seems to show that radical Gnosticism superseded rather than preceded Christianity as a target for the rabbinic debate. The rabbinic polemic seems to have been developed around doctrines like Christianity, to be applied later to more virulent dualisms.

This study began with the observation that rabbinic evidence cannot easily be used to solve the problems of the origin of Gnosticism. More than illustrating the difficulty of studying rabbinic texts, I have tried to show that some valuable information about Gnosticism can be gained when rabbinic exegetical issues can be placed in their appropriate contexts by comparison with Hellenistic writers like Philo and the church fathers. Hidden within the texts is the Jewish witness to the rise of Christianity even though the texts date from centuries later. They certainly give us a good idea of some of the issues over which Christianity and Judaism separated. In some ways, the more important point is methodological. Rabbinic evidence can sometimes be dated earlier than the redaction dates of the documents, when an exact and appropriate fit can be found with the better attested non-rabbinic evidence. Continued close study of rabbinic evidence and its non-rabbinic parallels may reveal more of this epoch-making period for all the religious traditions of the West.

TWO

THE RULER OF THIS WORLD

The problem of normative group self-definition is nowhere more evident than in the discussion of the rise of Gnosticism. Although the question of the origins of Gnosticism has occupied scholarly attention for a century, there has been surprisingly little interest in the social situation in which the orthodox and heretical groups separated or in how the various sects and denominations came to the conclusion that they were different from their neighbors. All too often a simple answer to the problem of gnostic self-definition has been assumed: Gnosticism is the inevitable outcome of the combination of Hebrew and Greek thought, a spirit of late antiquity, the dominant form of late Hellenistic spirituality. Just before, during, or after this encounter, Christian and Jewish orthodoxies arose to defend the faithful from such a radical synthesis.[1] Some form of

[1] This chapter appeared originally as "Ruler of this World: Attitudes towards Mediator Figures and the problem of a Sociology of Gnosticism," in *Jewish and Christian Self-Definition*, vol. 2, *Aspects of Judaism in the Greco-Roman Period*, ed. E. P. Sanders with A. I. Baumgarten and Alan Mendelson (Philadelphia: Fortress, 1981), 245–68, 403–13 and is used with permission. It would go too far afield now to summarize the many relationships which scholars have posited among Judaism, Christianity and Gnosticism. Perhaps since Gnosticism was first described by church fathers, Christian scholars have been the most interested in the problem. Although there is agreement among them in correlating Christianity with Gnosticism, there is hardly any agreement on a theory which would explain that correlation. Particularly thorny has been the problem of whether Gnosticism or Christianity is the chronological predecessor. Did Christianity grow out of a gnostic environment or did Gnosticism grow out of a Christian one? The early church fathers saw Gnosticism as a Christian heresy, and they first reported the term "gnostic" as a description of it. But from Graetz's time forward it became clear that the question of priority could not be addressed without careful study of Jewish texts. See Alan F. Segal, *Two Powers in Heaven: Early Rabbinic Reports about Christianity and Gnosticism* (Leiden: Brill, 1977), 1–30, esp. 14–18. Also see C. Colpe, *Die Religionsgeschichtliche Schule* (Göttingen: Vandenhoeck & Ruprecht, 1961); W. A. Meeks, *The Prophet-King: Moses Traditions and the*

this intellectual dialectic has been widely assumed by many recent scholars, perhaps to sidestep the overall problem of gnostic origins in order to address more specific exegetical problems within their own fields of competence. Of course, I do not mean to say that this enterprise has been profitless. Rather, it has been advantageous to set aside some of the larger textual problems inherent in the publication of the Nag Hammadi material.[2]

Though recent sociological studies on the rise of Gnosticism represent a different perspective they are nevertheless important and complementary.[3] By looking for the social forces which contributed to the rise of Gnosticism, their authors are attempting to get beyond the tacit assumption of an intellectual dialectic operating in history to face the social settings within which Gnosticism developed. The force of the new sociological perspective has been towards the general once again, but we should not feel prevented from trying to locate specific textual evidence about the issue of normative self-definition; for when it comes to this thorny problem, archaeology, the primary body of data available to

---

Johannine Christology (Leiden: Brill, 1967), 6–17; E. Yamauchi, *Pre-Christian Gnosticism: A Survey of the Proposed Evidence* (Grand Rapids: Eerdmans, 1973), 13–28; L. Ginzberg, *Die Haggada bei den Kirchenvaetem* (Amsterdam: 1899); I. Heinemann, *Darkhe ha-Agadah* (Jerusalem: Magnes, 1954); S. Lieberman, *Greek in Jewish Palestine: Studies in the Life and Manners in Jewish Palestine in the II–IV Centuries C.E.* (New York: Feldheim, 1965); idem, *Hellenism in Jewish Palestine: Studies in the Literary Transmission, Beliefs, and Manners of Palestine in the I Century B.C.E.–IV Century B.C.E.* (New York: Jewish Theological Seminary of America, 1962); E. E. Urbach, *The Sages: Their Concepts and Beliefs* (Jerusalem: Magnes, 1975); and idem, "Teshubat Anshe Ninevah ve-Havikuah Ha-Yehudi-Nozri," *Tarbiz* 20 (1950): 118–22.

[2] For a summary of research on the gnostic problem, see R. Haardt, "Zur Methodologie der Gnosisforschung," in *Gnosis und Neues testament: Studien aus Religionswissenschaft und Theologie*, ed. K. Tröger (Berlin: Evangelische Verlagsanstalt, 1973), 77–88.

[3] See E. M. Mendelson, "Some Notes on a Sociological Approach to Gnosticism," in *Le origini dello gnosticismo*, ed. U. Bianchi, Numen Supplement 12 (Leiden: Brill, 1967), 668–76; Hans Kippenberg, "Versuch einer soziologischen Verortung des antiken Gnostizismus," *Numen* 17 (1950): 211–31; Kurt Rudolph, "Das Problem einer Soziologie und sozialen Verortung der Gnosis," *Kairos* 19 (1977): 35–54; Petr Pokorny, "Der soziale Hintergrund der Gnosis," in Tröger, ed., *Gnosis und Neues Testament*, 77–88; Peter Munz, "The Problem of 'Die soziologische Verortung des antiken Gnostizismus,"' *Numen* 19 (1972): 41–51; Henry Green, "Gnosis and Gnosticism: A Study in Methodology," *Numen* 24 (1977): 95–134; idem, "Suggested Sociological Themes in the Study of Gnosticism," *VC* 31 (1977): 169–80; idem, *The Economic and Social Origins of Gnosticism* (Atlanta: Scholars, 1985); Elaine Pagels, "The Demiurge and His Archons," *HTR* 69 (1976): 3011.

the social historian of antiquity, has unfortunately been less helpful than one would first imagine. Rather than solve the problem of the origins of Gnosticism, these general sociological analyses have so far had the function of giving us a new set of questions about the role of sociological encounter in the development of a group's normative self-definition. In this chapter I shall try to show that a social-scientific perspective can help clarify the meaning of an ambiguous history of tradition precisely because it helps shift our emphasis from the issue of the origins of the tradition to the issue of its use within two communities in conflict. I hope I can show how conflict determines each party's self-definition and, at the same time, reveals an important clue in the origin of Gnosticism.

The tradition I have in mind is that of the "Ruler of the World." Though, as we shall see, the tradition is quite broad, the "Ruler of the World" remains one of the minor figures of the Gospel of John. He is nevertheless closely connected to the issue of the Gnosticism within that document. He occurs three times in the FG—John 12:31, 14:30 (in the attributive position but no change in meaning), and 16:11—and is probably related to the "God of this World" who appears in the Pauline corpus (2 Cor 4:4). "The rulers of the darkness of the world" appears in Ephesians 6:12, and "prince of the power of the air" appears in Ephesians 2:2. The title "Ruler of the World" is applied to Beliar in the earlier part of the Ascension of Isaiah (1:3; 2:4; 10:29). Ignatius uses similar terms several times (*Eph.* 17.1; 19.1). No terminological exactitude is maintained but the reference to supernatural opposition is unmistakable. Obviously, he is not a major character in the drama. Like Rosencranz or Guildenstern in Shakespeare's *Hamlet*, he performs a small and necessary if dishonorable function. He is the leader of the supernatural forces who oppose Jesus but "who already have been beaten" (John 16:11).

Most of the occurrences in the New Testament evince the theme of supernatural opposition, but I shall confine myself to the Gospel of John for the purpose of this chapter.[4] Though the Ruler of the World is

[4] See the article by A. W. Carr, "The Rulers of this Age—1 Corinthians 2:6-8," *NTS* 23 (1976): 20–35. Carr deals primarily with the Pauline corpus, while assuming that the Ruler of this World in the FG is Satan. He mounts an argument that the "rulers of this age" in Paul are the earthly rulers who crucified Jesus (which may or may not be correct). He is far too cavalier in dismissing Cullmann's theory of a double, divine and human, referent for the Pauline term. Nevertheless, his review of research on the subject is very useful, and so I have not reproduced his bibliographical entries. I do not think it is necessary to distinguish Pauline from other usages as carefully as he must to come to

not explicitly identified with Satan in the FG there can be no question that his demonic role is primary. In John 12:31 Jesus states that the Ruler of this World is about to be driven out, while Jesus shall draw all men to himself. In John 14:31 Jesus comments that the Ruler of this World approaches, but that he has no rights over Jesus. In John 16:11 Jesus says that he is about to pass from sight and return to the Father, while the Paraclete will convince the Jews that divine judgment will soon be upon them. The comment is occasioned as an answer to the synagogue, which has ostracized Johannine Christians from worship (John 9:22; 12:42; 16:2) and which is supposed to believe that persecuting Christians is a religious duty (John 16:2). The Paraclete provides an answer to this alleged hostility by revealing that divine judgment awaits the Jews from God because they are of this world. The sign of this coming judgment is that the Ruler of this World stands already condemned. Here the Ruler of the World is part of one of the strongest anti-Jewish polemics in the New Testament. For the moment I can only note that the supernatural figure and the anti-Jewish polemic are related; I want to return to the relationship later, to show that, ironically, where the gospel is being most anti-Jewish, it is relying heavily on Jewish traditions.[5] And it is precisely at this point that the problem of group definition will come clearly into focus.

In apocalyptic and Christian traditions, the demonic aspect of the Ruler of this World became more and more evident. Ignatius implies that the Ruler of this World is the captain of evil (*Eph.* 17.1; 19.1). In the Ascension of Isaiah the figure is Beliar, evidently identified with Melchira, which is probably one name for the evil angel opposing Melchizedek at Qumran.[6] Thus it seems clear that Christianity is using traditions which it shares with apocalyptic Judaism.

While these statements about the Ruler of this World may impress us as a strange corner of the Johannine universe, the really striking aspect of the tradition does not become clear until one contrasts the Pauline,

---

his conclusions. One can expect a certain residual parallel between rulers on earth and in heaven in most Hellenistic writing even if it is taken ironically. In a different way we both agree that the terms should be linked to human opponents. See below.

5 See W. A. Meeks, "'Am I a Jew?' Johannine Christianity and Judaism," in *Christianity, Judaism, and Other Greco-Roman Cults: Studies for Morton Smith at Sixty*, part 1: *New Testament*, ed. J. Neusner (Leiden: Brill, 1975), 163–86, here 172.

6 J. T. Milik, "Milki-sedeq et Milki-rasha dan les anciens écrits Juifs et Chrétiens," *JJS* 4 (1972): 95–144; and *RB* 79 (1972): 77–97.

Johannine, and apocalyptic portrayal of the Ruler of this World with the rabbinic one: *the rabbinic view contains no trace of the negative characterization which seems absolutely essential to the other portraits.*[7]

In rabbinic literature, the Prince of the World is regarded as the reciter of certain psalms in praise of God. For instance, in b. Yebam. 16b, he is said to be the speaker of Psalm 37:25: "I have been young, now I am old, yet I have not seen the righteous forsaken or his children begging bread."[8] In b. Hul. 60a, Psalm 104:31 is ascribed to the Prince of the World: "May the glory of the Lord endure forever. Let the Lord rejoice in His world." In b. Sanh. 94a, he appears in a puzzling discussion about the identity of the messiah. The Prince of the World becomes an advocate for the messiahship of Hezekiah by pointing out that during Hezekiah's time the earth fulfilled God's desire for a song of praise. The identity of the messiah, however, remains hidden as one of the secrets of God. In each case the Prince of the World offers praise, not opposition, to God. In 3 Enoch, the Prince of the World is sometimes the leader of the princes of the kingdoms of the earth. In other places, he is the ruler or prince of the heavenly bodies. In the Enoch-Metatron

[7] It is amazing how often this fact is ignored; J. H. Bernard, for instance (*The Gospel According to St John* [Edinburg: T&T Clark, 1928], 2:441), relies on Lightfoot to claim that the Prince of the World is a standard title for Satan in Jewish literature, without mentioning the significant rabbinic exception. Of course, it would be remarkable for an angel to be called the "God" of this world in rabbinic literature, although Moses is so called by the biblical Exodus account. ἄρχων is a standard translation for the Hebrew *SR* (שר, "Prince"); שר and ἄρχων are normal epithets for angelic beings in Hebrew and Greek literature respectively. For more information on the concept of mediator, see A. Oepke, "Μεσίτης," *TDNT* 4:602, 615; and J. Fossum, *The Name of God and the Angel of the Lord* (Tübingen: Mohr Siebeck, 1985). Herb Basser reminds me that many of the functions of the negative "Lord of this World" can be seen in rabbinic portrayals of Satan, *Sar Gehinnom*, and the *yetzer ha-ra*. See Eccles. Rab. 4:15; Num. Rab. 11:5; Ps. Rab. 9:5, p. 82; Tanh. Noah 19; Eqev 11; Exod. Rab. 41; b. Shabb. 104a, 105b; b. B. Bat. 16b; b. Sukk. 52a–b.

[8] R. Jonathan infers that the psalm must have been said by the Prince of this World because David was not old enough to see that the statement was true. Obviously R. Jonathan is aware that it is not easy to verify that righteousness is always rewarded in this world. He must then understand the psalm to describe the final retribution of souls in the next life, or else the comment about David makes no sense at all. One notes a rather similar argument in Acts 2:24-31 where Luke concludes that Ps 16:8-11 must refer to a future messiah, not David himself, since David died.

traditions, Metatron often takes over the functions essential to the Prince of the World.[9]

All these passages are quite late. But both Gershom Scholem[10] and Hugo Odeberg[11] (whatever their other differences) have noted that the Prince of the World also has a role in *merkabah* mysticism which would allow us to push the date of these traditions much further back. In fact, Scholem suggests that the figure of the Prince of the World has the same titles and functions—hierophant and angelic guardian of Israel—as does the archangel Michael. Furthermore, this makes him rather similar to Metatron or to the "angel of the Lord" or "YHWH the Lesser" in mystical speculation, all of whom are said to "carry the tetragrammaton."[12] This means that the intermediaries are not just angels but come

[9] See *3 Enoch*, trans. and ed. H. Odeberg (New York: Ktav, 1973), esp. 47 and 53 in the Hebrew section. In 30:2 the Prince of the World pleads in favor of the world before the Holy One. In 38:1 he is the ruler of the heavenly bodies. See also 10:3; 48:9(c); 46.2; and 14:1–3 where Metatron takes over these functions. In b. Hul. 60a, the Tosafot (s.v. *pasuk*) deny an identification between the two figures. But what is important is the existence of a primary angelic mediator with charge over the world, not whether tradition invariably called him Metatron or distinguished between him and the Lord of the World.

[10] See G. Scholem, *Major Trends in Jewish Mysticism* (New York Schocken Books, 1961), 40–79, and esp. *Jewish Gnosticism, Merkabah Mysticism, and Talmudic Tradition* (New York: Jewish Theological Seminary of America, 1965), 43f., 48–51, and notes.

[11] See Odeberg, *3 Enoch.*

[12] Odeberg and Scholem disagree about the relationship between the Prince of this World and Michael. Scholem notes that one of the Tosafot rejects the identification between the two and that they are never brought into relation by the talmudic or midrashic passages. In Pirqe de R. Eliezer, chap. 27, however, Michael is given the title Prince of this World, while a magic bowl inscription calls Metatron the Great Prince of All the World. (See C. D. Isbell, *Corpus of the Aramaic Incantation Bowls* [Missoula, Mont.: SBL, 1975], nos. 34.4; 49.1; 56.12). Scholem suggests that a previous linking of Metatron to Michael may account for the identification with the Prince of this World. The use of Ps 37:25 Scholem finds secondary, because the root idea of נער is "servant" at the divine throne rather than "youth." However, Scholem may not have taken adequate account of the psalm passage taken together with Daniel traditions where God, as the Ancient of Days, is helped through the Son of Man, who is views as a young warrior in rabbinic tradition. These speculations about God's human appearance are quite old. Scholem was forced to admit that one manuscript of Shiur Koma does mention the "Lord of the World" and that Metatron and he are described with the same language. In general, Scholem's caution is to be taken over Odeberg's enthusiasm. But in this case, Tosafot to b. Yebam. 16b explain the title נער as a reference to Ps 37:25 and I am inclined to agree, once the importance of Dan 7:13f. is seen. See MRI Shirta 4, Bahodesh 5 for an example of this tradition and the rabbinic condemnation of it by means of the designation "two powers." For a discussion of its antiquity, see my book *Two Powers in Heaven*,

dangerously close to being anthropomorphic hypostases of God himself. A first-century date for traditions of this type is virtually assured by the appearance of Yahoel in the Apocalypse of Abraham. The details of the tradition need not concern us. I merely want to point out that there is evidence for a positive portrayal of the figure in mystical and rabbinical speculation while Christianity and apocalypticism share the negative image of the Prince of the World.

The question is why? Why should the traditions differ so completely in the two literatures? A history of religions study might yield convincing evidence for the priority of either a negative or positive portrayal of the character. There is a rich classical and Jewish background to the titles. Biblical usage is probably the basis for all the speculation, but the Bible itself appears to be adopting the ancient Near Eastern usage in polemical fashion.[13]

Equally or more important for the Hellenistic period is the use of the titles similar to "Ruler of the World" in the cults of Syria and Palmyra. We know that Ba'al Shamin was called מרא עולם or Ζεύς μέγιστος κεραίος by the second century.[14] A similar history can be seen in the

chap. 2. For relevance to the Name of God traditions, see the work of G. Quispel, esp. "Qumran, John and Jewish Christianity," in *John and Qumran*, ed. J. H. Charlesworth, (London: Geoffrey Chapman, 1972), 137–55, esp. 149f.

[13] See "lord of all the earth" in Josh 3:11, 13; Mic 4:13; Zech 4:11; 6:5; Ps 97:5. In Jdt 2:5 the title is applied to Nebuchadnezzar. See W. Hallo, *Early Mesopotamian Royal Titles* (New Haven, Conn.: American Oriental Society, 1957), 21–29, 49–56; A. Petitjean, *Les oracles du Proto-Zacharie: Un programme de restauration pour la communauté juive après l'exil*, (Paris: Lecoffre, 1969). There are a series of problems in Ugaritic concerning the title אל עולם and its cognates and equivalents. It is difficult to say whether or not the title designates an independent divinity or is a standard epithet. Then too the meaning of the term is not so clear as it should be. Does it signify "eternal Lord," or "Lord of the World"? Apparently the original term was the former while the latter meaning is derivative. Also it is possible that the original term connoted the lord of the underworld; therefore, the Hebrew appropriation may have been a deliberate epithet favoring monotheism in that YHWH (not Mot or Shamash, etc.) was Lord of the Dead as well as the Living. See Alan Cooper, "Divine Names and Epithets in the Ugaritic Texts," in *Ras Shamra Parallels: The Texts from Ugaritic and the Hebrew Bible*, vol. 3, ed. Stan Rummel, Analecta Orientalia 51 (Rome: Pontifical Biblical Institute, 1981), 431–41.

[14] See W. H. Waddington, *Inscriptions grecques et latines de la Syrie* (Paris: Didot, 1870), 2631; *CIS* 2 (1889): 3912; A. J. Jaussen and R. Savignac, *Mission archéologique en Arabie*, vol. 1, *De Jérusalem au Hedjaz Médaine-Saleh* (Paris: Paul Geuthner, 1909), 172f., 177. J. Teixidor, in *The Pagan God: Popular Religion in the Greco-Roman Near East* (Princeton: Princeton University Press, 1977), concludes that by the mid-third century מרי עלמא is no longer

inscriptions of the Nabataeans. Ba'al Shamin and Bel are invoked as מרי עולם in Palmyrene.[15] Thus, the term is used both of earthly and heavenly rulers, in a normal corresponding fashion. As in the older material, there is confusion as to whether the title can be an independent divinity as well as an epithet.

Rabbinic literature directly parallels this usage.[16] Without reference to dating for the moment, we may note that the rabbis often called God, אדון העולם, "Lord of the World," or אדון העלמים, "Lord of the Worlds" (Derekh Bretz 4). In the targumim (see Exod 24:10) the term is frequently מדי די עולם (see, e.g., Exod 24:10 and Deut 32:8). In probable polemic against the Christian "Lord" the rabbis stress that God himself is to be called "Lord." Simeon b. Yohai is reported to have taught that Abraham first called God "Lord" (Gen 15:2; b. Ber. 7b) while R. Aha, a later rabbi, apparently contradicted his predecessor (Gen. Rab. 17:4, pp. 155–56; Ps. Rab. 8:26, p. 74; PRK, Parah, p. 61; Eccles. Rab. 7:23). R. Isaac speaks of God as אדון כל העולם (Gen. Rab. 39:1, p. 365). Of great importance is the polemic against the arrogation of the term by Pharaoh and the impudence of a man calling himself God (Exod. Rab. 5:19). This is substantiated as a Hellenistic polemic against tyranny in Philo's *Embassy to Gaius* 8, where Gaius is described as having succeeded to "rule over all the land and sea." In the MRSbY בעל העולם is reported as a title for God by "the contemptible," which perhaps reflects gnostic or Christian usage, because this term was employed in various ways in both Christianity and Gnosticism. The rabbinic term "contemptible" certainly reflects an opposing or heretical group. There are innumerable other references to God as "The Great One of Goodness" or "The Great One of the World" (העולם). Of course, the rabbis never call God

an epithet of Ba'al Shamin but a divine name to which a devotee might offer a separate invocation.

[15] G. A. Cooke, *A Text-Book of North-Semitic Inscriptions* (Oxford: Clarendon, 1903), 295 no. 133. At Efca, however, "Lord of the World" probably refers to Bel and not to Ba'al Shamin. See M. Gawlikowski, *Recueil d'inscriptions palmyréniennes provenant des fouilles syriennes et polonaises récentes à Palmyre* (Paris: Imprimerie National, 1974), 60n125f.

[16] The classic work on rabbinic titles for God was A. Marmorstein, *The Old Rabbinic Doctrine of God*, vol. 1, *The Names and Attributes of God* (Oxford: Oxford University Press, 1927). However, this has been supplemented by Urbach, *The Sages*, see esp. chaps. 4, 7 8, 9. See also J. G. Weiss, "On the Formula *Melekh Ha-'Olam* as Anti-Gnostic Protest," *JJS* 10 (1959): 169–71; E. J. Weisenberg, "The Liturgical Term *Melekh Ha-'Olam*," *JJS* 15 (1964): 1–56; J. Heinemann, "Once More *Melekh Ha-'Olam*," *JJS* 15 (1964): 149–54.

merely the God of this world. Whenever the subject is broached, they explicitly point out that He is God of this world and the next.[17]

A good many of these references are late and, like מלך מלכי המלכים, may reflect rabbinic reaction to an already existent title for earthly rulers and divinities. Nevertheless, some usage of the term "Lord of the World" is certainly antique, for Genesis 21:33 calls God אל עולם and Psalm 10:16 has מלך עולם. Furthermore, by the first century, there is certain evidence that usage like the rabbinic one had already evolved in Judaism, as is shown by the plural ending in 1QapGen ar II, 20, מרה עלמיה.

There is some evidence that the title was used even outside the semitic language group. In one of the fragments of the Acts of Paul the title "ruler of this world" is applied to "woman." The use, though late, may suggest some of the irony which must have figured in the development of the polemic against the Jews in the FG:

> Woman, ruler of this world, mistress of much gold, citizen of great luxury, splendid in thy raiment, sit down on the floor and forget thy riches and thy beauty and thy finery. For these will profit thee nothing if thou pray not to God. (Acts Paul 7)[18]

A certain reference to Adonai as Lord of the World occurs in the magical papyri,[19] in which the Hebrew God is reduced to an angelic demon, though still a positive one.

The evidence then is not meager but manifold. It gives us an enormous range of possibilities for deriving separate usages in Judaism and Christianity. In view of this extensive evidence it is unsatisfactory merely to claim that the Christian and apocalyptic evidence represents the entrance of a title for a pagan god into apocalyptic Judaism and Christianity as a demon while the rabbinic evidence represents an independent use of the tradition as an angelic figure. The title was a loose, not a close epithet. Though it was associated with pagan gods and with the Roman Emperor, it was also clearly a normal epithet for the Hebrew God as well. Thus we have to give up the idea of any simple development for the term. Whatever the origin and development of the term, the rabbinic and Christian uses represent opposing transformations of it.

[17] See my *Two Powers in Heaven*, 35–37.

[18] Translation in *New Testament Apocrypha*, vol. 2, *Writings Relating to the Apostles; Apocalypses and Related Topics*, ed. W. Schneemelcher, trans. R. McL. Wilson (Louisville, Ky.: Westminster, 1965), 370.

[19] *PGM* III. 211f.

The real question then is to discuss both the negative portrayal in Christianity and its contrast with the angelic figure in Judaism. We cannot be absolutely sure that a positive independent angelic *figure* existed in Judaism before the Christian usage, but it seems clear that the *term*[20] was at least used of God and was in the process of becoming a hypostasis in pagan usage and possibly even an angelic title in Judaism in the first century. My point is only that when the traditions differ so greatly one has to wonder if any information would be gained by attempting to clarify a multifaceted origin. Are we not falling prey to a kind of genetic fallacy in assuming that one single original usage could explain the development of the tradition? Since the bodies of material are so different we should be willing to posit many possible derivations and try to specify the conditions in each community which made the tradition evolve in unique ways. We have to ask the perplexing question: What are the different functions of these opposing portrayals of the Prince of the World?

It is already clear that we are dealing with communities in conflict and must seek a paradigm which will allow us to discuss friction and social change as well as a basic social charter. Mary Douglas, in *Natural Symbols*,[21] provides us with a summary statement of this kind of social paradigm, because she asks a key question in a very concise way: "Do definable relationships exist between a group's social position and its symbol system?"[22] Since her answer is positive, she goes on to develop a model of society which allows both for an analysis of social change and for cross-cultural comparisons.

[20] I.e., the title "Lord of the World" and closely similar titles, many of which are listed in the preceding discussion.

[21] See Mary Douglas, *Natural Symbols: Explorations in Cosmology*, 2nd ed. (London: Barrie & Jenkins, 1973), 91, 122, 144–45, 153, 199. See also Sheldon Isenberg and Dennis F. Owen, "Bodies, Natural and Contrived: The Work of Mary Douglas," *Religious Studies Review* 3 (1977): 1–17.

[22] Of course, Douglas is also interested in the relationship between social structure and religion and she is not the only scholar with these interests. One might easily mention Durkheim, Topitsch, or Fromm, all of whom posit a relationship between social and political structures and conceptual thinking about divinity. Douglas is representative of the position not only because she asks the question clearly but because she suggests that concepts of the human body might provide the link between the two. As we have already seen, the "Lord of the World" is clearly a human figure projected into heaven and hence grist for her mill. See Munz, "The Problem of 'Die soziologische Verortung.'"

In *Natural Symbols* Douglas designs a very elegant system which exposes the relationship between a society and its concept of divinity in a Durkheimian fashion. We do not need to discuss the merits of her entire scheme, whether or not she subscribes to Durkheimian social reductionism, or even whether Durkheim's social reductionism is desirable. Since Douglas' writing is being used here as an example of a general perspective we do not have to enter into the methodological issue of whether either variable, social structure or religion, is independent of the other. For our purposes we can assume that they are mutually dependent. Sometimes social structure affects theology; sometimes the opposite. All we have to note is the frequent parallel relationship between a given social structure and a society's idea of divinity. In this case we can be very pragmatic. We almost always know the ideology of early Jewish groups; we sometimes know their structure. If the relationship between them could be defined more completely, we might be able to discover why the figure of the Lord of the World has such different coloring in different communities. Based on Douglas' inquiry, we should expect that societies undergoing deep social conflicts would seek to express those conflicts in their ideologies and divine economy, if the chance for expression were presented. Douglas's description of the phenomenon, though still very general, would help us locate more details. Dualism, she finds, is characteristic of small, competitive communities: "Small competitive communities tend to believe themselves in a dangerous universe, threatened by sinister powers operated by fellow human beings."[23] She tries to show that groups which have negative opinions of the world and who personify it as hostile often live in small, closed communities with a characteristically high degree of internal social pressure. They often perceive themselves as passing through a period of persecution, a situation which may be partially confirmed in fact but which is often magnified and projected into hostility on the part of cosmic powers. It often serves as the justification for fission and expulsion, as in some African witchcraft accusations.[24]

[23] Douglas, *Natural Symbols*, 137.

[24] In the case of witchcraft accusations, the society's ideology has not developed the ability to comprehend the hostility from within, so that it posits an outside danger. This also seems partially true of the Johannine community. But the analogy is not complete. See below for a more complete discussion. I have not entered Douglas' specific theoretical constructions, not because she concentrates on African witchcraft belief, but

Obviously the "Prince of the World" occurs as part of a larger and very complicated symbolic system which, under the name of Johannine theology, has been a subject of New Testament scholarship for generations. Modern scholarship has also noted that the social context of Johannine Christianity is discoverable, and most scholars would agree that Douglas' descriptions of dualistic communities are generally applicable to the Johannine group.[25]

We may now return to the relationship between the Ruler of this World and the anti-Jewish polemics in which he participates. The references to the Ruler of this World appear in highly charged contexts where the targets of the hostility are specifically mentioned as Jews. Scholars have noticed the symbolic character of the FG's usage of the term "Jew." Unlike the other Gospels the FG uses the term "Jew" frequently and often uses it in places where the other Gospels would have distinguished between various Jewish sects in Palestine. Having noticed this shift, Rudolf Bultmann maintains that the Jews of the FG serve as symbolic representatives of the world in its hostility to the Christian God.[26] Although it is true that the Jews are often used in a typological way, it is equally important to note the obvious fact that it is the Jews and not some other group who have been chosen for this onerous symbol. The Johannine group is not using symbols arbitrarily. Some social reality must be reflected in the symbolic statement. We should therefore expect that the "Lord of the World" and "the God of the Jews" should be linked somehow.

It would be very difficult to characterize the social reality from the FG account alone; for, like most historical and religious documents, it

---

because I do not want us to be needlessly distracted from our major inquiry. But I do want to maintain that, no matter how much one would want to object to the analogy between African witchcraft and the early Christian community, her model does offer some important perspectives on our problem. Basically, she, like other social scientists, is pointing to a congruence between social structure on the one hand and theology on the other. This observation has been profitably used to study Qumran. See Sheldon Isenberg, "Mary Douglas and Hellenistic Religions: The Case of Qumran," in *SBL 1975 Seminary Papers*, 2 vols., SBLSP 9 (Missoula, Mont.: Scholars, 1975), 1:179–85.

[25] See, for instance, J. H. Charlesworth, "A Critical Comparison of the Dualism in 1QS 3.13–4.26 and the 'Dualism' Contained in the Gospel of John," *NTS* 15 (1968–1969): 389–418. It is clear from Charlesworth's article that the dualisms of the two communities have unique aspects and affinities and that it would be wrong to underestimate the this-worldly/otherworldly, above/below, good/evil dichotomies of John.

[26] See R. Bultmann, *The Gospel of John* (Louisville, Ky.: Westminster, 1971), 86.

is highly tendentious. Nevertheless, one can start by characterizing the Jewish position in the FG. For instance, according to John 9:22, if anyone confessed Jesus as Messiah, the Jews excluded him from the synagogue. This implies that the Johannine community feels itself ostracized as heretical from the Jewish synagogue and that it is quite bothered by the fact (see John 9:22; 12:42; 16:2).[27]

If the extent of the Jewish opposition is clear in the FG's portrayal, its nature and content come out only in polemical contradistinction to the Johannine position. The debates with the Jews concerning the identity of the messiah in the FG, and even those about the law and Sabbath observances (John 5:9-18; 7:21-24; 9:13-16), are but occasions for the question of the authority of Jesus.[28] When the Jews reject Jesus as messiah because he does not bring national redemption (John 6:15; 11:4-6; 19:12), the evangelist does not directly argue against them. Instead he states that they understand Jesus in a this-worldly way,[29] for the Johannine Christ, though called Messiah explicitly (1:41; 4:25), is far more than an anointed one, the usual Jewish understanding of messiah (18:33-37).

[27] While the report may be exaggerated by the evangelist or even refer to nonrabbinic synagogues, we certainly know some of the mechanisms by which rabbinic leaders sought to silence heresy. They standardized prayer and ritual, seeking to censor any leader of the congregation who inserted suspicious clauses in prayer (see m. Meg. 4.5 and parallels). The penalty was probably neither death, as the Gospel implies (John 16:2), nor *herem* (הרם), nor *nidui* (נדוי), which seem to be later and were primarily used within the rabbinic community, not as weapons against heretics. Instead, we should probably assume that this kind of opposition to the Christian heresy was restricted to special uses of already existent instruments such as exclusion from the synagogue service, the prayer against the *minim* (מינים), charges of magic, "leading astray," etc. See J. Louis Martyn, *History and Theology in the Fourth Gospel*, 2nd ed. (Nashville: Abingdon, 1979), 12–45; G. Forkman, *The Limits of the Religious Community: Expulsion from the Religious Community within the Qumran Sect, within Rabbinic Judaism, and within Primitive Christianity* (Lund: Gleerup, 1972); C. H. Hunzinger, "Die jüdische Bannpraxis im neutestamentlichen Zeitalter" (Ph..D diss., University of Göttingen, 1954); J. Heinemann, *Prayer in the Talmud: Forms and Patterns*, trans. Richard Sarason (Berlin: de Gruyter, 1977; from the 2nd Heb. ed. [Jerusalem: Hebrew University Press, 1966]); J. E. Mignard, "Jewish and Christian Cultic Discipline to the Middle of the Second Century" (Ph.D. diss., Boston University, 1966); and the essays of E. Urbach, L. Schiffman, and R. Kimelman in Sanders, ed., *Jewish and Christian Self-Definition*, vol. 2.

[28] On this issue, see the groundbreaking work of N. A. Dahl, "The Johannine Church and History," in *Current Issues in New Testament Interpretation*, ed. W. Klassen and G. Snyder (New York: Harper & Row, 1962), 129f.

[29] See W. A. Meeks, "The Man from Heaven in Johannine Sectarianism," *JBL* 91 (1972): 44–72.

He is the λόγος and the Savior of the world. It is particularly interesting that these claims give him the status of what might be described as a principal, angelic mediator in other kinds of Judaism, relating him to traditions about the figure of the Prince of the World in other Jewish communities. One unusual aspect of the Johannine description of Jesus, however, is the claim that he is a divine hypostasis. The evangelist states this claim clearly and unambiguously at the very opening of the Gospel. Obviously the link between the messiah and a divine hypostasis is an exceedingly important aspect of the Johannine church's beliefs. Furthermore, according to a commonly accepted interpretation of John 8:58, Jesus claims the divine name YHWH translated as ἐγώ εἰμί ("I am"). If this is correct, the FG makes an explicit identification with the divine mediator who is the Name of God:

> The Jews said to Him, "You are not fifty years old and you [claim to] have seen Abraham?" Jesus said to them, "Truly, truly, I say to you, before Abraham was, I am." So they took up stones to throw at him . . . (John 8:57-59)

True to form, it is the claim of the Messiah's divinity, not primarily the messianic claim itself, which accounts for Jewish opposition to Johannine Christianity, according to the Gospel. This is demonstrable by appeal to several passages in the FG where the issue between Jesus and the Jews is precisely that he seeks to make himself equal with God. Each time the penalty is stoning:

> For this reason, the Jews sought all the more to kill him—not only was he breaking the Sabbath; worse still he was speaking of God as his own father, thus making himself God's equal. (John 5:18)[30]

> "We stone you for no good work but for blasphemy; because you, being a man, make yourself a god." (10:33)

It is significant that the Jews oppose Jesus for claiming divinity and that the penalty is stoning, not crucifixion. These details suggest a setting in the life of the community and not from the life of Jesus. Though the social situation cannot be reconstructed in detail, it can be characterized. The Johannine community is obviously being criticized by a Jewish community (rabbinic or not) for the basic tenet of its faith. A considerable

[30] Translation from R. E. Brown, *The Gospel according to St. John*, AB 29–29A (New York: Doubleday, 1966).

breach is perceived on both sides. The generalized Johannine use of the term "Jew" (which does not distinguish between parties), therefore, appears to derive from a time when the rift between Jews and Christians had become irremediable. This must have occurred at the end of the first century or later, certainly not in the days of Jesus himself, though the FG explicitly says that the hostility started then (see, e.g., 12:42).[31] The Gospel expresses the breach between the Jewish and Christian communities and tries to come to terms with it in a number of ways. One of those ways, it seems to me, is through dualism. But it is a dualism of a specific type, a dualism which has helped the Johannine Christians understand how they can continue to consider themselves heirs to the prophecies of the Jewish Bible when the synagogue has rejected both them and their understanding of how biblical prophecy has been fulfilled.

The characterization of the Jews in the FG, though tendentious and exaggerated, must be based on a real Jewish charge against Christians, for the position attributed to them corresponds to the position rabbis take against unnamed heretics in rabbinic literature. The rabbis, as well as other Hellenistic Jews, objected to some concepts of divine mediators and to the redemptive role of angels.[32]

Rabbinic Judaism was especially intolerant of angelologies when the unity of God was in question. A brief look at those heretics called "those who believe in two powers in heaven" will illustrate the rabbinic position.[33] The rabbis objected to any biblical exegesis which implied a plurality in the divinity. The name of God in the Hebrew Bible represented a special problem. Elohim is an archaic plural and sometimes takes a plural complement. The tetragrammaton, YHWH, might also be taken as a divinity separate from Elohim. The rabbis stated that the divine name YHWH does not imply that there is either a creature

[31] See Martyn, *History and Theology in the Fourth Gospel*, esp. 17–45. One need not assume, however, that the opposition of the Jews involved the killing of Christians. The statements that the Jews sought to kill Jesus can be derived from the events of Jesus' life, the traditions of the church, and the fears of the Johannine community. They need not reflect the actual policy of the rabbis, although there may have been non-rabbinic vigilantes who went further than rabbinic law allowed. See below, n. 39.

[32] See J. Goldin, "Not by Means of an Angel and Not by Means of a Messenger," in *Religions in Antiquity: Essays in Memory of Erwin Ramsdell Goodenough* (Leiden: Brill, 1968), 412–24. See also D. Flusser, "Not by Means of an Angel . . ." *Toray Yeshurun* 29 (1971–1972): 18–20 (in Hebrew).

[33] See my *Two Powers in Heaven* and chap. 1 in this volume.

separate from God or a plurality of deities (MRI Bahodesh 5 and Shirta 4, to Exod 15:3 and 20:2; compare with MRSbY, at the same place). Most of the time, the heresy implied in the rabbinic description involved a heavenly hierarchy with two corresponding powers in heaven.

Occasionally the rabbinic description may imply an opposing configuration of divinities in heretical thought, but the emphasis in early rabbinic texts is almost completely on defeating the idea that a corresponding figure of angel is divine. The biblical passages at the heart of the heresy, however, are remarkably consistent throughout the many different reports. They include any place where a plural was used to describe God, such as Genesis 1:26, together with any reports of the physical shape of God or his angels, such as Exodus 24:10; Ezekiel 1; Daniel 7:13 etc. Since the Daniel 7 passage was crucial to Christian exegesis, many of these reports probably refer to Christians; but some aspects of the heretical traditions of the sort opposed by the rabbis are reported in the writings of Philo, who even describes the λόγος as a second divine manifestation and as a second God (*Somn.* 1.227–229; *QG* 2.62). It is clear from Philo's discussion that the terminology of "second God" or divinity is carefully chosen.

The assertion of divinity seems to be a way of avoiding making any intermediary equal with God. The creator and all angels and other forms of mediation are not separate creatures, rather part of God himself. Ironically the term "second God" is used by Philo to avoid the charge of dualism. One can perhaps see a similar strategy in the Johannine community. Asserting Jesus' divinity through identity with the λόγος has the effect of denying the possibility of any other mediation, or more exactly of tying up all mediations—exceptional, incarnate, and eschatological—in one figure. Of course, it opens the Johannine church to the charge of "two powers in heaven," a charge which the rabbis probably would also have levied against Philo or anyone of similar disposition, had they been familiar with their writings. The reference to "two powers" in rabbinic sources occurs without any uniquely Christian polemic, so that Christianity was probably seen as but one of a number of different systems of thought which the rabbis wanted to brand heretical.

The rabbinic defense against the threat is remarkably simple. The rabbis merely invoke the places in the Old Testament where God claims to be unique: Deuteronomy 6; Deuteronomy 32; Isaiah 44–47. They also note that claiming divine honors was the sin of the Prince of Tyre and the King of Babylon (see also Isa 14 in b. Sanh. 43a).

The Johannine community itself objected to several doctrines of mediation. In arguing with Nicodemus, the Pharisee and ruler of the Jews, Jesus is made to say: "No one has ever gone up to heaven except he who descended from heaven, the Son of Man" (3:13). The Johannine community seems to be limiting the class of mediators to a unique figure, Jesus, who was able to make a heavenly ascent because he is a heavenly creature. The FG claims that no simple man could ascend to heaven, a polemic against beliefs found in Enoch literature, mysticism, and other pseudepigrapha, where similar claims are often made for specific mediators,[34] to say nothing of Roman emperors who claimed to ascend to heaven after death.[35] The FG claimed that no one could make a mystical ascent to see God unless he really was a divine creature himself—a polemic against YHWH the Lesser, Yahoel, and other concepts for God's principal angel (by whatever names he was known), but whom the FG acknowledged only as λόγος, Messiah, or Son of Man. Evidence of this type has persuaded many New Testament scholars that the Johannine community was interested in clarifying the Christian message to a group of mystical Jewish-Christian sectarians whose beliefs may have included non-orthodox understandings of mediation and even loyalty to Jewish law (though probably not to the rabbinic canon of Torah).[36] Both rabbinic and Christian exegesis, then, oppose in differing degrees and in different ways the angelic mediator traditions of mystical and apocalyptic Judaism, such as those about YHWH the Lesser, Metatron (or even possibly the Prince of the World), and particularly those agents who began as humans and later achieved a kind of divine status in some communities, like Jacob-Israel, Moses, or Enoch-Metatron. Of course, the rabbis would object to the Christian confession as a variety of the latter.

Therefore, we have an intriguing and complicated historical phenomenon. On one hand, the Johannine community restricted ideas of mediation to the Christ, outlawing any other concept of mediation. On the other hand, the rabbinic community outlawed any idea of divine

[34] See, e.g., the article by Jonathan Z. Smith, "The Prayer of Joseph," in Neusner, ed., *Religions in Antiquity*, 254, where ascent traditions about Enoch, Moses, and especially Jacob are discussed.

[35] See my chapters on ascension, "Heavenly Ascent in Hellenistic Judaism, Early Christianity and Their Environment" (repr. in this volume).

[36] For a summary of the various possibilities, see Brown, *The Gospel according to St. John*, 1:lxxiiif. See also Martyn, *History and Theology in the Fourth Gospel*; and Quispel, "Qumran, John and Jewish Christianity."

mediation which implied that the Godhead is composed of two or more hypostases, a polemic which excluded Christianity among a wider variety of Jewish heresies. It therefore seems necessary to posit at least three rough groupings: the rabbinic community, the Johannine community, and other heterodox Jewish or Christian communities. The last grouping embraces a spectrum of belief about mediation from the divine to the human in ways outlawed in both the rabbinic and the Christian communities.

Though there appear to us to have been at least three logical groups in this spectrum, neither the Johannine nor the rabbinic community felt the need to distinguish more than two, an in-group and an out-group. The rabbis saw the dividing line to have been between orthodoxy and ("two powers") heresy. The Johannine community distinguished between the Jews and the followers of Jesus, who were the real Israel.[37]

The Jewish penalty for such crimes may have been exclusion from the synagogue, as the Johannine community stated.[38] But it probably was not accomplished exactly as the FG has it, by a direct threat against the life of Christians. The rabbis, for instance, excluded from leadership in synagogue services any *min* (מין) or sectarian whose beliefs were questionable. Rabbinic literature ascribes to R. Gamaliel the order to add a curse against sectarians to the service, which would have been tantamount to an invitation to leave synagogue life (b. Ber. 28b). Since the tradition has been ascribed to the rabbinic Sanhedrin at Yavneh in the late first century, it may correspond directly to the events described by the FG; but, at any rate, it provides a convincing background to the reports of Jewish opposition in the Johannine community.[39]

A fair consensus of the various views on the *birkat ha-minim* (ברכת המינים) would make the following points: A preexistent curse against informers and separatists appears to have been extended to sectarians and implicitly to Christians by R. Samuel's addition. The Christian community, in turn, appears to have correctly understood this as a criticism of their position. This action, as pointed out by Martyn, is

[37] In these paragraphs, I am relying on the consensus of Bultmann, Brown, and Martyn, without forgetting that they differ greatly in detail in characterizing the various groups.

[38] See n. 27.

[39] See above, pp. 56–57. The consensus among many scholars of Jewish liturgy (see Heinemann, *Prayer in the Talmud*) is that there was no single authoritative version.

more likely to have been the principal instrument of Jewish opposition than were *herem* or *nidui*. It would be unfair to say that this action was a watershed. It appears to have organized what was already the dominant Jewish reaction to Christianity. If the events in Acts have any historic validity, they appear to describe an instinctive reaction in synagogues to the preachings of Christianity without any necessary official sanction. The promulgation of the new text for the curse was but one natural step in the growing hostility.[40]

We should note that the rabbinic defense against Christianity, however strong it may be supposed, was not uniquely applied to Christians and probably predated the origin of Christianity. In other words, the rabbis used preexistent categories and penalties to attack Christian heresy, only adapting them for the Christian heresy.

Not only may this development be supposed to be the case with the *birkat ha-minim*, but it can be shown to be relevant in other midrashic reports of Christianity. In a baraita introduced in b. Sanh. 43a the charges adduced against Jesus are magic (מכשף), enticement (משית), and leading astray (מדויח). The former is a charge made by Jews in the

[40] It would be too much to say (*pace* R. Kimelman, "*Birkat Ha-Minim* and the Lack of Evidence for an Anti-Christian Prayer in Late Antiquity," in Sanders, ed., *Jewish and Christian Self-Definition*, 2:226–44) that the rise of Christianity had no effect on Judaism. The seriousness of the challenge of the *minim* (of whom the Christians are the principal and most important members, if not the only component) and the special enactments necessary to defeat them are surely everywhere reflected in rabbinic literature. It is impossible to say how much of rabbinic thought received encouragement from the Christian menace, since it evolves according to its own logic. But this does not mean that no effect was felt. Hence, though Kimelman is using sound judgment in warning against over-interpreting the *birkat ha-minim* as the equivalent to formal excommunication, one must also be on guard against undervaluing the evidence. Kimelman has emphasized the fact that the rabbis did not explicitly curse the Christians by name in the service. He has not shown that the *birkat ha-minim* was not taken by the Christians and Jews alike to have included Christians. One only has to allow for slight exaggeration (and the church fathers like Tertullian went far beyond slight exaggeration in their polemical zeal) to see that the church fathers' claims are in agreement with rabbinic evidence. One must posit only that *min* referred to "sectarian" or "heretic" in general, not a specific sect, to clarify this position. (Kimelman grants this as a possibility [231f.] but does not exploit the implications of his observations at this point.) Whether or not the Christians liked the idea of being called sectarians or heretics (i.e., *minim*), they appear to know that they are meant by the phrase. The reports of the church fathers are yet more puzzling if they do not apply to the *birkat ha-minim*. See William Horbury, "The Benediction of the Minim and the Early Jewish Christian Controversy," *JTS* 33 (1982): 19–61.

New Testament (see Mark 5 and parallels). The latter terms can easily be compared with the verb πλανεῖν, which appears as a charge against Jesus in John 7:42 and Revelation 2:20, as Martyn shows.[41] No doubt b. Sanhedrin 43a represents Jewish reaction to the gospel story of Jesus (and hence an implicit threat to Christians), but not a piece of historical evidence about Jesus. It corresponds to the evidence in John. The application of charges of this nature reflects the growing antagonism of the Jewish community to the preaching of the church.

Again, it does not seem necessary to conclude that the opposition reported by the Johannine community is more formal than the kind of opposition reported by Paul or in Luke-Acts in the diaspora. Cursing Christian heretics in synagogues is not the same as persecuting them. Examples of persecution appear to be mob actions which exceed rabbinic ordinances. This only underlines the fact that Jewish reaction to heresy has never been monolithic. The passage of time since Paul might also allow for changes and a more organized or prepared reaction. Yet, the Johannine community is far more bothered about the actions of the Jews than Luke was. Given the Johannine admission that members of the Christian community had been excluded and the allegations that some Jewish leaders believed in Jesus but would not confess him lest they be excluded (12:42), it is probably better to describe the Jewish reaction as "ostracism" rather than "excommunication." That action, together with threat of prosecution for capital offenses in midrash and occasional illegal or mob actions reported in other places in the New Testament, would be more than enough to raise the apprehension among the Johannine followers to the level evinced in the Gospel, since unlike other Christians they appear to have had a closer association with the Jewish community and may have continued to visit it. Justin says that Jews cursed Jesus in synagogues (*Dial.* 16f., 47f., 93f., 108, 123, 133f.).[42]

[41] Martyn, *History and Theology in the Fourth Gospel*, 160.

[42] See above, n. 27. A word must be said about L. Schiffman's argument in that it is halakically impossible to cease being Jewish. It is possible to exaggerate the importance of this conclusion since his evidence comes from a period in which rabbinic tradition was firmly accepted by the Jewish community. Even in rabbinic tradition ideological crimes like "denying the root" had the effect of exclusion from the reconstructed Israel of the world to come (b. Sanh. 10 and the talmudic comments).

Then, too, extrapolations from rabbinic law may not describe the entire social situation. What is more important in cases of self-definition is to see the perspective of each side. In the Johannine situation, the Johannine Christian community clearly considers

Here then are the theoretical possibilities for the history of tradition of the Lord of the World: If one accepts the evidence of Scholem that many Jews speculated about a principal angelic mediator hypostasis of God, which was another understanding of the name YHWH, then one sees that the existence of the principal angelic mediator per se was not debated in every community. Rather, it was the identity, role, and rank of the mediator that was at issue. Some people identified the figure as Yahoel, some as Michael or Gabriel, some as Enoch, and some as Melchizedek. Since the primary characteristic of this angel is that he manifests one of the names or titles of God, it is not inconceivable that the "Prince of the World" had already evolved from merely a title into a divine hypostasis, as previously happened in other Near Eastern cults. It is impossible to say for sure when the evolution took place. Thus, it is possible that the "Prince of this World," like YHWH the Lesser, signified the name of God, the Master of the World, re-understood as a separate angelic hypostasis.[43] Through such "mystical" speculation on the divine name a plausible (but not necessary) explanation can be found for the development of the positive term before the FG and the apocrypha.

---

itself distinct from the Jews, though it may be closer to the Jewish community than Luke and may contain members who were Jews at birth. The effect of considering Jewish Christians as Jews in rabbinic law may have been to obligate them to rabbinic law, but there is no evidence that Christians were treated in this way or that they desired to be obligated by rabbinic rulings. Furthermore, I see no certain evidence that synagogues opposing the Christian community in John (or Luke, for that matter) were yet fully rabbinic. The archaeological evidence of Tcherikover and Fuks in *CPJ*, to take a single example, would suggest that rabbinic hegemony came in Egypt only after the native community had been severely damaged by antisemitism. Edicts like the silencing of *minim* in synagogues are likely to reflect more general Jewish practice which the rabbis only standardized when they took over the control of synagogue life.

[43] This is speculative, of course, and so I shall not suggest that the positive view of the angel must have antedated the negative one. It is also possible that the Gospel community (or another community like it) understood the phrase polemically against the God of the Jews but not the Lord of Deliverance who was not "of this world." See Sifre Deut 329, pp. 379–80; MRI Shirta 4, Bahodesh 5 for the rabbinic answer that the God of Israel is God both of this world and the world to come. Evidence that the name of God was associated with the Lord of the World comes to us from the magical papyri (*PGM* III. 211f.) where Adonai is praised as "Lord of the World." Though it is impossible to be sure whether the figure is meant to be negative or positive, because magicians prayed to both demons and gods, one could surmise that he is meant to be positive because he is in good company (Zeus, Iao, Raphael, and Sabaoth). Furthermore, it is clear that ancient Jewish tradition ascribed to God the title "Lord of all worlds." See 1QapGen ar II, 4.

Of course, it is also possible that the negative figure developed from the rabbinic expression "Master of the World" or from the Near Eastern gods without the emergence of a prior positive figure. Then, the rabbinic traditions later on can be seen as being independent, or, less likely, as resulting from a deliberate revaluing of an explicitly demonic figure or even from the transfer of a divine title from another divinity.

What is not speculation is that Christians believed their mediator to be the Jesus who died as a messianic pretender and who was justified in the title "Messiah" ironically given to him by the Romans after he was believed by his followers to have been resurrected and ascended (or reascended) to divinity. As such he had a claim to the term κύριος, which is further interpreted as the "I am" tetragrammaton. Since Johannine Christianity had its own candidate for mediator and could accept no other candidates, all other titles and functions for a divine mediator, especially any title with reference to this world, could signify only the supernatural opposition to him. In the Gospel, "this world" could only contrast with the salvation of Jesus who was not of this world and was therefore beyond the reach of the synagogue which had excluded Christians from worship. Furthermore, the Johannine church would know that a mediator figure like Michael or Metatron, possibly with titles such as "Lord of the World," was viewed as Israel's guardian angel by many Jews. The negative reaction of the Jews towards Johannine Christianity, which had compromised monotheism from the rabbinic perspective, could then be projected into the heavenly realm by the FG as a reflection of the negative reaction of the "Lord of the World" (which was at the very least a name of the Jewish God, but could have been a title for God's principal angel even at that time). Thus, the guardian angel of Jewish sectarians could become a fitting opponent of Jesus in the supernatural sphere. As "Lord of the World" he became a symbol of the world's rejection of Jesus.

The later tradition of the Prince of the World in rabbinic Judaism is most anomalous since it reflects a positive view of the world, after the figure of the angel is unambiguously demoted to a subsidiary role and thus is not an independent power, but only God's supervisor on earth. Though no honest theory of the origin of the epithet and figure can be convincing, we are not completely unable to analyze the term, since the portrayal of the Prince of the World is not just doctrine. It is an allegory about the world written into the heavenly hosts, so that its interpretation lies in each community's experience in the world. For the Johannine

Christians (as for others), the Prince of the World became evil because the world (in this case in its opposition to the gospel) is evil; or, again for the Johannine community, the world is evil because the Jews, who symbolize the world, oppose the message of Christianity. The meaning of the allegory is parallel to the sociology of the Johannine church. The dualist theology is partly a symbolic portrayal of the sociological position of the church. Its function is to reassure and exhort the believer to remain uncompromisingly true to the uniqueness of the Christian message—even in the face of opposition from a variety of Jewish sects, indeed, from the whole world—because God's plan for the destruction of the opponents of his people would certainly soon be manifest. That social message is expressed by the FG's attitude towards a supernatural figure representing the heavenly opposition and at the same time is linked to the real Jewish earthly opposition Johannine Christians felt but could not explain as prophesied.

Now we can see why the FG constantly links Jesus' role as Savior with the theme of retribution. In John 12 Jesus reveals that his fate is to glorify the Name of God, an occupation clearly suitable to angels as well as connoting martyrdom. In this context the Lord of the World, Jesus' direct supernatural opponent, is said to be judged and defeated (John 12:31), though he still appears strong. In chapters 14 and 16, Jesus predicts that once he leaves, the church will have an angelic protector, called variously the Spirit of Truth or Paraclete. Other Jewish communities at this time were applying the same titles to principal angels.[44] In the FG it is clear that the Paraclete is supposed to function as the Holy Spirit, but this does not preclude or mask the angelic background of the concept.[45] Again, it is in the context of the prophecy of the Paraclete that the Ruler of the World is mentioned as Jesus' antagonist (John 14:31; 16:11). This

[44] For instance, on the Spirit of Truth, see T. Jud. 20:1–5. Compare with 1QS IV, 23–24. See also R. E. Brown, "The Paraclete," Appendix 5, *The Gospel according to St. John*, 2:1135–44; Otto Betz, *Der Paraklet: Fürsprecher im häretischen Spätjüdentum im Johannes-Evangelium und in neugefundenen gnostischen Schriften* (Leiden: Brill, 1963); George Johnston, *The Spirit-Paraclete in the Gospel of John* (Cambridge: Cambridge University Press, 1970); A. R. C. Leaney, "The Johannine Paraclete and the Qumran Scrolls," in Charlesworth, ed., *John and Qumran*, 38–61; H. Windisch, *The Spirit-Paraclete in the Fourth Gospel*, trans. J. Cox (Philadelphia: Fortress, 1968).

[45] Even in Pauline writings, e.g., 1 Cor 12:11 and Rom 8:16, the Holy Spirit performs voluntary actions.

usage is quite close to the theology of Qumran, where the angelic leader of the forces of the good is also called the Spirit of Truth.

Once the angelic battle is mentioned, the corresponding social significance of the allegory can be clarified. John 8:40f. shows us how this allegory works. The Jews say, "We are not base born; God is our father, and God alone." But Jesus says: "If God were your father, you would love me, for God is the source of my being. . . . Your father is the Devil and you choose to carry out your father's desires." The heavenly allegory explains why the earthly Jews oppose the Christian message. To be sure, the Prince of the World and the Devil are not overtly equated in the FG, but such a conclusion is not difficult to derive from it. Both the Prince of the World and the Jews are taken to be symbols of the opposition to God. The Jews are said to be the offspring of the Devil, while the Prince of the World is made into a demon. In this way the Prince of the World and Satan can be explicitly identified by later tradition. The difference between the Prince of the World traditions in each community can be understood as based on the antagonism and polemic between Christians and Jews.[46]

One of the ways in which this association is made can be seen in the Christian evidence. In the Ascension of Isaiah, an interesting combination of traditions about the Lord of this World, the Roman emperor, and Satan come together:

> And now Hezekiah and Josiah my son, these are the days of the completion of the world. After it is consummated, Beliar the great ruler, the king of this world, will descend, who hath ruled it since it came into being; yea, he will descend from his firmament in the likeness of a man, a lawless king, the slayer of his mother: who himself (even) this king will persecute the plant which the twelve apostles of the Beloved have planted. Of the twelve, one will be delivered into his hands. This ruler in the form of that king will come and there will come with him all the powers of this world, and they will hearken unto him in all that he desireth. And at his word the sun will rise at night and he will make the moon appear at sixth hour. And all that he hath desired he will do in the world: he will do and

[46] This phenomenon is somewhat analogous to the use of the phrase "first-born of Satan" as used in orthodox and heretical Christianity. See N. A. Dahl, "Der Erstgeborene Satans und der Vater des Tüfels (Polyk. 7:1 und Joh. 8:44)," in *Apophoreta: Festschrift fur Ernst Haenchen*, ed. W. Eltester, BZNW 30 (Berlin: Töpelmann, 1964), 70–84.

> speak like the Beloved and he will say: "I am God and before me there has been none." (Ascen. Isa. 4:1–6)[47]

The reference is apparently to Nero, who slew his mother Agrippina in 59 C.E.[48]

But note that besides calling Nero king of this world, the redactor of this document has equated Nero with Beliar, a supernatural opponent—in short, Satan. Furthermore, he adds to this description an application of prophecies concerning the Prince of Tyre (Ezek 28) and the King of Babylon (Isa 14), in which a great ruler has become corrupt because he considers himself a god. Now this move in itself is not an innovation. Nebuchadnezzar (Jdt 3:8; 6:12), Antiochus Epiphanes (Dan 11:36f.), probably Pompey (Pss. Sol. 2:28), Caligula (Philo, *Legat.* 22, 74–80, 93–97), and Nero (Sib. Or. 5.33–35, 137–154, 214–221) are all despised as those who tried to be gods. Nero is the first to be considered a supernatural evildoer, in the estimation of the writers. Hence, there is a new sense of irony in accepting the claim of supernatural aid, only transforming it into demonic opposition. The same irony may be presupposed to lie behind the FG's treatment of the Jews whose claim to supernatural mission is accepted but transformed into a demonic one. No doubt Paul's prophecies in 2 Thessalonians 2:3f. and Revelation 13:1, 5-6 are indicative of the Christian atmosphere causing this application. But it is the Gospel of John which is crucial, because it is John's usage which turns the figure of the Lord of this World into a technical term for Satan. Thus, in the Ascension of Isaiah we have a supernatural evildoer, identified with the earthly rulers of this world (no longer explicitly the Jews, though still in league with them). By the time of the Ascension of Isaiah, the Jews, the earthly powers, and Satan are seen as the demonic opposition to Christianity. The only part of that equation which is yet ambiguous is the political powers of this world, though a close alliance is certainly implied.

Thus, Douglas's typological hypothesis is useful in the study of sectarian Judaism. It has allowed us to form an idea of the function of the Prince of the World even when we cannot be sure of the genesis of the tradition. It has allowed us to see the value of the figure in explaining the

[47] 2 Thess 2:4; Rev 13:5f.; also Rev 13:4, 8, 12.

[48] J. H. Charlesworth, "Christian and Jewish Self-Definition in Light of the Christian Additions to the Apocryphal Writings," in Sanders, ed., *Jewish and Christian Self-Definition*, 2:27–55.

Christian fissure from Judaism, a fissure which grew more puzzling to Johannine Christianity as it grew more evident. The Prince of the World must be evil because the Johannine community perceived itself as under persecution from the synagogue in this world, even as it felt justified in the coming age. It knew that Jewish opposition was wrong. Yet it needed to rely on Jewish prophecy to legitimate its truth-claims.[49]

Social science could not provide an awareness of the historical dimension, for its models are of a general nature and must be constantly tailored to fit new situations. We historians cannot totally reconstruct the historical situation either, but we can see how the debate actually developed and how the exaggerations grew into dualism, when we are helped by the experience of observers of other religions.

Now, one may ask, is not the portrayal of the Prince of the World a minor aspect of Johannine Christology? So it is. But it still is a very important aspect, for within the conception of the Lord of the World lies the clue to the negative portrayal of the demiurge in Gnosticism. There is a very important analogy between this Johannine evidence and the traditions we find in extreme Gnosticism. Here I can only offer suggestions for further research.

It would be easy just to say that the Prince of the World is seen as evil because the Johannine Christians were gnostics. But there are important differences between the proto-Gnosticism in the Johannine community and the extreme Gnosticism witnessed by the church fathers and evidenced in some of the Nag Hammadi writings. First, the Lord of the World is not yet the gnostic demiurge, for he is not the creator of the world.[50] He is, at most, the Lord of the Demons, as he is in apocalyp-

[49] Douglas' model allows for some further distinctions. She plots two variables: group pressure (which she calls "group") against level of symbolic classification (which she calls "grid"), and proposes that societies can be described by the patterns which their individuals evince on the graph (see *Natural Symbols*, 49f., 83f.). It seems to me that the Jewish community should be defined as high grid/high group—or, at least, they are heading in that direction as they grow more and more rabbinized. With respect to the Roman Empire, of course, they should be classified as a small group, but they respond to that challenge in a specific way and in a way different from typical small groups. The rabbis see the only enemy as the outsider; within, all is governed to an extraordinary degree by social piety, purity rules, and sacralized institutions. The Johannine community, on the other hand, is still a small group with a dualist cosmology—i.e., it has a high group, but a low grid (see *Natural Symbols*, 91).

[50] J. Fossum has found the angel of the Lord as demiurge in Samaritan traditions. See his contribution on "The Samaritan Origin of the Concept of the Demiurge," paper

tic Jewish systems. Second, although the Johannine Christians maintain that the Jews are the offspring of Satan, they do not want to say that the God of the Old Testament is evil. Rather, they claim that Johannine Christians alone are loyal to the promises made to the prophets.[51] For instance, in a significant place (John 19) the Jews are made to say: "We have no king but Caesar!" The FG is saying by means of irony that the Jews themselves, in rejecting Jesus, have rejected the reign of God and hence have given up the title of Israel.[52] The FG may even be implying that the Jews are the agents of Caesar, Caesar being the embodiment of Satan in this place. This might imply the same situation as that reflected by Luke in Acts, namely that the Jews are complaining to civil authorities that Christians are disturbing their worship. Yet the complete identification of the Lord of the World with the creator demiurge (who is at the same time God of the Jews and Prince of the Demons) must be from a later, more desperate time. In many respects, the gnostic configuration is more logical and more effective argumentation against the Jews in the polemic, since it avoids the ambiguities in the status of the Jews which are reflected in the FG. In the less radical Gospel of John, some of the historical roots of the controversy are still evident and are being interpreted as part of the gospel narration. The radically gnostic solution, as I shall shortly outline, appears to be a later and neater way of dealing with the Jewish question; but it is a more polemical and mythologically antisemitic solution in the sense that even the historical roots for the polemical exaggeration have been obscured.

In the battle between these competing sects, the issue of normative group definition has been a strong undercurrent, but it has arisen in an unexpected way. We normally assume that basic theological differences lead to the formation of sects. This can be partially borne out here as well: the issue of the divinity of God's principal angel or mediator is

---

delivered at the Yale International Conference on Gnosticism, April 1978; and *The Name of God and the Angel of the Lord: Samaritan and Jewish Conceptions of Intermediation and the Origin of Gnosticism* (Tübingen: Mohr Siebeck, 1985).

[51] This may be compared with Origen who, in his commentary on John 2:34, criticizes gnostics for believing that the demiurge is the God of the Jews. See Elaine Pagels, "Origen and the Prophets of Israel," *JANES* 5 (1973): 335–44.

[52] See Meeks, *Prophet-King*, 76–78. See also idem, "The Divine Agent and His Counterfeit in Philo and the Fourth Gospel," in *Aspects of Religious Propaganda in Judaism and Early Christianity*, ed. E. Schüssler Fiorenza (Notre Dame: University of Notre Dame Press, 1976), 45–49.

a central defining issue in the split between the two communities. But significant social factors have also intervened, enforcing group self-definition and contributing to the fissure. One can summarize these factors by noting again the mythological loading around the term "Jew" in this Johannine context.[53] The oddity of this use of "Jew" in its new mythological context is that although it serves as a sanction or charter for the Johannine group definition (i.e., we are Israelites, not Jews) it functions equally well as polemic against opposing parties who claim to know the authoritative interpretation. While it is not a commonly listed function of myth,[54] clarification of one's worldview in the presence of opposition is, logically, a necessary part of the whole mythological process.

It is, as well, the very role which mythology will play in Gnosticism. In the gnostic documents from Nag Hammadi and in the reports of the church fathers, the gnostic demiurge speaks all the lines of the Old Testament God. He claims to be unique on the basis of Deuteronomy 32 and Isaiah 44–47. But, for the gnostics, this claim of the demiurge is ignorant. The gnostics know that there is a god of salvation above the god of the Jews who claims to be unique.

Now it is extremely interesting to note that the claim of the demiurge to be "God" in some gnostic documents not only reflects Isaiah 14 and Ezekiel 28 but is a re-understanding of the Scripture which the rabbis quote as a defense against the heresy of "two powers in heaven"—precisely the Scripture which was used against church fathers

[53] Here it seems to me fair to note that this predominantly mythological use of the term "Jew" contributes to antisemitism within the church. While the statements are antisemitic and have been used by antisemites within the church for generations, in its own context, the Johannine church was a minority group, not the persecutor.

[54] Normally one speaks of myth in a constitutive sense, e.g., B. Malinowski, *Myth in Primitive Psychology* (New York: W. W. Norton, 1926). One study of the polemical role of myth may be found in E. Leach, "Myth as a Justification for Faction and Social Change," in *Political Systems of Highland Burma* (London: Athlone, 1954), 264–78. See also R. Wilson, *Genealogy and History in the Biblical World* (New Haven, Conn.: Yale University Press, 1976); and L. Laeyendecker, *Religie en Conflict* (Meppel: J. A. Boom en Zoon, 1968). For the ancient Near East: P. Machinist, "Literature as Politics: The Tikulti-Ninurta Epic and the Bible," *CBQ* 38 (1976): 455–82; T. Jacobsen, *The Treasures of Darkness: A History of Mesopotamian Religion* (New Haven, Conn.: Yale University Press, 1976), 167–91, esp. 183–91: C. Loew, *Myth, Sacred History and Philosophy* (New York: Harcourt, Brace & Would, 1967), 21–32; A. Leo Oppenheim, *Ancient Mesopotamia: Portrait of a Dead Civilization*, rev. ed. (Chicago: University of Chicago Press, 1977), 171–83.

by docetists, monarchianists, and patripassionists.[55] It seems likely then that one ingredient of radical Gnosticism was social alienation by means of these arguments against monotheism. The gnostics accepted the scriptural proof that the Old Testament God claimed to be unique; they defended their position by radically reinterpreting Old Testament passages so that the god who spoke was not the highest God. More revealing still, according to recent studies by Pagels and Koschorke,[56] the gnostic description of the demiurge, together with the mythological description of evil archons, directly parallels gnostic description of the orthodox bishops. In other words, in radical gnostic interpretation, the same vague sociological condition existed as we saw in the Johannine community, but the radicalization of the role of the Jewish demiurge now signifies not primarily persecution of Christians by Jews but persecution of gnostics by Christians (and Jews?) who use Jewish Scriptures to bolster their point against the gnostics. Hence there is an analogy by opposition and polemical self-definition between Jewish and Christian self-definition on the one hand, and Christian and gnostic self-definition on the other. Though it is too much to say that it was Johannine Christianity that produced Gnosticism, it is not too much to say that the social situation which produced Johannine Christianity was parallel to that situation which eventually produced Gnosticism. One of the mythological contributions of John—clarifying that the Messiah was a unique divine mediator who preceded creation, effected it, was incarnated, and then returned to the Father in a milieu of supernatural opposition to the saving knowledge—is an important and necessary (though not a sufficient) step towards the mythological scenes in many of the Nag Hammadi documents.

I do not mean to suggest that the Gospel of John inevitably produced Gnosticism. Rather, I wish to point out only that similar social conflicts have a similar effect on theology and hence in normative group

[55] Cf. Segal, *Two Powers in Heaven*, 252ff. The ignorant gnostic demiurge is to a great degree a characterization of the monotheistic god of the rabbis. He it is who claims, ignorantly, to be unique (Deut 6:4; 32:39; Isa 44–47, etc.) when every gnostic would know that there is a higher god of salvation.

[56] Pagels argues that the same epithets characterize the demiurge and the orthodox bishops in gnostic exegesis (*The Gnostic Gospels* [New York: Random House, 1979], 28–47). After our study of the Johannine community, all these tactics ought to look familiar. See also K. Koschorke, *Die Polemik der Gnostiker gegen das kirchliche Christentum* (Leiden: Brill, 1978).

definition. In this case there is a sequence of perceived social conflicts between many competing groups of Jews and Christians, all of which tended to make each group's central definition stronger. The Gospel of John was important to Christian gnostics as it was to all varieties of Christians. Some of the themes in it were radicalized by extreme gnostics under analogous circumstances of perceived opposition. One of the results of social conflict is almost always the sharpening of any sect's understanding of its central principles in contradistinction to its feared and hated enemies. Yet, seen from the perspective of the dominant group, a dangerous heresy which occasions conflict is not necessarily perceived immediately in clear-cut categories. Rather the conflict itself may be the impetus to closer self-definition in answer to the heresy. Thus conflict, though normally thought dysfunctional, has one positive effect of aiding both the "sect" and the "orthodoxy" in defining themselves more closely.[57] One might even say that conflict is one of the strongest impetuses to group self-definition. Because the social situation in the community that produced the FG can be deciphered, I would caution my colleagues in the search for the social background of Gnosticism: it is not always necessary to jump immediately to the social malaise infecting the empire, when the reasons for gnostic propaganda may be more subtle and localized in nature. It may be granted that gnostic groups were alienated from the emperor's regime and that the gnostic division of mankind parallels the social distinctions in the empire, but such statements do not always differentiate gnostics from their neighbors and do not do justice to all the gnostic documents. When one looks into those documents, one discovers that although it is important that the gnostic demiurge resembles the Caesar, he also speaks the lines of the Old Testament God: "I am the first and the last; besides me there is no other."

[57] Throughout history men as disparate as Heracleides, Machiavelli, Marx, and Adam Smith have noted the importance of conflict in group definition. See Lewis Cozer, *The Functions of Social Conflict* (New York: Simon & Schuster, 1956); Joseph Himes, "The Function of Racial Conflict," *Social Forces* 45 (1966): 1–10; Raymond Mack and Richard Snyder, "The Analysis of Social Conflict—Toward an Overview and Synthesis," *Journal of Conflict Resolution* 1 (1957): 217–48; John Horton, "Order and Conflict: Theories of Social Problems as Competing Ideologies," *American Journal of Sociology* 71 (1966): 701–13; Georg Simmel, *Conflict and the Web of Group-Affiliations*, trans. Kurt Wolff and Reinhard Bendix (New York: Free Press, 1955); Pierre van den Berghe, "Dialectic and Functionalism: Toward a Theoretical Synthesis," *American Sociological Review* 28 (1963): 695–705.

The gnostics know that the statement is to be interpreted ironically, for the demiurge is ignorant of his own past. Similarly, the description of the archons parallels terminology used for the orthodox, non-gnostic bishops. It is clear that some of the gnostics' real enemies lie closer to home, and they want to link any description of the power of their enemies with counterfeit kingship exercised by unjust emperors and with demonic opposition to their message as well.

Now, from the evidence that we have reviewed, we can be sure that different ideas of divine mediation and agency were central to Johannine Christianity, as Bultmann said. It is undeniable that in the FG the Christ is portrayed as the mediator *par excellence*. This may, in part, distinguish Johannine from other varieties of dualism. Even so, we do not have a complete gnostic salvation myth. The obvious explanation for this is that the Johannine community is not an example of pre-Christian Gnosticism historicized, but of what turns out to have been, with our historical perspective, an important Christian step towards the later and not inevitable creation of extreme Gnosticism. Although there is no direct or inevitable link, one way in which gnostic writing evolved was by means of this progressive, polemical mythologizing, so evident in the cases under consideration. From the material we have reviewed, it seems to me that the FG demonstrates traditions which were originally part of Jewish lore but which have become Christian and have thereby taken on a specific polemical form. From communities like the Johannine one (though not always Christian ones) will come full-fledged extreme Gnosticism in the next century.[58] Therefore the steps towards radical Gnosticism were determined not just by the development of a "spirit of late antiquity," not just by an intellectual dialectic, but by the social position of the various groups (the Jewish gnostics, mystics, and hermetics) which did not overtly compromise monotheism from the rabbinic perspective, did not encounter strong rabbinic opposition, and had less need to polarize the world. Most of those who seemed to compromise monotheism were definitively evicted from the synagogue (as later some of them were evicted from the church). Among them were some who employed allegorical and mythological polemics to represent their position. We are beginning now to see some of the social dynamics which contributed towards the development of Gnosticism. But we must not assume facilely

[58] See Meeks, " 'Am I a Jew?' " esp. 120–21.

that the same social situation obtained all over the empire. Rather each document needs to be analyzed to yield its own specific data.

As in the witchcraft disputes discussed by Douglas,[59] we have seen how the Johannine community tried to enforce conformity within while meeting opposition from without. Its members were trying to understand contradiction and conflict in areas where none should have existed; for, according to the Christian perspective, all Jews should have accepted the message of their Messiah and certainly none should have opposed it. It may even be that they were trying to articulate the correct social role for a Jewish Christian party that was beset by the conflicting claims put on it by Judaism and Christianity.[60] But there is an important difference between the Johannine community and the typical society believing in witchcraft. In the normal witchcraft accusation, the offenders are expelled or recant so that the beliefs of the society are maintained without any further readjustment of ideology; that is, the function of the witchcraft accusation is to promote fission, after which it ceases to be an issue. The Johannine community, however, lacked this easy safety valve because it both cared about the promises of the Old Testament and was sensitive to the rejection by other Jews. It therefore had to develop a new, more sophisticated ideology—the movement towards Gnosticism—to explain its social situation. In Douglas' terms, Johannine Christians were meeting the challenge by developing a higher grid.

From the perspective of social science, we discover that we must go beyond the purely intellectualist interpretation of Gnosticism. Gnostic ideas do not inevitably emerge from the synthesis of Hebrew and Greek thought in some mysterious dialectic. Extreme Gnosticism, rather, is partly a social phenomenon. In the Johannine context it seems to have arisen among those groups interested in Judaism but excluded from the synagogue. The negative portrayal of the theology of the oppressor parallels opposition on the social level and enforces the pariah mentality of the sectarian group. It projects that opposition into the heavenly realm where the new revelation of the process of salvation, the gnosis, could indicate who would triumph. It is both a kind of oblique aggression and an attempt at consolation. Extreme Gnosticism was also partly a

[59] See Douglas, *Natural Symbols*; see also idem, "Thirty Years after *Witchcraft, Oracles, and Magic*," introduction to *Witchcraft: Confessions and Accusations* (London: Tavistock, 1970), xiii–xxxvi.

[60] See pp. 57f. above.

polemical attack against the ideology of a dominant group. The sectarian group which mounted such an attack, whether viewed as a Christian or Jewish heresy, must share the dominant ideology to an extent but must also resent its own expulsion from the congregation of the faithful.

THREE

HELLENISTIC MAGIC
Some Questions of Definition

It is a pleasure to contribute this chapter to a collection in honor of Dr. Quispel. His own work, like Jung's, has shown that magical texts reveal much about man's religious sentiments. Dr. Quispel has shown that magic, equally with religion, can be seen as an expression of humanity's deepest psychological processes.[1]

This chapter will be directed to some definitional questions raised by the continued attention of scholars to the phenomenon of magic. Although many different definitions of "magic" have been offered throughout the history of religious and anthropological research, no one definition has reached general use. Magic's relation both to religion and science has never been clearly delineated. Take the relationship between magic and religion: religious leaders are often interested in strict distinctions between magic and religion so that the purity of religion can be maintained.[2] Social scientists hope to isolate phenomena

[1] See, e.g., *Gnosis als Weltreligion* (Zurich: Origo, 1951), 40f; and "Gnosis und Religionswissenschaft," in *Gnostic Studies*, 2 vols. (Istanbul: Nederlands Historisch-Archaeologisch Instituut te Istanbul, 1975), 2:261.

[2] See esp. M. Smith, *Clement of Alexandria and a Secret Gospel of Mark* (Cambridge, Mass.: Harvard University Press, 1973); idem, *Jesus the Magician* (New York: Harper & Row, 1978). Also of interest are J. Z. Smith, "The Temple and the Magician," in *God's Christ and His People: Studies in Honor of N. A. Dahl*, ed. J. Jervell and W. A. Meeks (Oslo: Universitetsforlaget, 1977), 233–47; idem, "Good News is No News: Aretalogy and Gospel," in *Christianity, Judaism, and Other Greco-Roman Cults: Studies for Morton Smith at Sixty*, part 1: *New Testament*, ed. J. Neusner, SLJA (Leiden: Brill, 1975), 21–38. H. Remus (*Pagan-Christian Conflict over Miracle in the Second Century*, Patristic Monograph Series [Cambridge, Mass.: The Philadelphia Patristic Foundation, 1983]) outlines and surveys the traditional approach in admirable detail. He shows that, e.g., Rengsdorf in Kittel's *Worterbuch* and C. F. D. Moule attempt to distinguish between Christian miracles and pagan wonders on the basis of vocabulary, and hence preserve an essential difference between them in the texts. His conclusion is that the texts evince more fluid use of the words than either Rengsdorf or Moule allow. See also Howard Kee, *Miracle in the Early Christian World: A*

cross-culturally so that a consensus of methodology can be reached,[3] hence many attempts to make clear taxonomies. So both anthropologists and religionists seek to make extremely careful definitions in order to carry on their analyses. For instance, Malinowski defined the difference between magic and religion as sharply as possible. Religion refers to the fundamental issues of human existence, while magic always turns round specific, concrete, and detailed problems.[4] Religion is concerned with questions of ultimate concern—salvation, death, the meaning of existence—while magic is concerned with immediate goals—control of the weather, good health, achieving a specific position. Magic is characterized by manipulation and attempts to control nature. Religion is expressive; magic instrumental.

This should appear extremely sensible to us, since it amounts to a concise statement of one of our culture's definitions of magic. A surprising consequence of this definition is that magic can be viewed as an early form of science.[5] Neat though it is, such a clear-cut distinction leads to problems when cases are examined, as we shall see, since (1) it creates

Study in Sociohistorical Method (New Haven, Conn.: Yale University Press, 1983); C. R. Holladay, *Theios Anēr in Hellenistic Judaism*, SBLDS (Missoula, Mont.: Scholars, 1977); John M. Hull, *Hellenistic Magic and the Synoptic Tradition*, SBT (London: SCM Press, 1974); F. Martroye, "La répression de la magie et les cultes des gentils au IVe siècle," *Revue historique du droit français et étranger*, 4th series, 18 (1930): 669–701; E. Massonneau, *Le crime de magie et le droit romain* (Paris: Recueil Sirey, 1933); D. L. Tiede, *The Charismatic Figure as Miracle Worker*, SBLDS (Missoula, Mont.: Scholars, 1972); Gerd Theissen, *Urchristliche Wundergeschichten: Ein Beitrag zur formgeschichtlichen Erforschung der synoptischen Evangelien* (Gütersloh: Mohn, 1974); and H. van der Loos, *The Miracles of Jesus*, NovTSup (Leiden: Brill, 1965), 247f.

[3] See Ruth Benedict, "Magic," in the *Encyclopedia of the Social Sciences* (New York: Macmillan, 1933), 10:39–44 for the basic bibliography. More recently, R. and M. Wax, "The Magical World View," in *JSSR* 1 (1962): 179–88; idem, "The Notion of Magic," *Current Anthropology* 4 (1963): 495–503; Mary Douglas, *Purity and Danger* (London: Routledge & Kegan Paul, 1966); idem, "Thirty Years after *Witchcraft, Oracles, and Magic*," introduction to *Witchcraft Confessions and Accusations*, ed. Mary Douglas (London: Tavistock, 1970), xiii–xxxviii; Lucy Mair, *Witchcraft* (New York: McGraw-Hill, 1969). An interesting structural analysis is suggested by E. Leach, *Culture and Communication* (Cambridge: Cambridge University Press, 1966).

[4] B. Malinowski, *A Scientific Theory of Culture and Other Essays* (Chapel Hill: University of North Carolina Press, 1944), 200.

[5] This approach is typical of Frazer, Tylor, and Thorndike, for example.

an ideal type which can only be approximated by a specific occurrence and (2) it rarely describes what the magician himself thinks he is doing.[6]

I will argue that no definition of magic can be universally applicable because "magic" cannot and should not be construed as a properly scientific term. Its meaning changes as the context in which it is used changes. No single definition of magic can be absolute, since all definitions of magic are relative to the culture and subculture under discussion. Furthermore, it is my contention that we have been misled by our own cultural assumptions into making too strict a distinction between magic and religion in the Hellenistic world. As we shall see, in some places the distinction between magic and religion will depend purely on the social context.

Since we cannot agree on a suitable definition of magic beforehand, the only way to discuss magic in its Hellenistic contexts is to start with documents that claim to be magical and see what is in them. Only afterwards can we address the adequacy of our account of the phenomenon or offer a definition.

In spite of periodic suppression, considerable magical literature has come down to us. The easiest place to see the whole paradox of the definition of magic is in the magical papyri.[7] They use the terms "magic" and "magical"[8] while the practitioners call themselves μάγοι, "magicians."[9] However, scholars quickly discovered that this usage makes a

[6] See Remus for the complete history of research. Sensitive to these issues many anthropologists are inclined to resist a sharp distinction between magic and religion. Thus, e.g., R. Firth, P. Worsley talk about interpenetration of magic and religion. See also Douglas, *Purity and Danger*, 74ff. Jarl Fossum has called my attention to A. van Gennep, R. Williamson, R. Lowie, A. R. Radcliffe-Brown, W. J. Goode, E. Norbeck, C. G. Diehl and others who have noted the similarity between the two phenomena. Though it is not my purpose to outline or review a history of the study of magic in this chapter, the extent of this trend in the literature needs to be emphasized as well. Very often it seems to me as though theoretical work has tended to separate the two phenomena while field work has tended to combine them. My point is to recommend that we distinguish between the two enterprises and give more attention to how the term is actually used within the culture under consideration.

[7] See *PGM*.

[8] Μαγεια: αληθεια της περι αυτον μαγειας (IV. 2453); δυναμις της θειας αυτου μαγειας (IV. 2449); μυστης της ʽιερας μαγειας (I. 127); μαγειης της εμης βελος (IV. 2319). Μαγικος: μαγικην ψυχην εχων (IV. 210); εν τη μαγικη εμπειρια (I. 331).

[9] Μαγος: παντων μαγων αρχηγετης (IV. 2289); μαγων καθηγεμων (IV. 243); πλειστοι των μαγων (IV. 2081).

definition of magic harder, not easier. A. D. Nock published one of the earliest attempts to understand the magical papyri.[10] He thought of the phenomenon as having a Greco-Egyptian character, comparing it with many of the reports of magic in classical Greece. Though the papyri may have picked up Persian features, he basically saw them as Greek in character. Thus, he tried to understand them by comparison with the worship of Hecate in ancient Greece.[11] Martin Nilsson also turned his attention toward the papyri.[12] Though he found that the papyri were radically individualistic, he could not believe that the magicians wrote such beautiful hymns and spells without help. Their work must have been copied from some other source. For Nilsson and Nock, the most likely source for the writings of these magicians was Hellenistic religion. Based on the metric structure of the hymns, Nilsson suggested that there was an earlier body of literature, attached to the worship of various Greek gods, surviving only in late papyri. The magical texts witnessed to those religious hymns, though the magicians no longer understood them. Through this fairly elaborate theory of literary transmission, Nock and Nilsson were able to explain both the magical and the religious qualities of the writing. But the elaborate enterprise is necessary because they saw magic and religion as totally different and separate phenomena.

The greatest problem with the approach is that no direct literary connections between the magical hymns and religious hymns can be detected. Though there are many similarities between the "magical hymns" and the "religious hymns," no one has been able to demonstrate any direct borrowing. In the absence of such evidence, we should probably assume that the magicians were more creative men than either Nock or Nilsson thought, that hymns could be written in either magical

[10] A. D. Nock, "Greek Magical Papyri," *Journal of Egyptian Archaeology* 15 (1929): 219–35. See also his fine "Paul and the Magus," in *The Beginnings of Christianity: The Acts of the Apostles*, ed. F. J. Foakes-Jackson and K. Lake, 5 vols. (London: Macmillan, 1920–1933; repr., Grand Rapids: Baker, 1966), 5:171, and the many fine articles on magical themes now collected in his *Essays on Religion and the Ancient World* (Cambridge, Mass.: Harvard University Press, 1972).

[11] Though he and R. Reitzenstein agreed basically in seeing the papyri as *ignota pietas*, they disagreed as to the cultural milieu at the center. Reitzenstein ("Religionsgeschichte und Eschatologie," *ZNW* 13 [1912]: 1–28, here 13) thought that they had a Persian background.

[12] Martin P. Nilsson, "Die Religion in den griechischen Zaubetpapyri," in *Opuscula Selecta* (Lund: Gleerup, 1951–1960), 3:129–66.

or religious conditions, or, at least, that the material in the papyri is a *mélange* of different phenomena collected and written by people who saw no distinction between them.

E. R. Goodenough and Gershom Scholem have seen the hymns and charms in the Greek magical papyri in the context of sectarian Judaism and late Hellenistic syncretism. In his magnum opus, *Jewish Symbols in the Greco-Roman Period*, Goodenough quotes a charm like the ones found in *PGM*:

> By the power of those ten holy words of the Lord God, by the Name, I am that I am, God Almighty, Adonai, Lord of Hosts, I bind, excommunicate and destroy, I ward off and cause to vanish, all evil, accursed and maddening pains and sicknesses.[13]

As Goodenough indicated, one God alone is worshiped; the other deities are reduced to the levels of angels or demons. Goodenough's point is that these hymns reflect a sectarian Judaism, syncretized with a number of other influences. Although most of the spells are not "normative" Christianity or Judaism, they combine aspects of both. In order to maintain strict distinctions between magic and religion then, one would also have to define "orthodoxy" in an analytic way. Even if that could be done, it would take us too far afield. But one conclusion allows us to proceed with analysis: the documents are both religious and magical.

Goodenough and Scholem, though differing in other aspects, were united in their willingness to call some aspects of the *PGM* religious. The insights of Goodenough and Scholem can be profitably applied to all the significant hymns of the *PGM*. Many of these seem too sophisticated to be placed in the same category with charms and amulets. In particular, it would be worthwhile to note several of the texts analyzed by E. Peterson.[14] Peterson describes the celebrant as trying to escape from fate to return to the spiritual state from which he has fallen.

Although Peterson tries unsuccessfully to associate the ἄνθρωπος of IV. 1177f. with Adam,[15] his basic understanding of the magical praxis

[13] E. R. Goodenough, *The Archaeological Evidence from the Diaspora*, vol. 2 of *Jewish Symbols in the Greco-Roman Period* (New York: Pantheon), 164.

[14] E. Peterson, "La liberation d'Adam de l'Ανάγκη," *RB* 55 (1948): 199–214. This study has also appeared in a revised German edition, "Die Befreiung Adams aus der Ἀνάγκη," in Peterson's *Fruehkirche, Judentum, und Gnosis* (Freiburg: Herder, 1959), 107–28.

[15] The man (ἄνθρωπος) in IV. 1177f. is so-called in distinction to God's other creations: ὅτι ἐγώ εἰμί ἄνθρωπος, θεοῦ τοῦ εν οὐρανῷ πλάσμα κάλλιστον. This does not

appears to be correct. The celebrant prays that, although born mortal (θνητός γεννήθεις ἐκ θνητής ὕστερας; IV. 517–518) he may be transformed (βεβελτιωμενος) by the god, whose presence he seeks after having made the appropriate consecrations (ἅγιοις ἁγιάσθεις ἁγιάσμασι; IV. 522). The process of immortalization is accomplished through a heavenly journey, climaxed by a face-to-face vision of the divinity (καὶ ἀτενίζε τῶ θεῶ; IV. 711) in which the divinity of the god empowers the journey and appears to confer immortality:

> στας ουν ευθεως ελκε απο του θειου ατενιζων εις σεαυτον το πνευμα όταν ουν αποκατασταθη σου ή ψυχη, λεγε . . . (IV. 628–630)
>
> So stand still and at once draw breath from the divine into yourself, while you look intently. When your soul is restored, say: . . .
>
> συ δε ευθεως μυκωμα μακρον, βασανιζων την γαστερα, ίνα συνκινησης τας πεντε αισθησεις, μακρον, εις αποθεσιν, μυκω καταφιλων παλιν τα φυλακτηρια και λεγων ΜΟΚΡΙΜΟ ΦΕΡΙΜΟΦΕΡΕΡΙ ζωη μου, του δεινα, μενε συ, νεμε εν τη ψυχη μου, μη με καταλειψης. (IV. 704–710)
>
> And at once produce a long bellowing sound, straining your belly, that you may excite the five senseσ: Bellow long until the conclusion, and again kiss the amulets and say: MOKRIMO PHERIMOPHERERI, life of me, N, Stay, dwell in my soul, Do not abandon me.[16]

In the Mithras Liturgy, the salvation is brought by Helios, not Adam; but he grants both immortality and a new birth, implying a new horoscope as well.

> κυριε, παλινγενομενος απογιγνομαι αυξομενος και αυξηθεις τελευτω, απο γενεσεως ζωογονου γενομενος, εις απογενεσιαν αναλυθεις πορευομαι, ώς συ εκτισας, ώς συ ενομοθετησας και εποιησας μυστηριον. (IV. 718–723)

---

make him equivalent to the firstborn Adam who appears in III. 145–147. E. Peterson has been misled by Reitzenstein's formulation in *Poimandres: Studien zur griechisch-aegyptischen und frühchristlichen Literatur* (Leipzig: Teubner, 1904), 274. Rather, the passage explicitly emphasizes this man's earthly origin which needs to be ritually perfected into a σῶμα τέλειον, possibly his divine image after the rite. Thus, the "man" involved is not the supernatural Adam. See now *The Greek Magical Papyri in Translation: Including the Demotic Spells*, ed. Hans D. Betz (Chicago: University of Chicago Press, 1986), 61 and n. 162.

[16] The so-called Mithras Liturgy can be found at IV. 475–829 in Preisendanz. The translation is from *The Mithras Liturgy*, ed. and trans. Marvin Meyer (Missoula, Mont.: Scholars, 1976), 19, lines 629f. and 705f. See now *Greek Magical Papyri in Translation*, ed. Betz, 48–52, translation also by Marvin Meyer.

> O Lord, while being born again, I am passing away; while growing and having grown, I am dying; while being born from a life generating birth, I am passing on, released to death—as you have founded, as you have decreed, and have established the mystery.[17]

More important than whether or not the identity of the mediator figure is Adam is the use of the term "archangel" (ἀρχάγγελος) to describe the function[18] and the manifold use of a mediator in bringing the salvation from God to man (see I. 206f., 219ff.; IV. 1190ff., 1200, 1203f.).

Let us see what definition of magic and religion is presupposed by the texts. Even a brief look at the Mithras Liturgy emphasizes the religious character of the experience being related. The expected result of the long ceremony is not merely to understand the future, though that was involved as well. The expected result is to gain an immortal rebirth (μεταγεννηθέντος; IV. 647) or immortalization (ἀπαθανατίσθεις). The rebirth entails a new horoscope and is described often as a mystery. Furthermore, the adept's vision is described as ἐποπτεύσω (IV. 504), a technical term for participating in the mystery cults. The adept appears to gain his immortality through what he sees and experiences. He rises in an ecstatic heavenly journey by appeasing the various tutelary divinities. His soul is restored through breathing in the divine (IV. 630). At the end he appears to be vouchsafed a vision of the great god Helios Mithras, of whom the magician is the archangel. This is as sophisticated and spiritual an idea as one finds in the religious world of late antiquity.

Suffice it to say that we have discovered a document in which magic and religion are extraordinarily well mixed.[19] Apparently, in the Helle-

[17] See *Mithras Liturgy*, ed. Meyer, 21. This was the end of the Mithras Liturgy, according to Dieterich.

[18] There are a few places in Jewish tradition where Adam is called an angel or compared with one. See Mek. Exod. 4:29; Gen. Rab. 21:5. Also the material in b. Sanh. 38af. suggests Adam's angelic status.

[19] This paradox is also illustrated by the scholarly argument about the Mithras Liturgy. In 1903 Albrecht Dieterich proposed that lines 475–834 of the Paris Magical Papyrus were part of the official liturgy of the Mithras cult, hence religion (*Eine Mithrasliturgie* [Leipzig: Teubner, 1903]). Since the publication of Dieterich's book, many scholars, notably Cumont and Reitzenstein, have criticized his theory. (See the Nachträge to the 3rd ed. [1923]). By the third edition, Dieterich was forced to moderate his claims to admit that the Egyptian magicians had altered the text substantially. Most others have seen the text as Egyptian magic pure and simple, though all have seen significant parallels with the hermetic writings and solar piety. The argument has not ever been satisfactorily resolved. Dieterich's evidence that the document represents a religious mystery is partially sound,

nistic world, as in our own, the definition of magic was not firmly fixed. This is not surprising because the Hellenistic world was a complex and varied *assemblage* of cultures, resembling our own in its development of cosmopolitanism and individualism.[20] In order to address the real meaning of "magic" in the Hellenistic world then, we have to discuss both the ostensible definition of magic and the many social contexts in which magic existed.

To a certain extent ambiguity in the distinction between magic and religion is due to the semantic range of the terms for magic. The words μάγος, *magicus*, and μαγεία were used with a variety of connotations—from the religion of the Magi to scurrilous, harmful magic or witchcraft. The Magi were members of the priestly clan of the Persians and therefore could be considered to be honest religionists. But the Greeks and Romans who actually viewed the Persian Empire tended to bring their own intellectual prejudices to bear against religion when they described it. Herodotus, Pliny, and Plutarch tended at their harshest to view the religion as little more than fraud.[21] Furthermore, since Persia remained Rome's most potent enemy throughout the Imperial Era, any religion practiced there was bound to be viewed as subversive and dangerous.

Then too, many people in the Hellenistic world called themselves μάγοι, when they had no real connection with Persia. These people always courted the epithet γόης, a less ambiguous term usually meaning "quack." Though in the *Symposium* (202e) Plato grants γοητεία a measure of efficacy as a function of the daimon Eros and hence uses it as equivalent to what we have been calling μαγεία, almost all other uses of the

---

yet important aspects of his argument for its Mithraic origin can be dismissed. What is important for our current purposes is to note that scholars themselves cannot decide whether the text is magical or religious. The complementary problem is found in some of Morton Smith's writings. Smith notes that the ascent motif is characteristic of magical rites and tries to maintain that Jesus is a magician because he sees evidence of the same practices in Jesus' ministry and teachings. See below, pp. 97–100.

[20] See, e.g., E. Brehier, *The Hellenistic and Roman Age*, trans. Wade Baskin (Chicago: University of Chicago Press, 1965). I am glad to see that this is also H. D. Betz's opinion in his new introduction to *Greek Magical Papyri in English*, xlv–xlvi. Note his suggestions and his description of the mixing of motifs.

[21] See Smith, *Jesus the Magician*, 71f. See also A. Abt, *Die Apologie des Apuleius von Madaura und die antike Zauberei: Beiträge zur Erläuterung der Schrift der Mageia* (Giessen: Töpelmann, 1908).

term are derogatory.[22] The problems of candidates for the title "divine man" was to convince the world that they were not *magi* and certainly not γοήτες, as detractors might have called them.[23]

Magic was subversive. When magic is mentioned in Roman laws, it is always discussed in a negative context. A consensus was established early which viewed harmful acts (and only harmful acts) of magic as criminal. The Laws of the Twelve Tablets (451–450 B.C.E.) expressly forbid anyone from enticing his neighbor's crops into his own field by magic. Furthermore, the maleficent arts were often considered to be identical with death by poisoning and punishable with equal severity.[24] An actual trial for alleged violation of these laws was held before Spurius Albinus in 157 B.C.E.[25] Cornelius Hispallus expelled the Chaldaean astrologers from Rome in 139 B.C.E.—ostensibly on the grounds that they were magicians.[26] In 33 B.C.E. astrologers and magicians are explicitly mentioned as having been driven from Rome. Twenty years later, Augustus ordered all books on occult subjects to be burned. In 16 C.E. magicians and astrologers were expelled from Italy, which was reinforced by edicts from other emperors in 69 C.E. and 89 C.E. Later, Constantine issued a ruling to cover all charges of magic. In it he distinguished between helpful charms, not punishable, and antagonistic spells:

> If any are discovered to have been using magic arts so as to threaten men's safety or pervert modest persons to libidinous practices, their science is to be punished and deservedly penalized according to the severest

[22] Josephus (*J.W.* 2.261f.; *Ant.* 20.92, 167, 188), e.g., dismisses miracle-workers with the term.

[23] In the case of Apollonius of Tyana the apologetic is present right at the start. Philostratus, his official biographer, shows that, like philosophers, Apollonius was not afraid to learn about occult subjects, but that he never practiced magic. He is also capable of using the same word μάγος to describe the priests of Persia, who though not all-knowing, are nevertheless in wise in certain matters. The emphasis is on becoming wise: ομιλησαντες μαγοις και πολλα δαιμονια ειποντες, ουπω ὑπηχθησαν τη τεχνη (*Vit. Apoll.* 1.2). Compare with 1.26: τι ὁι μαγοι; τον δε αποκρινασθαι σοφοι μεν, αλλ' ου παντα. See also Anitra B. Kolenkow, "A Problem of Power: How Miracle Workers Counter Charges of Magic in the Hellenistic World," in *SBL 1976 Seminar Papers*, ed. G. MacRae (Missoula, Mont.: Scholars, 1976), 105–10.

[24] Smith, *Jesus the Magician*, 75f.

[25] Pliny, *Nat.* 18.41–43.

[26] See Eugene Tavenner, *Studies in Magic from Latin Literature* (New York: Columbia University Press, 1916), 13; and J. E. Lowe, *Magic in Greek and Latin Literature* (Oxford: Basil Blackwell, 1929).

> laws. However, no accusations are to be heard against remedies sought out for human bodies or, in rural districts, to protect mature grapes from fear of rains or from being crushed by the pounding of hailstones.[27]

Several observations can be made on the basis of the history of the crime of magic. First, magic was clearly viewed as efficacious; otherwise it would have been prosecuted as fraud.[28] Second, though illegal, it must have been widely practiced, or at least believed to be so, to have occasioned such frequent condemnation. Third, it is the *maleficium*, witchcraft, which is proscribed; presumably what we call "white" or non-aggressive magic was no crime, though, to be sure, much that they called "religion" might appear to us to be magic. "White" magic or nonaggressive magic could easily appear to be religion by their standards. But notice the further ambiguity: though the Chaldaean astrologers were religionists and presumably were not aggressive by definition, once their ideology was deemed dangerous, they could be expelled as magicians, on the ground that they presented a danger to society. This illustrates Morton Smith's observation that, while in our culture "magic" has the connotation of trickery, in Roman culture it often had the connotation of subversion as well.[29]

The great witches of Greek legend, including Medea and Erichtho among others, were literary creations, but the fear of witchcraft and the use of sorcery were obviously quite common. Among the Romans, especially those in the lower classes, sorcery, though illegal, was often practiced or hired as a service by people who were in situations of competition and uncertainty. The charioteer owed his position to personal

[27] From Smith, *Jesus the Magician*, 76. See *Theodosiani Libri XVI cum Constitutionibus Sirmondianis*, ed. Th. Mommsen (Berlin: Weidmann, 1905; repr. 1954 and 1962), 9.16.3, p. 460; translated as *The Theodosian Code and Novels, and Sirmondia Constitutions* (Princeton: Princeton University Press, 1952), 237:

> Eorum est scientia punienda et severissimus merito legibus vendicanda, qui magicis adcincti artibus aut contra hominum molite salutem aut pudicos ad libidinem deflexisse animos detegentur. Nullis vero criminationibus inplicanda sunt remedia humanis quaesita corporibus aut in agrestibus locis, ne maturis vindemiis metuerentur imbres aut ruentis grandinis lapidatione quaterentur, innocenter adhibita suffragia, quibus non cuiusque salus aut existimatio laederetur, sed quorum proficerent actus, ne divina munera et labores hominum sternerentur.

[28] For a rare example of the charge of fraud, see Lucian, *Alexander the False Prophet*. See also Smith, *Jesus the Magician*, 88.

[29] See *A Secret Gospel of Mark*, 221.

skill, which was both increased and frequently attacked by magic. So it is not infrequent to find this sort of evocative masterpiece among the collections of curse tablets:

> I conjure you up, holy beings and holy names; join in aiding this spell and bind, enchant, thwart, strike, overturn, conspire against, destroy, kill, and break Eucherius, the charioteer and all his horses tomorrow in the circus at Rome. May he not leave the barriers well, may he not be quick in the contest, may he not outstrip anyone; may he not make the turns well; may he not win any prizes; and, if he has pressed someone hard, may he not come off the victor; and, if he follows someone from behind, may he not overtake him; but may he meet with an accident, may he be bound, may he be broken, may he be dragged along by your power in the morning and afternoon races. Now! Now! Quickly! Quickly![30]

This *defixio* is clearly aggressive magic, it is clearly *maleficium*, and it is definitely illegal. No one would have practiced it with the impression he was practicing a legal and wholesome religious rite, however richly deserved was the damage to the intended victim. Peter Brown gives a special explanation of the frequency of references to chariot races in the tablets.[31] The competition faced by the charioteer extended beyond his time in the circus. The charioteer was an undefined mediator in urban society. He was both the client of local aristocracies and the leader of organized groups of fans. As a public figure with considerable popular

[30] This curse may be found in *Inscriptiones Graecae ad Res Romanas Pertinentes*, vol. 1, ed. R. Cagnat (Paris: Leroux, 1906), no. 117. The English translation is from *Roman Civilization Sourcebook II: The Empire*, ed. N. Lewis and M. Reinhold (New York: Columbia University Press, 1955), 570. Three hundred examples of *defixionum tabellae* were published by Audollent (1904). A supplementary list from central and northern Europe was made by Preisendanz, in *AR* 11 (1933). The Attic examples known before 1897 were separately edited by R. Wunsch (*IG* III.3). Additional Attic curse tablets have been published by Ziebarb (*NAWG* 1899, 105ff. and SPAW 1934, 1022f.). Others have been found subsequently. There seem to be only a few that can be assigned to the fifth century B.C.E. or earlier; on the other hand, a good many can be shown to belong to the fourth. Still, the majority are Roman and come from much later times. For a complete bibliography, see E. R. Dodds, *The Greeks and the Irrational* (Berkeley: University of California Press, 1968), 204f.

[31] On the issue of black magic and witchcraft, see Peter Brown, "Sorcery, Demons, and the Rise of Christianity from Late Antiquity into the Middle Ages," in Douglas, ed., *Witchcraft: Confessions and Accusations*, 17–46. Also see Mair, *Witchcraft*, cited above and G. Parrinder, *Witchcraft: European and African* (London: Faber & Faber, 1963).

following, he became a potential leader in urban rioting.[32] Because of the anxiety and charisma associated with such an uncertain life, some charioteers and many of their fans were driven to seek sorcerers. This keen observation anticipates the necessity for more social-scientific attention to the phenomenon of Hellenistic magic.

Thus, when magic was viewed as benign it might easily be coterminous with religion, whereas in the crucial contexts where magic was viewed as antagonistic and illegal it was carefully differentiated. The definition of this crime of "black" magic was made on the basis of its presumed injury, and it was treated in many respects as other practices banned for the protection of the body politic. Common sense tells us that, whenever an accusation of magic was made, a distinction between magic and legitimate forms of religion was being made by the accuser. The accuser is claiming that the accused meant to harm society. It is not necessarily true, however, that the accuser would say that the "magic" practiced is not religion—since the Persian Magi, Jews, *Mathematici*, and philosophers are often grouped together in a ban—only that the practice was aggressive or primitive. Therefore, the defendant in an accusation of magic might have a different view of what he was doing.

In order to specify further the conditions under which "black" magic and religion were distinguished in the Hellenistic world, we have to review a few actual cases of witchcraft accusations. The rhetor Libanius successfully defended himself against the charge of sorcery several times.[33] His righteous indignation at being so wrongly accused, an insult to his ability as a rhetor, tempts one to view him as a strict rationalist. But this is far from the case. When his old injury (from being struck by lightning) begins to act up, causing him to suffer unsettling dreams, he suspects sorcery. Finding a dead chameleon in his classroom, he becomes convinced that he has been made a victim of some malevolent force invoked by an enemy. On this basis he is able to blame recent losses in debate on the sorcery of his opponents instead of their superior skill. This phenomenon has also been admirably discussed by Peter Brown.[34] Brown sees

[32] See R. MacMullen, *Enemies of the Roman Order: Treason, Unrest, and Alienation in the Empire* (Cambridge, Mass.: Harvard University Press, 1967), 171 and nn. 10–12, 339–41.

[33] *Libanius' Autobiography (Oration 1)*, ed. and trans. A. F. Norman (London: Oxford University Press, 1965); see esp. viii–xii, 31, 35, 39–41, 61, 93, 127–29.

[34] Brown, "Sorcery, Demons, and the Rise of Christianity," 17–46. This is indeed a valuable and exciting article. See also MacMullen, *Enemies of the Roman Order*.

Libanius as an example of how sorcery beliefs coalesce around areas of competition and uncertainty—conditions which are being aggravated in the third century in a society becoming more and more committed to a vested hierarchy in church and state.[35] Certainly this is a case of how sorcery "explains unfortunate events," to rely on Kluckhohn's functionalist description of Navajo witchcraft. The sorcery attacks can be seen to counter and explain misfortune in competitive situations in ways that allowed the ostensible victim to escape without damage to his feelings of professional competency. In this case, magic or sorcery is seen as discontinuous with religion because it is aggressive and mean. The accusation is made against colleagues and presumably in the case of Libanius, the accusation of witchcraft was quite straightforward.

In other, more revealing contexts, the definition of magic is the subject of the controversy. This is illustrated by the experience of Apuleius. In Apuleius' time, many archaeological finds begin to be evidenced on expensive media like papyrus and parchment. Amulets begin to be fashioned of jewels, gold, or silver. All of this suggests that the people with more money were beginning to become interested in magic. When Apuleius is accused of witchcraft by the relatives of his newly married wife, he expresses an ambiguous opinion of μαγεια, which will help us clarify how "magic" and "religion" were differentiated:

> I will now deal with the actual charge of magic. You spared no violence in fanning the flame of hatred against me. . . . I should therefore like to ask his most learned advocates how precisely they would define a magician? If what I read in a large number of authors be true, namely that "magician" is the Persian word for priest, what is there criminal in being a priest and having due knowledge, science and skill? . . . [36] But, if you

[35] Brown, "Sorcery, Demons, and the Rise of Christianity," 25. See also C. Kluckhohn, *Navajo Witchcraft* (Cambridge: Cambridge University Press, 1944), esp. 79–128 for the psychological functions of witchcraft.

[36] His opinion of the Magi was shared widely. When Ps.-Aristotle affirms that the Magi are not acquainted with τήν γοητίκην μαγείαν, he is referring to the orthodox clergy of Persia. In many places, Greek authors go out of their way to declare that the Magi practice μαγεία, not γοητεία, therefore they are not magicians: "Μαγεία Ζωρουάστρου ἐστί θεῶν θεραπεία." See J. Bidez and F. Cumont, *Les mages héllenisés: Zoroastre, Ostanès, and Hystaspe d'après la tradition grecque*, 2 vols. (Paris: Les Belles Lettres, 1938), 1:144 n. 2. In point of fact sorcery was equally demonic in Persia, where it was considered to be service to the *devas* (demons) by the *druj* (evil ones). Cf. *The Zend-Avesta*, trans. J. Darmesteter, 2 vols. (Oxford: Clarendon, 1880–1883), 1:76 n. 8, 90 n. 53; 2:12 n. 252; F. Cumont, *Textes et monuments figurés relatifs aux mystères de Mithra*, 2 vols. (Brussels: Lamertin, 1899), 1:141.

> accusers of mine, after the fashions of the common herd, define a magician as one who, by communion or speech with the immortal gods, has the power to do all the marvels that he will through a strange power of incantation, I really wonder that they are not afraid to attack one whom they acknowledge to be so powerful. (*Apol.* 25–26)[37]

Since Apuleius, a young man, had managed to marry an elderly woman of considerable fortune, her relatives feared that they might be disinherited. Yet Apuleius had violated no specific law, so they attempted to press their claim by maintaining that he used magic to win his wealthy wife. This is surely an example of the use of the charge of magic to clarify an ambiguous and threatening situation, a use which we will investigate further. The threat to the traditional expectation about inheritance is countered by a charge that the social order was upset by demonic action.

More interesting still is Apuleius' reply to the charge. In wonderful rhetorical fashion, he rebukes the illogicality of his accusers. If "magicus" is a Persian priest, he has done no harm. On the other hand, if it is what the common herd thinks it is, he marvels that they are not afraid to attack one they acknowledge to be so powerful!

Though Apuleius admits that the common people see magicians as all-powerful, he denies only that he has the power to do what he will. The possibility that he might be a Persian priest is taken as an unjustified compliment. This is to be explained by the trend in the first centuries

[37] *The Apologia and Florida of Apuleius of Madaura*, trans. H. E. Butler (Oxford: Clarendon, 1909), 55–56. See Apulee, *Apologie et Florides*, ed. Paul Vallette (Paris: Les Belles Lettres, 1960), 31, 33.

> Aggredior enim iam ad ipsum crimen magiae, quod ingenti tumult ad inuidiam mei accensum frustrata exspectatione omnium per nescio quas anilis fabulas defraglauit . . . et ideo mihi libet quaerere ab eruditissimis eius aduocatis quid sit magus.
>
> Nam si, quod ego apud plurimos lego, Persarum lingua magus est qui nostra sacerdos, quod tandem est crimen sacerdotem esse et rite nosse atque scire atque callere leges cerimoniarum, fas sacrorum, ius religionum? . . . Sin uero more uulgari eum isti proprie magum existimant, qui communione loquendi cum deis immortalibus ad omnia quae uelit incredibili quadam ui contaminum polleat, oppido miror cur accusare non timuerint quem posse tantum fatentur. Neque enim tam occulta et diuina potentia caueri potest itidem ut cetera. Sicarium qui in iudicium uocat, comitatus uenit; qui uenenarium accusat, scrupolosius cibatur; qui furem uenit, sau custodit; enimuero qui magum qualem isti dicunt in discrimen capitis deducit, quibus comitibus, quibus scrupulis, quibus custodibus perniciem caecam et ineuitabilem prohibeat? Nullis scilicet; et ideo id genus crimen non est eius accusare, qui credit.

of our era to see magic, philosophy, and wonder-working as essentially similar, as Morton Smith and others have shown us. Hence, there arises quite often a distinction between what a critical outsider might call the act in question and the experience of the participant.

Apuleius' usage reflects a growing upper-class flirtation with "magical" arts. But Apuleius' full view of magic per se is most fully expressed in his picaresque novel, *The Golden Ass*. The hero of this novel, Lucius, is led by a mistress (herself a servant of a witch) into careless experimentation with magic. The result is that Lucius is transformed into an ass, a predicament which continues until the end of the novel, when Lucius finally regains his original shape because of a rose-leaf antidote.

No doubt, Apuleius' story about a human in the shape of a donkey made the Romans behave more circumspectly in the presence of their beasts. But it was more than a comic invention of a burlesque novel. The antidote to the witchcraft is a very serious account of the hero's salvation through the intervention of Isis. After this is accomplished, the priest of Isis delivers a speech which explains the basic meaning of the whole story (11.15):

> After enduring many different troubles and after being driven by the wildest storms of Fortune and her heaviest gales, at last, Lucius, you have come to the haven of Rest and the altar of Mercy. Your high birth was of no avail to you nor even your position in society, nor yet the learning in which you are so rich, but on the slippery path of your hotheaded youth you fell into low pleasures and you have gained a grim reward for your ill-starred curiosity. Nevertheless the blindness of Fortune, while it tortured you with the worst of dangers, yet led you in its unforeseeing evil to your state of religious bliss. Let her quit now and rage in her wildest frenzy and seek another object for her cruelty. For hostile fate has no power over those whose lives have been claimed by the majesty of our goddess. What avail to wicked Fortune were the robbers, the wild beasts, the slavery, the hardships of journeys that winded on and back, and the daily fear of death? Now you have been received into the protection of a Fortune who is not blind, but sees, and who illumines the other gods too with the radiance of her light.
>
> Show, then, a happier face in keeping with the white cloak you have assumed. Follow the procession of the Savior Goddess with triumphant step. Let the unbelievers take note, let them take note and acknowledge their mistake: behold, here is Lucius! He has been freed from his former sufferings and, rejoicing in the providence of mighty Isis, he is victorious over his Fortune. But to be safer and better equipped, enroll your name

> in this holy military service, whose solemn oath you were asked to take not long ago, and vow yourself from this moment to the ministry of our religion. Accept of your own free will the yoke of service. For when you have begun to serve the goddess, then will you better realize the result of your freedom.[38]

Apuleius' final understanding of "magic" is negative. Magic represents the world under the power of blind chance, a world in which Lucius had been enslaved until the grace of the goddess saved him. Just as magic represents the ill-starred world under the influence of fate, so the religion of Isis is defined as the special knowledge and care of the goddess that saves from fate. Lucius' salvation is through the mystery cult of Isis, whose public ceremonies were known to all in the Hellenistic world but whose secrets were known only to the initiates. We have no better description of the inner ritual or goals of the mystery religions than Apuleius' work. It is this specific characteristic of the cult which makes it a legitimate religion for Apuleius.

The striking aspect of Apuleius' account, however, is how completely it resembles the experience in the magical papyri. The magical adept, like Lucius, is seeking the power to be free of the fates and demons, through a heavenly ascent and theurgic power. Thus, while the insider

[38] *Apuleius of Madauros: The Isis-Book*, ed. J. G. Griffiths, EPRO 39 (Leiden: Brill, 1975), 87–89.

> Multis et variis exanclatis laboribus magnisque Fortunae tempestatibus et maximis actus procellis ad portum Quietis et aram Misericordiae tandem, Luci, venisti, nec tibi natales ac ne dignitas quidem, vel ipsa, qua flores, usquam doctrina profuit, sed lubrico virentis aetatulae ad serviles delapsus voluptates curiositatis inprosperae sinistrum praemium reportasti, sed utcumque Fortunae caecitas, dum te pessimis periculis discruciat, ad religiosam istam beatitudinem inprovida produxit malitia eat nunc et summo furore saeviat et crudelitati suae materiem quaerat aliam; nam in eos, quorum sibi vitas deae nostrae maiestas vindicavit, non habet locum casus infestus, quid latrones, quid ferae, quid servitium, quid asperrimorum itinerum ambages reciprocae, quid metus mortis cotidianae nefariae Fortunae profuit? In tutelam iam receptus es Fortunae, sed videntis, quae suae lucis splendore ceteros etiam deos illuminat. Sume iam vultum laetiorem candido isto habitu tuo congruentem, comitare pompam deae sospitatricis inovanti gradu. Videant inreligiosi, videant et errorem suum recognoscant: en ecce pristinis aerumnis absolutus Isidis magnae providentia gaudens Lucius de sua Fortuna triumphat. Quo tamen tutior sis atque munitior, da nomen sanctae huic militiae, cuius non olim sacramento etiam rogabaris, teque iam nunc obsequio religionis nostrae dedica et ministerii iugum subi voluntarium. Nam cum coeperis deae servire, tunc magis senties fructum tuae libertatis.

in this case distinguishes between magic and religion, his description of true religion matches some aspects of magical practice elsewhere.

Theurgy, more than anything else, represents the force that transformed "magical" acts into acceptable religion in the Roman Empire. Theurgy itself had been brought into the Roman Empire through the agency of the Chaldaeans. As far as we know, the earliest person claiming this art was Julianus, a contemporary of Marcus Aurelius.[39] He, in turn, claimed an association with an earlier Julianus, who gave him the secrets of the Chaldaean Oracles. The technique of theurgy became more and more associated with the late Neoplatonic school, to such an extent that Proclus could define theurgy grandly as "a power higher than all human wisdom, embracing the powers of divination, the purifying powers of initiation, and, in short, all the operations of divine possession" (*Theol. Plat.* 1.26).[40] This explains why magic became acceptable in some aristocratic circles. Simply, it became a consistent religion, appealing to philosophers as well as their aristocratic students because of its independence from organized cults.

Even in this particular context, however, the term "magic" often continued to be viewed with contempt. Porphyry accused Iamblichus of dealing only with demons and so forced Iamblichus to write a long justification of theurgy as a means of controlling gods as well as demons. It is not difficult to see in this conflict an attempt to define magic again. Iamblichus is actually defending himself against the charge that he is merely dealing in magic by attempting to show that his beliefs form a philosophically coherent system and involve communications with the gods.

This is a clue to the most obvious reason why the definition of magic continued to be ambiguous even in nonaggressive contexts. It appears that magic was often tacitly defined as worship of demons, while religion was defined as worship of the gods. Since both gods and demons were most often invisible, their effects alone being palpable, it was difficult to tell who was at work. Before it was clear whether "magic" or "religion"

[39] See M. Smith, "Observations on Hekhaloth Rabbati," in *Biblical and Other Studies*, ed. A. Altmann (Cambridge, Mass.: Harvard University Press, 1963), 142–60. See also *Jamblique, Les Mysteres d'Egypte*, ed. and trans. É. des Places (Paris: Les Belles Lettres, 1966); *Oracles Chaldaïques*, ed. and trans. É. des Places (Paris: Les Belles Lettres, 1971).

[40] *Proclus, Théologie platonicienne*, vol. 1., ed. and trans. H. Saffrey and L. Westerink (Paris: Les Belles Lettres, 1968), 113.

was the best explanation of the marvelous event, a complicated social ambiguity had to be resolved.

The most important example of this distinction may be found in Porphyry's *Life of Plotinus*, 10:

> Among those making profession of philosophy at Rome was one Olympius, an Alexandrian, who had been for a while a pupil of Ammonius. This man's jealous envy showed itself in continual insolence, and finally he grew so bitter that he even ventured sorcery, seeking to crush Plotinus by star-spells. But he found his experiments recoiling upon himself, and he confessed to his associates that Plotinus possessed "a mighty soul, so powerful as to be able to hurl every assault back upon those that sought his ruin." Plotinus had felt the operation and declared that at that moment Olympius' limbs "were convulsed and his body shriveling like a money-bag pulled tight." Olympius, perceiving on several attempts that he was endangering himself rather than Plotinus, desisted.
>
> In fact, Plotinus possessed by birth something more than is accorded to other men. An Egyptian priest who had arrived in Rome and, through some friend, had been presented to the philosopher, became desirous of displaying his powers to him, and he offered to evoke a visible manifestation of Plotinus' presiding spirit. Plotinus readily consented and the evocation was made in the Temple of Isis, the only place, they say, which the Egyptian could find pure in Rome.
>
> At the summons, a divinity appeared, not a being of the spirit ranks, and the Egyptian exclaimed: "You are singularly blessed; the guiding-spirit within you is none of the lower degree, but a God." It was not possible, however, to interrogate or even to contemplate this God any further, for the priest's assistant, who had been holding the birds to prevent them from flying away, strangled them, whether through jealousy or in terror. Thus, Plotinus had for indwelling spirit a being of the more divine degree, and he kept his own divine spirit unceasingly intent upon that inner presence. It was this preoccupation that led him to write his treatise upon *Our Tutelary Spirit*, an essay in the explanation of the differences among spirit-guides.
>
> Amelius was scrupulous in observing the Day of the New Moon and other holy days, and once asked Plotinus to join in such celebration: Plotinus refused: "It is for such beings to come to me, not for me to go to them." What was in his mind in so lofty an utterance we could not explain to ourselves and we dared not ask him.[41]

[41] Porphyry, "On the Life of Plotinus and the Arrangement of His Works," in *The Enneads of Plotinus*, trans. Stephen MacKenna, 3rd rev. ed. by B. S. Page (London: Faber, 1965), 8.

There are very complicated and ambiguous relationships between magic and religion here. In the first paragraph Plotinus' power is distinguished from pure magic on the basis of superiority in quantity, not essence. Therefore, either Plotinus is being called a magician or Porphyry sees a continuum between religion and magic. In the second and succeeding paragraphs, it is clear that the latter alternative is to be chosen. Plotinus is to be distinguished from magicians because his power (as a god or coming from a god) is greater. Plotinus' claim to have divine power is upheld by a religious authority of some stature—an Egyptian priest. Though the practice sounds magical to us, it is clear that Porphyry is interested in it precisely because a priest of Isis is a religious defender of Plotinus' great power. Thus, after Porphyry has proven that Plotinus is a "divine man" with a god as tutelary spirit, he can digress to tell us of several great feats which were performed by him. In this context, as with other divine men, we are to interpret the great feats as "miracles," not as magical manipulations, precisely because a religious claim is being made about the performer.

In other words, there is no universal definition of magical procedure in Hellenistic culture. Instead, the charge of magic and its meaning depended on a complicated series of assumptions, not all of which were clear at the beginning of the social interaction. One of the results of the interaction was to produce that clarity. Thus, the charge of "magic" helps distinguish between various groups of people from the perspective of the speaker but does not necessarily imply any essential difference in the actions of the participants. In a narrative about the event, the narrator will attempt to clarify his grounds for distinction.

It is in this context that I believe we should put the disputes about Jesus in Mark 2, 3; Matthew 10; John 7, and many others, as well as the accusations against Apollonius of Tyana and the other evidence that Morton Smith has given us.[42] As we would expect, the exorcism stories have been edited to discuss the question of the source of Jesus' power. In the Beelzebul controversy (Mark 3:19-27; Matt 12:22-30; Luke 11:14-16, 17-23) the ambiguity over the source of Jesus' power is clear, but it is also combined with the issue of dissent within the movement, which serves to obscure the conclusion of the Gospel writer on the question of magic. The first question is raised by Jesus' followers (ὁι παρ' αὐτοῦ) in

[42] Note Smith, *Jesus the Magician*. See also Kolenkow, "A Problem of Power."

the Markan version. Seeing the overwhelming crowds and anticipating the difficulty feeding them, some of his own disciples begin either to think that Jesus is insane or unaware of the problem by virtue of an ecstatic trance (ἔλεγον γάρ ὅτι ἐξέστη).[43] After this situation is outlined, the charge of the scribes of Jerusalem is introduced, combining a different but similar tradition of attack on the motivation for Jesus' actions, this time from outside the movement. The scribes are represented as believing that Jesus' power is not from God but from Beelzebul. This is logical because, if Jesus were from God, he could not oppose the legitimate authorities of Judea. Since he does, his power must have other sources. The New Testament portrayal, however, takes no account of the opponents' position. Jesus points out that he is casting out demons, therefore he must be from God, since Satan would not consent to overthrow his own kingdom. This argument only makes sense if one assumes a unified evil hegemony in opposition to God and that the demons, now considered helpers of Satan, are evil—a presupposition central to the New Testament, which is only partly shared by the Pharisees and certainly not by all Jews, as Goodenough showed us above. In any event, in the New Testament it is enough to silence the opposition from the outside. Therefore the New Testament is not really interested in analyzing the social situation. More important to the story in the present context is the lesson that follows. Those followers who criticize the marvelous deeds of the Savior risk blasphemy in the name of the Holy Spirit, a sin much worse than the accusation of the scribes, which appears only as external hostility. So the story of the charge of magic is combined with the issue of internal dissent which becomes the central issue for the church.

In Luke and Matthew, the controversy is complicated by a *tu quoque* argument which destroys the logic of the parable of the house divided but again reflects the unsolved ambiguity of the charge of magic: "If I cast out demons in the name of Beelzebul, in whose name do your sons exorcise?" This implies what we knew all along—that there were Jews who claimed to work similar acts to what Jesus had accomplished and who also claimed divine favor. Therefore, this version spells out the implication that Christianity is certainly "religion" if other kinds of Jewish exorcism can be. But the conclusion about magic is purchased at the price of the logic of the Markan version. The later Gospels then fasten

[43] See the rabbinic comment on Simeon b. Zoma, b. Hag. 15a.

on the term "kingdom" and convert the story to a kingdom saying about the coming of the end of time. Matthew even eliminates the original charge of Jesus' followers, as a sensitive issue, by attributing the entire charge to Jesus' outside enemies, who are called "Pharisees" for the first time. No doubt this reflects a later time when Pharisees could have been expected to have made just such a charge, based on their conviction that Jesus' power, was not from God, just as the scribes could have done so in Jesus' lifetime. Each additional comment gives us a further example of the difficulty in defining magic. If someone called himself a magician, that was one thing. But more often, people who appeared to have divine favor or who exercised supernatural power could be charged with the crime of magic by their detractors. There were no objective criteria separating the miracle worker from the magician. So, it was often necessary for an adept to prove himself a miracle worker and not a magician.

Furthermore, one sees from this particular context that the conflict has slightly different overtones than in the pagan examples. Here, worship or partnership with demons is not merely viewed as low, unsophisticated, and potentially harmful. It is also heresy, a threat to monotheism. Even when accepted as tutelary spirits, one had to decide whether the "demons" were angels, as some Jewish exorcists were evidently claiming,[44] or devils. Most often the judgment of the orthodox group was that these demons were evil, hence our use of the term "demonic" in contradistinction to the less morally loaded pagan understanding of the term.

Particularly striking in this respect is the remarkable similarity between Jesus' "I am" statements and the claims of magicians in the magical papyri.[45] To find such little noted similarities takes an acute mind and years of research. The data clearly demonstrate the essential unity of all men claiming spiritual powers in late antiquity. Such similarities further demonstrate why the Gospel writers were sensitive to the charge of magic brought against Jesus. A defense against the charge of magic is not only characteristic of the polemics of the church fathers and evangelists, it goes back to the earliest traditions of the church. But it does not prove that Jesus was a magician. The early charge of magic against Jesus is not so much clear proof that Jesus was a magician as a

[44] The Jewish exorcists described in the Gospel of Matthew certainly existed. See *Sefer Harazim*, where Jewish magicians prayed to inferior "angels" to help them accomplish their ends.

[45] See Smith, *Jesus the Magician*, 126.

clear example of the social manipulation of the charge of magic. When Jesus is accused of magic, it is his credentials as miracle worker that are under scrutiny. Since the determinants of Jesus' credentials are not objectively verifiable, whether or not he is a magician is the subject of the controversy. There is no evidence that Jesus wished to claim the title of magician. To the contrary, the Gospel presents his teachings as well as the titles of divine favor as a defense against the accusation, just as Plotinus and Porphyry defend themselves.

The most interesting question for scholarship, as I see it, is not whether the charge of magic against Jesus is true or not. Since he does not claim the title, there can be no possible demonstration or disproof of a charge which is a matter of interpretation in the Hellenistic world. The most interesting question for scholarship is to define the social and cultural conditions and presuppositions that allow such charges and countercharges to be made.

Though I have been arguing that no single generalization can hold for the use of the charge of magic in Hellenistic society, a few general statements can be made, if they are understood as probabilities rather than essential distinctions. The charge of magic is likely to be made by legitimate religious leaders against people who are viewed as threatening the social order but who have as yet done no other prosecutable criminal offense. For instance, *Mathematici*, Jews, and Christians could be seen as subversive by the Roman government, so it was logical to charge them with "magic" even though the charge might be factually groundless and impress us as absurd. On the other hand, there were real Jewish and Christian sorcerers, whose existence was probably all the more detested because they could get the entire group into trouble. With this observation most of the usages of the word "magic" can be easily explained. In succeeding centuries, Christians and Jews shared the upper-class disgust for magic for different reasons. Orthodox Christians and Jews appear to have generalized the negative implication of magic to every outside group, including each other. Since every other religion was false, it stands to reason that every other religion was working with demons, not God. Therefore, every other religion was either magic (if it was puissant), or it was nothing at all. In this sense, both orthodox Christianity and Judaism appeared as a kind of "anti-witchcraft cult," a characteristic which was to add to their success considerably. Their enemies—Jesus in Judaism, Simon in Christianity—could be called magicians. Both could promise that their believers were free from the powers of fate. Hence, they serve the same function as did the cult of Isis from Lucius in Apuleius' novel. But the impetus against witchcraft was the belief in one God.

Even as the orthodox Christianity and Judaism opposed magic as worship of the demons, pagan opinions of magic seem to have grown more tolerant. But, since the late Neoplatonic schools, those most famous for indulging in magic, were sensitive to the charge of magic, how then are we to explain the magical papyri's mixture of magic and religion? The answer, it seems to me, has to do with a situation outside of a strict Jewish or Christian setting, and outside of the aristocratic setting in a context where no accusation of magic is overtly made. An important factor is Egypt itself where spells and curses to protect the dead had been part of state religion since its inception. In these cases magic is most clearly a "conflict" crime—that is, a criminal act to some but not to all members of the society. This was the "ecological niche" of the Hellenized magi.

One of the clearest examples of the use of the term "magic" as a religious act comes from the autobiography of Thessalos.[46] Thessalos, after finding both that Greek rhetoric and traditional magic are not satisfactory, wanders in Egypt in search of a revelation. His question is whether any "magical energy" might still survive (εἰ τὶ τῆς μαγικῆς ἐνέργειας σώζεται; 1.13).[47] The priests are either afraid of the legal repercussions of the term "magic" or, more likely, merely embarrassed by the belief in an act they could not practice.[48] After much searching, one priest promises him a vision, if he can accomplish the requisite purification. At a prearranged place,[49] Thessalos asks to see Asclepius, alone, "one to one."[50]

[46] See Smith, "Temple and the Magician," who summarizes all the research done on this document and presents the experience in it as characteristic of the religious life of late antiquity. He shows that the traditional forms of religion represented by the temple are in decay, making necessary a new form of individual experience with the divine.

[47] *Thessalos von Tralles*, ed. and trans. H. Friedrich (Meisenheim am Glan: Hain, 1968), 49 line 16.

[48] See Smith, "Temple and the Magician," 235 on this point.

[49] Called an οἶκος but not a temple. See Smith, "Temple and the Magician," 235 on this point.

[50] Like "face to face," this term has an obvious theophanic association. See refs. brought by Smith, "Temple and the Magician," 243 n. 40 to Plotinus, Porphyry, Proclus, Numenius, and Eusebius from E. Peterson, "Herkunft und Bedeutung der *Monos pros Monon*-Formel bei Platon," *Philologus* 88 (1933): 30–41.

Interestingly enough, though the promise of divinization is made through this theophany, it is the gift of the knowledge of proper times and places which occupies the attention of the narrator. Again, as in the magical papyri, the mix of overtly magical claims with clearly religious desire of individual divinization makes it impractical to distinguish between magic and religion, for now magic is even taken, in opposition to the temple cults, to be the only really effective religion.

Although there is an implicit polemic against established religion, there is no social competition in the document, rather a description of the internal working of the minds that produced such documents and their location on the social map of the Roman Empire. A most helpful way of understanding the mix of what we call "vulgar magic" and "religion" in these syncretistic works is suggested by the anthropological study of the Aladura cult in Africa. Robin Horton postulates that

> a basic African cosmology . . . has a two tier structure, the first tier being that of the lesser spirits and the second that of the supreme being. The lesser spirits underpin events and processes in the microcosm of the local community and its environment, whilst the supreme being underpins events and processes in the macrocosm—i.e., in the world as a whole.[51]

This theory suggests that the distinction between lesser deities and the high god is not an arbitrary one. Obviously, the African analogy cannot be taken over in entirety. But it appears likely that the celebrants of the rites described in the magical papyri had a similar concept of the world. For the microcosmic aspects of life, the little micropolitical battles, it was enough to call on one or more demons to help balance the score. But when the meaning of processes in the macrocosm was sought, a greater kind of salvation was needed. Therefore the cosmos needs to contain two orders of divinity. In both black Africa and Egypt, it is the everyday affairs of local community which are being ordered when the divine inhabitants of the second rung are invoked. A rich plethora of lesser spirits and a wealth of techniques for manipulating them form the matrix of the second order of the cosmos. As with other magical

[51] R. Horton, "On the Rationality of Conversion, Pt. 1," *Africa* 45 (1975): 219–35, here 220. Part 2 is found on pp. 373–99. See also idem, "African Conversion," *Africa* 41 (1971): 85–107. Against Horton, see H. Fisher, "Conversion Reconsidered: Some Historical Aspects of Religious Conversion in Black Africa," *Africa* 43 (1973): 27–40. Also Richard Bruce, "Conversion amongst the Pyem" (unpublished paper, Dept. of Sociology, Ahmadu Bello University, Zaria).

charms, presumed control handles the anxiety of daily life. The bulk of the magical papyri contain description of rites important to the local community. But as individuals find themselves in the larger world of the empire, they begin to perceive a higher moral code and spirituality for the governance of this wider life. Since the demons are not necessarily evil creatures in Egypt, and the papyri are specifically addressed to gods as well, the path from magic to religion could be seen as continuous in the papyri—even if among other subgroups a distinction between magic and religion was necessary. Our confusion is that, following our Jewish and Christian forebears, we call the worship of demons and other gods "magic," which we take as contrary to religion. In the minds of those who were interested in the magical papyri, magic and religion were united.[52] Magic was religion.

There is no precise analogy between the African high god and the upper tier of the Hellenistic magical system. Although the Hellenistic texts give us a high god often, the really significant pattern of religion in the third century is not the name or attribute of the high god but the theophanic encounter with him through theurgic praxis (as in Thessalos' case) or the heavenly journey of the soul to him by means of the psychopomp (as in *PGM*).

Now, this analysis of the similarity of magic and religion is intellectualist and structuralist. Nevertheless, the analysis does have social consequences. Following Horton's train of thought, we ought to be able to define some of the social circumstances under which "magic" will be acceptable (i.e., under local micropolitical pressures) as opposed to times when it will be necessary to rely on one of the higher religious ideologies and when any magical interpretation will be excluded. Where social relations are limited (i.e., confined to the microcosm), we should expect religious life to be centered on the demons or lesser spirits. But when social life grows more broad to involve greater contact with the macrocosm, religious life is likely to be somewhat different. Less attention will be paid to the spirits and more to the underpinning of events and processes in the macrocosm. Whether the processes are called "magic" or religion depends on the context.

[52] This sociological observation is independently confirmed by J. Teixidor, *The Pagan God: Popular Religion in the Greco-Roman Near East* (Princeton: Princeton University Press, 1977). See p. 4, e.g.: "To discuss the immortality of the soul or how to acquire true gnosis were not popular concerns."

These suggestions of Horton can be helpful to us in studying the syncretistic activities of the late empire. The magical scrolls pay an inordinate amount of attention to the tutelary deities of Hellenistic society. But the story of Thessalos and other aspects of the scrolls reflect a sophisticated sense of the greater world. Indeed, the story of Thessalos is interested in showing precisely that the traditional religions are bankrupt, that a new dispensation is needed in imperial times. It is arguing that the information found within magic is the only true science of spirituality. No doubt some magicians were trying to compete with other religions in the area, but this does not change the fact that the people who valued the magic scrolls understood and were occasionally interested in the great spiritual problems of the Roman Empire. We should then expect that some of the clientele of the magicians like Thessalos himself were educated in international sciences and were groping towards a more elaborate concept of deity, one that was in greater consonance with the world religions of their day. However, the acceptance of the rites of those religions appears to have been selective and serendipitous.

This suggests that the phenomenon which we call syncretism (as a term of reproach) may equally well be understood as the coming to knowledge of various groups within the empire of the vast system of political, economic, and cultural exchange to which they belonged. Furthermore, it would suggest that the great religions of the empire faced the same social problems, understood something similar about imperial rule, and expressed it through similar structures, either as ascent to or descent of the god, which imparted knowledge of how to attain personal immortality. For a while the similarity in structure was enough. Finally, it was the Christian variety of the ascent-descent myth which was to serve as the single ideology which united the entire empire.

As for the definitional problems in the study of magic, this survey has tried to show that functionalist definitions (and to some degree certain structuralists as well) have ignored several crucial factors "internal" to the situation. These approaches tend to produce definitions of concepts for analytical use, but they often miss the subtleties and dramatic presentment of the term in the situation itself or, in their drive for taxonomic clarity, fail adequately to distinguish between social perspectives.

FOUR

THE SACRIFICE OF ISAAC IN EARLY JUDAISM AND CHRISTIANITY

The church was interested in the story of Isaac, as was Judaism, because, as an example of Abraham's steadfast obedience to God, it could also be understood as a story of martyrdom—the death of the innocent to fulfill the will of God.[1] My interest in the exegesis of the Akedah will be neither solely literary nor exhaustive. There has already been a good deal of criticism on the topic. Rather I want to recover the pre-Christian Jewish traditions about the question of martyrdom, explore how that theme related to the story of Abraham's sacrifice of Isaac, and find out how the question of the martyrdom of lsaac affected the birth of Christianity. Of course, to the completely uninitiated, the story of the sacrifice of Isaac will seem of dubious importance to Christianity. But those who know a little Jewish tradition will know that occasionally Isaac was viewed by the rabbis as being sacrificed and his ashes used to atone for Israel's sins.[2]

Though there have been dozens of studies of the Akedah, the major methodological steps can be summed up with the three major studies of the material.[3] The most influential contributor to the study of the tra-

[1] This chapter was originally published as "'He Who Did Not Spare His Only Son . . .' (Romans 8:32): Jesus, Paul, and the Sacrifice of Isaac," in *From Jesus to Paul: Studies in Honour of F. W. Beare*, ed. Peter Richardson and John C. Hurd (Waterloo, Ont.: Wilfrid Laurier, 1984), 169–84 and is republished with permission.

[2] See *Mechilta d' Rabbi Ismael*, ed. H. Horowitz and A. Rabin (Frankfort: J. Kaufman, 1931), 24–25, 38–39 for examples. Also Midr. Rab. ad loc. and the relevant chapters in S. Spiegel, *The Last Trial: On the Legends and Lore of the Command to Abraham to Offer Isaac As a Sacrifice*, trans. Judah Goldin (New York: Random House, 1976; orig. pub. 1950).

[3] See *The Sacrifice of Isaac: Studies in the Development of a Literary Tradition*, ed. Eli Yassif (Jerusalem: Makor, 1978), 34f in the Hebrew section. After this work was published the following publications should be of interest: P. R. Davies and B. D. Chilton, "The Akedah: A Revised Tradition History," *CBQ* 40 (1978): 514–46. The fullest treatment to

dition of the Akedah is Shalom Spiegel, in "Me-Aggadot Ha-Akedah."[4] This is a delicate and disinterested literary study of the context of the *Piyyut* of Rabbi Ephraim ben Jacob of Bonn, trying to show what is assumed by the poet when he writes.

Part of Spiegel's genius is surely to have seen the importance of this theme within Judaism and the need to make that theme explicit—whether in its biblical version, as a model for the Maccabean martyrs, as a model for the suffering messiah, or as a model for the Jewish martyrs of the crusades. The martyrs of the medieval European pogroms saw themselves as Isaacs prepared for the slaughter and even described the knife as a sharpened instrument with no nicks, implying that the rules for sacrifice (hence the rules for appropriate dietary slaughter) had been observed. In the modern period, the theme of the sacrifice of Isaac has continued to draw artistic attention when the problem of theodicy must be raised—from Britten's *Requiem* to Kierkegaard's concept of the "leap of faith" to Segal's memorial statue to the fallen at Kent State. Apparently the frequency of the model in discussions of theodicy points to its deep symbolic effect upon our sensibilities. The fact that Spiegel turned his attention to it when he did was surely influenced by the growing recognition of the horror of the European holocaust.

Even in the presence of such a masterpiece as Spiegel's work, however, hard questions about the adequacy of his method must be asked. We must take the force of Vermes' criticism of previous studies on the midrash.[5] Vermes himself defines two fundamentally different ways of approaching the midrash. The first can be represented in its best light by Louis Ginzberg's masterful *The Legends of the Jews*,[6] a giant anthology collecting all the available material from every possible source and "paying little attention to chronological data, to construct a synthesis of the various interpretations." The second way, of course, is to be a

date is James Swetnam, *Jesus and Isaac: A Study of the Epistle to the Hebrews in the Light of the Akedah* (Rome: Pontifical Biblical Institute, 1981).

[4] S. Spiegel, "Me-Aggadot ha-Akedah: Piyyut 'al shehitat Yizhaq u-tehiyato le-Efrayim mi-Buna," in *Alexander Marks: Jubilee Volume on the Occasion of His Seventieth Birthday* (*Sefer Ha-yovel Icvod Alexander Marx*) (New York: Jewish Theological Seminary, 1950), Hebrew section, 471–574, here 519. The English translation is *The Last Trial.*

[5] G. Vermes, *Scripture and Tradition in Judaism* (Leiden: Brill, 1961). Spiegel's idea that the source of the story is entirely in pagan thought is probably Israeli romanticism and is certainly unfounded in evidence.

[6] L. Ginzberg, *The Legends of the Jews* (Philadelphia: Jewish Publication Society, 1900).

self-description of Vermes: ". . . to follow the development of exegetical principles by means of historical criticism"[7] and thereby to identify the particular text read by a particular audience and to fill in the historical, social, cultural, and religious contexts—or, in short, the entire semantic context of the time. At first one would think that Spiegel will fail this simple test while Vermes may succeed, since Vermes identifies the methodological issue so well. However, answers are rarely as simple as they appear at first. Though Spiegel gives us a thematic (and hence by definition a homogenized) view of the theme of the sacrifice of Isaac in the Middle Ages, he does not entirely lose the possibility of defining a text. One must not forget that the purpose of Spiegel's book is to fill in the context of the *Piyyut* of Rabbi Ephraim ben Jacob of Bonn. Though he homogenizes the tradition in the period of Jesus, he gives us an extremely well-defined picture of the traditions that preceded Rabbi Ephraim ben Jacob, in addition to a very well-informed reading of the poem itself.

Vermes, on the other hand, has given us not a literary so much as an historical argument, the background for a literary analysis, in which he attempts to show us that the midrash about Isaac in the first century became a paradigm to express the expectations of the disciples in Jesus' mission. We must take his arguments much more slowly, so as to see exactly what the tradition of the Akedah was in just barely pre-Christian times, to define what the Christian additions to that text were and finally to define what may have been the Jewish reaction to the Christian interpretation. That is a far less interesting task than to read Spiegel or even to reread him. Nevertheless, it is quite necessary in light of the hard questions which Vermes has asked.

The first thing which must be said about Vermes is that his arguments are based upon a bold thesis: the Palestinian Targum tradition contains a core of first-century tradition which can be self-consciously isolated, besides containing the material which has entered the text much later. Vermes' conclusion, based on this hypothesis and his supporting evidence, is that the account of the sacrifice of Isaac and not the suffering servant of Isaiah 53 may be the most important model of the early church in its understanding of Jesus' passion, for, according to Vermes, the Jewish community had already begun to use the death and

[7] Vermes, *Scripture and Tradition*, 1.

resurrection of Isaac as the model for the reward of the martyrs, and hence this naturally became the paradigm for the suffering of Jesus.

At the outset, the hypothesis seems rash, for there are only a very few references to Isaac in the New Testament. But scholars[8] have consistently reminded us that in spite of the common assumption, Isaiah 53 is rarely quoted in the New Testament, and rarer yet is any use of it to show vicarious atonement. Since one of the central aspects of the Isaac story in the midrash is vicarious atonement, or *zecuth aboth* (זכות אבות) as the rabbis put it, the story of the sacrifice of Isaac may well give us a source for vicarious atonement in Christianity.

Now, Vermes' hypothesis of the early date of the Palestinian Targum (in its present shape) may one day be proved. We know that targumim were in use in the first century. But it has so far been almost impossible to develop consistent criteria for isolating the first-century traditions in the targumim. In such a case, though we may appreciate the creativity of the targum and must come to some understanding of its method, we must bracket the targumic evidence of Vermes to bring the historical problem to the fore again: Just what can be established as the commonly understood text of Genesis 22 in the first century? Vermes' methodological question about the meaning of the biblical text comes back to haunt him when one takes away the targumic evidence on which he builds his own case.

The evidence against Vermes has been best summarized by our third example of methodology in P. R. Davies and B. D. Chilton:

> We propose to deal with the poem of the four nights and the Targums to Genesis 22 after we have reconstructed the development of the Akedah from rabbinic sources. Our reasons for this approach are straightforward, but the vogue for dating targums early is so strong that a word of explanation may be necessary. Daly, for example, cites Le Deaut and McNamara in asserting the antiquity of the targumic Akedah. In the light of the very strong objections to assuming the antiquity of targums raised by J. A. Fitzmyer and P. Grelot, it is necessary to look again at the arguments cited. McNamara is confident that the Akedah is in the main pre-Christian seeing that many of its themes are attested in the works of Josephus, Philo in the Biblical Antiquities of Ps.-Philo and the Mekhilta. The last mentioned source is, of course, a rabbinic composition with a second century C.E. *terminus a quo*; its testimony is beside the point for

[8] M. D. Hooker, *Jesus and the Servant* (London: SPCK, 1959).

> this purpose. The first three documents cited are among those which we will deal with presently and in which we find no trace of the Akedah, so that McNamara's argument does not convince us. The same applies, *mutatis mutandis*, to Le Deaut's citation of Jubilees and G. Vermes' appeal to 4 Maccabees.[9]

This short quotation should show how difficult it is to find agreement among the scholars about the correct dating of targumic evidence. The correct method in such a case is to bracket the targumic evidence as unsure witnesses to the state of affairs in the first century. Against Vermes, the position of Davies and Chilton is that the targums are not pre-Christian. But they go on to say that there is no mention of the Akedah in any other pre-Christian literature. This is an extreme position—one which has merit only in the literal sense of the word. For it is literally true that the term "Akedah" is not used in Scripture. It occurs first in the rabbinic tractate Tamid, as a reference to the daily sacrificial lamb offering. The use of the term "Akedah" is dependent upon a tradition that we cannot satisfactorily date before the second century. With this warning against anachronism, however, there is clear evidence for the hermeneutic interpretation of the sacrifice of Isaac as an example of martyrdom and as a temple sacrifice before Christianity. Davies' and Chilton's overly strict caution leaves out important parts of the evidence, because they appear to want to preserve the integrity of the concept of atoning sacrifice in Christianity.

Much of Davies' and Chilton's arguments against Vermes can be discounted. While it is true that the term "Akedah" is rabbinic, not all associations between sacrifice and the story of Isaac are post-Christian. The history of interpretation of the sacrifice of Isaac begins right in the Bible. In 2 Chronicles 3:1, Mount Moriah, scene of the sacrifice, is identified with the Temple Mount; so an explicit connection between the story of the sacrifice of Isaac and the sacrificial cult in Jerusalem is established. Secondly, the criticism of Davies and Chilton to the contrary, the book of Jubilees does contain an explicit connection between the sacrifice of Isaac (or "Akedah," loosely speaking) and the Passover.[10] The

[9] Davies and Chilton, "The Akedah," 514f.

[10] See Jub. 17:15–18:19. The heavenly discussion takes place on the twelfth of Nisan. Three days later (Gen 22:4) would bring us to Passover for the sacrifice itself. Jubilees also connects Noah's ark, Abraham at Shechem, and Jacob at Bethel. The sacrifice of Isaac is related to the liberation from Egypt and all future liberations as well.

fact that Jubilees also connects other events in the lives of the patriarchs with other holidays does not override the obvious fact that a significant connection between Passover and the sacrifice of Isaac has been made.

The passage is clearly the subject of much popular hermeneutical activity before Jesus. We have fragments of Philo the Elder,[11] Demetrius, and Alexander Polyhistor (Eusebius, *Praep. ev.* 9.20.1) as well as a passage from Sirach 44:19-21, which is devoted to the subject.[12] The fragment from Philo the Elder, though puzzling in many respects, is a reference to the sacrificial scene. Polyhistor's reference is clearer but he follows the biblical story without major alteration. The book of Judith 8:25-27 certainly links the sacrifice of Isaac with the trials which the Jewish community is facing, since it uses the same word (πειραζειν) as does the LXX in describing the testing of Abraham. But it is quite true that the focus of the event is Abraham's steadfastness rather than Isaac's. The testing of Isaac to which the text refers may be a reference to Rebecca's barrenness in Genesis 25:21.[13] However, the Greek version of the text singles out Isaac as having been the object of God's testing, thus implying the martyrological analogy.

Philo does not give us many discussions of the sacrifice of Isaac. It is missing from his *seriatim* interpretation of the Pentateuch. However, he does give us some interesting traditions about the sacrifice of Isaac in *de Abrahamo*. There, the emphasis is on Abraham as priest officiating at a sacrifice (even though the sacrifice does not take place). The sacrifice which Philo has in mind must be the *tamid* (תמיד) offering: "Perhaps, too, following the law of burnt offering, he would have dismembered his son and offered him limb by limb." He also clearly understands the concept of giving one's life for others' benefit (*Abr.* 198).

Josephus' version of the sacrifice of Isaac appears in *Antiquities* 1.13.1–4,[14] a work probably completed in 94 C.E. For the most part, Josephus follows the biblical story closely. As with Philo, Josephus is interested in Abraham, rather than Isaac, and he takes special pains to show that Abraham's piety (θρεσκεία) is tested, his piety rewarded. Josephus has Isaac greet the news of his impending sacrifice with great joy,

[11] See Eusebius, *Praep. ev.* 9.20.1 (*Praeparatio evangelica*, ed. K. Mras, *Eusebius Werke, Band 8*, 2 vols., GCS 43 [Berlin: Akademie, 1954], 1:506f.)

[12] See Swetnam, *Jesus and Isaac*, 29f.

[13] See Swetnam, *Jesus and Isaac*, 35.

[14] See also 20.12; 1.267.

rushing in anticipation to the altar. He is twenty-four or five when the event takes place, apparently an interpretation of *na'ar* (נער), paralleled in the story of Jephthah's daughter, and designed to show that the victim was not a minor, rather a willing adult. This is a major aspect of martyrological tradition.

If Davies and Chilton have pointed up the need to treat the dating of the targum conservatively, they have surely erred in finding no significant references to the Akedah before Christianity. In other words, one may go too far on either extreme, as Vermes on the one hand or Davies and Chilton on the other respectively do, in evaluating the traditions which precede the Christian version of the Isaac legend. It is clearly wrong to say that there was no Jewish tradition of the sacrifice of Isaac before Christianity or that the exegesis of that biblical passage was not involved in martyrology or traditions of vicarious atonement. On the other hand, it is also wrong to assume that there was a single paradigmatic tradition which could be picked up by the church as a *typos* for Jesus, as does Vermes. Either is, as I will try to show, a misrepresentation of the literary quality of the texts. Clearly one must go over the texts one more time, with new sensitivities.

Some reference to the broad context must be made before entering into a more detailed criticism of Davies and Chilton. Resurrection was still a new idea within Judaism in Hellenistic times. It appears to enter the Bible in the book of Daniel (ca. 165 B.C.E.) although there may be hints in the difficult to date parts of Isaiah and Ezekiel.

Presumably, the concept of resurrection is linked to the problem of theodicy occasioned by the Maccabean revolt. Thereafter, discussions of martyrdom are often associated with resurrection or eternal life.[15] Resurrection is first of all the reward of martyrs and only secondarily a general reward. In the time of Jesus the theme of resurrection was still hotly debated in the religio-political life of the Jews. Pharisees accepted it; Sadducees rejected it. Concomitant with the idea of resurrection, the idea of ascension and heavenly exaltation developed in Judaism. Martyrs were thought to live with God in holiness. Now ascension itself was not originally a Hebrew idea of what happened after death. In fact, since

[15] See G. W. E. Nickelsburg Jr., *Resurrection, Immortality, and Eternal Life in Intertestamental Judaism* (Missoula, Mont.: Scholars, 1972); H. C. C. Cavallin, *Life After Death: Paul's Argument for the Resurrection of the Dead in I Corinthians 15,* part 1: *An Inquiry into the Jewish Background* (Lund: CWK Gleerup, 1974).

Sheol, the abode of the dead, was underground, the only ascensions that took place in the early biblical period were those of figures like Elijah or Enoch who were supposed by the text to have avoided death completely by going to heaven while still alive. Originally ascension was a very special reward for extraordinary people. But since ascension became a favorite theme of late antiquity in general (for reasons that cannot be analyzed here) it also found a place in Daniel and other Jewish literature of the Hellenistic period. These developments served to connect ideas of life after death with the apocalyptic idea of resurrection in extremely complex and varying ways. The one generalization about this complex constellation of material which still seems valid is that the Hebrew versions of the theme of ascension are almost always associated with the problem of theodicy.[16]

The problem of the martyrdom, the person who dies a painful death precisely in staying true to the commands of God, is a Hebrew expression of a broad ethical and moral question which was being debated actively in the Hellenistic world. While the themes of martyrdom and resurrection are clearly connected and developed by the book of Daniel and 2 Maccabees and especially by the addition of the story of Hannah and her seven sons to the text of 2 Maccabees 7, the motif of Isaac's sacrifice as the example *par excellence* of martyrdom does not appear until the first century, preeminently in the book of 4 Maccabees dated to the early 30's, but devoid of Christian influence.[17] This, not the targumim and

[16] See my work, "Heavenly Ascent in Hellenistic Judaism, Early Christianity and their Environments," *ANRW* 23.2:1333–94 (repr. in this volume).

[17] Davies and Chilton, "The Akedah," 517, do not see anything of importance in 4 Maccabees and note that the work has been variously attributed to dates in the first and second centuries. See, e.g., U. Breitenstein, *Beachtungen an Sprache, Stil und Gedankgut des vierten Maccabärbuches* (Basel: Swabe, 1976) and A. Dupont Sommer, *Le quatrième livre des Maccabées* (Paris: H. Champion, 1939). They have their own reasons for accepting a late date in spite of the lack of evidence for Christian influence in 4 Maccabees, and their unsupported contention that it is of no importance to the development of the tradition is mistaken, as I will try to show below. For my part, I find the evidence of Bickermann ("The Date of 4 Maccabees," in *Louis Ginzberg: Jubilee Volume on the Occasion of His Seventieth Birthday* [New York: American Academy for Jewish Research, 1945], 105–12) to be persuasive. The word θρεσκεία is never used for religion until the period of Augustus, yet the book conceives of the temple and its service as still existing, which naturally dates it before 70 C.E.

Furthermore, the title of Apollonius in 4:9, "governor of Syria, Phoenicia and Cilicia," refers to an administrative arrangement that lasted only from 20 to 54 C.E.

not Jubilees, seems to me the best evidence supporting Vermes' general observations that some preexistent Jewish tradition formed the basis of the Christian view of Jesus as a type for Isaac. More interesting still is the occurrence of the concept of vicarious atonement in this book. Eleazar prays that his death may serve not only to atone for his own sins but also for the sins of the people as a whole:

> Thou knowest God that though I might have saved myself, I die in fiery torment for the sake of the Law. Be merciful to thy people and let my punishment be sufficient for their sake. Make my blood an expiation for them and take my life as a ransom for theirs. (4 Macc 6:27f.)[18]

Isaac's sacrifice is brought in later on as a paradigm of martyrdom. This work seems to me evidence of extraordinary importance, especially when one notes the absence of Isaiah 53 as a significant part of martyrological discussion in the pre-Christian era. Instead, there are discussions of the paradigmatic value of the innocent sufferer, of which many could be adduced.[19]

Even in the Greek paraenesis of 4 Maccabees, Isaac's sacrifice itself is never directly linked with vicarious atonement. Martyrdom is associated with vicarious atonement while Isaac is preeminent among the martyrs. Fourth Maccabees may even imply that Isaac actually underwent martyrdom: ὑπομένω, the word used at that point, may mean "to suffer" or "undergo" or "await." This is in line with the editor's desire to use Isaac's example as a type for martyrdom, while yet preserving the biblical story intact. Jewish tradition required that for atonement to be effected, sacrificial blood must be spilt. We find that the midrashic spirit is not present in 4 Maccabees. Since the editor evidently wanted to preserve the original story, he could not link Isaac's sacrifice with vicarious atonement directly. All the ideas clearly come together in this work, but the explicit relationship between the themes depends on the scriptural

---

Splitting the difference, we can provisionally assign the book to the reign of Caligula, which was certainly a period in which Jews needed to consider the problem of martyrdom. See *The Third and Fourth Books of Maccabees*, ed. and trans. Moses Hadas (New York: Harper & Brothers, 1953), esp. 95f. Also, *Encyclopedia Judaica*, "kiddush ha-shem," for an independent evaluation of the importance of 4 Maccabees in the development of Jewish martyrology.

[18] Translation from Hadas, ed. and trans., *Third and Fourth Books of Maccabees*.

[19] See *Ideal Figures in Ancient Judaism: Profiles and Paradigms*, ed. John J. Collins and G. W. E. Nickelsburg Jr. (Chico, Calif.: Scholars, 1980).

passage under consideration. Since the exegete will not contradict the text, 4 Maccabees does not mention Isaac's death and subsequent resurrection, the most important part of the story from the Christian perspective.

From the early Jewish exegesis of the Akedah, several conclusions are possible. First, the Akedah was heavily used in Jewish exegesis and had already gained a firm grip on Jewish sensibilities by the time of Jesus. Like all exegetical *cruces*, it could be used in many ways, but this particular passage was used especially to clarify the meaning of martyrdom and encourage Jews in persecution. Associated concepts of death and resurrection are clearly present in 4 Maccabees but they are not attracted to the Genesis 22 passage because of the biblical text itself. Although there are occasional references to the righteous character of the sufferer, the focus of the story is still on the trial of Abraham and his obedience. Finally, and this is the most important part, the story is nowhere used as a prototype of messianic suffering.

How different is the Christian material! Here, one finds that the identification of the martyred figure as the messiah is absolutely central to the typology. Paul's use of the Scripture immediately shows this distinction. Like the exegetes before him, Paul does not subject these traditions to systematic comparison. At most, one can say that he is using the Isaac story with considerable exegetical functionalism. Possible references to Isaac come up only twice and only in indirect ways in Paul: "He who did not spare his own Son but gave him up for us all" (Rom 8:32) clearly sounds the note of vicarious atonement, but it neither mentions Isaiah 53 nor the temple service nor blood.[20] Rather it appears to make a kind of implicit analogy between God's action and the action of Abraham in sacrificing his son. Like Abraham, God compensated mankind in a kind of "measure for measure" (*middah k'neged middah*, מידה כנגד מידה)

[20] It is possible that the language of this passage implies a direct relationship with Isa 53, as both Martin Hengel (*The Atonement: The Origins of the Doctrine in the New Testament*, trans. John Bowden [Philadelphia: Fortress, 1981]) and before him E. Lohse (*Märtyrer und Gottesknecht* [Göttingen: Vandenhoeck & Ruprecht, 1963]) have implied. The evidence for this is the use of the terms παραδίδοναι and περί. It appears to me that literary evidence based on this general use of language is very suspect. The general idea of vicarious atonement, however, is not rare; nor is this language particularly rare in Hellenistic Jewish contexts. In any case, I would be prepared to concede some use of Isa 53, although it would be much less explicit even than the figure of the sacrifice of Isaac, which itself is very allusive!

argument that is elsewhere found in rabbinic midrash. Of course, the understanding that Christ died for sins is not really in need of proof for Paul. It can be found in 1 Corinthians 15:3b and frequently elsewhere. But only here in 1 Corinthians does he say that this saving death is in accordance with Scripture. He does not explicitly tell us that Isaiah 53 is the Scripture he has in mind, although it is possible that he meant Isaiah 53 in any case. Almost all scholars agree that he is using traditions which were taught to him by the community which he joined and which therefore antedate his entrance into Christianity.[21]

Note that in Romans 8:32, in discussing the sacrifice of Isaac, the focus of the passage is Abraham, not Isaac, just as in the earlier Jewish interpretations. The "us" in Romans is left unspecified. But by means of Galatians 3:13-14 the reference can be further clarified. "That . . . the blessing of Abraham might come upon the Gentiles" is a paraphrase of Genesis 22:18, "and in your offspring shall all the nations of the earth be blessed," although the expression "blessing of Abraham" may have been taken from Genesis 28:4 where it occurs explicitly. In any case, "in Christ Jesus" has been substituted for the original "in your offspring."[22]

Deuteronomy 21:23 curses a man hanged upon a tree. But Paul, who applies the reference to Jesus, says that the curse has been turned into a blessing. He may thus be playing upon the Genesis story of the lamb caught in the thicket.[23] However, in this case, the analogy would be between the ram and Jesus, since both are seen as the sacrifice provided by God.

The novel aspect for Paul is a story of a crucified messiah, the obvious aspect of the story missing from the pre-Christian Jewish exegesis, where Isaac is never understood as a type of the messiah. Paul takes the crucified Jesus to be Messiah and Son of God because of his faith commitment, not because of a preexisting development of the midrash. Only because of his prior faith can he say that as Abraham had offered up his son, so too God offered up his son for Isaac's children so that all

[21] See Hengel, *Atonement*, 36f.

[22] This is the argument of N. A. Dahl, *The Crucified Messiah* (Minneapolis: Augsburg, 1974), 153, which is very persuasive.

[23] These themes are actually fairly common in the ancient Near East. See T. W. Doane, *Bible Myths and their Parallels in Other Religions*, 7th ed. (New York: Truth Seeker, 1948), 94f.; E. O. James, *Sacrifice and Sacrament* (London: Thames & Hudson, 1962), 68–73; R. Graves and R. Patai, *Hebrew Myths: The Book of Genesis* (Garden City, N.Y.: Doubleday, 1964), 166–69.

the families of man would be blessed. It is a new idea totally absent from Jewish exegesis, even when Jewish exegesis stresses the vicariousness of the sacrifice. The received Jewish midrash, which certainly post-dates Paul, does not use the Scripture for that particular purpose. Again, the most probable explanation for this event is Paul's own personal experience and exegetical freedom which that experience placed upon him. He was more interested in the consequences of this passage for a gentile mission than had any Jew been previously.

In fact, if one looks at the fragments of Melito of Sardis,[24] one sees that even in the second century, one of the important points that the church fathers made about this passage was that Jesus actually suffered while Isaac did not. We see here the converse use of the very Jewish tradition which made for conservatism in 4 Maccabees—that blood must be spilled to effect atonement. But, we also learn that it was unlikely that Melito and the other fathers following his point had heard any Jewish tradition that Isaac actually underwent martyrdom. Rather, as is clear from the frequency of the reference, they knew only the Jewish tradition linking Isaac with martyrdom. From the Christian perspective the typology was even more appealing when applied to Jesus. Yet there is no evidence of an explicit Jewish tradition about Isaac's death and resurrection which was known to those fathers who stressed that Jesus' sacrifice was greater on account of his actual suffering. This suspicion, arising from the Christian evidence, is entirely confirmed by the Jewish material which we have already surveyed. There is no good evidence for a lost pre-Christian Jewish tradition of Isaac's resurrection.

At this point one wonders if the previous scholars' mistakes are not a bit more subtle than at first seemed evident. The hypothesis that the targumim must be early is one thing. Vermes is certainly right to emphasize the use of these little employed documents. But, it is quite another thing to assume that, because many of the motifs which dominate Christian exegesis are present in Jewish exegesis, Christianity merely took them all over, effecting no transformation in the traditions as it employed them. Rather, Christian exegesis was founded on various Jewish exegeses (*pace* Chilton and Davies) but the method was carried out with an entirely

[24] See M. J. Routh, *Reliquiae sacrae*, vol. 1 (Oxford: Oxford University Press, 1814); J. C. Th. Otto, *Corpus apologetarum christianorum*, vol. 9 (Jena: 1872); A. Harnack, *Geschichte der altchristlichen Literatur* (Leipzig: 1893); and see the discussion of David Lerch in *Isaaks Opferung, christlich gedeutet* (Tübingen: Mohr Siebeck, 1950), 29f.

new understanding of what exegesis was meant to demonstrate. In other words, the method of Jewish midrash was brought to an entirely new purpose in Paul, the purpose of exposing the actual victory of an ostensibly failed messianic candidate.

When one looks carefully, the methodological mistake the previous scholars make is a literary one. It is quite close to the implied methodological mistake which Vermes imputes to Ginzberg. Despite his respect for Ginzberg, Vermes complained that earlier studies had "homogenized" the text, destroying the historical context. Though he has uniquely seen the role of the Jewish past in the tradition of the sacrifice of Isaac and is certainly blazing an important new methodological trail in his use of targumim, Vermes is in danger of "homogenizing" the text in a slightly different way. Although he notes where important themes are missing in each document, in sum he operates as if the whole constellation is always present once all the parts of the tradition are attested.

Vermes describes a figure of Isaac the vicarious martyr which can merely be taken over into Christianity. Since this is clearly not the impression that the evidence gives, the criticism of Davies and Chilton, which is wildly off in some respects, has some validity. They note that the missing terms in the pre-Christian interpretation are just as important as the attested ones because they underline the thought processes of the Jewish interpreters before Jesus as well as emphasize the central aspect of the new Christian interpretation. I have tried to show, even in taking issue with Davies and Chilton's under-interpretation of the material, that the midrash is not a single text but an anthology made up of different interpretations of individual commentators. Each single interpretation takes on some but not all the themes of later Christianity, while none interprets the Isaac passage messianically. Christianity takes themes of (1) death, (2) resurrection, (3) martyrology, (4) vicarious atonement, and (5) messiahship from Judaism, but it does not find any of them ready-made or united in one place in Jewish tradition. Instead it hunts for what it needs and applies it to the events which it is seeking to explain. Thus we cannot define a single text giving us a single sum of past experiences as Vermes does, even though his use of Jewish tradition is to be commended.

Midrash records a complex mixture of past traditions being reinterpreted in light of new events. As a corollary to this conclusion, one can strongly suspect that there is no figure with the title "suffering servant" whose identity could be searched in the way that past Christian scholarship has often implied.[25] There is no figure in Judaism approximating what scholars have called THE Suffering Servant. There is not even an overarching understanding of the referent of the servant songs in Judaism. The midrashic process (unlike the Christian interpretation in this respect) does not ask "Who is the suffering servant?" so much as "What can be further known about the 'servants of God' from the passage under consideration?" By a process of analogy, Isaiah 53 is often viewed in light of other passages in which "servants of God" are mentioned. In various places in the Bible, Abraham, Phineas, as well as others and preeminently Moses are called "servant."[26] The rabbis note this and associate the various occurrences in various ways depending on the import of the midrash.

For our purposes it is important to note that a targum to Job does identify Isaac as the servant of God on the basis of a rather imaginative exegesis.[27]

Although we know from Qumran fragments that a Job targum did exist in the first century, the extant targum, the one linking Isaac with the servant, does not agree with the Qumran fragments where it overlaps. Hence it is dubious evidence of the identification of Isaac as a servant of God in pre-Christian times. But it is suggestive of the importance of Isaac in martyrologies and the possible link with servant imagery.

Some exegetical hints do exist about the various identities of servants of God in the first century. Another person who is called servant is David.[28] This can be shown on the basis of Ezekiel 34:23; 37:24. David is called "servant" in Psalm 89 in four places (89:3, 20, 38, 50), and in

[25] W. Zimmerli and J. Jeremias, *The Servant of God*, trans. Harold Knight (London: SCM Press, 1957), an English translation of their article "παις θεου" in *TWNT* (in English as *TDNT*).

[26] See Donald Juel, "The Image of the Servant Christ in the New Testament," *SwJT* 21 (1979): 7–22. His important book *Messianic Exegesis* (Philadelphia: Fortress, 1988) expands his careful and sensitive reading of midrash to other aspects of New Testament studies.

[27] Here is the passage in Job 3:17-19: "There the wicked cease from troubling and there the weary are at rest. There the prisoners are at ease together, they hear not the voice of the slave driver. The small and the great are there; and the *servant* is free from his master." Here is the targum to the passage: "Jacob, called the young one, and Abraham, called the old one, and Isaac, the servant of the Lord (*'abda d'YHWH*, עבדא דיי) who was delivered from the bonds by his Master."

[28] Zimmerli and Jeremias say that this is "The Messiah," but they are mistaken. It is the historical personage of David who is so designated, not a future king.

one place is called "the branch" (Zech 3:8),[29] a messianic term. So there is some evidence that the messiah could have been thought of as one of God's servants.[30] In other words, there is in Jewish exegesis an attempt to specify the meaning of a biblical text by bringing other biblical texts with similar usage to bear upon them. But there is no attempt to see any particular passage as a prophecy. This looks rather like modern methodology, except for one glaring difference. No historical framework is developed for understanding the two references. What is learned from one reference is simply inserted into the second occurrence of the term. If one looks at the midrashic enterprise from an overall perspective, one sees a constellation of associations of various figures and values rather than a system of preexistent titles whose identities were subject to constant identification.

This brings up another strand of the tradition under consideration—the use of the word for "son." In Greek, παῖς can mean either "son" or "servant." As "servant," παῖς can be associated with the term "messiah" in Christianity. As "son," παῖς can also pick up messianic interpretations. God calls the Davidic king "son" several times in the Old Testament.[31] The interesting aspect concerning sonship occurs in the Greek Old Testament whose significance is unstressed by Vermes.[32] The term *yahid* (יחיד) in Hebrew, meaning "only son," is translated by LXX as ἀγαπητός ("loved one").[33] It occurs in reference to Genesis 22:2, 12, 16 speaking of Isaac's sacrifice and, interestingly, also in Judges 11:34 of Jephthah's daughter, who was also a sacrifice. The other occurrences of the term—Amos 8:10; Jeremiah 6:26; Zechariah 12:10—are metaphoric, comparing grief over the destruction of the temple with grief at the death of an only child. Jesus is called ἀγαπητός, "only or beloved

[29] "Servant" also occurs here.

[30] "The" messiah is also a misnomer, since many different kinds of figures could be described as messianic.

[31] Zimmerli and Jeremias, "παῖς θεοῦ," *TDNT* 5:664.

[32] See Davies and Chilton, "The Akedah," 529 and esp. 530. See also C. H. Turner, "ὁ υἱός μου ὁ ἀγαπητός," *JTS* 27 (1926): 113–29; W. Dekker, "De Geliefde Zoon in de synoptische Evangelien," *NedTT* 16 (1961–1962): 94–106; A. Scattolon, "*L'Agapetos* sinnotteco milla luce della traditione giudaica," *RivB* 26 (1978): 3–32.

[33] Aquila has: μονογενή (Ms. 135 reads: μοναχός; see Wevers, *Septuaginta 1: Genesis* [Göttingen: Vandenhoeck & Ruprecht, 1974], 213). Symmachus has τόν μόνον σου; see Field, *Origenis Hexaplorium* (Oxford: Clarendon, 1875), 37. Otherwise in Greek, the word is ἀγαπητός, used in Genesis, Amos, Judges, Jeremiah, and Zechariah, as specified above.

son" at the baptism (Mark 1:11 and parallels) and transfiguration (Mark 9:7 and parallels). Davies and Chilton to the contrary, it is impossible not to feel an implicit analogy between Isaac, Jephthah's sacrificed daughter, other martyred children, and Jesus in these places. All this is especially important if one notes that the word for servant, παῖς, is never used in Mark with the context of Isaiah 53 clarified. It seems to me that one important aspect of the Gospels' use of the idea of sonship is the implicit analogy between Jesus and Isaac as only sons who were sacrificed. The reasons for thinking so are implicit in Bible translations, not explicit in the targumim.

In other words, as we would expect from Jewish tradition, we can find many contexts which link some parts of this tradition together in Jewish thought. However, if one wants an explicit reference to the messiah or to Isaac's resurrection, one does not find it until later Christianity. The reason, it seems to me, is to be found not in exegetical tradition but in the events surrounding Jesus' life. This is what Vermes discounts but Davies and Chilton take too much in isolation. It makes no sense to begin the discussion of Christian exegesis in any other place than in the Easter event accepted as fact by Christians, that Jesus, who was manifestly crucified as a messianic pretender by the Romans ("King of the Jews,")[34] and taunted by that title in his execution, was believed to have merited the title ironically when his followers experienced what they took to be his resurrection. That experience, which is predictable if not normal on the part of a Jewish community of the first century, most often in the case of martyrdom, justified the earliest Christian community in thinking for the first time in Judaism that there could be such a thing as a crucified messiah. From this oxymoron everything else derives and, of course, all of it is post-resurrection in formulation.

In other words, there is no historical evidence for an expectation of a crucified or suffering messiah until the events of Jesus' life proved to the early church that this was the true and secret meaning of Scripture. All discussions of suffering in the Bible thereafter take on a new meaning, as prophecies of Jesus' suffering. But no Jew would have seen them in this way before Jesus' crucifixion. Rather, like a magnet, everything dealing with "sonship" or "messiah" or "suffering" or "servant" is attracted to

[34] See N. A. Dahl, "The Crucified Messiah," in *The Crucified Messiah* (Minneapolis: Augsburg, 1974), 10–36.

Jesus.[35] When applied to Jesus all traditions collapse into a single figure, in order to show how prophecy was fulfilled in the person of Jesus. One can see this at work in Paul's writing. Although his Christian commitment is evident, the strands of Jewish tradition are still intact. Paul talks about vicarious atonement and suffering but normally uses no scriptural references to demonstrate his point. In fact, he does not need them, for vicarious atonement is a widely accepted understanding of the significance of the suffering of the martyrs. When he brings in the sacrifice of Isaac, it is to prove Jesus' sonship. He also knows why a crucified messiah is a stumbling block to the Jews, folly to the gentiles, in a way that would be incomprehensible only a few generations later, for instance, to the readers of Acts.

Of course, Paul's use of the material represents only the beginning of the tradition. John's use of the Akedah in 3:16 provides another allusive reference to reinforce the concept of sonship. So do James and Hebrews, but they each develop the theme in new and interesting ways. In the church's later interpretation, the elaborate typologies comparing the three-day journey with the Easter event, the wood for the sacrifice with the cross, one need not look for any further influences than the New Testament.

A word should also be said about the later Jewish material, although it too has been often reviewed in detail. On the Jewish side, in the first century, it is easy to see that the discussion of the Akedah was greatly elaborated after the destruction of the temple. The placing of the Akedah at Rosh Hashanah, rather than Passover, the motif of the shofar as the horn of the ram caught in the thicket, the reading of Genesis 22 on the second day of Rosh Hashanah, with the first day being reserved

[35] Strangely however, Isa 53 is brought in relatively late, as Hooker has shown us. Even then, it is brought in to show that Jesus must suffer, not that the suffering was vicarious, which was apparently in no need of proof to those that accepted it. See Hengel, *Atonement.* Hengel first notes the widespread Hellenistic notion that dying for others is heroic. The context is fairly often one of sacrificial death to appease the gods, as well. So one must not get the idea that vicarious atonement was entirely a semitic idea. Hengel himself feels that the particularly Hebrew aspect of the notion can be seen in Isa 53, which is, in turn, used by the church (and even Jesus in his estimation) to understand Jesus' sacrificial death. Thus, the Pauline use of the notion of vicarious atonement only reflects the pre-Pauline idea, which in turn, goes back to the earliest notions in Christianity. While I have my own ideas about the value of Isa 53 to the early church, I think it safe to say, on the basis of Hengel and others, that the notion of vicarious atonement is quite widespread.

for the biblical passage describing the sin-offering, all of these motifs make sense if one sees the Jewish community trying to understand the destruction of the temple by means of an Isaac martyrology and anything else at its disposal. The process starts as early as Yohanan ben Zakkai with the *takkanah* about the blowing of the shofar in the synagogue. This simple action of moving a temple ritual to the synagogue is in many ways the ritual and symbolic equivalent of the Christian community's understanding of the crucifixion. Seemingly impossible events must be understood within the context of meaning available to the community. A new understanding of history had to be found on account of an anomalous event. Therefore, the Scripture was reread in new eyes until the event could be appropriated into a new web of meaning.

Rabbinic exegesis followed entirely different directions from Christianity as the tradition about Isaac emphasizes. But this tradition-history also shows that they operated by very similar methods. From a methodological perspective, it is Christianity with its known history which serves as a model for the unknown but reconstructable rabbinic tradition-history. From my perspective, Isaac's relationship with the New Year festival of Rosh Hashanah is most appropriately dated to post-70 C.E. Judaism, when a substitution, as it were, for temple service had to be found. It is then, after the temple is destroyed and sacrifice is only possible in a symbolic way, that the connection between Isaac and the word "Akedah" through the agency of the *tamid* sacrifice is most likely to have been developed, though again, it is theoretically possible for the connection to have been formulated even earlier. It is beyond dispute that the midrashim stressing explicit sacrificial typologies developed more strongly at this time.

But, it is also reasonable to expect that the Passover tradition of Isaac's martyrdom in rabbinic midrash received further development at this time. Rabbinic exegesis, being a compilation of individual homiletics, need not be entirely consistent even when it is compiled into a single midrashic work, as we all know. There is no reason why rabbis should not have continued to discuss Isaac's relationship to the Passover holiday. Furthermore, it is not out of the question that rabbis continued to discuss this connection in competition with the church fathers' use of Isaac as a *typos* for Christ. The Amoraic traditions of the death and ashes of Isaac and his subsequent resurrection can be reasonably understood as an attempt to enrich Judaism with a figure that was as colorful as the one known to Christian exegesis. This rather astounding possibility, that the rabbis learned from Christian exegesis, must be investigated further. Considering the sure rabbinic knowledge of the central aspect of Christian doctrine, one does not even need to posit very much cultural contact between the two communities to allow for such a development. Furthermore, while Vermes must be right in stressing the role of the targumim in the development of Jewish midrash, he is not necessarily right in predating any Christian tradition which is later found in targumim. Unless one can find specific reasons for an early dating of the material, the safest hypothesis is always to consider it together with the midrash in date. Indeed, it is the Christian material itself which provides the best evidence that any tradition later found in rabbinic Judaism was already present in the Jewish world of the first century. Ironically, it is Christianity that often demonstrates first-century Jewish traditions, rather than the other way around, as is the normal method in New Testament studies. But using Christian documents to demonstrate Jewish traditions may only be attempted when the specific motivations and goals of Christian exegesis are carefully outlined.

In sum then, we can outline two different routes taken by the two developing communities, in line with the events which shaped those communities. Both in some ways use the Akedah tradition to explain the founding events of the community. Both the Christian and the rabbinic exegesis of Isaac's sacrifice is based upon the pre-Christian, Jewish exegetical tradition, which stressed martyrdom. But each community makes its own significance of the tradition from its own experience and also listens to what the other community is saying to an extent. The pattern is simple enough but, in order to see it, one must give up the idea of traditions of hypothetical figures circulating in Judaism (as they did in later times among the church fathers). Instead one is left with an appreciation of how the Jewish community sought the meaning of its Scriptures through hermeneutical reinterpretation. We have also come to the position of appreciating much more strongly the *Sitz im Leben* of each tradition that we have traced. These traditions did not develop under the pressure of literary transmission alone. They are the result of the response of exegetes to specific events within their community.

FIVE

TORAH AND *NOMOS* IN RECENT SCHOLARLY DISCUSSION

When I began my studies in Hellenistic Judaism, the issue of *nomos* (νομός) and torah (תורה) had already been satisfactorily resolved.[1] A consensus had been reached, becoming the basis of one of the distinctions between Judaism and Christianity. My introduction to the subject matter was through Samuel Sandmel, who put the blame for the separation between Judaism and Christianity upon the intellectuals of Hellenistic Judaism. They had misunderstood the very basis of Judaism when they translated torah as *nomos*.

> For Hellenistic Judaism, the casualness with which the Hebrew word Torah was translated by the Greek word *nomos*, "law," is apparent on every page of the surviving literature. Greek Jews nowhere raised the question of whether Torah really means *nomos*, law! And whenever they defended their Jewish convictions, it was always on the premise, startling to modern Jewish students, that *nomos* did adequately translate Torah. To Palestinian Jews, and their Spiritual descendants, the word Torah never had so restricted a connotation; they equated *Torah* with our word "revelation.". . .
>
> The whole cast of mind of Greek Jews, especially as evidenced by Philo, is shaped by the unquestioning acceptance of the premise that Torah meant Law. Philo even undertakes to defend the proposition that Genesis, with its relatively few laws and its narratives about the Patriarchs, is nevertheless basically a book of law. . . .
>
> Philo's acceptance of Torah as *nomos* is paralleled, though not precisely, by Paul. At times, as in Romans 2:17-18, Paul seems to regard the entire Pentateuch as Law, though his emphasis on legal matters would seem to indicate that by Law he refers only to the legalistic section which

[1] This chapter originally appeared in *Studies in Religion/Sciences Religieuses* 13 (1984): 19–28 and is used with permission.

> begins, as is usually considered, in Exodus 12 . . . in graeco-Jewish terms, Paul considers outmoded not the Law but the laws.
>
> The graeco-Jewish equation of Torah and law was picked up and propagated by the church fathers. This dubious identification appears in some of the scholarship of our own day. Out of the misunderstanding of what Torah meant to rabbinic Jews, there emerged two reactions among Protestants, in particular since the 1870's (1) the identification of Judaism with "legalism" and (2) a supercilious and condescending attitude both to Judaism and to legalism itself. Out of some of this Protestant literature one would infer something which no Jew has ever experienced: that the Torah was a burden.[2]

Essentially, Professor Sandmel assumes that the poor translation of the Hellenistic Jewish community has been the root of a mammoth misunderstanding of Judaism, first by the Hellenistic world, then by Philo, then by Paul and Christianity, finally by all Western culture. Ever since my college days, Professor Sandmel's books have been my teacher and guide. I mean no disrespect for his talents. But upon the second reflection necessary for the Canadian Society for Biblical Study seminar on torah and *nomos*, his position in this matter is both representative of the consensus and exaggerated. The argument that Hellenistic Judaism produced a primary misunderstanding of Judaism, which was then followed by Paul among others, smacks of ideology and apology rather than scholarship. It gives Sandmel a very convenient way to show that every non-rabbinic understanding of Judaism was wrong, starting with Hellenistic Judaism, developing principally in the theology of Paul, and ending with modern Protestant theology.

The importance of the issue probably drove Professor Sandmel to the rhetorical and unsupportable position that no Jew ever found the ceremonial laws burdensome. There is considerable evidence in the first century to suggest that some Jews did break with the ceremonial laws, first from Philo in *On the Migration of Abraham* 84–89 and especially in Christianity. Add to this an obvious argument from silence in the first paragraph of Sandmel's description of the problem, that there is no example of Jews objecting to the translation of the torah as *nomos*, and there are sufficient grounds to be suspicious of the motives and judgment of even such a balanced and impartial critic as Professor Sandmel.

[2] S. Sandmel, *The Genius of Paul* (New York: Farrar, Straus & Cudahy, 1958), 46–47.

Let us try to track down where these peculiar notions came from. Samuel Sandmel says,

> The foremost example of Greco-Jewish writing is the Greek version—indeed versions—of the Bible. We have already encountered (p. x) the account of the translation of the Letter of Aristeas and the tradition recorded there that seventy-two priests, as fluent in Greek as in Hebrew, prepared the translation that gives us the title the Septuagint. The translation presumably took place around 250 b.c., and encompassed at that time only the five books of Moses. It is a matter of utmost consequence, as we shall see, that Greek Jews gave to the five books the title Nomos ("Law"), a word with a ring quite different from that of Torah ("divine teaching").[3]

This is paralleled by similar statements by Samuel Belkin.[4] It is easy to see why a position of this sort would appeal to a modern Jewish scholar. But lest one get the idea that this approach is a Jewish observation whose real import will be turned upon Paul (which it is in part), it bears noting that one of the most influential proponents of this position is C. H. Dodd in his *Bible and the Greeks*.

> Thus, over a wide range the rendering of Torah by *nomos* is thoroughly misleading, and it is to be regretted that the English versions followed the LXX (via the Vulgate) in so many cases. But while the translation is often misleading as a representation of the original meaning, it is most instructive in its bearing upon Hellenistic Judaism. It is clear that for the Jews of Egypt in the Hellenistic period, the developed meaning of Torah as a code of religious observance, a "law" for a religious community, was the normal and regulative meaning, and they made this meaning cover the whole use of the word in the Old Testament.[5]

It is the writing of Paul, so completely devoted to the issue of *nomos*, that is the keystone in the argument. C. H. Dodd remarks,

> In all these cases it is not denied that Paul had in the back of his mind the thought of *nomos* = Torah. But because he was using a Greek and not a Hebrew word he was able to use expressions which would have been

[3] S. Sandmel, *Judaism and Christian Beginnings* (New York: Oxford University Press, 1978).

[4] S. Belkin, *Philo and the Oral Law* (Cambridge, Mass.: Harvard University Press, 1940).

[5] C. H. Dodd, *The Bible and the Greeks* (London: Hodder & Stoughton, 1935), 33–34.

impossible but for the fact that Torah by becoming *nomos* had entered into a new field of associated ideas."[6]

It is possible that C. H. Dodd independently originated the observation that the problem of Paul's attitude toward the law was solved by the LXX's translation of torah. He certainly has given us one of the clearest Venn diagrams of semantic range.[7] It is also clear that Belkin and Sandmel take Dodd much further than Dodd himself would want to go.

While I feel that my analysis will show that Sandmel misunderstood the issues within Hellenistic Judaism, I do not feel that he would have blundered in this way, were it not for the similar judgment of C. H. Dodd, who found the translation of torah as *nomos* to be a significant translation problem in the study of ancient Judaism. Ultimately the suggestion appears to go back to Solomon Schechter, where it was an aside in his broader criticism of Wellhausen and the biblical critical method.[8]

This opinion has certainly constituted a common British-American consensus on the problem, but it has not been entirely uncontested. I have recently found an article by James Sanders which criticizes this scholarly consensus in a number of important ways.[9] He emphasizes that the distinction between Hellenistic and Palestinian Judaism implicit in this categorization cannot be maintained any longer. Besides that, the rabbinic movement was only one among a variety of sects in Palestine until well into the second century, and thereafter it was still only a significant part of a brokered power system. Therefore, we must conclude that there were many so-called Hellenistic Jews in Palestine and that it is possible, if not probable, that they had an exalted and transcendental view of torah.

Since Professor Sanders' article is extremely compressed, the intuition he shows there needs fleshing out in order to be a persuasive argument. On the other hand, it is amazing how much ammunition for the defeat of the Dodd position can be found in a perusal of the Kleinknecht

[6] Dodd, *Bible and the Greeks*, 37.

[7] Dodd, *Bible and the Greeks*, 41.

[8] Solomon Schechter, *Aspects of Rabbinic Theology* (New York: Schocken, 1961; from the 1909 ed.), 117. For the full story, see the fine essay of Stephen Westerholm, "Torah, *Nomos*, and Law: A Question of 'Meaning,'" *Studies in Religion/Sciences Religieuses* 15, no. 3 (1986): 327–36.

[9] J. Sanders, "Torah," in *The Interpreter's Dictionary of the Bible: Supplementary Volume*, ed. V. P. Furnish, K. R. Crim, and L. R. Bailey (Nashville: Abingdon, 1976), 909–11.

and Gutbrod article on *nomos* in the *Theological Dictionary of the New Testament*, though it is presented there without any apparent emphasis on its importance.

Nomos belongs etymologically to the verb νεμω, "to allot," and thus has the sense both of what is proper and what the gods have allotted, having both a human and a transcendent meaning. In ancient times, it had a comprehensive range of meaning, embracing any kind of existing or accepted norm, order, custom, or usage. On the one hand, it can refer to social dealings and customs that are rooted in religion, with all the transcendence that is usually implied in that term. On the other, it practically refers to the customs or laws of any particular place and therefore has a very relative and local connotation.

Professor Sandmel is right in observing that in Hellenistic Jewish literature *nomos* is used quite regularly to refer to the torah. This is viewed as a surprising development, presumably because most non-Jewish Hellenistic literature ignored or left unexplored any transcendent connotations of *nomos*. But Hellenistic Judaism, starting with the LXX, most commonly used it to translate torah. For instance, in Josephus and Maccabees, *nomos* is normally used to denote the Jewish religious law, as well as the Pentateuch itself. Josephus can talk about bringing the law or having the law, when obviously the possession of a book is meant. There are also longer expressions like νομός θεοῦ, which serve to remove the ambiguity about the divine authorship of the law. Besides using the term to refer to Jewish religious law, however, Josephus can use the term to refer to the laws of the other nations. The question of transcendence or personification must remain moot in these cases, but as good Greek allows, Josephus uses the term *nomos* as the subject of active sentences, implying that the law commands or enacts. It is clear, however, that these Jews did not neglect the divine or the transcendent aspects of the Jewish law by calling it *nomos*.

According to Kleinknecht and Gutbrod's article in Kittel's dictionary, Philo uses the term *nomos* in identical ways to the rest of Hellenistic Judaism.[10] *Nomos* is primarily to be understood as the torah of God. The φιλανθρωπία νομοῦ (*Spec. Leg.* 2.138) is the love of the Old Testament law. But the laws of the state can also be όι νομοί (*Jos.* 63). More broadly than Josephus, Philo uses *nomos* for the order and law of nature (ὁ τῆς

[10] H. Kleinknecht and W. Gutbrod, "νομος," *TDNT* 4:1052, quoting E. Schürer, *Geschichte der jüdischen Volkes im Zeitalter Jesus Christi*, vol. 3, 2nd ed. (Leipzig: Hinrichs, 1886).

φύσεως νομός; *Abr.* 135). Philo uses it to mean either order or ordinance, which are not really distinguishable senses, even in the mind of a German dictionary writer. Finally, a man can be figuratively the *nomos* as the embodiment of the law (*empsychos nomos*). Before Moses became a lawgiver, he was made: αὔτος ἐγίνετο νομός ἔμψυχος τε καὶ λογικός θείαι προνοίαε (*Mos.* 162). The life of Abraham is not merely a νόμιμος βίος but also νομός αὔτος τῶν καὶ τέσμος ἄγραφος (*Abr.* 276, cf. 5).

Thereafter Gutbrod offers the opinion that law was not the center of Philo's spiritual life, which was really that of a spiritual ecstatic. Philo, therefore, was a kind of contradiction in action because he would not give up the centrality of the law overtly, though it really had nothing to do with the sources of his religiosity.[11] Yet this *TDNT* article portrays the use of *nomos* in Philo to be otherwise entirely without controversy, which is important when one is trying to understand just what the usage of *nomos* was in Hellenistic Judaism.

This conclusion also misses some interesting developments in Philo's writing. To begin with, Helmut Koester has shown that Philo propounds a new understanding of the term *nomos physeos* in order to do justice both to the Greek and Hebrew bases of ethics.[12] Koester shows how infrequent is the use of the term νομός φύσεως in the philosophical literature before Philo's time. Philo is the first writer in Greek literature to employ the term "law of nature" frequently (about thirty times) in his writing. Koester argues that the sudden appearance of this term in Philo is a result of Philo's attempt to unite basic elements of Jewish tradition with the general Hellenistic thought world.

For Philo, the Platonist, there were two basic terms, *physis* (nature) and *nomos* (law), which designated two different realms of endeavor. *Nomos* existed in the world of men and reflected human endeavor to find some order in human "activities, customs, and morality." *Physis*, on the other hand, is not a function of human activity but the realm of nature to which man's *nomos* ought to correspond. But that is no simple matter if

[11] Kleinknecht and Gutbrod, "νομός," 700. With all due respect to Gutbrod's fine research, it is hard to attribute to Philo the notion that the law should be given up. This is one of Gutbrod's more ideological positions. Sandmel was not the only scholar to bring a hidden agenda to the study of *nomos*.

[12] H. Koester, "*Nomos Phuseos*: The Concept of Natural Law in Greek Thought," in *Religions in Antiquity: Essays in Memory of Erwin Ramsdell Goodenough*, ed. J. Neusner (Leiden: Brill, 1968), 521–41.

one superimposes the cosmology and metaphysics of Platonism. Everything in the human, sensible realm is an imperfect imitation of the "real" world of ideas. Therefore, *nomos* can only be an imitation of the real heavenly *physis*. Nomos is the imitation; *physis* the reality. Therefore, says Koester, the realm of *nomos* is not an extension but in many ways the very opposite of *physis*.

If torah were merely law this would be no problem at all. Philo would just accede to his Platonic training. But he did not, and the reason is quite clear. Degrading the torah is an impossible sentiment for anyone with a high view of *nomos* as torah. The solution becomes evident in Philo's discussion of cosmology or *physis*. *Physis* and *nomos* become blended as the *nomos physeos*, the law of nature. The commandments which begin in Exodus 20 are the *nomos* of Moses, and that *nomos* in the sensible world is the imitation of "law of nature." Therefore, the pre-Mosaic patriarchs lived by laws inherent in nature. Afterwards, the Hebrews lived by the laws of Moses.

In relegating the literal *nomos* of Moses to an imitation of or substitute for *physis*, Philo is on the verge of denigrating the torah, which he calls the *nomos* of Moses.[13] Instead, Philo terms the *nomos* of Moses as the best possible imitation of *physis*, contrasting the *nomos* of Moses with the *nomos* of the city-states. In the latter, a new king can rescind old laws or introduce new ones; the *nomos* of Moses is eternal and unchangeable. The laws of Moses then, though they look like the laws of other localities, are different and superior because they are the best possible approximations of the *physis*.[14] "Only a philosophical and theological setting in which the Greek concept of nature was fused with the belief in a divine legislator and with a doctrine of the most perfect (written!) law could produce such a theory, and only here could the Greek dichotomy of the realms of law and nature be overcome."[15]

Let us summarize what we have been able to discover about Philo's concept of *nomos* so far. Professor Koester's argument illustrates Philo's individual genius for making a synthesis of Hebrew and Greek thought. But, at the same time, Koester also shows that Philo is able to use *nomos*

[13] See S. Sandmel, *Philo of Alexandria: An Introduction* (New York: Oxford University Press, 1979), 119.

[14] See *Mos*. 2.13–14, where Philo contrasts the laws of the other countries with the laws of God which "stand firm, unshaken . . . stamped with the seals of nature herself."

[15] Koester, "*Nomos Phuseos*," 536.

in a human sense and is sensitive to the problem of the translation of the term *nomos*. Philo's apology for the Hebrew *nomos* entirely depends on his knowledge of the common Hellenistic definition of *nomos* as both a divine and a very human endeavor. But it also implies that Philo was well aware that in this case *nomos* could mean much more. The question is: Are there Greek as well as Hebrew precedents for the amelioration of *nomos*? The answer, I feel, is yes! But before that conclusion can be established there is another aspect of the problem which must be emphasized.

What should immediately occur to us is that this is a direct contradiction to the argument from silence of Professor Sandmel that no Jew in the diaspora ever objected to or showed the least sensitivity to the word *nomos* as a translation of torah. "Greek Jews nowhere raised the question of whether Torah really means *nomos*, Law."[16] To the contrary, we have just seen that Philo, the diaspora Jew *par excellence*, knew the ambiguity of *nomos* and endeavored to clarify the term for his Hellenistic colleagues.

One possible, though mistaken explanation for this state of events is that Philo is absolutely unique. He knew that the term *nomos* was used for the Hebrew word "torah" because he had some special external information about the usage of the Hebrew term "torah." In an all too simple form, the argument would run that Philo knew the correct understanding of the term *nomos* because he had studied oral tradition or midrash as to the real meaning of the word in Judaism. Thus, Philo's usage is usually mustered as evidence for his knowledge of the oral law.[17]

Now, I am of the opinion that Philo knew quite a bit about how the torah was interpreted in the land of Israel. For one thing, he tells us that he has learned traditions from the elders (*Mos.*, beginning). But it is quite another thing to assume that what he learned was rabbinic tradition, or that this was the only kind of Judaism taught in the diaspora, or that Jerusalem itself was solidly rabbinic in the first century. Not all traditions valuing the torah have to be rabbinic. Philo could just as easily have heard Sadducean traditions or common traditions, for all Jewish traditions of this time valorized torah (which is probably what Sandmel meant above when he said that no Jew ever felt the commandments were a burden). The point here is precisely that Philo, in spite of the appreciation of his unique development of the concept of natural law, is completely in the mainstream of Hellenistic Jewish tradition of using *nomos*

[16] Sandmel, *Genius of Paul*, 47n1.

[17] Belkin, *Philo and the Oral Law*, 36f.

to translate the word "torah," so he need not be considered a special case. What he adds is a new understanding of natural law because of the special constraints of using Platonic thought to exegete the Bible. This is precisely because he and probably the majority of Hellenistic Judaism understood torah quite properly to be a transcendent law.

Only now can one raise the question of the propriety or impropriety of translating torah as *nomos*. Was every other Greek convinced of the *immanent* meaning of *nomos* to the exclusion of the transcendent one? Can it really be that every Jew in the Hellenistic world was so seriously misinformed about the translation of the word *nomos*? Can it be that the term *nomos* was understood only platonically everywhere in the Hellenistic Jewish world except for Philo, whose usage can be explained by virtue of the fact that he had private communications with Judea? Everyone writing in that period seemed to use the same vocabulary (no doubt influenced by the LXX very much). There is something not only illogical but also uneconomical about these conclusions. It is much simpler to assume that the Greek term maintained both its transcendent and immanent senses and that Philo need not have had a unique or a special intuition about the term. Luckily, the difference between the very long and convoluted series of assumptions about usage and the shorter and more practical series of assumptions can be decided by looking at a variety of evidence, including just how the Hellenistic world did use the term *nomos*.

Nomos is not nearly as bad a translation for torah as first appears, especially if one removes the Platonic framework, which clearly drove Philo to his inventive and fortunate solution. In defense of the translators of the LXX, let me say that there is clear and constant evidence of the divine origin and nature of the *nomos* in Greek literature of the Hellenistic period. Starting in the drama of Antigone, for instance, neither Zeus nor Dike commands Antigone to do what she does, but the ἄγραπτα κασφαλῆ θεῶν νόμιμα (454f.), which can only mean that there is another law above the state which is divine and which the state, when it is just, should emulate. Usually, this is judged to reflect the crisis of confidence in religion in the fifth century B.C.E., where *nomos* is demoted, as part of the general disinclination to honor the traditional gods. In this respect, the theorizing of Plato about *nomos*, which Koester reports to be so suggestive in Philo's case, was a kind of rescue operation which Plato attempts by making *nomos* the child of *nous* (νοῦς), hence related to the soul and thus also to *physis*. Though this was intended to safeguard the sanctity of law and democratic or oligarchical principles, the *Theological Dictionary of the New Testament* article shows how the concept was interpreted in Hellenistic political theory to make the king an embodiment of *nomos*, a phenomenon which is reflected in Philo's theories, at least in an apologetic way. Here *nomos* no longer rules the polis but, instead, the will and person of the *basileus* become itself the *nomos*. This is clearly something which Philo abhorred.

The usage which is reflected in the LXX and upon which Philo and the other Jewish writers depended is one that ordinarily assumed that *nomos* was divine and encountered the newer Hellenistic justification for divine kingship only in a polemical way. That the older understanding of *nomos* remained alive in the Hellenistic world is clear through a number of texts influenced by Stoicism but not bound to recognizing the king necessarily as the personified law, as we shall see momentarily. The individual of the Hellenistic world seeks and finds the one true and divine *nomos* only in the cosmos. Since he is the citizen of the world, the world is his state and its *nomos* the law of the *kosmos*, parallel with Platonism to an extent. But as general and supreme reason, *nomos* permeates all nature and determines the moral conduct of men. The spiritually determined order of the world is identical with the concept of law, whether as *nomos* directly or as equated with *theos*, and is therefore often made into a religious discussion. This more popular conception was far more attractive to Jewish writers. In fact, in popular religion, the name Zeus is often given to the cosmic *nomos*.[18] In the Cleanthes hymn (fr. 537),[19] too, all-powerful Zeus controls the world by *nomos*. In the final verses, he is himself identified with the cosmic order. Though the strict Platonist could find this system limiting, it was possible to ignore the limitations of *nomos* in the more eclectic climate.

To this list of references to the continued use of *nomos* as a transcendent principle, I can add one more important Hellenistic appearance, that of the Orphic Hymns usually supposed to be third- or fourth-century popular religiosity, which contain a very short but affecting hymn to *nomos* as the cosmic principle who rules over men and gods:

> Upon the holy lord of men and gods I call,
> heavenly *Nomos* who arranges the stars and sets a

[18] See Diogenes Laertius, and Kleinknecht and Gutbrod, "νομός."

[19] *Stoicorum veterum fragmenta*, vol. 1, ed. J. Arnim (Leipzig: Teubner, 1905), 121–23.

> fair limit between earth and the sea's waters and
> who by his laws
> ever preserves nature's balance obedient and steady.
> Journeying on the heavens he brings the laws from
> above and drives malicious envy out with a roar.
> *Nomos* summons a good end to mortal life and he
> alone steers the course of everything that
> breathes,
> ever the steadfast companion of righteous thought.
> Primeval and wise, in peace he shares the same
> house with all who abide by the law, while he
> visits harsh vengeance upon the lawless. But, O
> Blessed bringer of prosperity, beloved of all and
> honored, have kindness of heart and make me
> mindful of your lordship. (Hymn 64)[20]

These verses are, of course, supposed by the collector to be ancient. But they are usually viewed by scholars to belong to the second, third, or fourth centuries C.E. where they became part of the widespread Hellenistic popular spirituality. The popularity of the writings is to be underlined in this context. There can be no doubt of the continued high regard which *nomos* had in Hellenistic circles. To *nomos* is given the sole rule of the world; but not only that, *nomos* steers the course of everything that breathes, visiting vengeance on sinners and rewards upon the righteous. *Nomos* also summons a good end to mortal life.

Outside of strict Platonism in the more popular Stoic tradition, where *nomos* was given a special usage which gave Philo trouble, *nomos* continued to have a good reputation as divine regulation of the universe. In short, we have all been misled by Philo's Platonism into thinking that all the Hellenistic world believed the *nomos* to be mundane and secular. Instead, we should have been appreciating the special constraints of Philo's exegesis by taking both Stoicism and Platonism seriously; issues which made difficult his explanation of Judaism. Then we could have been more attentive to the creative ways in which he solved his intercultural problems.

Annie Jaubert has said, "Il est donc assez normal que dans une atmosphere stoicien on ail tendu à assimiler la loi (*nomos*) et la raison

[20] *The Orphic Hymns: Texts, Translation and Notes*, ed. and trans. Apostolos N. Athanassakis (Missoula, Mont.: Scholars, 1977), 85.

(*logismos*)."[21] In Stoic thought, which was considerably more political than Platonic thought, enacted laws ought never be abrogated, because they ought to be based upon reason and therefore ought to be in accord with nature. It is at this point that Philo's contentions make sense. Only a law which was revealed by God, who is the creator of nature, can be in accordance with nature in the true sense of the term, for such a law, being the work of God, is like nature itself—universal, eternal, and immutable. As Wolfson shows,[22] whenever Philo tries to make this point, he naturally moves through three arguments: (1) what is meant by natural law; (2) the prevailing laws of the cities are not always in accordance with nature; and (3) the Mosaic law is in the true sense of the term a law in accordance with nature. The agenda of the Jewish community involved removing an unwanted association from a term which was ambiguous to gentiles sometimes (though certainly not always), but appears never to have been ambiguous to Jews at all. Philo shows us clearly that this clarity had to be maintained, even at the risk of his philosophy.

The use which Philo makes of the word *nomos* has never been thought controversial, and with this I can agree. But it is special in a number of respects, as Koester has shown us. Like other Jews before and after him, Philo understood perfectly that *nomos* meant law in the narrow sense, but at no time did this meaning negate the broader meaning of torah or the divine origin of the legislation for him. The ordinary meaning of the word *nomos* in Greek—statutory enactment, legal corpus, or existing custom—had already been used consistently by the LXX to refer to Hebrew Scriptures, because the Greek term was continuously and popularly associated with transcendent values. Philo uses the same term as the LXX does, to refer to the Hebrew Scriptures. He does so, not because he misunderstood what torah was. To the contrary, he argues forcefully and often for the correct meaning of torah. Rather he does so for the same reason that the LXX did, because the word *nomos* in Greek normally had transcendent and divine associations as well, which Philo, *pace* Sandmel and Dodd, takes the time to spell out in detail. The difference between the Hebrew use of torah and the Greek use of *nomos*, which is made to be the unfortunate genesis of much misunderstanding between Hellenistic

[21] A. Jaubert, *La notion d'alliance dans le Judaïsme aux abords de l'ère Chrétienne*, Patristica Sorbonensis 6 (Paris: Editions du Seuil, 1963).

[22] Harry A. Wolfson, *Philo: Foundations of Philosophy in Judaism, Christianity, and Islam*, 2 vols. (Cambridge, Mass.: Harvard University Press, 1947), 2:180f.

Jewish and Christian exegesis on the one hand—as, for instance, in the writings of Paul—and Palestinian, rabbinic Jewish exegesis on the other, is not evidenced in Philo. To be sure, Philo applies the term presumably as no Greek would ever do, even to the non-legal material of the Bible. He does this not because he misunderstands what torah is but because he knows that the word *nomos* in Greek can support this interpretation of divine revelation. But in this enterprise he appears to be entirely in agreement with his Hellenistic brethren like Josephus. What Philo adds is not so much an apologetic for the divinity of law, something which every other Jew naturally understood. He offers a special apologetic for the law as the closest embodiment to Platonic forms. The narratives of the Bible he calls *ho nomos* or *hoi nomoi*.[23] The stories of the patriarchs, of the Tower of Babel, and the flood are considered *nomoi*. The Hebrew Bible is the personification or embodiment of divinity, and even the translators of the LXX are to be viewed as prophets (see *Spec. Leg.*, at the beginning).

If *nomos* did not merely mean law or custom in Philo or any other Jewish writing of the Hellenistic world, then what did *nomos* mean in Paul? I can give no systematic answer here. But it seems to me that one possibility is virtually eliminated: Paul did not merely misunderstand what Jewish law was. Given the unlikelihood of the Sandmel proposal, it seems much more likely that Paul deliberately revalued torah, knowing full well what it meant both in Hellenistic and Palestinian Judaism. And I would argue that he did so on the basis of what we might call a radical conversion experience, even if it was not the conversion experience which Acts describes three times in contradictory fashion.

[23] See. E. R. Goodenough, *By Light, Light: The Mystic Gospel of Hellenistic Judaism* (New Haven, Conn.: Yale University Press, 1935), 73–74.

SIX

COVENANT IN RABBINIC WRITINGS

Earlier Studies

Both Judaism and Christianity inherited the covenant tradition.[1] Unfortunately, the inheritance has been contested, leading directly into a theological lawsuit about the validity of each other's claims of possession. Scholars have tried a number of ways to arbitrate the suit, most effectively by studying the actual use of the terms in the two communities of the first century. But scholars have theologies too (some contribute significantly to theological debate), so that a related and equally heated theological contest has erupted between scholars on the subject of covenant.

The basic theological argument is that Judaism gave up its claim to being a covenantal community as the Christian community picked it up. The history of the position is best summed up by two of the many scholars who wish to correct this wrong emphasis. E. P. Sanders, in his *Paul and Palestinian Judaism*[2] has given us a thorough introduction to the misreading of rabbinic Judaism among Christian biblical scholars. For instance, he singles out Dietrich Rössler[3] as an example of the extreme position that covenant passed from apocalyptic Judaism to Christianity, by-passing rabbinic Judaism. Charlotte Klein, who traces the same line

[1] This chapter originally appeared in *Studies in Religion/Sciences Religieuses* 14 (1985): 53–62, and is used with permission. It has been changed substantially since then.

[2] E. P. Sanders, *Paul and Palestinian Judaism: A Comparison of Patterns of Religion* (Philadelphia: Fortress, 1977), 33–59.

[3] D. Rössler, *Gesetz und Geschichte: Untersuchungen zur Theologie der jüdischen Apokalyptik und der pharisäischen Orthodoxie*, WMANT 3 (Neukirchen: Neukirchener, 1960).

of thought in her interesting book, *Anti-Judaism in Christian Theology*,[4] is able to show a bias in the writings of such scholars as Martin Noth, who claimed that, during the restoration of the Second Temple period and sometime before the birth of Christianity, Judaism gave up any real concept of interrelatedness with God. Charlotte Klein characterizes Noth's description of Second Temple Judaism in this fashion:

> All that remained was for the law to be turned into an independent reality, taking the place, as it were, of God himself. Only at this stage did the concepts of merit and penalty, the whole idea of retribution and legalistic piety for the sake of merit, emerge in Judaism.[5]

When the Dead Sea Scrolls were discovered, it became clear that the term *brith* (ברית) or covenant was used extensively within the Qumran community. The fine study of Annie Jaubert[6] has shown how important was the term "covenant" to this newfound Essene community. In the process of studying this term, Annie Jaubert also showed how frequently the term and concept of covenant appears in the attendant Jewish communities.

Word Studies of Covenant in Rabbinic Judaism

In spite of the success of Annie Jaubert in avoiding earlier pitfalls, she was only able to put together a short description of the use of the term "covenant" in rabbinic Judaism, seven pages of a five-hundred-page book, to measure the attention crudely. This same lack of emphasis can be seen in the article on διαθήκη in the *TDNT*, a thirty-page article by Quell and Behm, which devotes one and one-half pages to the usage of the term in Jewish literature and only one short paragraph to the use of the term in rabbinic Judaism.

[4] C. Klein, *Anti-Judaism in Christian Theology*, trans. Edward Quinn (Philadelphia: Fortress, 1975), esp. chap. 3, "Law and Legalistic Piety," 39–66.

[5] Klein, *Anti-Judaism*, 53. This is especially ironic when one realizes that Noth was defending the relatively liberal idea that covenant continued to inform Israelite notions of law well into the exilic period, a position which corrects the negative evaluation of Deuteronomy as a "legalistic" work, an opinion which is all too common today. See J. Behm and G. Quell, "διαθήκη," *TDNT* 2:124, for example.

[6] A. Jaubert, *La notion d'alliance dans le Judaïsme aux abords de l'ère Chrétienne*, Patristica Sorbonensis 6 (Paris: Editions du Seuil, 1963).

The Complexity of Early Rabbinic Judaism

No one today would be foolish enough to conclude that there was no rabbinic concept of covenant on the basis of the study of one word. In order to understand why early rabbinic Judaism lacks the term *brith* in profusion, one must read the contemporary debates on the nature of rabbinic literature. The fact is that the organizing principles and functions of rabbinic literature are still something of a mystery, even to those who are skilled in reading Mishnah, midrash, and Talmud.

The mystery has been partly illuminated by form-critical studies of rabbinic Judaism. For instance, Jacob Neusner has shown that the Mishnah and Tosefta are the only consistently reliable rabbinic traditions of the first two centuries, and that they themselves are likely to have been extensively edited during the last decades of the second century. Since these rabbinic writings are halakic rather than aggadic, they show not the theology of the rabbis, so much as their attempt to build a new community of law (torah) on the basis of the Pharisaic sect, but with the new desire to define a catholic Israel. A second perception in the solution to this mystery has come from Christian scholars who want to take an unbiased view of Jewish tradition. E. P. Sanders, for instance, has discussed the general Jewish worldview of the first two centuries as "covenantal nomism." All the varieties of Judaism in the first century seem united in their interest in covenant. The fact that rabbinic writing does not take the word ברית as central is puzzling, but one cannot conclude that the rabbis neglected the issue. Perhaps "covenant" had become so identified with circumcision that it could not be used for the more general concept.

Were Sanders explicitly responding to Professor Neusner, he would perhaps have argued that the term "covenant" is found in the sectarian literature of the first century and it is found in rabbinic writing after the first century, therefore it must be assumed to be present in the earliest rabbinic thought as well, though there is no written record of it.[7] In

[7] Neusner and Sanders have subsequently carried on a scholarly debate over these issues since Professor Neusner's reviews of Sander's books in *History of Religions* 18 (1978): 177–91 and 24 (1985): 285–86. The published debate may be found in *Approaches to Ancient Judaism* vol. 2, ed. William Scott Green, Brown Judaica Studies 9 (Atlanta: Scholars, 1980), 43–79. The debate has been continued with papers at more recent meetings of the AAR. Professor Sanders has shared his latest response with me. I have assessed their positions in a review of the volume for the *AJS Newsletter* (Spring 1982). Michel Desjardins has more recently summarized the debate in his paper for the CSBS meeting in

doing so, he would observe that in the rabbinic movement the covenantal aspects of the worldview are crucial but, for whatever reasons, they were left largely unspecified. As Professor Sanders himself says,

> Although the word "covenant" has thus far not occurred in Sifre, it is clear that the entirety of Sifre Num. 1 presupposes a firm belief in a covenant between God and Israel. God dwells with his people and they are to keep His commandments precisely. *The bulk of the halakic material deals with the elaboration and definition of Israel's obligation to God under the covenant. This is what accounts for the halakic material in general.* . . . Very seldom is God's role in the covenant directly discussed. It is assumed so thoroughly that it need not be mentioned. But that role is nevertheless the presupposition upon which all the halakic material rests.[8]

Sanders maintains that in Tannaitic literature, the basic theological concepts are assumed, rather than stated. And his concept of "covenantal nomism" has been a convenient summary against which to redress previous misunderstandings of rabbinic Judaism. For instance, by looking carefully at the writings, Sanders has put to rest the misapprehension that rabbinic Judaism was "a scoreboard religion" in which one's good deeds were merely totaled against one's bad deeds. He showed how important was the working of God's grace to the rabbis; but he had to demonstrate this contention through the rabbinic rules of repentance, because the rabbis do not just state that God's grace is omnipresent. That is neither their vocabulary nor their style. Rather they are interested in legal distinctions to be used within the nation's actual jurisprudence. Mishnah is not a fortuitous genre for theological writing because theological exposition is not its purpose. Nevertheless, theological assumptions may be distilled from the writing, provided one is careful to explain how they are derived.

Possible Methodological Emphases

Although prejudice and lack of sensitive reading may have been involved in the original contention that the rabbis had little concept of covenant, there is still some justification for the slowness of scholarship to

---

Winnipeg in 1986, as preparation for reviewing Sanders' newest book, *Jesus and Judaism* (Philadelphia: Fortress, 1985). The positions in the debate are not nearly as important for our purposes as are the terms under which the debate is being held.

[8] Sanders, *Paul and Palestinian Judaism*, 84.

understand the rabbinic view of covenant. There is not a lot of explicit evidence on which to found a rabbinic view of covenant.

One way to resolve this issue would be to emphasize that the term "torah" has very broad implications in Judaism and that it subsumes "grace" and "covenant," which only needed to be distinguished from "law" in Christianity. There is no question that this is true, yet it does not give us a positive doctrine with which to work.

Another way to attack the issue is to add the midrash into the discussion of rabbinic literature, which is more or less what Sanders does. When one adds the midrash into the equation, the job of finding theological discussion of covenant in rabbinic Judaism becomes much easier (as Sanders has noted and Neusner has criticized so strongly). One of the major themes of the Mekhiltas, for instance, is how the Sinai covenant was a covenant freely ratified by both Israel and God, emphasizing the value of the covenant for all future Israelites.

Yet, this is precisely what is forbidden methodologically by saying that the midrash is of uncertain date and cannot be used with surety for reconstructing the precedents for rabbinic Judaism of the first century. Of course, this is an entirely different problem from the previous state of affairs, which was largely caused by prejudice or ignorance. The new issue is an artifact of our renewed understanding of the nature and dating of rabbinic literature. The new constraints come from the method in the study of rabbinic literature and have nothing to do with the theological problems of covenant at all. But they do add to the problem of trying to come to a more balanced view of rabbinic theology.

Some Personal Opinions

I have maintained that, when there is consistent outside evidence for the existence of similar traditions in other Jewish sectarian communities, one can count midrashic evidence towards the understanding of the first century.[9] Philonic and Christian evidence have seemed to me to be crucially important when faced with the results of form criticism in rabbinic writing. From a form-critical analysis of rabbinic tradition we can sometimes get a relative chronology of the tradition. But we cannot firmly establish absolute dates unless we can find an appropriate and close parallel in Philonic or Christian writing. One could easily argue that the importance

[9] See Alan F. Segal, *Two Powers in Heaven* (Leiden: Brill, 1977; repr. Waco, Tex.: Baylor University Press, 2012).

of the concept of covenant in the Christian community points to its continued presence in other first-century varieties of Judaism, an argument which I think has some limited validity in and of itself.

Yet, using Christian evidence to posit the importance of the term "covenant" in rabbinic literature would violate the nature of this debate, since the previous positions have tacitly maintained the (methodologically dubious) idea that the Christian emphasis on covenant is historically and theologically unique. Because of studies like Jaubert's and Sanders' we are now more free to compare the rabbinic evidence with the sectarian Jewish evidence. One learns from this, I think, that there is a consensus of covenantal theology underlying all of first-century Judaism. But the issue here is to prove that rabbinic Judaism shares in that consensus.

The Methodological Quandary: An Argument from Silence

Many scholars have accepted the fundamental point that since covenantal nomism is characteristic of all first-century sects of Judaism and since it is characteristic of rabbinic Judaism in succeeding centuries, when we have firmer evidence, it is likely to have been presupposed by the Tannaitic community as well. The problem is, as Neusner has shown, that we have very little positive evidence that the early rabbis grappled with these ideas. But this is a problem inherent in all studies of rabbinic literature. It has as much to do with our constraints in studying rabbinic Judaism as with the rabbis' interests.

Let us try to discover if there are unexamined parts of rabbinic literature which deal with covenant in a more thorough way. To be sure, we have some early traditions about the value of circumcision as a covenantal event, a report which is confirmed by Josephus and Philo as well as the New Testament in the most graphic ways. Otherwise, we have the problem of an argument from silence. In spite of most contemporary scholars' desire to believe that covenant was a part of rabbinic thinking we still have only little demonstrable evidence for it in rabbinic literature. Even though we are sure that rabbinic Judaism depended on a concept of covenant, we are still left with the anomaly that we are arguing from silence, in part a silence of scholarly caution in dating rabbinic evidence and in part a silence of knowing that rabbinic literature itself is not the basis for such a discussion.

Liturgy and Ritual: Untapped Sources of Information

There is, however, a significant body of evidence which has been overlooked in this discussion: liturgy. In liturgy we find not only texts expressing the value of covenant but also rituals which do the same. The connection between liturgy and the expression of covenant should have already been clear, since the one area in which covenant is clearly expressed in rabbinic writing is universally admitted to be circumcision and there is a developed liturgy for every Jewish ritual. However, almost no one has systematically studied the ritual or liturgical expressions of the concept of covenant. This is unfortunate since it is exactly in the area of liturgy that the concept of covenant is most strongly expressed. I have no intention of surveying the area of liturgy systematically, since even a casual perusal of the service will establish the importance of the discussion of covenant.

Of course, by moving into liturgy we do not completely eliminate the problem of dating, and we add to that problem the dimension that ritual activities are rich symbolic actions with very imprecise doctrinal implications. That is one reason that they are so powerful as unifying factors in a religious community. They appeal directly to religious instincts, bypassing many sources of theological argument. That is simply a given when one studies symbolic actions, but we can simplify some of the problem by relying on the liturgical expressions of what the ritual means.

Of necessity, the problem of dating comes right back to the fore. Furthermore, we will have to investigate the relationship between the rabbinic movement and liturgy. It could be maintained that the rabbis had little to do with the liturgy of the synagogue and did not subscribe to it. But I think there is sufficient evidence in the liturgy and in mishnaic rabbinic Judaism, especially in the Tractates Berakhot and Shabat, which discuss the proper format of prayer, to prove that this is not the case.

I will also have to rely on some texts which are likely to be later than the Mishnah. But a great many aspects of liturgy are extremely stable and can be established from external evidence to be early in the Jewish community. Parts of the liturgy may antedate the rabbinic movement, in some sense expressing the general Jewish consensus which Sanders has been describing. *Lex orandi* is still *lex credendi*, even when modified by scholarly constraints.

Let us first look at some of the texts of prayers without attending to date, to show that the liturgical interest in covenant is neither insignificant nor arbitrary. First of all, we find many prayers in which the covenant is itself used as the standard by which righteousness is to be judged. In the Musaf *Tefillah* of the festivals, the people state that they have betrayed the covenant: "On account of our sins we were exiled from our land, and removed far from our country." This is balanced by the call to remember the covenant and restore the Jewish people to its homeland. Obviously this is later than first century. In the same vein are the penitential prayers recited on Monday and Thursday mornings: "Remember unto us the covenant of our fathers, and save us for Thy name's sake," is one *Tahanun*. Another is "Remember unto us the covenant of our fathers, and the testimony we bear every day that the Lord is one." It would not be unreasonable to suppose some polemical point against Christianity in the latter phrase.

In morning benedictions, there is a moment in which the congregation states, ". . . we are Thy people, the children of Thy covenant." Later in the morning service there is a quotation of a covenantal passage from Nehemiah 9:8: "[And Thou] . . . made a covenant with [Abraham] to give the land of the Canaanite . . . unto his seed."

In the Rosh Hashanah service, Leviticus 26:45 is used to support Israel's reminder of God's obligations, due under the covenant:

> Remember unto us, O Lord, the covenant and the lovingkindness and the oath which Thou swearest unto Abraham our father. . . . As it is said: "I will remember . . . the covenant with the ancients, whom I freed from the land of Egypt in the sight of the nations to be their God."[10]

Thus, while none of these passages are undeniably first-century, like the midrash they demonstrate that the concept of covenant is not only assumed but definitely discussed throughout rabbinic literature.

Circumcision

The one area in which scholars have emphasized the concept of covenant in rabbinic Judaism is circumcision. Besides noting the obvious relevance to Paul's letter to the Galatians, scholarship has not notably moved into the area of liturgy to see what the concept of circumcision signified for the rabbinic or the general Jewish community. This may be because of the difficulty in describing significance of ritual as compared

[10] See Abraham Millgrom, *Jewish Worship: A Guide to the Prayer Book and the Synagogue Service* (Philadelphia: Jewish Publication Society, 1971), 403–6.

with written, textual expressions of religious sentiment. Nor do we know much about services in the first century, though we can evaluate the Mishnah's evidence from this new perspective.

Circumcision was the symbolic act *par excellence* for entrance into Judaism in the first century, even while the temple still stood and even though baptism or immersion was sufficient for half of those who entered Judaism. Whether that entrance took place at birth or after proselytism, circumcision marked the boundary, even though it only applied to a fraction of the community. The symbolic dimension of calling circumcision a *brith millah*, a covenant of circumcision, cannot be denied. This is the technical term throughout the rabbinic literature, though *millah* alone for circumcision certainly is found as well. The covenant with Abraham was to be made ritually present on every Jew virtually at birth. This is precisely what the circumcision service was meant to certify, whenever it became normative:

> Our rabbis taught: He who circumcises must recite: "Who has sanctified us with Thy commandments and has commanded us concerning circumcision." The father of the infant recites, ". . . Who has sanctified us with Thy commandments and hast commanded us to lead him into the covenant of our father Abraham." The bystanders exclaim, "Even as he has entered the covenant, so may he enter into the Torah, the marriage canopy, and good deeds." And he who pronounces the benediction recites: ". . . Who hast sanctified the beloved one from the womb; He set a statute in his flesh, and his offsprings he sealed with the sign of the holy covenant. Therefore as a reward for this, O living God who art our portion, give command to save the beloved of our flesh from the pit, for the sake of Thy covenant which Thou has set in our flesh. Blessed art Thou, O Lord, Who makes the covenant." He who circumcises proselytes says, "Blessed art Thou, O Lord our God, King of the universe, who hast sanctified us with Thy commandments and hast commanded us concerning circumcision." He who pronounces the benediction recites, ". . . Who hast sanctified us with Thy commandments and hast commanded us to circumcise proselytes and to cause the drops of the blood of the covenant to flow from them, since but for the blood of the covenant heaven and earth would not endure, as it is said, *If not my covenant by day and by night, I had not appointed the ordinances of heaven and earth*. Blessed art Thou, O Lord, who makest the covenant." He who circumcises slaves recites: ". . . Who hast sanctified us with Thy commandments and has commanded us concerning circumcision." While he who pronounces the benediction recites: ". . . Who hast sanctified with Thy commandments and hast commanded us to cause the drops of the blood of the covenant

to flow from them, since but for the blood of the covenant the ordinances of heaven and earth would not endure, as it is said, *If not my covenant by day and by night I had not appointed the ordinances of heaven and earth.* Blessed art Thou, O Lord, who makest the covenant." (b. Shabb. 137b)

The passage is introduced as a Tannaitic teaching; so although it appears in an Amoraic discussion, it was already regarded as old. Note the occurrence of the word "covenant" frequently, but also the direct reference to the mutuality of the agreement, the taking of oaths, not to mention the description of circumcision as a ritual sign of the covenant. Oaths, mutuality, and the use of blood sacrifice to seal covenant are, of course, directly in line with the biblical and ancient Near Eastern view of the institution. The blood of the covenant explicitly is mentioned as allowing the ordinances of heaven and earth to endure, valorizing the ritual deed itself, as if in polemical contradistinction to Philo's radical allegorizers (*Migr.* 89ff.) and Christian notions of covenant. *Brith millah* is thereby represented as a covenant reenactment ceremony, liturgically celebrated. This is directly parallel to biblical understandings of the rite. Not only is the theme of covenant still known in rabbinic Judaism but the liturgy is aware of the cultic requirements of the custom in ancient semitic culture. *Prima facie*, the evidence appears to promote a hypothesis of the continuity of understanding the importance of the belief from biblical to rabbinic times.

The specific blessings of the liturgy are no doubt ancient already in the third century, since they are noted as a Tannaitic tradition. It is substantial but not decisive proof of the antiquity of the use of covenant within Jewish liturgy. One can always maintain that the importance of circumcision changed in relationship to the Christian peril. (No doubt that is partly true, as we shall see.) But the question to be asked is: did the concept or importance of circumcision change so as to recover a lost notion of covenant? This seems unlikely, given the continuity of covenantal language in rabbinic discussions of circumcision and the biblical passages it quotes. These passages show us that there is an enormous amount of liturgical emphasis to the concept of *brith* in *brith millah*, which deserves far more attention than scholars have so far given it. But we still must find a sign that the liturgy can be traced to the first century.

Daily Service

The basic structure of the public liturgy, both for everyday and holidays, intersperses the voices of the congregation with the answers of God in Scripture in an antiphonal way, suggesting a conversation between Israel and God, the mutuality implied by a covenant obligation. The most recent full-scale study of Jewish prayer forms, by Joseph Heinemann, illustrates the point.[11] In chapter 4, on use of the second person in prayer, Professor Heinemann shows that the usual formula is to address God in the second person. Referring to someone else than God in the second person in prayer is exceptional and mainly indicates that the blessing emanates from or is directed into the congregation. The basic format of the service is discussed as early as the Tannaim but the conversational style is noted by their successors. The reason for this preference for direct address to God, according to the Amoraim, is that a man should not dissociate himself from the congregation. By referring to God in the third person, a supplicant tends to remove himself from the congregation of Israel, which is speaking directly to God, and become an observer. In any event, the usual form of address, direct address to God followed by passages illustrating God's address to Israel, is one standard format, often indicating that the prayer originated in a private, devotional context. There is good evidence from the Mishnah that originally the worshiper was not obliged to use a fixed word-for-word formulation of these private prayers but might spontaneously compose his own formulation. As in Orthodox services today, each congregant continues at his or her own pace until an agreed upon pause is reached.

Some synagogue prayers are statutory, which is often a clue that they were taken over from the temple service. Since the center of the temple cult is sacrifice and the sacrifice is widely reported as silent, the liturgy which is transferred from the temple to the synagogue was not necessarily the centerpiece of temple worship. Psalms and doxologies (notably the Hallel and Hoshana of Sukkoth) as well as petitionary and supplicatory prayers (*Tahanunim*) come directly from temple service. Not all petitionary prayer in the temple is recorded in a litany, however. There is also evidence that during the prostrations of the priestly benediction

[11] See J. Heinemann, *Prayer in the Talmud: Forms and Patterns*, trans. Richard S. Sarason (Berlin: de Gruyter, 1977; from the 2nd Heb. ed. [Jerusalem: Hebrew University Press, 1966]).

and after the incense offering, each worshiper might offer up his own individual supplication (m. Tamid 7:3). The result is that, except for the special ceremonies which were transferred to the synagogue after the destruction of the temple, the prayer service in the synagogue preferred the personal form of address to God, with the exact wording of prayer often left to the congregant, implying that it was meant to be a very personal as well as communal conversation between God and His people. The content of that conversation enacted covenantal themes both in ritual and explicitly in liturgy, as we shall see.

Sabbath Service and Torah Reading

Anyone who has ever attended a Jewish Sabbath service knows that there are two major special characteristics of the service: (1) valorization of the Sabbath and (2) Torah reading. Both of these characteristics are occasionally described by the liturgy as covenantal. Added to the Kedusha for the Sabbath is the phrase:

> And the children of Israel shall keep the Sabbath, to do the Sabbath in all their generations as a perpetual covenant between Me and the children of Israel. It is a sign forever, that the Lord made heaven and earth in six days and on the seventh day He rested and refreshed himself.[12]

The Sabbath itself again is one of the well-attested differentia of Judaism in the first century. Everybody—Jew, Christian, and gentile—noted Jewish Sabbath observance. It is one of the Ten Commandments, which were also recited in the ancient synagogue. So what really needs proving in this context is the relationship between the Ten Commandments and covenant in liturgical contexts. In a moment the relationship will become clear.

In returning the Torah to the ark the liturgy quotes the Bible in saying: " 'This is my covenant with you,' says the Lord." It is clear in context that the Torah itself is meant to be the proof that the Lord himself

[12] The Kedusha is supposed to be a post-Yavnean addition to the prayers, so the antiquity of the prayer is not the point. Rather it is the emphasis or location of the motif of covenant which is important for the moment. Later, we shall see that the Sabbath is itself understood as sign of the covenant and that it was indeed prominently mentioned in the Ten Commandments. The Kedusha was certainly in place in the fifth century in Babylonia, when the Shema was added on account of persecution. See H. H. Donin, *To Pray as a Jew: A Guide to the Prayer Book and the Synagogue Service* (New York: Basic Books, 1991), 124f. and Millgrom, *Jewish Worship*, 134f.

will be the redeemer of Zion's captivity. The particular exegesis may be post-Christian. But the value of Torah as covenant might just as easily be much older.

The practice of public Torah reading is clearly antique, older than the first century of our era by centuries. The Torah was publicly read during the reform of Josiah and during Ezra and Nehemiah's time, explicitly as a covenant ratification ceremony. On the other hand, the liturgy itself cannot be traced that far back. It may be that it had lost its covenantal signification over the centuries, to regain it again later, a cumbersome assumption, which needs only a thread of factual evidence to disprove it. But we need to find that thread. Luckily the relationship between the Shema and tefillin provides it.

The Shema and Tefillin

This is the most interesting part of the liturgical emphasis on covenant. Four biblical passages command the Jew to put the words of the law for "a sign upon the hand and a frontlet between the eyes"—Exodus 13:1-10, 11-16; Deuteronomy 6:4-9; 11:13-21. Except for the biblical injunction there is no independent witness that the practice of putting on tefillin on all weekday morning services was earlier than the rabbis. We know from the tefillin found at Wadi Qumran and Wadi Murabba'at that they were in use in the first century. Apart from that fortunate archaeological find which verifies that they are closely related to the articles used today (those at Murabba'at have been deemed kosher; the Qumran ones seem sectarian), they are mentioned in Aristeas (159), Josephus (*Ant.* 4:213), and the New Testament (φυλακτηρία; Matt 23:5). While the laws governing them are recognized by the rabbis to be *miderabbanan* (i.e., rabbinical ordinances), it is clear that they are not merely a sectarian custom of the Pharisees.

The one important difference between the tefillin of today and those of the Dead Sea Scroll community is that the ancient ones include a text of the Ten Commandments. According to the Mishnah (Tamid 5:1), in the temple the priests used to recite the Decalogue together with the three paragraphs of the Shema, but this was discontinued in the synagogue "because of the errors of the sectarians that they should not say 'these alone were given to Moses in Sinai'" (y. Ber. 1:8, 3c; b. Ber. 12a). The Sifre to Deuteronomy 4:6, which deals with the tefillin, used two exegetical interpretations to justify the exclusion of the Decalogue from the tefillin. On this basis, it was plausibly assumed and now confirmed by archaeological remains from the first century that the tefillin actually contained the Decalogue, which was later excluded from the tefillin for the same danger of sectarian exegesis. So we have some independent witnesses that in this case the midrash records a tradition at least as old as the first century, shows that the rabbinic tradition rests on an antique earlier custom, and emphasizes that the rabbis made changes in ritual when it was deemed necessary. This passage also indissolubly links the Shema, the Ten Commandments, and the tefillin to first-century prayer. Thus, it provides us with a datable demonstration of the value of covenant to the early rabbinic community.

The passages included in the tefillin are exceptionally important because, not only do they include the biblical injunction to tie them between the eyes and upon the hand, they also specifically mention several times the exodus from Egypt, God's swearing to give Israel the land ("which I swore to your fathers to give to you"), and the sanctification of the firstborn son. The act of God's swearing to save Israel and Israel's ratification by keeping the specific commandment as a sign of the covenant is clearly patterned in this almost daily occasion. It is evident that the function of the articles is to confirm the covenant by means of remembering the oath on God's part as well. If a non-scriptural origin for this practice is ever found, it would not surprise me if they were related to commemoration, oath-swearing or curse avoidance in the ancient Near East.

The act of swearing was so clear a connotation of putting on tefillin that the Amoraim even pictured God as wearing his own tefillin and swearing the appropriate counter-oaths to Israel's professions of faithfulness every morning. In b. Ber. 6a, Rab Abin bar Rab Ada begins the discussion by asking how we know that God puts on tefillin. The proof comes from Psalm 62:8 which is understood to mean that God has sworn by His torah and by His tefillin. "His right hand" refers to torah, as we learn from Deuteronomy 33:2. More relevant is the proposition that "arm of His strength" refers to tefillin. This is demonstrated by relying on two more quotations: Psalm 29:11 and Deuteronomy 2:8, 10. The first verse says that the Lord will give strength unto His people and the second says that the people of the world shall fear Him. (One must assume that a visible sign makes the people afraid, hence the tefillin are meant.) Rav Abin (fourth-century Amora) quotes a person of the previous generation as saying that God puts on (מניח) tefillin, with a significant variant from codex Assemani of the Vatican that God "swears" (נשבע) by His tefillin. The passages in God's tefillin make the appropriate counter-oaths to Israel's promises: Deuteronomy 4:7-8, 34; 26:19; 33:29.

The antiquity of the practice of putting the same passages in the tefillin and their appropriateness to covenant ceremonies makes the point clear. The act of wearing tefillin had clear covenantal associations of the most literal kind. It was an action of remembering by the signs of the covenant that the covenant obligations would be continued as well as a caution that backsliding had tragic consequences. It also harkened back to the exodus event directly.

Now tefillin are not a distinctively rabbinic practice, since we find them at Qumran and the zealot caves, but they are characteristic of rabbinic Jews. Since their use depends upon the idea of covenant, tefillin are one vivid symbol of the continuity of the covenant idea in rabbinic Judaism. The later rabbinic discussions of God's daily oaths only spells out that the idea was never lost. It also demonstrates, if any demonstration is really required, that the rabbis shared a certain number of cultural presuppositions with other Jews of that time, reproducing them rather than inventing them in their literature.

The Shema and the Ten Commandments

Since the tefillin ritual is adjacent to and underlines the importance of the paragraphs known as the Shema in Jewish liturgy (Deut 6:4ff.), I should probably mention them explicitly. The Shema is said antiphonally in every single synagogue service, as well as every morning and evening by Jews. It is the centerpiece of rabbinic liturgy. Its position as the first subject of the Mishnah only emphasizes this fact.

The content of the Shema is covenantal. After its first stirring line, it is a call to hear the word of God, to love Him totally and mentions the covenantal signs, tefillin, and tsitsith, as a reminder (*zikkaron*) that the promised benefits of the covenant will be manifest to those who keep commandments, the opposite to those who are forsworn. It explicitly mentions the increase of the nation that follows obedience. The ancient words of Deuteronomy, stressing love and faithfulness, are explicitly covenantal language. By multiple daily repetition ("when thou liest down and when thou risest up"), the Jew is reminded of his covenantal obligations "to walk in His ways, and to observe His laws and commandments and norms." The consequences of betrayal are also specified: the land will become a curse and the children of Israel will be ejected.

It was at this point that the Ten Commandments were recited in ancient times, though they were later removed on account of sectarians who believed that the Ten Commandments were all which was required. Christians were one principal group among those who were causing the problem, though they were not unique in opposing aspects of rabbinic law. There is therefore evidence that the rabbis altered Jewish liturgical practice because of Christian pressures. But it does not verify the idea that the Jews gave up the concept of covenant because the Christians used it so often. If anything, it shows the converse, that the rabbis attempted never to let the idea of covenant be limited to one aspect of legal obligations.

On the positive side, what is clear from the development of rabbinic liturgy is that the daily prayers and observances of the Jews of the first century were a kind of dramatic enactment of covenantal swearing in the most obvious and literal way. It seems evident why we get only hints of the covenantal obligations of the Jews in the Mishnah: it was already present in the liturgy of the people.

Here we must remember another aspect of the sociology of the first century. We are misled if we think that the Mishnah was the only religious expression of the Pharisaic-rabbinic movement in the first century. The Mishnah reflects their distinctive legal contribution to Judaism, but it does not subsume all that they thought about Judaism.

The Pharisaic-rabbinic community also inherited what the synagogue was saying and clearly affirmed it. But the synagogue was not limited to Pharisaic rule; it had a much broader clientele. As the rabbinic movement gradually extended its rule over all Israel, it did not seek to create an entirely new ritual. Rather it reinterpreted the ritual, deciding which customs and ceremonies were most in keeping with its understanding of the ancient past. It therefore took over and retailored the rites of the synagogue. Those who participated and listened to Tannaitic discussion of how to observe the torah had already sworn daily to uphold it in ritually dramatized covenant renewal ceremonies. It is this constant and emphatic use of ritual to express the fundamentals of covenant in Judaism that makes it possible for the internal legal meditations of the Tannaitic community often to pass over covenantal discussion in silence. It is the specialized function of the rabbinic literature, not any theological blindspot, which accounts for its silence on a number of important theological issues.

SEVEN

ROMANS 7 AND JEWISH DIETARY LAWS

In the thicket of Pauline scholarship, the brambles grow most densely around Paul's attitude toward torah.[1] And Romans 7 is no doubt the center of the darkest, thorniest, and most disputed territory. In this passage Paul begins his discussion of the value of torah for salvation. He speaks in the first person about his inability to do "the good" which he desired while he was keeping torah. Readers of the New Testament from the second century onward have disputed about Paul's meaning. Paul appears to be meditating on the problem of volition and self-salvation. Is Paul speaking about his own experience? Does he have a guilty conscience? Does he refer to experience before or after being a Christian? All the logical possibilities have been investigated, though none seems to satisfy all the data. If Paul refers to his Christian experience, why is he making uncharacteristically critical statements about the Christian life? If he is speaking universally only, with no reference to himself specifically, why does he adopt the first person in so straightforward a way? Any argument about the meaning of these passages must begin with a new exegesis that appears to fit Paul's words.[2]

Some scholars have suggested that Paul's first person is merely an impersonal figure of speech signifying all Israel, citing the Psalms and

[1] This chapter first appeared in *Studies in Religion/Sciences Religieuses* 15, no. 3 (1986): 361–74, and is used with permission.

[2] For a review of the literature on this problem, see Anders Nygren, *Commentary on Romans* (Philadelphia: Fortress, 1949), 284–85. Also see O. Kuss, *Der Römerbrief*, 2nd ed. (Regensburg: F. Pustet, 1963), 479. My thanks to the Torah-Nomos seminar of the Canadian Society of Biblical Studies for their informed discussion of this thesis, and to David Weiss-Halivni, Jarl Fossum, John Gager, Harold Remus, Thomas Boslooper, Holland Hendrix, and Peter Richardson for reading this work and offering criticisms and suggestions.

especially the Hodayoth of the Dead Sea Scrolls as examples of an impersonal "I."[3] But the most convincing analogies produced in biblical and later Qumranic psalms come from confessional poetry appropriated into liturgy, which is quite a different *Sitz im Leben* from Paul's letters. Throughout his letters Paul consistently uses the first person in the ordinary way. Even in Romans he addresses himself to his readers both in the first person singular and plural in order to generalize from their mutual experience to conclusions about the life of faith in general.[4] But Paul cannot here be using liturgy.[5] For me, Romans 7:22-24, which is purely a private observation, makes an impersonal reading of Romans 7 virtually impossible:

> For I delight in the law of God in my inmost self, but I see in my members another law at war with the law of my mind and making me captive to the law of sin which dwells in my members. Wretched man that I am! Who will deliver me from this body of death?

These words seem to me to have special and personal meaning, which I shall try to describe below.

The most obvious place to begin the inquiry into Romans 7 then is that Paul is speaking personally.[6] But this does not mean that Paul

[3] E.g., 1QH III, 23ff.; IV, 29ff. See W. Wrede, "Paulus," reissued in R. Rengstorf, ed., *Das Paulusbild* (Darmstadt: Wissenschaftliche Buchsgesellschaft, 1907), 1–97; W. G. Kummel, *Römer 7 und die Bekehrung des Paulus* (Leipzig: Hinrichs, 1929); and esp. O. Michel, *Römerbrief*, 14th ed., Meyer's Commentary (Göttingen: Vandenhoeck & Ruprecht, 1977), ad loc.

[4] "I" is found 845 times in the letters of Paul and 180 times in Romans. "We" is found 637 times in the letters of Paul and 141 in Romans. E. Stauffer, "εγω," *TDNT* 2:356–62 and bibliography there. See esp. E. Dobschütz, "Wir und Ich bei Paulus," *Zeitschrift für systematische Theologie* 10 (1933): 251–77; and J. M. E. Cruvellier, *L'Exégèse de Romains 7 et le mouvement de Keswick* (Amsterdam: Academisch Proefschrift, Universiteit te Amsterdam, 1961), 131. I am going against the opinions of these august scholars as well as, in other ways, against the opinion of Kümmel, Bultmann, Althaus, Fuchs, Gutbrod, Lekkerkerker, Gaugler, Schlatter, Bornkamm, Lohmeyer, Michel, Schoeps, and Braun. Quite a formidable group! I do not undertake this line of reasoning lightly.

[5] See E. Gerstenberger, "Jeremiah's Complaints: Observations on Jer 15.10-21," *JBL* 82 (1963): 393–408.

[6] Other recent studies agreeing with me are: J. Christiaan Beker, *Paul the Apostle: The Triumph of God in Life and Thought* (Philadelphia: Fortress, 1980), 236–43, although Professor Beker sees Paul as evincing a heretofore secret dissatisfaction with the law; also Paul Meyer, "Romans 10:4 and the End of the Law," in *The Divine Helmsman: Studies on God's Control of Human Events, Presented to Lou H. Silberman*, ed. J. L. Crenshaw and S. Sandmel

feels his experience to be eccentric. Rather, he mentions his own experience precisely because it illustrates a general religious principle which he hopes his audience will come to share.

Paul's Jewish Audience

Though Paul was aware of a wider audience, the letter to the Romans is addressed to the church or churches in Rome, which evidently included both Jews and gentiles. Much of the letter is directed to the gentiles, cautioning them not to pride themselves over against the Jews and Jewish Christians because they have understood the obsolescence of Jewish ceremonial laws. At the beginning of chapter 7, however, Paul defines a special audience. He speaks first of all to his ἀδελφοί, fellow Christians, and furthermore "to those who know the Law" (Rom 7:1). At this crucial point he addresses himself primarily to the Jewish Christians and their followers in the community at Rome, immediately mentioning Jewish marriage and divorce law. Whether or not he speaks to a Jerusalem audience as well or a specific problem within that community he deliberately assumes a shared experience with the Jewish Christians in Rome. By first examining this experience then raising the issues of doctrine which depend on these experiences, Paul hopes to convince his compatriots of his position.

Paul's basic point appears in 7:4-7, in which he says that since they, the Jewish Christians, have entered the Christian community, they are discharged from torah, dead to that which held them captive, so that they now have a new freedom. He has previously made a similar point to the gentile Christians in the Roman community, with regard to sin. But with the Jewish Christian community he finds it necessary to add a few personal notes, since like him they had come to Christianity from a Jewish past where torah is paramount. Romans 7 makes good sense when read as a personal statement.

Yet Romans 7:9-12 gives trouble:

> I was once alive apart from the law, but when the commandment came, sin revived and I died; the very commandment which promised life proved to be death to me. For sin, finding opportunity in the commandment,

---

(New York: Ktav, 1980), 67, although Professor Meyer sees an existential reason behind the rejection of righteousness in the law. See E. P. Sanders, *Paul, the Law and the Jewish People* (Philadelphia: Fortress, 1983), 76–77, 88–91.

> deceived me and by it killed me. So the law is holy, and the commandment is holy and just and good.

These verses appear to state that Paul gave up torah at a particular point and then returned to it. Paul nowhere explicitly states that he stopped observing the torah, and some New Testament scholars justifiably maintain that Paul continued to be an observant Jew throughout his life.[7] If this report is to be taken personally, Paul is saying that there was a period of time when he did not observe the torah. For some reason he returned to it and sin revived in him. The passage may, hence, contradict Paul's statements in Galatians and Corinthians where he says he gave up the law!

Let us consider the logical possibilities for making sense of this statement:

(1) Paul can be referring to prelapsarian times. A personal reading of Romans 7 would logically rule this meaning out. But in addition, Paul's language is clearly inappropriate for a description of paradise.[8]

(2) "Apart from the law" may refer to the time before Paul reached the age of legal majority (i.e., what would later be called *bar mitzvah*), but this seems artificial because Paul's minority in torah learning, like every other child's, would have made him subject to the torah before he became responsible for keeping torah.[9]

(3) There may have been a time before Paul became a Pharisee when he did not keep the law. Acts 23:6 records that Paul came from a Pharisaic family in Tarsus but several scholars have questioned the meaning of being a Pharisee in the Diaspora.[10] Paul might then be following a pattern of religious questing when he became a Pharisee, even before he entered Christianity. Though this theory has much to recommend it, I find no evidence supporting it in Paul's writing.

[7] E.g., W. D. Davies, *Paul and Rabbinic Judaism* (London: SPCK, 1948), 321.

[8] E. Gaugler, *Der Brief an die Römer* (Zurich: Zwingli, 1945), 233; F. J. Leenhardt, *L'Épître de St. Paul aux Romains* (Paris: Delachaux et Niestle, 1957). 106; P. Althaus, *Der Brief an die Römer*, NTD 6 (Göttingen: Vandenhoeck & Ruprecht, 1953), 65, 221.

[9] This suggestion has been often made. See, e.g., Michel, *Römerbrief.*

[10] Claude G. Montefiore, "Rabbinic Judaism and the Epistles of St. Paul," *JQR* 13 (1900): 161–217; idem, *Judaism and St. Paul* (London: Max Goschen, 1914). See also James W. Parkes, *Jesus, Paul, and the Jews* (London: SCM Press, 1934).

(4) Paul may be describing his life as a Pharisee when he talks about his inability to do the good that he wants: though the torah is good and holy, it led him to some wrong conclusions and, therefore, needs to be revalued. Paul's statements of the blamelessness of his behavior as a Pharisee in Galatians 1 and Philippians 3 may argue against understanding Romans 7 as referring to his Pharisaic days, but this is not conclusive since Paul may have been guilty of no infraction against torah, yet had a "guilty conscience" while he was a Pharisee. Some modern converts report a great dissatisfaction with their previous life retrospectively, so the interpretation may have some plausibility but, in that case, his statement of being outside the torah is too obscure for us to unravel. Of course, the most cogent argument against this position is that Paul had a "robust conscience."[11] Paul's discussion of these issues will prove to be less ethereal and more practical, as I will show below.

(5) Paul may be describing his experience with torah after his conversion. This is not a new interpretation: Augustine and various other Latin fathers, as well as Luther, Calvin, Barth, Nygren, and Cranfield among others have read Paul in this way. I will try to show that this is in fact the most profitable possibility.

The strongest and most often raised objection to understanding Romans 7 as Paul's experience after conversion comes from interpreting Romans 8. Many scholars have noted that the two sections naturally set each other off, so that chapter 7 describes a person under torah, while chapter 8 describes a person redeemed by grace. But it does not necessarily follow that Paul is distinguishing between Judaism and Christianity. He may just as easily be talking about the distinction between two types of Christianity, being under torah as a Christian and being saved

[11] Krister Stendahl, "Paul and the Introspective Conscience of the West." Originally a paper delivered before the annual meeting of the American Psychological Association, the article was published first in *HTR* 56 (1963): 199–215. It subsequently appeared in many places, including Professor Stendahl's own book *Paul Among Jews and Gentiles and Other Essays* (Philadelphia: Fortress, 1976). While I would maintain that understanding the psychological concomitants of Paul's conversion is crucial to understanding Paul, Professor Stendahl's observations about psychoanalytic and existential positions are well founded. Other aspects of contemporary psychology are far more helpful than psychoanalysis in understanding Paul. See my *Rebecca's Children: Judaism and Christianity in the Roman World* (Cambridge, Mass.: Harvard University Press, 1986), 96–116.

by faith as a Christian, for the distinction between the two religions was hardly clear in Paul's day. The sense is apposite because he is trying to convince Jewish Christians of his personal view of salvation by faith. Since Paul is a kind of Jewish Christian (albeit an unorthodox one), Paul may be speaking as a Jewish Christian to other Jewish Christians about the value of torah to Christians. In 8:3 when Paul describes torah, he can be describing both pre-Christian and Christian observance of torah from the point of view of a Christian. If so, what he would be saying is that torah has no positive value for salvation even for the Christian redeemed, even though it may continue meaningful as prophecy and divinely directed history. This is precisely what he has said many times before. But to understand what he means in saying he returned to the law we must return to Paul's discussions of Jewish ceremonies.

The Weak and the Strong in Corinth

Evidence that Paul did change his opinions about observing the ceremonial laws of the torah comes from his famous statement about his devotion to his mission:

> To the Jews I became as a Jew, in order to win Jews; to those under the law I became as one under the law—though not being myself under the law—that I might win those under the law. To those outside the law I became as one outside the law—not being without law toward God but under the law of Christ—that I might win those outside the law. To the weak I became weak, that I might win the weak. I have become all things to all men, that I might by all means save some. (1 Cor 9:20-22)

It is puzzling here for Paul to claim participation in a Jewish mission as well as a gentile one. The context of Paul's statements is crucial for understanding his referents. In fact, it seems to me that Paul is not discussing a Jewish mission so much as his attempt to mollify Jewish Christian criticism, as I shall explain.

Paul is not just discussing torah in general or how to honor local customs while missionizing. He is discussing the issue of the "weak" and the "strong," his terms for parties in the controversy about things sacrificed to idols (εἰδωλόθυτα), the same issue that Paul takes up again in Romans. He admits to abridging torah when he mentions his own behavior, for only someone who felt torah to have a limited role would be able to say that he merely followed the conventions of the community he was visiting. A Jew fully following torah does not have this choice.

Many scholars have pointed to the idealism of Paul's ethical principles in these passages. But few scholars have pointed out that the passage appears as well to be an apology of Paul's own behavior: "This is my defense (ἀπολογία) to those who would examine me" (1 Cor 9:3). Paul's defense must surely be against those who saw this behavior as transgression or apostasy.[12] A very likely possibility, then, has been insufficiently investigated in New Testament literature: *In Romans 7:9 Paul may be reflecting on his personal experience after giving up serious allegiance to the ceremonial torah. However, he still saw a reason to return to various customs afterwards, as a courtesy to those whose sensibilities might be offended by his private beliefs. That moment was the crucial one in which sin again entered his actions. Indeed, as we shall see, it is a significant factor in his troubles within the Jewish and Jewish Christian community.*

Paul's position about observing torah is spelled out as often in terms of ritual requirements as it is in terms of principles. This is in keeping with the Pharisaic approach to the problem of law. Moral principles are adduced through legal principles or cases, which become boundary marking precedents for the community. Paul often uses the same method for discussing the overriding principles. Paul warns the Corinthians not to eat meat sacrificed to idols. Paul approves of eating meat at another's house (even if the ritual circumstances of its slaughter are not known), yet he disapproves of sharing in the sacrificial meal at a public temple service of a pagan cult. Christians must not be seen at idolatrous sacrifices because this gives the impression that Christians still believe in the idols. Though pagan gods have no real existence, behind them are demons tempting the righteous to destruction, because those who eat the pagan sacrifices become communal partners (κοινόνοι) with the demons (1 Cor 10:18-22). This warning is, as we shall see, consonant with (though less stringent than) the standard rabbinic warnings about the dangers of idolatry, which Paul apparently learned in his Pharisaic past.

[12] Furthermore, as John C. Hurd Jr. has pointed out so clearly, the entire passage must be part of one letter, not several letter fragments. See *The Origin of 1 Corinthians* (London: SPCK, 1965; new ed., Macon, Ga.: Mercer University Press, 1985). But are the opponents Jews or other Christians and what precisely is the charge? The opponents of Paul and his gentile Christians in Corinth are likely to be Jewish Christians rather than Jews because, as Peter Richardson has pointed out, there is little explicitly "Anti-Judaistic" language in 1 Corinthians, especially by comparison with Galatians, for instance. See "On the Absence of 'Anti-Judaism' in 1 Corinthians," in *Anti-Judaism in Early Christianity*, vol. 1, *Paul and the Gospels*, ed. P. Richardson and D. Granskou (Waterloo, Ont.: Wilfred Laurier University Press, 1986), 59–74.

In Galatians 2:11-12 Paul says that he opposed Cephas and James. Cephas ate with gentiles, but then drew back and separated himself, fearing "the circumcision party." Paul criticizes Cephas for changing his stance and jeopardizing the unity of the Christian community. There is a crucial difference between Paul and Cephas. For Cephas the change in practice was motivated by indecision about the value of torah; for Paul, who had clarified his opinion about the limitations of torah, the issue was not the distinction in purity between Jews and gentiles but church unity. Paul would not tolerate any distinctions between the saved within the Christian community and, one assumes, he would not have altered his practice for the purpose of making distinctions between Christians, only for removing them.

This has obvious repercussions in how Peter and Paul would have analyzed the question of food laws. For Peter (Cephas) in the Pauline letter as well as the Peter described by Luke, the issue might well have been the continuance of the kosher laws per se, as Acts maintains. But for Paul, the basic issue was much narrower: the correct procedure for eating with gentiles. Although eating only with one's coreligionists is not a law explicitly enjoined on Jews, Paul, when he was a Pharisee, would not have eaten either with gentiles or impure Jews, because they carried ritual impurities to the table. This position is an extreme on the spectrum of possible Jewish approaches to dietary law, because the Pharisees were noted for their punctilious observance of food laws. From his Pharisaic past Paul also learned how important table fellowship is for unifying a community. Paul carried "the oral, unwritten law" and his legal acumen into his new community, but he left the rabbinic solutions behind.

Although Jewish commensality was frequently noted by Roman and Greek writers, we do not know exactly how ordinary Jews, as opposed to strict Pharisees, observed the dietary laws in the first century. There was obviously a range of practice which we cannot precisely define, since we have to rely on the mishnaic laws, codified a century and a half after Paul, from the point of view of the successors to the Pharisees.

We can get some hints from rabbinic literature. It is too inexact to consider that the issue separating Peter and Paul is *kashrut*, as many scholars have done.[13] The issue in Paul's community is how Jews may eat with gentiles, which is a more clearly defined problem. Rabbinic law

[13] See the new discussion of food laws in regard to Jesus in E. P Sanders, *Jesus and Judaism* (Philadelphia: Fortress, 1985), 175–221.

actually discusses a similar problem in mentioning the kind of foodstuffs produced by gentiles which may be eaten. Mishnah Avodah Zarah 2:3 specifically mentions that gentile wine and meat offered to idols should not be eaten:

> These things that belong to gentiles are forbidden, and it is forbidden to have any benefit at all from them: wine, or the vinegar of gentiles that at first was wine. . . . Flesh that is entering in unto an idol is permitted, but what comes forth is forbidden, for it as the sacrifices of the dead (Ps 106:29)—the words of Rabbi Akiba.

The issue here is not *kashrut* but avoiding foodstuff used in idolatrous service. The rules could not overrule the other laws of *kashrut*. A Jew who eats foodstuffs produced or marketed by gentiles is assumed to be following the rules of *kashrut*. Eating meat which has been dedicated at a temple is thus forbidden, though eating meat obtained from gentiles itself is not. This leniency in regard to meat is usually attributed to rabbinic attention to economic hardship. Since meat was too great a luxury to be wasted, some compromise means of avoiding the stigma of idolatry (and thus making use of the meat) were deemed appropriate. Such leniency is often characteristic of rabbinic writings.

Buying and using gentile wine is forbidden because it is assumed to have been used for a libation. The "sacrifices of the dead" are probably discussed in relation to all gentile foodstuffs and are elsewhere mentioned both by R. Akiba (d. 135 C.E.) and R. Simeon (Aboth 3:3; see also Ps 106:28; Prov 21:27; 15:8). By the mid- and late second century, these reviled gentile customs probably referred to the commemorative libations for heroes and ancestors, which were frequent at Greco-Roman dinners, and which evidently displeased the rabbis. This may also mean that the very central rite of Christianity, the Lord's Supper, had attracted rabbinic suspicion, since it commemorates a person who died and is worshiped as a God. (The other differences between Christian and pagan dinner customs would then obviously have been overlooked.)

Much can be learned of the rites of first-century Judaism by comparing the differing solutions to the problem in the various Jewish and Christian communities. The rabbis may well be codifying in the second century what was common practice in the first. For sure, a Pharisee who observed the purity rules and tithes would have difficulty eating with any Jew who did not observe these rules. We can speculate about other possible areas of conflict between Paul's congregations and a variety of Jewish Christians. If a Jewish Christian were observing rules about wine, he might have insisted that the Eucharist be dispensed by a Jew to avoid the problems of a gentile serving wine. Whatever else may have been at issue, Paul certainly had to deal with the questions of serving meat and wine.

Not stated explicitly in the mishnaic laws but an implication of the discussion is that, whenever there is a question, many Jews would entirely avoid eating with gentiles, as Cephas himself does, or, as a lesser safeguard, limit eating with gentiles to vegetables, bread, and fish, (assuming that the other laws could be observed). Since "ritual vegetarianism" avoids issues of slaughter and possibly even some of the issues of tithing, which had specific implications for produce of Israel's land, vegetarianism continues to be a natural choice available to some pious Jews in a similar situation today. The New Testament seems to bear out that this common ritual strategy was also in use in the Christian community, in discussing the difficulties between the "strong" and the "weak."

The "Weak" and the "Strong" in Romans and Elsewhere

In Romans Paul discusses his gentile converts with a primarily Jewish audience, stating his own private opinions about the further relevance of food laws. He is not dealing with a different issue in Romans so much as the converse side of the issue in Corinth. In Corinth, Paul specifically addressed a gentile clientele, answering their query by explaining Jewish sensibilities about idolatry and its relevance to the gentile church. Thus, the problem in Corinth may be that gentile Christians are attending pagan shrines. But that is not the whole story. The rest of the problem is that, whatever they are doing, they are being chastised for their behavior by some Jewish Christians who refuse to eat with them because they may be attending pagan ceremonies. Paul explains to them what the issue is. Though he does not personally see the relevance of dietary prohibitions in Christianity, he cautions the gentiles against falling back into idol worship (1 Cor 8; 10:25-30). According to the Mishnah, idolatry is exactly the issue that necessitated the prohibition against eating gentile meat and wine, so Paul is merely expressing a Pharisaic sentiment to his gentile audience, as he clarifies the issue to them. But he has brought his Pharisaic sensibility into an entirely new environment, where the issue has become acute as a communal problem, rather than a problem for an individual Jew as he pursued his livelihood.

In Romans Paul explains to Jewish Christians why his radical opinion of food laws is correct.[14] Speaking about food prohibitions generally in Romans 14:1-6, 15-20, Paul argues that all Christians should eat together without fear. He addresses two different groups: the "weak," who eat only vegetables with their comrades, and the "strong," who eat together with their fellow Christians with no qualms or reservations. As we have seen, the "strong" position represents mostly gentile Christians while the "weak" position in Romans and Corinthians clearly reflects Jewish sensibilities. That does not mean that they are strict ethnic denominations, for Paul himself is an exception to the rule. Any person, Jew or gentile, who embraced the "strong" position would naturally point out that the rule applies to all food prohibitions and all religious holidays, hence it must apply to all parties within the church.

No matter which audience he addresses, Paul cautions against scorning the other position, which is consonant with his general theme of the danger of pride in Romans and his constant interest in the unity of the church.

In harkening to the criticism that gentile Christians may be idolaters, Peter (Cephas) then is probably urging one position from among the spectrum of ordinary Jewish practice found in the early Christian community. Ironically, the New Testament becomes a source for Jewish history. It inadvertently records some of the ritual strategies available to ordinary Jews in the first century for dealing with commensality with gentiles, the very kind of evidence which we cannot get from the Mishnah, because it deals in legal theory and is redacted a century and a half after Paul. The "weak" and "strong" positions may even have originated before Christianity, among more acculturated Jews, for instance, who were forced by commerce into closer association with gentiles. But the Jewish legal issue is clearly evidenced by Christianity alone in the first century because of two facts: (1) the Mishnah did not approve of the

[14] Paul Minear in his book *The Obedience of Faith: The Purposes of Paul in the Epistle to the Romans* (Napierville, Ill.: Alec Allenson, 1971) has suggested the relevance of these passages to Jewish food laws, but he does not sufficiently recognize that the basic issue is the rules about idolatry. Gerd Theissen, in his article "The Strong and the Weak in Corinth," from the 1974 German article, in *The Social Setting of Pauline Christianity: Essays on Corinth*, ed. and trans. J. H. Shütz (Philadelphia: Fortress, 1982), 121–43, has made very interesting suggestions about the gentile sociological situation in Corinth and has specially noted the generality of Paul's statements, but he has failed to unpack the basic Jewish custom underlying the controversies at Corinth and Rome.

violation of ritual status, so it would not discuss such open accommodations; and (2) avoiding meals with gentiles was not an appropriate communal strategy for Christianity, or at least, this is the position of Paul and his supporters.[15] Partial commensality appears to be the kind of practical solution which could have been precedented among diaspora Jews with sensitivity to dietary issues before the rise of Christianity.

So far as Paul is concerned even partial commensality is an inadequate ethical solution to the problem. His private opinion, that the rules are totally irrelevant now, is unique and radical, similar to the most acculturated position one can imagine in pre-Christian Judaism, though the ethical function of Paul's position is the same as the function of food laws among Jews: to preserve the unity of the community. Though Paul also represents a Jewish perspective in warning the Corinthians not to fall back into idol worship, his opinion of ritual observance certainly opposes his Pharisaic past and much of ordinary Judaism besides.

Paul's personal feelings are clearly with the "strong" (cf. "we the strong" in Rom 15:1), so he can confidently say that no food is unclean of itself, only to him who thinks it so (Rom 14:14). His personal opinion, perhaps a result of his vision of the crucified Christ, could be argued as communal rule according to his interpretation of Deuteronomy 21:23.

But, in his capacity as apostle he is prepared to compromise. He outlines two axioms, an ideological position of strength and a diplomatic principle of conciliation. All Christians should eat with each other, even if doing so means that the "strong" diplomatically avoid foods which the "weak" despise, a position which he argues to each side of the controversy (Rom 14:15; 1 Cor 8:12). Paul feels that the church's unity is more important than any food prohibitions or even the principle that all foods are clean: "Do not, for the sake of food, destroy the work of God" (Rom 14:20).

Paul's ideological position, as commonplace as it may seem to Christianity today, was an extreme position in his own time; even his diplomatic principle would have been controversial in the church, to say nothing about the Jewish community. The Apostolic Decree, as formulated in Acts 15:20, 29; 21:25, virtually sets aside the radical position of Paul, regardless of Acts' contention that Paul was a participant in the

[15] See Raymond E. Brown and John P. Meier, *Antioch and Rome: New Testament Cradles of Catholic Christianity* (Ramsey, N.J.: Paulist, 1983), for a discussion of the broad spectrum of Christian opinion on Jewish law.

decree.[16] Revelation (2:14, 20) predicts damnation for any who put a stumbling block in front of Israel by leading them to eat food sacrificed to idols. For the Didache, proper behavior includes keeping away from all food offered to idols. It uses language that is more reminiscent of the Mishnah than Paul's letters: "Now about food: undertake what you can. But keep strictly away from what is offered to idols, for that implies worship of dead gods" (6:3). The Didache exhorts Christians to observe as much of the dietary laws as possible. It even mirrors the mishnaic reference to worship of the dead, though it interprets the phrase differently, as pagan gods now known to be "dead." Throughout early church history, the dominant position is quite likely to have been more like the Didache and the Apostolic Decree, not Paul's ideological position.[17]

Paul's Accommodations

With his opinions, Paul could not have been a practicing Pharisee, though he might still consider himself a Jew and honor torah in other ways. Paul's ideological position could only be seen as yet more extreme by the Jewish community than by the Christian community, even a radical antinomian revolution. As C. K. Barrett points out, Paul is nowhere less Pharisaic than when he recommends that food laws are of no consequence. It is no wonder that Paul does not stress his position but counsels a diplomatic principle of conciliation.

Strangely enough, having come to a radical analysis of the situation, Paul's principle of reconciliation actually goes beyond the position of the "weak" in the opposite direction. If Acts is correct in regard to circumcision as well, Paul was likewise there willing to go beyond even his compromise position in order to preserve the unity of the church. He does the same with the issue of dietary rules. In 1 Corinthians Paul does not merely recommend that the "strong" be respectful of the misguided "weak" sensibilities; he swears not to eat any flesh, if eating flesh offends his fellow Christians. This oath is in the first person singular: "If meat offends my brother, *I will not eat meat forever, lest I offend my brother*" (1 Cor 8:13). There is no reason to believe that this oath was merely rhetorical. It is an honest obligation taken in writing. Since it was a written and

[16] H. Lietzmann, *The Beginnings of the Christian Church*, trans. L. B. Woolf (London: Lutterworth, 1937), 199.

[17] See the extremely helpful article, C. K. Barrett, "Things Sacrificed to Idols," in *Essays on Paul* (Philadelphia: Westminster, 1982), 40–59.

unambiguous pledge, it appears even to be valid in a rabbinic court (see m. Ned. 1).[18]

Using oaths in this way is a sensible ritual strategy in later Judaism, pledging to avoid a material of suspicious purity. Thus, Paul again evidences Jewish practice otherwise unmentioned in the earliest rabbinic writings but known from later ones. While the legal situation raised by communal meals in Christian communities is unusual for first-century Judaism, and while Paul personally may have felt that food laws were entirely irrelevant, and while Paul's compromise position may have been only to avoid meat when the idolatrous connection might tempt others to sin, he also can take the principle of reconciliation to its furthest extreme, by volunteering to abide by an even more conservative position, one that is stricter than either the "weak" Corinthians' position or the Jewish practice outlined in the Mishnah. But he goes much further than Pharisaism to make his point. By seeking the most stringent answers in matters of ritual, Paul takes the normal Pharisaic way to avoid a situation in which doubt could be thrown on his ritual status.

There must have been a strong reason for such an accommodation. Since Paul says specifically that he would swear to avoid offending his fellow Christian, he wants at the very least to appease the most conservative members of the Christian church. He may also have his fellow Jews in mind as well, for it is likely that first-century Jewish opinion contained legal positions far more conservative than the rabbinic one of the second century. To counter the charge that he is unclean or untrustworthy for having eaten meat sacrificed to idols, he swears that he is willing to become a total vegetarian. For even the most stringent Pharisee, this would have the effect of eliminating the issues of acceptable slaughter of meat, idolatry, and even tithes on fruit, leaving only the relatively minor problem of tithing vegetables, which was irrelevant outside of the land of Israel, in any case. But, in approaching Jerusalem, it would have had the effect of removing the major issue preventing Paul's full acceptance by observant Jews, whether they be Christians or not.

[18] It is an oath rather than a vow, for it is a promise assumed by the person. See m. Shav. 3 and 4. The rabbinic desire to limit oaths and vows to those that can be taken seriously has been discussed by Saul Lieberman, in "Oaths and Vows (in Ordinary Speech)," in *Greek in Jewish Palestine: Studies in the Life and Manners of Jewish Palestine in the II–IV Centuries C.E.* (New York: Feldheim, 1965), 115–43.

Acts also maintains that Paul took a nazirite vow (Acts 18:18) in Cenchreae on his way to Jerusalem. Although Acts does not specify what the oath was, and the text allows for the alternative interpretation that Aquila performed the rite, Acts appears to be describing the unique conditions under which (temporary) nazirite vows can be terminated, if a minimum of a month had passed after the vow.[19] After cutting his hair, Paul needed to bring a temple offering, which would mark the completion of the vow. Acts implies that this is what happened. It records that Paul was indicted in Jerusalem in spite of his attempt to prove his loyalty to Judaism by paying for the guilt and thanksgiving sacrifices of four other nazirites who underwent purification with him (Acts 21:17-26).

We do not know if Acts is historically accurate. But paying for the sacrifices of others completing nazirite vows was a contemporary Jewish piety and would have been understood as a desire for communal respect.[20] Of course, for Paul to have taken on a nazirite vow would have had further strong implications beyond the immediate context of table fellowship with gentiles, but taking on either obligation would have meant subjecting himself to the torah in precisely the area that he claimed is irrelevant to Christian salvation. However, when salvation itself is not the issue, and especially when church unity is the issue, Paul seems far more ready to compromise. The compromise may even have been, as Acts seems to maintain, that if the Jewish Christians will abide by the apostolic decree, so will Paul, though his own position is far more radical. Although this is a compromise ritual position, it is quite important to note that Paul is not compromising his ideological position. Since Paul believes that the ritual is of no importance for salvation, whether Paul observes it or not is entirely irrelevant.

[19] There are many difficulties with this passage. Cutting one's hair so far from Jerusalem presents a kind of problem, since there is no example of the ritual being performed outside of Jerusalem. Furthermore, the grammar of the passage is so loose that it is possible to understand the subject of the shearing to be Aquila rather than Paul. This seems rather far-fetched given the subsequent narration, so, for the sake of argument, Paul's participation (which is the usual interpretation) is assumed. But, as above, Acts' witness is used as support but nothing definitive is concluded from Acts' narrative itself. See Ernst Hänchen, *Die Apostelgeschichte* (Göttingen: Vandenhoeck & Ruprecht, 1955), 483; and Robert Jewett, *A Chronology of Paul's Life* (Philadelphia: Fortress, 1979), 18.

[20] See m. Naz., esp. chap. 1, and David Weiss-Halivni, "On the Supposed Anti-Asceticism or Anti-Naziritism of Simon the Just," *JQR* 58 (1968): 243–52.

I suppose this means that Paul is willing to compromise in ways that most modern scholars would find impossible. But the point here is that the compromise is itself a normal Jewish way of handling differences in ritual practice, and does not necessarily reflect Paul's personal position. In Acts this conflict is expressly linked to Paul's last visit to Jerusalem and his pilgrimage to the temple. This makes perfect sense if the halakic strategy of Paul's behavior is admitted. Yet even Paul's most conservative behavior does not assuage the ire of some of the Jews, who accuse him of teaching others to overthrow the torah. Acts, of course, implies that the charge is false. Although Acts again is not above reproach as an historical source, it may be correct in portraying Paul's decision at this juncture, for Paul himself tries to avoid open conflict (e.g., in 2 Cor 1:23).

The journey to Jerusalem is also a logical place for these issues to come to a head. The charge against Paul is also logical, given Acts' historical scheme, because Paul comes close actually to overthrowing the torah in his opinion of its inapplicability to food laws or circumcision. From his own letters we know that Paul's conservative Christian brethren are angry (and Paul himself is angry as well). The Jewish community could only have reflected still more conservative sentiments.

If we consider the nature of the charge, there is a sense in which it is true from the Jewish point of view. Paul could himself have lived as a Jew "in order to win Jews" in Jewish communities, and he could also have lived "lawlessly" around gentiles in order to win them (1 Cor 9:20). But he could not have done both at once, which is exactly the problem when Jewish and gentile Christians ate together. In Jerusalem, with both communities present, Paul could not have practiced both. Nor would the strategy have worked as well where the Pharisaic issues of tithing fruits and vegetables were relevant. Paul's compromise fails when members of the two communities eat together or directly confront each other. It can only work if there is mutual support, no boasting of one group over the other. And that is why Paul is so careful to point out the sin of boasting.

Thus, the real issue is not merely what Paul himself did; it was that his practice became the gentile community's definition of piety. That standard differed radically from the standard practiced in the Jewish Christian community. The result, according to Acts, is that Paul is put in danger by the allegations of Jewish Christians who denounce him to the Jewish authorities. This begins the process which brings him eventually to Rome and, as legend has it, to his martyrdom.

Even without accepting Acts' contentions, it is logical that one place where Paul could not have avoided open conflict is on his trip to Jerusalem. Paul's insistence on his gentile brother, Titus, as well as other unnamed members of his party, is likely to have been a provocation (2 Cor 8:20-23). Of course, Paul not only left open the road for compromise, by bringing gentiles with him, he also made sure that his actual position was properly represented. He offered both the compromise and the confrontation. But to see the full issue in Romans 7, one must realize that Paul offered a clear compromise (which was rejected by the most conservative members of the church in Jerusalem).

Paul's Clarification to the Gentile Community

Paul's actions in swearing not to eat meat and possibly in taking a nazirite vow, while troublesome to almost anyone in the church, would even be troublesome to his followers "the strong," because his promise not to eat flesh appears to observe Jewish law, reversing his previous position. Questions of this nature had been raised in Galatians, when it seemed to some converts that Paul was preaching circumcision (Gal 1:10). If Acts' account of Timothy's circumcision is to be believed, the question is all the sharper, because Paul did circumcise Timothy, who looked like a gentile, for all intents and purposes, although he was really an uncircumcised Jew. There is no reason why Acts could not be right in maintaining all of this. But, in any event, Paul's conciliatory actions put in doubt Paul's position outlined in Corinthians that the ritual laws are no longer relevant in Christianity.

Though much must remain in doubt, the importance of the symbolic messages which Paul was sending throughout the Jewish world must be noted. Paul's vow in 1 Corinthians 8:32 had halakic consequences and would itself have led to ambiguities in his position on his Christian freedom. As Paul himself says in Galatians, where the primary issue is circumcision but where the food laws surface immediately: "But if, in our endeavor to be justified in Christ, we ourselves were found to be sinners, is Christ then an agent of sin? Certainly not! But if I build up again those things which I tore down, then I prove myself a transgressor" (Gal 2:17-18). It was precisely the charge that Paul had again subjected himself to the law, hence accepted the designation transgressor, which Paul attempted to rebut in Romans.[21]

Of course, in his role as apostle Paul was not being inconsistent in retreating to a diplomatic compromise with the conservative position in the church. But this consistency would not necessarily have been self-evident to anyone else, especially in the light of the Jewish-Christian opposition to Paul's view of community. The fact that we ourselves do not know exactly what happened is probably no different from the perspective of most of Paul's contemporary observers. Paul would need to resolve the seeming contradiction between his conciliatory actions and his ideological position, especially since these are complex legal issues which might be argued and construed in a number of ways.

Paul uses his letter to the Romans to attempt his clarification and justification and, in so doing, meditates on the value of law (the apostolic decree as well as Pharisaic interpretations?). Thus, Romans 7 describes neither a psychoanalytic nor an existential predicament. Rather it is the apologia of a pragmatic man who formulated a radical solution to the problem of food laws in Christianity, but who, as an apostle, was willing to compromise when his solution was not accepted by the more conservative members of the Christian community.

Romans 7

Let us read Romans 7 with this historical context in mind, to see if it makes a new, more plausible sense of the puzzling soliloquy which comes just before Paul's discussion of "weak" and "strong":

> I was once alive apart from the law, but when the commandment came, sin revived and I died; the very commandment which promised life proved to be death for me. For sin, finding opportunity in the commandment, deceived me and by it killed me. So the law is holy, and the commandment is holy and just and good. Did that which is good, then, bring death to me? By no means! It was sin working death in me through what is good, in order that sin might be shown to be sin, and through the commandment might become sinful beyond measure. . . . I do not understand my own actions. For I do not do what I want, but I do the

[21] For a different but related interpretation of this passage, see Lloyd Gaston, "Paul and the Law in Galatians Two and Three," in P. Richardson, ed., *Anti-Judaism in Early Christianity*, 1:37–58; and John Gager, *The Origins of Anti-Semitism: Attitudes toward Judaism in Pagan and Christian Antiquity* (New York: Oxford University Press, 1983), 233.

> very thing I hate. Now if I do what I do not want, I agree that the law is good. . . . (Rom 7:9-15)

While the death that Paul mentions may be linked to his baptism, as many scholars have noted, such an explanation does not take the chronology of Romans 7:9-12 very seriously. Certainly Paul mentions rebirth when describing his baptism. But chronologically the death Paul mentions here has to come after his conversion, so it may just as easily be an expression of his risk of eternal life after baptism, if his faith in Christ fails, or even an anticipation of capital punishment if charges against him are sustained. We shall never know precisely what the death is that Paul mentions. But it is clear that it is the overthrow of all his plans.

In other words Paul is talking about his experience as a Christian after already rejecting the claim of Jewish observance. He begins *in medias res* as a convert without the law: ". . . since I was once alive apart from the law." Sin is thereafter pictured as "deceiving" and bringing to death, "finding an opportunity in the commandment" (7:11). Paul's opinion in Romans 7 is that the law is good although, since flesh is under the sway of sin, and the law is concerned with flesh, it also brings one to death. This observation may easily be literal as well, based on legal difficulties in Paul's life: he is aware that he can be judged an apostate by means of the law. There is no reason not to suppose that the phrases are meant literally as well as metaphorically. It is misleading to jump immediately to a theological analysis of the human situation when Paul is underlining his personal experience so emphatically by use of the personal pronoun. Sin's deception of him through the law began not when he was a Pharisee and not when he lived without the law as a gentile Christian but afterwards, when as a Christian he compromised with it, because he was so concerned to achieve Christian unity by trying to heal the breach between Jewish and gentile Christians. By journeying to Jerusalem, which is where Paul is to go before he goes to Rome, he would have been subjecting himself to scrutiny by torah-true Christians and Jews alike. Thus, to journey to Jerusalem was to put himself in real danger and to realize that he was caught in a situation which might prove his downfall.

In spite of the dire personal straits Paul has encountered or may be anticipating, this meditation is a softening of Paul's other positions on law. Previously Paul virtually equated law both with sin and the flesh (see Gal 3:19; Rom 3:20; 4:15; 5:20; 6), in keeping with a strictly apocalyptic view of the fallen world and its depraved inhabitants. But this crucial passage, based on Paul's personal post-conversion experience with the law, represents a less radical intuition about the place of law. The law is just, but the flesh brings about law's failure to give life.[22] Does Paul say this out of a very human desire to persuade his readers, since the Roman church probably contains more Jewish-Christians than do the other churches to which he has sent letters? Perhaps. He may anticipate an equally mixed audience in Jerusalem, where his letter could have preceded him. But it is also likely that the mixed audience, consisting of Jewish and gentile Christians, also presents Paul with a greater opportunity: to try to unite the entire Christian community with a more thorough treatment of the issue of law and Israel's place in God's plan.

Paul's attempt to mediate between the different customs in the early church has created misunderstandings so great as to put him in danger. Placed in this position, his conclusion is breathtaking. He shows that his personal difficulty is neither accidental nor abstractly existential. It is the same material predicament of all Christians under the torah. He discusses the good that he wishes to do and suggests that attempting to follow the ceremonial torah as a Christian inevitably leads to sin, whether intentional or not: "For I do not do what I want . . . it is no longer I that do it, but sin which dwells in me" (7:15, 17). This may be an another admission to his listeners that he is not recanting his position on law but that he did not at first foresee that the effects of his compromise attempts might put him in real danger (7:15) (though obviously he has no need to feel guilty about it). At the same time, he reiterates, as he always believed, both that the torah is good and that he enjoyed fulfilling it, but Christ has saved him from observing those laws after he died and was reborn in Christ.

Paul is not a man who was constitutionally unable to practice the law. In this passage he appears to a person who is tempted to return to the law, since he enjoyed it, and since it might save some internal dissension. He represents the struggle in this way: "For I delight in the law of God in my inmost self, but I see in my members another law at war with the law of my mind and making me captive to the law of sin which dwells in my members" (7:22-23). Though the law is holy and good, the ceremonial laws, which in dealing with circumcision and proper food

[22] See Sanders, *Paul, The Law and the Jewish People*, 70–80, for the perception that Paul is pulling back from his earlier positions.

are literally and metaphorically the laws of his members, have brought him under the sway of sin. Indeed, keeping the law, for whatever reasons of conciliation, is not a means for his salvation, though the torah is good and holy and points out what sin is. His perception that the law of sin dwells in his members arises from his diplomatic struggle to find an accommodation to ceremonial laws in the new Christian community. Stendahl is right that the problem in Romans is salvation history, but he is right only when one realizes that the crisis which precipitated the discussion is a personal and legal crisis in Paul's life.

A New Vocabulary for Discussing Torah

No Jew or gentile observer of torah previous to Paul made a systematic distinction between ceremonial and ethical laws. Torah was a body of divine wisdom that had to be adopted in its entirety. The only question was how torah was to be interpreted; it was here, by means of allegory, pesher, or midrash that first-century Jews found grounds for latitude in practice. Even though Paul had given up Pharisaism, and even though the laws of idolatry were part of oral torah, Paul did not simply recommend that his community observe the ethical requirements of torah while ignoring the ceremonial parts. There was little precedent or vocabulary for such a policy. Yet, Paul's argument has that force. Paul begins with his own situation about the law and in chapter 8 discusses a relationship between sin and the law, based on his own post-conversion experience. There is no ready-made vocabulary on which Paul can depend. Paul takes an unprecedented position when he says: "With the mind, I serve the law of God, but with the flesh, the law of sin" (7:25b). He thus invents a new vocabulary for dealing with his problem. Though Paul's mature position is unique, it does have certain affinities with the extreme allegorizers to whom Philo gives credit for having found philosophical wisdom but whom he described as trying to be souls without bodies:

> There are some who, regarding laws in their literal sense in the light of symbols of matters belonging to the intellect, are overpunctilious about the latter, while treating the former with easy-going neglect. Such men I for my part should blame for handling the matter in too easy and off-hand a manner: they ought to have given careful attention to both aims, to a more full and exact investigation of what is not seen and in what is seen to be stewards without reproach. As it is, as though they were living alone by themselves in a wilderness, or as though they had become disembodied souls, and knew neither city nor village nor household nor

> any company of human beings at all, overlooking all that the mass of men regard, they explore reality in its naked absoluteness. These men are taught by the sacred word to have thoughts for good repute, and to let go nothing that is part of the customs fixed by divinely empowered men greater than those of our time. (*Migr.* 89–93)

Although Philo's criticism of the extreme allegorizers is that they ignore their ordinary daily life, imagining themselves to be disembodied souls without bodies, he tempers his criticism with an appreciation of their higher purpose. He does not believe them to be merely apostates; rather they make the mistake of thinking that they live in the wilderness and "overlook all that the mass of men regard." This would suggest that Philo, had he known Paul, would have considered him one of the radical allegorizers. Though Paul certainly did not ignore the body, he preached its transcendence through mystical identification with Christ not Torah, opening him to a criticism similar to Philo's criticism of the extreme allegorizers, in claiming to have left behind the body of flesh and entered the one spiritual body of the Lord (1 Cor 6:17). Furthermore, Philo's observation that extreme allegorizers "overlook what the mass of men regard" would be an understandable criticism of Paul from a Jewish perspective, and probably represents the closest we will get to a contemporary diaspora Jewish reaction to Pauline Christianity. If Acts is right, both Jewish-Christians and Palestinian Jews were far more critical of Paul's view of the ritual aspects of torah than Philo would have been, as long as no apostasy was committed.

Paul would have been well advised to have remained figuratively "in the wilderness" and stayed away from Jerusalem. But this is exactly what Paul could not do, because he hoped to bring an acceptable collection and, in gaining acceptance for his gentile brethren, produce a single church community. He must have seen this issue as an attempt to heal the incipient fissure in the church, though, ironically it was just this desire to make sure that Jewish and gentile Christians could eat and pray together which put him in greater danger than any radical allegorizer. The irony is that Paul's desire for Christian unity, not specifically his thoughts about torah, brought him into danger, since he apparently could have stayed out of harm's way by not going to Jerusalem.

Thus Romans 8 still does deal with the contrast between being under law and being under faith. But it is a personal distinction in Paul's life as a Christian. There was a period in Paul's Christian life during which he struggled with the torah "in the flesh" as he says, before he understood that its true value was "in the spirit" as prophecies of the coming of the Christ: "in order that the just requirement of the law might be fulfilled in us, who walk not according to the flesh but according to the spirit" (8:4). During this period he may have observed the torah in Jewish-Christian contexts, while ignoring it in his gentile mission. But this was an unacceptable compromise to those who still valued the torah because episodic observance was inconsistent. Paul's final ideological point is always that, although the law is spiritual, it is played out in the flesh, which is unredeemable. Faith is spiritual and conquers fleshly attempts at salvation. Therefore, the law has been replaced by faith (8:2). All of this is a clearly understandable intellectual position, but it is not possible to make a single acceptable ritual practice out of it. Therefore whenever Paul encountered a mixed group of Christians, as when he entered Jerusalem and deliberately produced one, he was doomed to be misunderstood by one side or the other, if judged on the basis of his ritual actions.

> For the law of the Spirit of life in Christ Jesus has set me free from the law of sin and death. For God has done what the law, weakened by the flesh, could not do: sending his own Son in the likeness of sinful flesh and for sin, he condemned sin in the flesh. (8:2-3)

It is further ironic that Paul should make his strongest statements about the relationship between torah and grace in Romans, in the context of having to justify a seeming retreat. But he conquers the bitterness of his misfortune. Rather he turns that reverse of fortune into an occasion for meditation. By means of his personal predicament, he illustrates that it is the flesh and not the law itself which causes the law to bring men to death rather than to life. But his rhetoric has the added advantage of addressing his Jewish-Christian listeners precisely in the same position, those who were wondering how and whether to keep the law of the flesh while they had already become persons of the spirit. While Paul does not begin with an evaluation of the torah in general so much as describe his experience, he feels he can generalize in warning them that their new Christian commitment has implications vis-à-vis all Jewish Christians' previously learned attitude toward torah. While one can avoid the foods which offend the weak's sensibilities, and one can even swear to avoid all flesh in order to satisfy those who demand it, it is faith and not torah which brings about salvation. He may even be warning his readers that his attempt to compromise is unwise.

In Romans Paul is talking about his own experience. Like many Jews of his time, he argues about the intention and symbolic meanings of the rites of Jewish practice. His later readers, however, who had lost the fine appreciation for the importance of the symbolic value of ritual in Jewish life, jump immediately to the theological implications. Paul's reflections are a perfectly natural aspect of a strongly debated issue of Jewish law in Christianity, which has subsequently been lost because later Christians no longer felt the legal implications of his actions in so poignant a way. Paul, however, felt that his experience was relevant to the legal point because he was counseling tolerance of "antinomian" Christians to the Jewish Christians of Rome and vice versa. He was pointedly asking Jewish Christians to understand his behavior on the basis of a presumed shared experience, a move which has rhetorical motivations as well as personal and doctrinal implications. In doing so he illustrates an entirely new understanding of the value of torah. But any doctrinal conclusions from Paul's discussion must begin with an appreciation of Paul's very personal voice and the reasons for his apologia. Paul's intention was to meld two communities together; the result was that he himself was brought into danger. Paul's own commitment to Christian unity and to bringing the Jewish and gentile wings of the church into fellowship spelled disaster for him. Though neither Jewish nor Christian tradition has sufficiently appreciated it, Paul's soliloquy in Romans 7 is the stuff of tragedy.

PART TWO

HEAVENLY ASCENT IN HELLENISTIC JUDAISM, EARLY CHRISTIANITY, AND THEIR ENVIRONMENT

ONE

THEORETICAL CONSIDERATIONS: THE CULTURAL BACKGROUND OF ASCENSION IN THE HELLENISTIC WORLD

Criticism of Reitzenstein[1] and the whole history of religions school has been the focus of scholarly concentration for many years.[2] In the course of time it has grown clear that they were misled. First, they have fallen victim to more than their share of misdated texts and provenances. But, more important perhaps is their contention that the Christology of the New Testament and, in particular, the Gospel of John has been deeply influenced by a pre-Christian, gnostic salvation myth.[3] In general, this theory presupposed the existence of a redeemer figure (sometimes called the Anthropos and combined with the Iranian-Indian idea of the primal man), who arrives on earth in corporeal form to reveal the fallen condition of souls, to uncover the saving gnosis of the soul's necessary liberation, and to show the way back to its original divine rest in heaven. This pre-Christian, gnostic myth of the redeemed redeemer, often combined with myths of the primal man, was believed by Reitzenstein and Bultmann to have been historicized by the Johannine Christian community

[1] *Die hellenistischen Mysterienreligionen nach ihren Grundgedanken und Wirkungen* (Leipzig: Teubner, 1910); *Hellenistic Mystery Religions: Their Basic Ideas and Significance*, trans. J. E. Steely, PTS Monographs 15 (Pittsburgh: Pickwick, 1978); *Poimandres: Studien zur Griechischägyptischen und frühchristlichen Literatur* (Leipzig: Teubner, 1904); *Das Iranische Erlösungsmysterium* (Bonn: Marcus & Weber, 1921). See C. Colpe, *Die Religionsgeschichtliche Schule: Darstellung und Kritik ihres Eildes vom gnostischen Erloscrmythus* (Göttingen: Vandenhoeck & Ruprecht, 1961) for complete bibliography.

[2] The most important summaries and histories of research in light of the history of religions school have been Colpe, *Die Religionsgeschichtliche Schule* and in English E. Yamauchi, *Pre-Christian Gnosticism: A Survey of the Proposed Evidences* (Grand Rapids: Eerdmans, 1973). The bibliography in each book is excellent.

[3] The foremost critic developing this position is, of course, R. Bultmann, *Das Evangelium des Johannes*, Meyer's Commentary (Göttingen: Vandenhoeck & Ruprecht, 1941), 1950–53 mit Ergänzungsheft.

which saw the events in the life of its Savior as the enactment of this myth in actual, historical form. There are many and admirable scholars who feel there is reason to continue believing in such a theory.[4] But most scholars find the evidence against it to be overwhelming. So preponderant is the evidence that it must be taken up in categories:

(1) *Pre-Christian*: The texts evincing the so-called salvation myth were rich and varied. But the "Hermetica," the "Hymn of the Pearl," the Mandaic and Manichaean evidence, the Avestan Yasht 22, even possibly the "Parables" of Enoch, when properly identified and dated, all turn out to be post-Christian. This forces most proponents to admit that the gnostic Redeemer myth appears nowhere in a pure form after the end of the first century.[5] However, this argument is misleading, for we do not find the complete pre-Christian, gnostic salvation myth anywhere before the first century either. Pre-Christian traditions about the messiah, Logos, Sophia, Anthropos, and the Angel of YHWH are all important for the study of the rise of Christianity and Gnosticism. But no one of them demonstrates the complete cycle of descent, revelation, and return, or even all the other traits ascribed to the salvation myth. This has convinced many (and among them myself) that the entirety is an ingenious product of modern scholarship, not a creation of the ancient mind.

(2) *Gnostic*: Criticism of this part of the argument is analogous to the failure to show the pre-Christian nature of the evidence. While many of the themes which are important to Reitzenstein become part of Gnosticism, there is no evidence that they are "gnostic" wherever they occur. The whole enterprise stands or falls on a clear definition of Gnosticism. Sadly, no convincing definition has yet appeared. The problem caused by this lack of consensus among scholars is best illustrated by the first international conference which was called specifically to find the definition. Meeting at Messina in 1965, the world's leading scholars of

[4] See, for instance, K. Rudolf, "Stand und Aufgaben in der Erforschung des Gnostizismus," in *Tagung für allgemeine Religionsgeschichte* (Jena: 1963; repr. in *Gnosis und Gnostizismus*, ed. K. Rudolf [Darmstadt: Wissenschaftliche Buchgesellschaft, 1975], 510–53) and his discussion of the evidence, as quoted in J. M. Robinson and Helmut Koester, *Trajectories through Early Christianity* (Philadelphia: Fortress, 1971), 264f. See also Yamauchi, *Pre-Christian Gnosticism*, chap. 1.

[5] W. Schmithals, *Gnosticism in Corinth: An Investigation of the Letters to the Corinthians*, trans. John E. Steely (Nashville: Abingdon, 1971), 79, an English translation of *Die Gnosis in Korinth*, FRLANT 66 (Göttingen: Vandenhoeck & Ruprecht, 1956).

Gnosticism agreed to distinguish between the full-fledged gnostic documents of the second century and a variety of related phenomena in the first century by calling the former "Gnosticism," the latter "gnosis." Thereafter agreement failed. There was no accord as to whether the first-century phenomena could be called proto-Gnosticism (already essentially gnostic) or merely pre-Gnosticism (containing elements which would appear in Gnosticism).[6] No one single element was taken by the scholars to be the sine qua non or definitive factor producing Gnosticism. This is because none of the major contenders as the essence of Gnosticism (i.e., dualism, anti-cosmism) can be demonstrated to pervade the documentary evidence before the second century. To make matters worse, the adjective derived from either gnosis or Gnosticism is "gnostic," obfuscating what any particular scholar means unless he specifically chooses to clarify the issue. The second meeting of scholars of Gnosticism in New Haven in 1978 generally avoided these difficult questions and concentrated on the fascinating and as yet little-studied texts from Nag Hammadi (a fourth-century find). Thus, to posit that the mythology used by the disciples and apostles to understand Jesus was "gnostic" is tendentious and effectively places another unknown variable into the already difficult Christian equation.

(3) *Salvation*: Nowhere in Iranian mythology, the supposed origin of the myth in question, does the primal man bring salvation. This fact necessitated changes in the early theory that made a blending of two myths necessary—a primeval man myth accounted for creation, while a redeemed redeemer accounted for the final deliverance. But we cannot isolate these two strands at all in most literature. Furthermore, there is not even any unambiguous pre-Christian evidence for a "son of man" figure in Judaism.[7] Other mediators in Jewish tradition which serve as precursors to the savior—Logos, Wisdom, Sophia—are not usually redeemer figures. Still others like Moses, the prophets, Elijah, though important eschatological figures in their own right, are as often

[6] *Le origini dello Gnosticismo*, ed. U. Bianchi (Leiden: Brill, 1967).

[7] The supposed evidence in Enoch can no longer be dated to pre-Christian times, since En. 37–71 does not appear in the Aramaic fragments of Enoch found at Qumran and can possibly be understood as a special Jewish or Christian writing which made its way into the Ethiopic church. For a reaffirmation of their Jewish provenance see J. H. Charlesworth, "The SNTS Pseudepigrapha Seminar at Tübingen and Paris on the Books of Enoch," *NTS* 25 (1979): 315–29.

described as intercessors but not redeemers. Angels such as the angel of YHWH may sometimes be described as redeemers, but no single angelic mediator emerges from the pre-Christian evidence, and, in any case, redemption is most often reserved for God. The most consistent earthly redeemer figure in Judaism is the messiah, who did not attain any standard description before Christianity (or, in Judaism, after it) and certainly cannot be said to be the redeemed redeemer which Reitzenstein and Bultmann outlined.

While it is clear that the pre-Christian gnostic salvation myth is neither unified, "pre-Christian" nor "gnostic," it yet remains that Reitzenstein noted the existence and use of "myth" as constant and crucial in the gnostic message. Although this has been accepted as a commonplace, and has received extensive discussion on account of R. Bultmann's *The New Testament and Mythology*,[8] it has rarely been examined outside of theological discussion. Because of Reitzenstein's use and understanding of the term "mythology," I think, parts of his theory can be salvaged, for we now have more sophistication about what myth is and an enormous literature devoted to discovering its properties.[9] What most illuminated my reflection on myth in Reitzenstein's work was the suspicion that he had in mind not a specific myth nor a motif but what, since the work of Lévi-Strauss, has been, called a "mythical structure." The kinds of evidence that Reitzenstein described point not to the existence of a single myth which preceded Christianity nor yet merely to a series of motifs which can be taken up later by Gnosticism[10] but rather to a deep struc-

[8] See, e.g., *Kerygma and Myth*, ed. by H. W. Bartsch (London: SPCK, 1953) containing Bultmann's article and contributions by Lohmeyer, Schniewind, and Thielicke, trans. H. R. Fuller, Farrer's contribution in English.

[9] A number of points which could be made about the evolution of our understanding of myth in the intervening years will have to go undiscussed for lack of space. For instance, it is commonly assumed by Reitzenstein and his followers (and esp. Bultmann) that myth and history are totally opposed disciplines, when it seems to me that nonempirical paradigms are as central to the writing of history as they are to myth and that uncritical history serves as myth in every modern nation state, just as it did for the ancient Hebrews, Jews, and Christians. For Bultmann, the meaning of the myth is describable in existentialist terms, hence the importance of hermeneutics. But I think that the meaning of a myth is not so easily translated, for it is a subtle blend of its structural and functional aspects as well as interaction with historical events.

[10] See the excellent work of G. Widengren on the ascent motif: *The Ascension of the Apostle and the Heavenly Book*, vol. 3 of *King and Saviour: Studies in Manichaen, Mandaean, and Syrian-gnostic Religion* (Uppsala: Uppsala Universitets Arsskrift, 1950, 1957).

ture of Hellenistic thought which indeed predates Christianity. Possibly a mythic structure was the object of the purview of the history of religions school, even if it was, on account of the state of the discipline, unable to come to an adequate description of the phenomenon. Such a common structure could not be specifically gnostic or otherwise; it rather would be susceptible to gnostic, Jewish, or Christian interpretations, for while structural studies are concerned to discover the overall pattern, communities understand the meaning of the pattern in unique ways.

Before we proceed further to explore this issue two disclaimers will need to be voiced and discussed, at least in brief: (1) I do not have exactly the same thing in mind as Lévi-Strauss when I say that there is a deep structure inherent in Hellenistic mythologies which has been too inexactly expressed as the gnostic salvation myth. (2) The underlying structure behind the various myths which predate Christianity is not the pre-Christian gnostic salvation myth which Reitzenstein defined; it is only implicit in his discussion.

The structural study of myth is no longer new. The seminal works by Lévi-Strauss[11] have been available for a considerable period of time in English and a gigantic body of literature has grown up around them, demonstrating both Lévi-Strauss' genius and that some of his analyses of myth are in fundamental need of correction. What I want to discuss briefly is one of the central theoretical aspects of his work. Lévi-Strauss believes that a certain universal property of the human mind generates the structure of a myth, in the same way that the human mind generates the deep structures of language. Just as syntax can be described by a series of formal transformations in accordance with certain rules, so the specific events in a mythical narrative are reducible to a number of formal transformations governed by a few simple rules. Secondly, Lévi-Strauss says that mythic structures are reducible to binary contrasts, just as computers operate on binary systems, perceived by the mind as a dilemma, then bridged or solved by an anomalous term that mediates between the opposing terms. His most famous example is the nature culture dilemma

[11] Most influential in English have been: *Structural Anthropology*, trans. C. Jacobson and Brooke Grundfest Schoepf (New York: Basic Books, 1963); *The Raw and the Cooked*, trans. John and Doreen Weightman (New York: Harper & Row, 1969); *From Honey to Ashes* (New York: Harper & Row, 1966); *The Savage Mind* (Chicago: University of Chicago Press, 1962).

expressed, for instance, in foods as "raw" and "cooked," a contrast bridged by certain anomalous substances like honey and tobacco.

I propose to examine the second proposition I have attributed to Lévi-Strauss in light of serious questions raised to the first. The Lévi-Straussian assumption that myths are generated from the human mind in exactly the same way as language has been widely criticized, but this criticism has been no better expressed than by Dan Sperber. I quote from the new English edition of his work, *Rethinking Symbolism*:

> A grammar is a device that generates the sentences of the language it describes by means of given axioms and by the operation of rules, independently of all external input. All sentences, the whole language, are contained in its grammar. Inversely, according to Lévi-Strauss' myths are generated by the transformation of other myths or of texts which carry a certain mysticism; in other words, by a device that allows infinite and non-enumerable sets of possible inputs. No grammar therefore generates by itself the set of myths, any more than the mechanism of visual perception generates by itself the set of possible perceptions. The device that would generate myths depends on an external stimulus; it is thus similar to cognitive devices and opposed to semiological devices; it is an interpretative, and not a generative, system.[12]

The deep structures of myth differ from the deep structures of language in that the former can be more easily affected by external stimuli—by borrowings and events, etc.—as well as the internal rules of perception. The structural study of myth may be analogous to the structural study of language to the extent that both are analyses of the formal aspects of a complex symbolic system—analyses of the system itself rather than the individual components of the system, "holistic" analyses rather than exegeses of the parts of the system. But the properties of the structure of language and the structure of myth are not identical. It is, therefore, unnecessary for the current purpose to enter the province of theory, except to add that an underlying mythical uniformity in the Hellenistic world will dictate a similarity of meaning in different communities, though different social structures, histories, and theologies will work towards unique cultural understanding.[13] Is the so-called pre-

[12] D. Sperber, *Rethinking Symbolism*, trans. A. L. Morton (Cambridge: Cambridge University Press, 1975; repr., 1975; orig. French ed., 1974). See Sperber, as well as Daniel Patte, *What is Structural Exegesis?* (Philadelphia: Fortress, 1976), 82–83.

[13] See below p. 206f.

Christian gnostic salvation myth amenable to structural description? Do all examples noted by Reitzenstein and Bultmann contain formal similarities which may be analogous to the deep structures of language? Yes, I think so. Furthermore, there are reasons to analyze late Hellenistic culture in this manner, if only to get at some of the uniformities of Hellenistic life. Many of the different ascension myths (and it ought to be clear now to us that we can speak of them as different myths, not examples of the same myth) seem to me to show a fundamentally similar structure. They speak of a god who lives in a perfect realm, usually called heaven, and men who live in an extremely imperfect realm usually called earth. Communication between the two ought to be impossible; so when it occurs, it can only be accomplished through the movement of a mediator. The metaphor is so deceptively simple that many will ask whether it adds to our understanding. The reduction of such complicated legends to this simple pattern will not determine the entire meaning of the pattern in any individual culture, but I think it does point at the uniformities which Reitzenstein and the history of religions school had in mind. Furthermore, there is a striking similarity between this Hellenistic pattern and the basic binary mythological pattern which Lévi-Strauss delimits. I personally am somewhat surprised by this simple finding because, like Victor Turner[14] and Mary Douglas,[15] I am convinced that there are more important and different structures than binary ones. If myth is a different order of structure than language, there is no reason to suppose that its structure needs to be binary, even supposing that language must be binary. It merely happens that the opposing structures of earth and heaven with their contrasting properties, bridged by a mediating figure, describes the primary structure most simply in this case.

One advantage of a structural theory is that it implies that simple operations called transformations account for differences in the myths, in the same way that different sentences can be generated by transforming its elements, even as the deep structures remain constant. And that is why I feel we need to adopt it. Structurally, mediation from above to below is equivalent to mediation from below to above: both accomplish the desired communication. It is easy to see that they are transformations of one another—a simple opposition of vectors:

[14] See esp. *Drama, Fields and Metaphors* (Ithaca, N.Y.: Cornell University Press, 1974).

[15] See esp. *Implicit Meanings: Essays in Anthropology* (London: Routledge, 1975), esp. 142–72.

Chart I

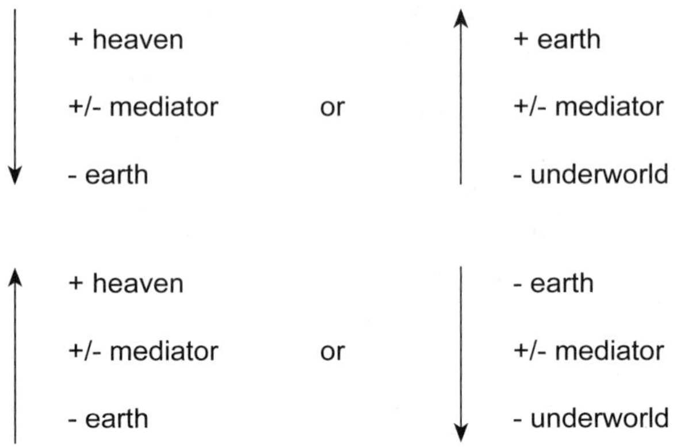

There is a parallel historical development to this hypothesis that the journey up and the journey down are structurally equivalent—that is, the changing concept of the abode of the dead from subterranean to celestial realms. When the dead were believed to live under the earth, the necessary journey was to be downward, as, for example, the orphics maintained.

Chart II

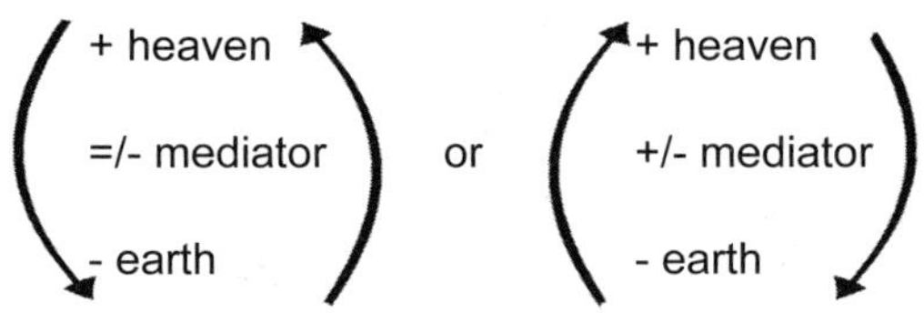

However, when a concept of astral immortality evolved, a journey to the stars became necessary and a whole new constellation of meanings specifically symbolizing a desire for immortality was generated. The journey motif itself can sometimes be emphasized as a primary theme, giving rise, for example, to the Jungian interpretation that journey expresses a basic human archetype. This chapter does not contradict such analyses; however there will be no attempt to postulate a "therapeutic" role or value to the image.[16] In the Hellenistic world, when the direction of the journey is downward, the so-called *katabasis* pattern, we normally expect divine mediators such as the Logos, an angel, Word, Son, Wisdom, etc. to figure in creation and revelation texts. When the direction is upward, the so-called *anabasis* pattern, we normally expect the mediator to be a man or men, the soul, psyche or figures of that kind and the interest is normally associated with the question of death. Though the *katabasis* and the *anabasis* patterns are formally transformations of one another, in pre-Christian times it is more normal to find only one pattern—a man may ascend and return, a divine mediator may descend and return. One formal journey does not necessarily imply the other. Though the mediator often returns, only one half of the cycle is important. The return is necessary but of no special importance. In other words, though the two patterns are structurally equivalent, they are not necessarily exegetically equivalent. The first pattern we normally associate with cosmologies, theophanies or angelophanies, and prophetic mediation; the second is normally associated with ascensions, ecstatic ascents, journeys to heaven, and the heavenly journey of the soul. The former have received much study of late as part of the enterprise to understand the wisdom component of Christianity and Gnosticism.[17] The latter were studied by Reitzenstein and the History of Religion School but have largely languished since their time.[18] I think it is time to renew the scholarship of heavenly journey, and so will concentrate on the *anabasis* pattern, making whatever reference is necessary for the others.

W. Bousset's "Die Himmelsreise der Seele" still remains the classic work on heavenly journey. While Bousset, unlike Reitzenstein, did not overvalue the antiquity of the Avestan evidence, he felt that the

[16] See R. J. Z. Werblowsky, "Structure and Archetype," in *Festschrift for T. Gaster = Journal of the Ancient Near Eastern Society of Columbia* 5 (1973): 435–42.

[17] See, e. g. B. L. Mack, *Logos und Sophia: Untersuchungen zur Weisheitstheologie im hellenistischen Judentum*, SUNT 10 (Göttingen: Vandenhoeck & Ruprecht, 1973); H. Hegermann, *Die Vorstellung vom Schöpfungsmittler im hellenistischen Judentum und Urchristentum*, TUGAL 82 (Berlin: Akademie, 1961); H. F. Weiss, *Untersuchungen zur Kosmologie des hellenistischen und palästinischen Judentums*, TUGAL 97 (Berlin: Akademie, 1966).

[18] Perhaps the most complete study of the material and the most complete history of research can be found in G. Lohfink, *Die Himmelfahrt Jesu—Erfindung oder Erfahrung*, SANT 26 (München: Kösel, 1971). Though I have significant differences in approach, his discussion of the history of research is an extremely good, short introduction on the subject. See p. 13f.

presuppositions for the heavenly journey were already present in Persian thought in the earliest Avestan evidence.[19] He may have been right, for much of the later material on heavenly journeys probably contains Persian influence through untraceable sources. But it is not true that a Persian origin sufficiently explains the motif of the heavenly journey wherever it appears. The theme has a native version in Greek, Egyptian, Babylonian, Eastern European, and biblical thought, where it is understood with similar (but not identical) categories and similar (but not identical) morals are derived from it. The date of the first occurrence of the tradition is of secondary importance compared to Bousset's observation, at the beginning of his article:

> Die Ekstase, vermoege deren man sich durch den Himmel zum hoechsten Gott erhebt, is ja nichts anderes als eine Anticipation der Himmelsreise def Seele nach dem Tode des Menschen.[20]

His perception of the parallel between ecstatic trance journeys to heaven and the supposed journey of the soul after death is a remarkable intuition into the almost universal structure of the ascent myth. Though there are a few crucial cases in which the heavenly journey is not explicitly interpreted as a prefiguration of a particular soul's journey after death, the structural similarity between the ecstatic journey and the final journey of humans after death is so widespread as to be crucially important. There may be many different understandings of the prefigurations. For instance, the ecstatic journey may or may not itself confer immorality. It often serves only to confirm that a "traditional" cosmology is true when brought into question by crisis. But the migration of souls from this existence is always part of the cosmology in question. To search for an expression to comprehend such a widespread religious concept one needs to interpret Bousset's observation in a more structural mode: It appears that all of the mediation stories are somehow concerned with the contradiction between the evanescent and enduring, life and death, impermanent earthly existence and permanent heavenly reward, seeming injustice or suffering and heavenly justice—a contradiction which is often made plain by a mythical or historical crisis which then must be overcome, in so far as possible, by the mediation of the intermediary

[19] W. Bousset, "Die Himmelsreise der Seele," *AR* 4 (1901): 136–69; 228–73 (repr., Darmstadt: 1960); here 156f.

[20] Bousset, "Die Himmelsreise," 136.

figure. For instance, the crisis may be brought on by the apparent disconfirmation of an important religious belief. But there is always a relation between the mythic heavenly journey and notions of afterlife. This, in turn, is always related to mythical cosmologies. Since the Hellenistic world came to share certain gross assumptions about the world, it is not surprising that they also evinced certain similarities in dealing with the problems of human existence. Of course, such mediation, in Lévi-Strauss' terms, can never, by means of symbolic interplay, actually overcome the contradiction between the opposite forces. But, I think we will see, as we review the evidence, that within individual cultures they must provide credible and plausible structures for resolving the opposition between life and death—hence, they are part of the constitution of reality. The paradigm of understanding—in this case, the heavenly journey—is, like a scientific theory, an informing and driving intellectual impulse which continues to govern the speculation on the issue in transformation until it has reached the limits of its potential for explanation.[21]

Since there was a time before the ascension became dominant in Hellenistic culture, it is relevant to ask about origins. Usually Persia has been seen as the birthplace. The problem of Persian influence is likely never to be satisfactorily resolved. Though the heavenly journey of the soul is a prominent feature of later Persian literature, there is no way to verify how early these ideas became part of Persian religion. Furthermore, it is nearly impossible to establish Persian influence because the borrowers would be hardly aware of their dependence. Even had they been aware of their sources they were unlikely to have acknowledged them and thereby indicate any reliance on Persian ideas.

The Persians' version of the heavenly journey was explicitly held to be the fate of every soul after death. The principal text exists only in fragments and is of uncertain import. It is often called the "XXII Yasht," since the language appears to be younger Avestan. The book is called the *Hadokht Nask* by the Parsis, although it seems not to correspond with the early document named and described by the "Denkart."[22]

[21] Lévi-Strauss, *Structural Anthropology*, 229.

[22] See E. W. West, *Pahlavi Texts*, part 1: *The Bundahis, Bahman Yast, and Shayast La-Shayast*, Sacred Books of the East 5 (Oxford: Clarendon, 1880), 224 n. 8. A Pahlavi translation of the book has been edited and translated by M. Haug and E. W. West in *The Book of Arda Viraf* (London: Trübner, 1872; repr., 1971).

The Yasht is a description of the fate awaiting the soul of the righteous and the soul of the wicked. After three days of either enjoyment or pain, depending on its earthly conduct, the soul meets a feminine figure who personifies his own conscience—either a splendid maiden or a vile old woman. Afterwards the soul is brought to a three-tiered heaven or hell.

Since the pattern of reward or punishment after death is clear,[23] the later drug-induced heavenly journey of Arda Viraf in the book attributed to him[24] must be seen as confirmation of the truth of the Zoroastrian religion. In his vision he sees all the good that Zoroastrianism preached rewarded, all the sins of the religion punished; as well, his journey confirms for all who value his testimony the structure of the universe on which Zoroastrian morality depended. Therefore it is written as an historical event and the kernel may be factual.

The text appears with various introductions, one making Arda Viraf a contemporary with Zarathustra and King Gushtasp. But the most reliable text dates Arda Viraf to the period after the overthrow of Alexandrian Greek hegemony. Thus the incident upon which the ascent is based is the crisis of faith brought about by the Greek conquest and the necessity of finding out what should be done to reestablish it. However, as the editors admit, the text also appears to reflect Sassanian times, so that the Greek conquest may actually be a cipher for the Muslim conquest. If this is correct, it is equally possible that some of the pseudepigrapha influenced the "Arda Viraf Namah" as it is to be their source.

Tempting as it may have been to present the Persian evidence as the genesis of the heavenly journey motif when the Persian documents had just been discovered, there are important and early precedents within many traditions, including Greek culture, which are likely to be more important, though they can only be mentioned in passing.

The Mesopotamian background of ascension has been well summarized by Geo Widengren in *The Ascension of the Apostle and the Heavenly Book*. For instance, the eponymous ancestor of the *baru* cult prophecy school, King Enmeduranki of Sippar, is called to the divine *puhru* by

[23] See also Yasht 24: 53–65; *Minokhired* II, 123–194 (in West, *Pahlavi Texts,* part 3: *Dina-I Mainog-i Khirad, Sikand-gumanik Vigar, and the Sad Dar*, Sacred Books of the East 24 [Oxford: Clarendon, 1885]).

[24] See West, *Pahlavi Texts*, part 1; Haugh and West, *Arda Viraf.*

the gods and placed upon a golden throne.[25] Shamash and Ada, who are known as the gods of oracles, give him tablets, the knowledge of oil and water divination, the bag with the mystery of heaven and earth, and a cedar staff. According to Widengren, the tablets are special symbols of sovereignty, which are pondered by the high god and his court at the New Year's festival as part of the process of deciding the fate of the coming year. With other texts, Widengren shows that the tablets of destiny themselves are seen as the oracles for the coming year; hence, he who possesses them possesses the rulership of the world. Thus, the Mesopotamian king is viewed as commissioned from heaven itself and responsible for a portion of god's providence. For this reason, he is glorified as possessing surpassing wisdom.

This commissioning or sending forth of the king is explicitly ritualized in a text Widengren brings from Lipit Ishtar. It invokes (1) entering the heavenly palace, (2) reception by the god, (3) naming with glorious names, (4) handing over the sovereignty of the world, (5) promise or firmness of rule, (6) exhortation to proceed like daylight. The importance of such a theme for the Hebrew evidence is striking. Similar commissionings can be seen in prophets, in the Daniel throne scene (Dan 7:9f.), in the Enoch literature, and even in Moses' ascent of Sinai, as Widengren pointed out. Some kind of connection seems undoubtable. Yet even so, Hebrew society imposed its own ideology on this interpretation.

The Greeks told stories of heroes like Hercules, Castor, and Pollux, who after dying mounted to heaven to become apotheosized. Immortality and immortalization are frequent interests of the Greek version of the journey. However, it is not always the primary exegesis of the event. In an extremely interesting fragment at the beginning of Parmenides' epic poem,[26] the philosopher-poet relates how he is escorted out of the realm of the night toward the light. He is carried in a chariot with maidens leading the way at enormous speed.

> There are the gates (separating) the ways of day and night and they are enclosed by a lintel and a threshold of stone; and the ethereal gates

[25] E. Dhorme, *Choix de textes religieux assyro-babyloniens*, Études bibliques 7 (Paris: Gabalda, 1907), 140ff. Also J. A. Craig, *Assyrian and Babylonian Religious Texts*, vol. 1, *Prayers, Oracles, Hymns* (Leipzig: Hinrichs, 1895), pl. 64, ac, quoted in Widengren, *Ascension of the Apostle*, 8 n. 1.

[26] *Parmenides: A Text with Translation, Commentary, and Critical Essay*, ed. and trans. L. Tarán (Princeton: Princeton University Press, 1965).

> themselves are covered with big wingdoors, of which Dike, whose vengeance is stern, possesses the rewarding keys. The maidens appeased her with gentle words and knowingly persuaded her to push back quickly from the gates the bolted bar. (Parmenides, 1.11–17)[27]

(Appeasing of the gatekeepers will be a major theme in the later Markabah evidence.) The goddess then addresses the poet for the remainder of the poem. The first lines however are directly relevant:

> O young man coming to our abode joined with immortal charioteers with the horses which carry you, welcome, since it is by no means an evil lot that sent you forth to travel on this road (for it is far away from the wandering of men), but right and justice. It is necessary that you learn all things, as well the unshaken heart of well-rounded truth as the opinions of mortals in which there is no true belief. Nevertheless, you shall learn these (opinions) also, how the appearances, which pervade all things, had to be acceptable. (Parmenides, 1.24–32)[28]

The objection that this is not specifically a heavenly journey can be easily silenced by noting the solar imagery (chariot, daughters of the sun, day, night, gates, etc.), the goddess at the end of the journey, and especially the use of the word "ether" to describe the gates to which the *dikē* has the keys.[29] Sextus, who provides us with the best version of the poem, interprets the experience under the influence of the allegory of the soul as a chariot in Plato's *Phaedrus* (246A 4–7). But, in the text before us, no such analogy is supplied by the poet. We are probably dealing with an independent use of legends of the chariot of the god by the poet in order to provide a setting for his philosophy, which then assumes the authority of a revelation.[30] Tarán's strongly worded condemnation against over-interpretation is surely meant to dissuade us from believing that the text is the record of an actual shamanic journey or heavenly journey of the soul. But that does not mean that astral journey is not supposed

[27] *Parmenides*, ed. and trans. Tarán, 8.

[28] *Parmenides*, ed. and trans. Tarán, 9.

[29] Tarán, in his desire to emphasize the philosophical worth of the piece, seems not to acknowledge the concreteness of the metaphor used as a literary device. See below.

[30] P. 30. He notes parallel occurrences of chariots of Zeus and Poseidon in Homer, *Il.* 8.41–50, 38–40; 13.23–38. Also, Sappho fr. 1.9 (in *Poetarum Lesbiorum Fragmenta*, ed. E. Lobel and D. Page [Oxford: Clarendon, 1955]); the Homeric *Hymn to Artemis* 9–4; Bacchylides 13.194 (in *Bacchylides Carmina Cum Fragmentis*, ed. B. Snell and H. Maehler [Leipzig: Teubner, 1961]). Tarán suggests that it was Plato himself who first identified the symbol of the chariot with the soul (since Ps.-Isocrates, *Demonicea* 32 is later).

to take place. Rather it appears to be a journey to heaven related without a reference to an explicit doctrine of the soul. Its literary purpose only points out the strategy underlying almost all heavenly journeys—to guarantee and legitimate that heaven attests to the values which will be propounded in the document. Not only is the contrast between light and darkness, mortality and immortality specifically noted, but portentously, so is the contrast between fate and freedom, mortality and immortality, justice and injustice. These are the basic contrasts which the journey from heaven to earth and back will mediate in the Hellenistic period. Of course, in this short description, almost no account is made of the mediator figure himself. But no emphasis on mediation is necessary in the literary text under consideration.[31]

It is precisely the problem of theodicy which occupies first place in the story of Er, the Pamphylian, who returns alive after twelve days of death and reports on the fortunes of souls after their death:

> "Such then while he lives are the prizes, the wages, and the gifts that the just man receives from gods and men in addition to those blessings which justice herself bestowed, and right fair and abiding rewards," he said. "Well, these," I said, "are nothing in number and magnitude compared with those that await both after death. And we must listen to the tale of them," said I, "in order that each may have received in full what is due to be said of him by our argument." "Tell me," he said, "since there are not many things to which I would more gladly listen." "It is not, let me tell you," said I, "the tale to Alcinous told that I shall unfold, but the tale of a warrior bold, Er, the son of Armenius, by race a Pamphylian. He once upon a time was slain in battle and when the corpses were taken up on the tenth day, already decayed, was found intact, and having been brought home, at the moment of his funeral, on the twelfth day, as he lay upon the pyre, revived, and after coming to life related what, he said he had seen in the world beyond." (Plato, *Rep.* 10.614Bff.)[32]

Er then relates how he was chosen to be the messenger (*angelos*) to mankind to tell them what awaits us in the other world. The story which he

[31] See Lohfink, *Die Himmelfahrt*, chap. 1, for a general review of the literature on heavenly journey. It seems to me, however, that he distinguishes between genres of heavenly journeys too closely.

[32] Translation from *The Republic*, ed. and trans. Paul Shorey (London: 1888). See *The Republic of Plato*, ed. James Adam, 2nd ed. by D. A. Rees, 2 vols. (Cambridge: Cambridge University Press, 1963), 2:433f.; see also the introduction, p. lf. for a good bibliography on the myth of Er.

relates is one of punishments and rewards for those unrequited during their own life—those who had committed great wrongs were condemned to ten times the punishment in measures of one hundred years.

The structure of this heavenly journey is clear. Those punished go into the earth. Those rewarded go to heaven. The central figure, Er, crosses from the lower realm to the other and returns to tell us that the universe conforms to just rules. The story confirms that justice exists in the universe by claiming that the voyage is parallel to the one which the soul will take at death. Its purpose is to warn men of the implications of their actions upon the earth and exhort them to righteousness.

One of the dominant motifs is that of the *agōn*. The soul struggles in life as in the games and thereafter receives the reward. Plato seemingly has his doubts about such tales and ends with this correction:

> But if we are guided by me we shall believe that the soul is immortal and capable of enduring all extremes of good and evil, and so we shall hold ever to the upward way and pursue righteousness with wisdom always and ever" (Plato, *Rep*. 10.621C)[33]

The same function can be seen in Plutarch's *Moralia* in his essay "On Those Who Are Punished by the Deity Late" (or "On the Delays of the Divine Vengeance"). He wants to correct some of the story while confirming the idea of the heavenly journey of the soul. After first making the point that the cruelest punishment is to see our loved ones and offspring suffering on account of our own misdeeds, Plutarch relates the story of one Aridaeus (renamed Thespesius after the adventure) who lived as a reprobate until one day he had a complete change of heart. The reason for his conversion to an ethical life was a heavenly journey:

> For he told them that, when his soul left the body, the change he first underwent was as if he were a pilot thrown violently into the sea out of a ship. Then raising himself up a little, he thought he recovered the power of breathing again altogether and looked round him in every direction, as if one eye of the soul was open. But he saw none of the things he had ever seen before, but stars enormous in size and at immense distance from one another, sending forth a wonderful and intense brightness of colour, so that the soul was borne along and moved about everywhere quickly and easily like a ship in fair weather. But omitting most of what he saw, he said that the souls of the dead mounted into the air, which

[33] *The Republic*, ed. and trans. Shorey, 2:488f.

> yielded to them and formed fiery bubbles, and then, when each bubble quietly broke, they assumed human forms, light in weight but with different kinds of motion . . . (Plutarch, *Mor.*, "On Those Who are Punished by the Deity Late" 22)[34]

The mechanism by which he traveled was not the same as those fully dead:

> For assuredly you are not dead, but by the will of the gods, you have left your body like an anchor; and as a proof of what I say both now and hereafter notice that the souls of the dead have no shadow and do not move their eyelids. ("On Those Who are Punished by the Deity Late" 22)[35]

Several mysteries are revealed to Thespesius—including the ultimate destination of souls, and the punishment of Nero. But it is clear that, whatever else the author may relate, the tale functions as a theodicy, precisely because it parallels the journey of the soul after death.

If it is true that both Greek and Roman societies from Plato to Plutarch, from one end of the span of Hellenistic culture to the other, know of the journey to the heavens, it is also clear that the Romans adapted the motif and structure to express some enduring and important thoughts about their native style of government and their rulers. In "The Dream of Scipio" (Cicero, *Rep.* 6.9–26) Cicero reflects on the values of the Republic and its defenders. Scipio the Elder (Africanus) returns to tell his younger namesake the future and ultimate rewards of the state:

> But Africanus, bear this in mind, in order that you may be more zealous in the defense of your country, all who have preserved, aided or advanced their country have a definite place in heaven where the blessed enjoy eternal life. For there is no earthly happening which is more acceptable to that sovereign God who rules all the universe than the councils and assemblies of men joined together by law, which are called states; the rulers and preservers of these go from here and to here they return. (Cicero, *Rep.* 6.13)

The narration continues with description of the organization of the universe in its spheres and constellations. The purpose of the trip is not merely the revelation of the structure of the universe, now clearly

[34] *Plutarch's Morals*, ed. and trans. A. R. Shilleto (London: George Bell & Sons, 1888), 358.

[35] *Plutarch's Morals*, ed. and trans. Shilleto, 359.

described as spheres within spheres, but the inculcation of values that preserved the Republic:

> And the noblest concerns are those assumed for the safety of your country; a soul stirred and trained by these pursuits will have a quicker flight to this abode, its own home; and this will be the faster, if even now, while imprisoned in the body, it reaches out and by contemplating what is beyond itself, detaches itself as much as possible from the body. (*Rep*. 6.26)

Even as Cicero strived to preserve the values and government that had made a Republic possible; so too the ascension and heavenly journey motif was brought into the debate about the correct government of the empire.

Before the emperors could arrogate to themselves the complete trappings of divinity, the story of the ascension of Romulus, a lawgiver and sole ruler, could be made to serve as the model for Julius, the second founder of Rome—thus forming the mythical basis of the emperor's right to rule:

> There, Romulus was giving his friendly laws to the citizens, and Mars caught Ilia's son up. His mortal body became thin, dissolving in the air, as a lead pellet shot by a broad sling will melt in the sky. Suddenly a beautiful form more worthy of the high couches (of the gods), is the form of Quirinus, who is now wearing a sacred robe. (Ovid, *Metam*. 14.823–828 [Meller, LCL])

Livy discusses Romulus' death and the rumors of it in terms reminiscent of the death of Julius Caesar:

> Then at first a few, then all, joyfully declared Romulus, the king and father of the city of Rome, to be a God, the son of God. They asked him with prayers for peace; so that he would always be pleased to wish favor for his children. I believe there were some even then who argued secretly that the king had been torn apart by the hands of the senators. Indeed, this rumor spread also, but very obscurely; the other version was enhanced by men's admiration for Romulus and their panic. (Livy, *Hist*. 1.16)[36]

But the rumors are calmed by the ascension story:

[36] See H. Temporini, *Die Frauen am Hofe Trajans: Ein Beitrag zur Stellung der Augustae im Principat* (Berlin: de Gruyter, 1979), 245f.

> Further, the stratagem of one man is said to have added to the credibility of the story. For, when the citizens were disturbed by the loss of the king and were hostile toward the senators, Julius Proculus as it is told, a man of repute, (at least he was the author of this important thing) addressed the assembly. "Romulus, Quirites," he said, "the father of this city, at the first light of this day, descended from the sky and clearly showed himself to me. While I was awed with holy fright, I stood reverently before him asking in prayer that I might look at him without sin.' 'Go,' he said, 'announce to the Romans that Heaven wishes that my Rome shall be the capital of the earth; therefore, they shall cultivate the military; they and their descendants shall know that no human might can resist Roman arms.' He said this and went on high." It is a great marvel what credence was generated by the man's tale, and how the loss of Romulus, for which the common people and the army grieved, was assuaged by the belief in his immortality. (*Hist.* 1.16)

Livy's ironic attitude points out the value of the heavenly journey as a proof of immortality and as mythical underpinning of the imperial system. A complete ascent-descent mythology can be found already in Vergil's fourth *Eclogue*. Apollo's descent and return is not the self-conscious theme of the writer—rather, the birth of Augustus is viewed as the redemptive act in the cycle:

> The last age of Sibyl's poem is now come . . . Now a new offspring is sent down from high heaven. Do thou, chaste Lucina, favour the birth of the child under whom the iron breed will first cease and a golden race arise throughout the world. Now shall thine own Apollo bear sway. (Vergil, *Ecl.* 4.8–10)[37]

In the cult of the emperor, the ascension of the dead ruler was viewed in very literal terms. A quick look through the descriptions of the cult and the collections of iconography will verify that. The emperor could ascend in a chariot, or on the back of an eagle. A shooting star signaled his demise.[38] The eagle was especially closely linked to the imperial cult. The practice arose of releasing a caged eagle from the top of the

[37] See W. Kraus, "Vergils vierte Ekloge: Ein kritisches Hypomnema," *ANRW* 31.1 (1980): 604–45; S. Benko, "Vergil's Fourth Eclogue in Christian Interpretation," *ANRW* 31.1 (1980): 646–705.

[38] See e.g., Pliny, *Nat.* 2.8.68. He remains skeptical. But Seneca and Dio make references to a comet at the death of Augustus. See further.

funeral pyre of the emperor.[39] Dio notes that centurions lit the pyre from below as an eagle was released—encouraging the belief that the soul was carried to heaven (*Rom. Hist.* 56.42.3). Beginning with Nero, coinage represents the motion of ascension with an eagle flying upwards.[40]

A remarkable diptych in the British museum depicts various symbols of apotheosis which had become part of the cult.[41] There are several intricate scenes. But the most relevant is the funeral scene with a pyre in the center from which a quadriga is about to take off for heaven. The chariot is driven by a youth (probably Helios) whose pose and garment suggest great speed. To the right of the funeral pyre are two soaring eagles, probably symbolizing the divinized Emperor and Empress together. The *divus* is represented at the top, being born aloft by two winged beings. Looking down arc the previously divinized ancestors and the signs of the zodiac.

That the charioteer and psychopomp is Helios supported by other archaeological evidence—this time a pyre recovered at Rome, which even bears the inscription *Sol me rapuit*, "The Sun has seized me."[42]

In the literary sources, the concept of the journey normally involved the soul of the deceased, while bodily ascension was limited to heroes, great men, and demigods like Romulus. Indeed, the physics of the day insisted that the stars and souls were the same substance. Pliny attributed this discovery to Hipparchus:

> Hipparchus will never receive all the praise he deserves since no one has better established the relation between man and the stars, or shown more clearly that our souls are particles of divine fire. (Pliny, *Nat.* 2.26.95)

The use (and abuse) of divinization in the imperial cult is well known. A century after the imperial system took hold, Hadrian could decree that the soul of his deceased lover, Antinous, had ascended to heaven

[39] F. Cumont, *Afterlife in Roman Paganism* (New Haven, Conn.: Yale University Press, 1922). See also idem, *Astrology and Religion among the Greeks and Romans* (New York: G. P. Putnam's Sons, 1912; repr., 1960) and idem, *Lux Perpetua* (Paris: P. Geuthner, 1949).

[40] See P. Fossing, *Catalogue of the Antique Engraved Gems and Cameos* (Copenhagen: 1929), 177 no. 1199, also 1203f.

[41] O. M. Dalton, *Catalogue of Ivory Carvings of the Christian Era* (London: Trustees of the British Museum, 1909), 1 and pl. 1 ("The Apotheosis of Romulus"). See the useful bibliography of Dominique Cuss, *Imperial Cults and Honorary Terms in the New Testament* (Fribourg: University Press, 1974), from whom I first heard of the triptych.

[42] *CIL* VI, 29954.

and become a divinity.[43] But if astral immortality was promulgated of the emperors, it was scarcely in less demand by the people. Astral piety was itself a movement created by combining many different versions of ascent and descent myths. Egypt was the source of one of the most potent ideas of immortality that entered Rome. The outer forms of Egyptian religion evoked ridicule by the Romans. Philo himself attacks the animal menagerie of the Egyptian pantheon while Roman satirists scoff at the adulation of cats, crocodiles, leeks, and onions (*De Decal.* 16). Juvenal comments ironically on the "holiness" of Egypt by saying that even their kitchen garden produces gods (*Sat.* 15.10). Yet the issues and liturgies of the Egyptian religion penetrated deep into Roman consciousness. More than any other religion, Egyptian texts from the earliest periods are obsessed with the notion of life after death. In its classic form, Egyptian religion narrated a journey of the dead to live in the underworld presided over by Osiris. Yet, even in ancient times, a heavenly journey could be part of the voyage to the underworld in the West where the sun went in the evening and could as easily be made by ladder as by ship:

> N. Ascends on the ladder which his father Re made for him.[44]

or

> Atum brought to N. the gods belonging to heaven, he assembled to him the gods belonging to earth.
> They put their arms under him.
> They made a ladder for N. that he might ascend to heaven on it.[45]

There are many casual Roman reports of the ceremonies of the "Isis mysteries," marking the death, dismemberment, and revivication of Osiris. If the deceased had served Osiris he was assimilated to that god and shared his immortality.[46] So the initiate in his mystery initiation felt

[43] Cassius Dio 69.2; Pausanias, *Description of Greece* 8.9.7–8; Eusebius, *Hist. Eccl.* 4.8.2; Justin Martyr, *1 Apol.* 1.29; Clement of Alexandria, *Prot.* 4.

[44] A. B. Meiser, *Pyramid Texts* (New York: Longmans & Green, 1952), 1.92, I. 390a, from E. R. Goodenough, *Pagan Symbols in Judaism*, vol. 8 of *Jewish Symbols in the Greco-Roman Period* (New York: Pantheon, 1958).

[45] Meiser, *Pyramid Texts*, 234, 1473–6–1474b. For further quotations, see Goodenough, *Pagan Symbols in Judaism*, 149f.

[46] See F. Cumont, *The Oriental Religions in Roman Paganism* (Chicago: Open Court, 1911), 100.

himself born again, the equal of the gods. He imagined that he actually viewed the gods face to face and returned as a superman transformed by divine presence. As described by Apuleius, the initiation involved rites of mortification followed by and perhaps triggering an ecstatic vision in which the initiate felt himself to be transported to heaven for a "one-to-one" encounter with the goddess. The result of the experience was eternal admission to the company of the gods (*Metam.* 11.24).[47]

Indeed, all of the mystery cults seemed to promise immortality and not a few of them contained considerable astral, planetary and solar imagery, together with astral journey of the initiate. The astrological imagery had its origin in Babylon and Chaldaea but was acclimated to the Hellenistic worldview. The mysteries of Mithras, for instance, contain much astrological material, a seven-graded ladder of initiation of which the highest was *heliodromos*. The structure for a heavenly journey is certainly mirrored in the organization, though the dearth of textual evidence makes it impossible to confirm that a journey was actually enacted.[48]

The imagery of ascension, albeit a spiritual one through the various systems of neoplatonic emanations, is so widespread in philosophy as to defy all but the simplest generalizations. Stoic notions of the universality of the fiery *logos* within man and its source in the sun were also molded into the philosophical synthesis. Though the idea that men rose to the sun and stars contradicted the traditional ideas of life after death, the empire did not lack philosophers to reconcile the two. Iamblichus, for instance, said that the sun and moon were "the Isles of the Blessed" (*Vit. Pyth.* 18.82). By the time of Proclus, an elaborate psychology had evolved to account for this ascending property of the soul.[49] The history

[47] Cumont, *Oriental Religions in Roman Paganism*, 100.

[48] M. J. Vermaseren, *Mithras: The Secret God* (New York: Barnes & Noble, 1963); Cumont, *The Mysteries of Mithra* (Chicago: Open Court, 1903; repr., New York: Dover, 1956); and see *Mithraic Studies: Proceedings of the First International Congress of Mithraic Studies*, 2 vols., ed. J. Hinnels (Manchester: Manchester University Press, 1975). It would take too much time and space to summarize the reports of the mysteries relevant to this topic. See the convenient bibliography of mystery religions available in English compiled by E. J. Epp, articles in *OCD* and PW, as well as the series edited by Vermaseren, *Études préliminaires aux religions orientales dans l'Empire Romaín* (Leiden: Brill, 1961–).

[49] See *Proclus, The Elements of Theology*, ed. and trans. R. Dodds (Oxford: Oxford University Press 1963), app. 2, "The Astral Body in Neo-Platonism."

and popularity of astral piety has been fascinatingly chronicled by Franz Cumont in many publications.[50]

Other cultures also related native traditions of ascent. Many scholars have posited a shamanic influence on the Hellenistic world to explain the introduction of Bacchic rites and associate this with barbarian influence of Phrygia, Dacia, and eastern Europe.[51] Here, there are two common patterns. On the one hand, an ecstatic shamanistic journey may have the heavens as its goal with the purpose of healing or representing the community, leading a soul to its reward or even solely seeking supernatural experience. More often the motif of the underground journey appears, ostensibly an ancestor or contributor to orphic mysteries. The foremost example of this pattern—a transformation of the ascension motif—is among the Getae, who worshipped Zalmoxis through an underground rite.

[50] Cumont, *After Life in Roman Paganism.*

[51] Mircea Eliade, *Zalmoxis, the Vanishing God: Comparative Studies in the Religions and Folklore of Dacia and Eastern Europe* (Chicago: University of Chicago Press, 1972); idem, *Shamanism: Archaic Techniques of Ecstasy* (Princeton: Princeton University Press, 1964); E. R. Danos, *The Greeks and the Irrational* (Berkeley: University of California Press, 1951). The orphic tradition has been outlined by W. F. C. Guthrie, *Orpheus and Greek Religion* (Princeton: Princeton University Press, 1935) and I. M. Linforth, *The Arts of Orpheus* (Berkeley: University of California Press, 1941). More recent evidence suggesting the antiquity of the tradition can be found in the Derveni Papyrus; see R. van den Broek, "The Serapis Oracle in Macrobius Sat. 1, 20, 16-17," in *Hommages à Maarten J. Vermaseren*, ed. T. A. Edridge and M. Boer, 2 vols. (Leiden: Brill, 1978), 1:123f.

TWO

ASCENSION IN HELLENISTIC JUDAISM

The argument of the last chapter necessarily cut across several historical periods. Though the cosmological structure and apparatus for ascent and descent was known generally throughout the Hellenistic world, one cannot assume that it was always and in every place interpreted to have the same meaning. The structure was general, its meaning and exegesis was localized, dependent on the cultural assumptions of the society in question. The Hellenistic world was a complex cosmopolitan culture since general acceptance of Greek language made cross-cultural contact both possible and desirable; but not all distinctions between class, ideology, religion, and culture melted away. Indeed, against the general mythological structure of the Hellenistic world, differences between individual cultures only show up more clearly.

The Hebrew Bible provides but one clear example of a heavenly journey—the ascension of Elijah in the whirlwind in 2 Kings 2:2-15. It is not related as a theodicy, rather as the demonstration that Elisha will continue the work of Elijah as his divinely appointed successor.

> When they had crossed, Elijah said to Elisha, "Ask what I shall do for you, before I am taken from you." And Elisha said, "I pray you, let me inherit a double share of your spirit."
>
> And he said, "You have asked a hard thing; yet, if you see me as I am being taken from you, it shall be so for you; but if you do not see me, it shall not be so." And as they still went on and talked, behold, a chariot of fire and horses of fire separated the two of them. And Elijah went up by a whirlwind into heaven. And Elisha saw it and he cried, "My father, my father! the chariots of Israel and its horsemen!" And he saw him no more. Then he took hold of his own clothes and rent them in two pieces. And he took up the mantle of Elijah that had fallen from him, and went back and stood on the bank of the Jordan.

> Then he took the mantle of Elijah that had fallen from him, and struck the water, saying, "Where is the Lord, the God of Elijah?" And when he had struck the water, the water was parted to the one side and to the other; and Elisha went over. (2 Kgs 2:9-14)

Though the extraordinary vision is taken as a sign of divine favor, there is scarce attention to the journey itself. Elijah's experience is not related per se; rather it serves as a sign in the present narrative that Elisha will continue the work of Elijah and that a double portion of the Spirit of YHWH rests upon him. To have been privileged to see Elijah's ascension places Elisha in the special category of God's favored, just as his subsequent miracles do. Nevertheless, since the ascent appears at the end of Elijah's earthly career, it is tied to the structural pattern we have been tracing. Thus, later tradition, which will work out a general theory of immortality, can make Elijah into a messenger of God, revisiting earth from time to time to accomplish specific tasks and to announce the eschatological end.[1]

Other explicit biblical references to journeys to heaven are always put in a negative context. The most evident example is Isaiah's prophecy on "the King of Babylon" who is cut down to the ground because he tried to ascend to heaven:

> You said in your heart,
> I will ascend to heaven, above the stars of God . . .
> But you are brought down to Sheol. (Isa 14:13a, 15a)

I cannot see this in any other way than as part of the polemic against Mesopotamian religion, with its concepts of ascension of the king on his enthronement, as was described above.[2] YHWH prevents man from

[1] The identification of Elijah and Phineas, together with their martyrdom may be due to Mal 2:4-7 in relationship to Num 25:12-13, then Mal 3:23. See Ps.-Philo, where Phineas has been lifted up. See A. Zeron, "The Martyrdom of Phineas-Elijah," *JBL* 98 (1979): 99–100; also R. Bauckham, "The Martyrdom of Enoch and Elijah," *JBL* 95 (1976): 447–58 and A. Spiro, "The Ascension of Phinehas," *PAAJR* 22 (1955): 91–114. See especially the following for the study of ascension in its Judaic context: M. Smith, *Clement of Alexandria and a Secret Gospel of Mark* (Cambridge: Cambridge University Press, 1973); H. C. Cavallin, "Leben nach dem Tode im Spätjudentum und im frühen Christentum, 1. Spätjudentum," *ANRW* 19.1 (1979): 240–345; G. W. E. Nickelsburg Jr., *Resurrection, Immortality, and Eternal Life in Intertestamental Judaism* (Missoula, Mont.: Scholars, 1972).

[2] Pp. 192–93.

ascending. The boundary between earth and heaven is not breached from below. It rather is mediated from above. The legitimate direction for mediation is most often from above to below. God Himself descends on a number of occasions. The angel of the Lord is sometimes indistinguishable from God.[3] Elsewhere the angel looks like a man (Gen 18:2, 22). Even so, the angel appears to carry God's name and direct God's actions (Gen 19:1, 13; 16;13; Exod 23:20). The angel is often explicitly described as descending and ascending (Exod 3:8; Judg 13:20). These reports will greatly interest Hellenistic Jews, for whom speculation about the meaning of mediation will provide a medium to synthesize native Hebrew thought with the then contemporary worldview.

The other area in which mediation from above provided an opening to Hellenistic interpretation was wisdom literature. According to the Bible, wisdom is available to all men on earth and not hidden. By the Hellenistic period, Wisdom is a figure sent from the heavens, often identified with "the law" or the Stoic *logos*.[4]

In view of the clear polemic against such claims to firsthand knowledge of God together with the biblical statement that no man can see God and live (Exod 33:20), it is rather surprising that so many ascension and ecstatic journeys are reported in intertestamental literature. The influence of foreign cultures is surely a major factor contributing to the popularity of the ascension structure. But the ascending heroes are personages important to Jews, the morals derived are Jewish morals. Those who rank foremost as mediators are Moses (who ascends Sinai to see God "face to face" [Exod 33:11; Num 12:7-8; Deut 34:10-12]) and Enoch (whom God "took" and thus, like Elijah, has no recorded death). But ascensions are also told of Levi, Baruch, Phineas, Ezra, Adam, Zephaniah, and Isaiah.[5]

[3] See Gerhard von Rad, *Old Testament Theology* (New York: Harper, 1962), 1:287.

[4] See Sir 24; Bar 3:27–4:4; Wis 9:10; 7:27; 8:10. Wisdom is the agent of salvation in 9:18; 10:1, 4, 6, 13, I5. Of late, these formulations have been extensively studied. See B. L. Mack, "Wisdom, Myth and Mythology," *Int* 24 (1970): 46–60, 51–53 and idem, *Logos und Sophia: Untersuchungen zur Weisheitstheologie im hellenistischen Judentum*, SUNT 10 (Göttingen: Vandenhoeck & Ruprecht, 1973); Charles Talbert, "The Myth of a Descending-Ascending Redeemer in Mediterranean Antiquity," *NTS* 22 (1977): 418–39.

[5] For Enoch's ascension, see Gen 5:24; Job 4:23; Eccl 44:16; 49:14; Wis 4:10-11; 1 En. 39:3ff.; 70–71; 2 En.; Heb 11:5; 1 Clem. 9:3. For Levi, see T. Levi 2:5f. For Elijah, see 2 Kgs 2:1-12; 1 Macc 2:58; 1 En. 89:52; 93:8; Eccl 48:9; Mark 9:28 and par.; Rev

Philo is a logical place to begin tracing the history of the Jewish traditions, not because he is the earliest Jew to deal with these ideas but because, in giving the ideas philosophical clarity, he achieved a brilliant synthesis of Greek thought and native Hebrew tradition.

Philo, as well, represents a full actualization of philosophic possibilities of the ascension structure which were developed in the Hellenistic Age. In spite of the dearth of specific Hebrew texts implying intermediation between earth and heaven by figures other than God, the Greek intellectual and philosophical atmosphere virtually necessitated such an idea. In order to protect the perfection of God, Philo speaks of a Logos which is God's principal mediator, communicating His desires, making it possible for us in impermanent existence to know His will. He regularly allegorizes all references to the angels in the Bible as referring to this mediating Logos-figure which he even calls a son of God. In order to discuss mediation in the other direction, he makes many Old Testament worthies into examples of the success of Greek education and philosophical acumen.[6] The patriarchs, Aaron, Levi, Melchizedek, and especially Moses are allegorized as ascending through various levels of discipline, thought, and contemplation to be called into the divine presence. This can often be seen as a heavenly journey of the type we have been describing. Though it is allegorized and spiritualized, the same general structural configuration can be seen, which disposes scholars like Dey to speak of "patterns" and "exemplars" of perfection. The structural pattern emerges when one notes that the specific exegeses Philo brings are secondary to his overarching system of ascent to God.

Philo expressed the distinction between life and death, heaven and earth, permanence and impermanence, immutability and mutability in Greek philosophical terms. God, being the perfect and most complete existent, is so beyond human ken that nothing on earth can have direct knowledge of Him. The gap between the divine and human is bridged by a series of intermediaries—God's powers, which are infinite but can

---

11:3-12. For Baruch's ascension, see 2 Bar. 13:3; 25:1; 46:7; 76; 3 Bar. For Ezra, see 4 Ezra 14:9; 49. For Moses, see Josephus, *Ant.* 4.8.49; As. Mos.; Mark 9:28 and par.; Rev 11:3-12; Jude 9; Clement, *Strom.* 6.15. For Isaiah, see Ascen. Isa. For Abraham, see Apoc. Ab. and T. Ab. For Adam, see LAE 25–29. For Zephaniah, see Apoc. Zephaniah in Clement, *Strom.* 5.11.

[6] See L. K. K. Dey, *The Intermediary World and Patterns of Perfection in Philo and Hebrews* (Missoula, Mont.: Scholars, 1975).

be categorized in various ways.[7] The summary of these powers he calls by the Stoic term, *logos*, which for him is structurally equivalent to the *nous* of Platonic thought. Thus, the structure of the Hellenistic cosmology is asserted once more.

Even more interesting is Philo's use of these concepts to demythologize and to remythologize the Bible. The Logos or other of God's powers are used by Philo to explain all of the scriptural traditions wherein are human representations of God. Places where He is represented with human feelings and emotions are seen by Philo to be descriptions of His Logos or intermediary who is divine—in fact, a second God—but who participates in our world as well.[8] The purpose of God's human form, according to Philo, is to educate man to His ways.[9] He appears as a man in order to educate men to his real incorporeal nature. Since incorporeality is only knowable to the human mind by extrapolation, God's human figure is necessary as a propaedeutic. So even God's manifestations—as He actually is in Himself and as He is seen in the world—mirror this underlying juxtaposition of mortality versus immortality, earthly versus heavenly life. Philo, of course, attempts to discuss these subjects in a scriptural framework, although we know that is has its basis as well in Greek philosophy and indeed in the accepted late Hellenistic worldview:

> There was a time when I had leisure for philosophy and for the contemplation of the universe and its contexts, when I made its spirit my own in all its beauty and loveliness and true blessedness, when my constant companions were divine themes and verities, wherein I rejoiced with a joy that never cloyed nor sated. I had no base or abject thoughts nor groveled in search of reputation or of wealth or bodily comforts, but seemed always to be borne aloft into the heights with a soul possessed by some God-sent inspiration, a fellow-traveller with the sun and moon and the whole heaven and universe. Ah then I gazed down from the upper air, and straining the mind's eye beheld, as from some commanding peak, the multitudinous world-wide spectacles of earthly things, and blessed my lot in that I had escaped by main force from the plagues of mortal life. But as it proved, my steps were dogged by the deadliest of mischiefs,

[7] H. A. Wolfson, *Philo: Foundations of Religious Philosophy in Judaism, Christianity, and Islam* (Cambridge, Mass.: Harvard University Press, 1947), 1:219; see esp. *Cher.* 9.27f., *Fug.* 18.95.100.

[8] *Somn.* 1.227–229; *QG* 2.62.

[9] *Deus* 51–73; *QG* 1.35 or 55; 2.54; *Somn.* 1.235–237. See N. A. Dahl, "Widersprüche in der Bibel," *ST* 25 (1971): 9–11.

> the hater of the good, envy, which suddenly set upon me and ceased not to pull me down with violence till it had plunged me in the ocean of civil cares, in which I am swept away, unable even to raise my head above the water. Yet amid my groans I hold my own, for, planted in my soul from my earliest days I keep the yearning for culture which ever has pity and compassion for me, lifts me up and relieves my pain. To this I owe it that sometimes I raise my head and with the soul's eyes—dimly indeed because the mist of extraneous affairs has clouded their clear vision—I yet make shift to look around me in my desire to inhale a breath of life pure and unmixed with evil. And if unexpectedly I obtain a spell of fine weather and a calm from civil turmoils, I get me wings and ride the waves and almost tread the lower air, wafted by the breezes of knowledge which often urges me to come to spend my days with her, a truant, as it were from merciless masters in the shape not only of men but of affairs, which pour in upon me like a torrent from different sides. Yet it is well for me to give thanks to God even for this, that though submerged I am not sucked down into the depths, but can also open the soul's eyes, which in my despair of comforting hope I thought had now lost their sight, and am irradiated by the lift of wisdom, and am not given over to lifelong darkness. O behold me daring, not only to read the sacred messages of Moses, but also in my love of knowledge to peer into each of them and unfold and reveal what is not known to the multitude. (Philo, *Spec. Leg.* 1–6 [Colson, LCL])

These personal observations begin without reference to a particular Scripture. They imply that in his youth, perhaps as a student, he had time for pure meditations and thus his soul would soar in the universe along with the other divine objects, the sun and moon and heavenly bodies (which are, of course, viewed as more perfect ensouled creatures). Though he sadly reports his present inability to continue such scholarly, rhapsodic ascents into mystical thought, at the end of the passage Philo maintains that he can still ascend through his mind's meditations of divine Scripture. Thus, for Philo, the activity of the mind, under the guidance of Scripture, leads to ascent to the divine.

Even a quick perusal of Philo's biblical exegesis is enough to convince us that behind this metaphor of ascent stand traditions of an actual journey to God:

> After all the rest, as I have said, Moses tells us that man was created after the image of God and after His likeness (Gen. 1:26). Right well does he say this, for nothing earth-born is more like God than man. Let no one represent the likeness as one to a bodily form; for neither is God in

> human form, nor is the human body God-like. No, it is in respect of the Mind, the sovereign element of the soul, that the word "image" is used; for after the pattern of a single Mind, even the Mind of the Universe as an archetype, the mind in each of those who successively came into being was moulded. It is in a fashion a god to him who carries and enshrines it as an object of reverence; for the human mind evidently occupies a position in men precisely answering to that which the great Ruler occupies in all the world. It is invisible while itself seeing all things, and while comprehending the substances of others, it is as to its own substance unperceived; and while it opens by arts and sciences roads branching in many directions, all of them great highways, it comes through land and sea investigating what either element contains. Again, when on soaring wing it has contemplated the atmosphere and all its phases, it is borne yet higher to the ether and the circuit of heaven, and is whirled round with the dances of planets and fixed stars, in accordance with the laws of perfect music, following that love of wisdom which guides its steps. And so, carrying its gaze beyond the confines of all substance discernible by sense, it comes to a point at which it reaches out after the intelligible world, and on descrying in that world sights of surpassing loveliness, even the patterns and the originals of the things of sense which it saw here, it is seized by a sober intoxication, like those filled with Corybantic frenzy, and is inspired, possessed by a longing far other than theirs and a nobler desire. Wafted by this to the topmost arch of the things perceptible to mind, it seems to be on its way to the Great King Himself; but, amid its longing to see Him, pure and untempered rays of concentrated light stream forth like a torrent, so that by its gleams the eye of the understanding is dazzled. (Philo, *Opif.* 69–71 [Colson, LCL])

In commenting on Genesis 1:26, Philo allegorizes the mind as the likeness of God while maintaining that the mind is a kind of God in itself, for, within the body, it provides a model for God's relationship to the world. By the power of the mind, man ascends, first to the atmosphere then to the heavens. Finally, seized by "a sober intoxication"[10]—a term which Philo uses often to describe religious ecstasy—man can ascend to within sight of God, whose majesty is firmly protected from human sight by the brilliant light stream.

[10] Hans Lewy, *Sobria Ebrietas: Untersuchungen zur Geschichte der antiken Mystik*, *ZNW* 9 (Giessen: Töpelmann, 1929).

According to Philo, Scripture gives us clear examples of this mystical ascent so that he feels free to allegorize the figures of Abraham, Jacob, Melchizedek, Levi, and Moses as mystical voyageurs:[11]

> These no doubt are truly admirable persons and superior to the other classes. They have, as I said, advanced from down to up by a sort of heavenly ladder and by reason and reflection happily inferred the creator from his works. But, those if such there be, who have had the power to apprehend Him through Himself without the cooperation of any reasoning process to lead them to the sight, must be recorded as holy and genuine worshippers and friends of God in truth, In their company is he who in the Hebrew is called Israel but in our tongue, the God-seer who sees not His real nature, for that, as I said, is impossible—but that He is. (Philo, *Praem.* 43f. [Colson, LCL])

The chief reward for this ascent is a vision of God. Indeed, the name Israel for Philo is considered to mean "He who sees God." However, the chief model for heavenly ascent is Moses for Philo. Moses ascends Mount Sinai, not only to receive the Ten Commandments, but in the process to receive a mystical vision of God. In *Questions on Exodus* 40 Moses is allegorized as the soul ascending not just Sinai but the very heavens:

> Ex. 24, 12 a: What is the meaning of the words, "Come up to me to the mountain and be there?" This signifies that a holy soul is divinized by ascending not to the air or to the ether or to heaven (which is) higher than all but to (a region) above the heavens. And beyond the world there is no place but God. And He determines the stability of the removal by saying "be there" (thus) demonstrating the placelessness and the unchanging habitation of the divine place. For those who have a quickly satiated passion for reflexion fly upward for only a short distance under divine inspiration and then they immediately return. They do not fly so much as they are drawn downwards, I mean, to the depths of Tartarus. But those who do not return from the holy and divine city, to which they have migrated, have God as their chief leader in the migration. (Philo, *QE* 2.40 [Marcus, LCL])[12]

[11] See Dey, *Patterns of Perfection in Philo and Hebrews.*

[12] For a more complete study of the Moses traditions, see W. A. Meeks, *The Prophet-King* (Leiden: Brill, 1967). Besides Moses' preeminent role in Judaism, the fact that his burial place is undisclosed (Deut 34:5) may explain the legend of his ascension. See, e.g., Josephus, *Ant.* 4.8.47f.; As. Mos.

As an interpretation of the Song of Moses, Philo relies on the description of ecstatic trance to portray the ascent of the soul in contemplation. In fact, since these ascents are all that are available to man before death, they serve as the experiential guarantee that death is transcended in immortality. Though Philo may also have other important philosophical problems on his mind, the structure of his thought reveals an underlying concern of the Hellenistic Age.

Similar concerns and structures are visible in the less Hellenized Jewish literature of the time. Although apocalyptic literature may have many different functions and purposes, an underlying ascent structure can be isolated. Due to the recent publication of the Aramaic fragments of Enoch found in the Dead Sea Scroll community, attention has been drawn to the antiquity of the Enoch legends.[13] Since the books were found in Aramaic at Qumran, which was destroyed at the end of the first century, it has become clear that the Enoch traditions are much older than one might expect merely from the Slavic, Greek, and Ethiopic fragments heretofore extant. Parts of the tradition seem as old as the throne visions in Daniel, and Milik even suggests that the biblical book of Daniel actually relies on a preexistent corpus of Enoch writings of which the Aramaic fragments are later witnesses.

As in Philo's writings, heavenly ascent is tied to scriptural citations, which for a Jew must provide a legitimate basis for the speculation; just as in Philo, however, the Enoch traditions go far beyond anything which Scripture explicitly says. In this case, the biblical pretext is an omission in Scripture. Enoch appears in the list of antediluvian heroes in Genesis 5:21-25 occupying the same position as Utnapishtim in the Babylonian version.[14] Besides living to inordinate age, like other legendary figures,

[13] *The Books of Enoch: Aramaic Fragments of Qumran Cave 4*, ed. J. T. Milik with Matthew Black (Oxford: Clarendon, 1976). Translations are from R. H. Charles, *The Apocrypha and Pseudepigrapha of the Old Testament* (Oxford: Clarendon, 1912). For more bibliography, see G. Delling, *Bibliographie zur jüdisch-hellenistischen und intertestamentarischen Literatur 1900–1965* (Berlin: Akademie, 1969) and J. H. Charlesworth, *The Pseudepigrapha and Modern Research* (Missoula, Mont.: Scholars, 1976). For a study of tours of heaven and hell, see the dissertation of Martha Himmelfarb, University of Pennsylvania (published as *Tours of Hell: An Apocalyptic Form in Jewish and Christian Literature* [Philadelphia: Fortress, 1985]), where the complete history of the vision of hell and the "question and answer" form is to be surveyed. The approach here is of necessity more selective.

[14] Utnapishtim was also granted immortality and a divine abode. Other parallels to Enoch's journey may be found in Sir 44:16; 49:14; Wis 4:10f.; Jub. 4:23; T. Isaac 4:2; Philo, *Mut.* 4 (34); *Abr.* 3 (17); Josephus, *Ant.* 1.3.4; 9.2.2; Heb 11:5; Ps.-Philo, 1:16;

Scripture says many unusual things about Enoch. For instance, it says, not once but twice, that Enoch walked with God (Gen 5:22, 24). Scripture further reports that Enoch disappeared: "he was not, for God took him," together with a most strange omission of a report of his death. The story provides an opening for speculation about Enoch's ascent to heaven, for it takes no great leap of the imagination to conclude that Enoch's walk with God was in heaven where he is still alive, having been transported physically before the time of his demise. Though the occasion is natural enough for discussion of heavenly journey, the wonder is that so many speculations on this particular biblical pericope have come down to us, speculation on mortality and immortality but also on the order of heaven and its contents.

First Enoch reads like a fabulous travelogue. No doubt, wonderment at strange sights and dangerous journeys was part of the fascination of the literature, but the same contradiction between heavenly permanence and earthly impermanence which we saw in Philo and the Greek texts can be seen here.

However, while Philo maintained that personal ethics and righteousness were necessary for the rigors of intellectual meditation and ascent, the Enoch material is far more interested in a communal question of the ultimate rewards of the righteous, punishment for the sinners. For Enoch the question is framed in cosmic rather than human terms. The writers of Enoch are quite bothered by the seeming lack of justice on earth, but the perplexity is not confined to the acts of men. Even the angels express shock that God has allowed violence to cover the earth (9:1–5). The atrocities, however, are the work of evil angels, not of mere men (9:6–9). God's answer is that all has been foreseen (9:9–10).

In this context, Enoch's ascent has the primary purpose of explaining some of the great evil on earth while confirming that both the suffering of the righteous and the success of sinful forces will be righted hereafter. First, Enoch tells us that he had a vision in which he is asked to intercede for the evil angels who are by then, repentant (12). Even so they are not forgiven and are forbidden to ascend to heaven (14:5). After telling them of the uncompromising divine verdict, Enoch relates his journey to heaven (14:8f.). Thus we note that, as in the Arda Viraf legends, the ascent is set at a time of crisis (albeit here a mythical one)

---

1 Clem. 9.3; Ps.-Clem, *Recog.* 1.52.4; 4.12.1; Acts Pil. 6.6; Justin, *Dial.* 19.3; Irenaeus, *Haer.* 4.16.2; 5.5.1; Tertullian, *An.* 50.

when the traditional understanding of the universe has come into question. The ascent serves to verify that the society's basic values are still valid, though now in a mysterious and secret way. Even if chaos appears to rule on earth, God's heavenly plan will soon be evident. The contrast and contradiction between the perfect heavenly realm and the imperfect earthly one is mediated again by Enoch's heavenly journey.[15]

Fantastic though it is, the journey is composed of snatches of descriptions of the heavenly realm in Daniel, Ezekiel, and other Scriptures, culminating in a divine audience before the Great Glory, a privilege even the angels could not bear (14:21).

After the audience, Enoch is given a guided tour of heaven, which confirms what is supposed to be the moral as well as the geographical order of the world described in Scripture (14:9). Innovations in the worldview give us important evidence for the actual date of the document.[16] Besides the heavenly bodies, the prison of punishment for the fallen and the hollow places of assembly for the righteous are described. Of overriding importance is merely that they exist—as does the garden of Eden. They are, in a sense, waiting for each righteous man's "eschatological verification." Therefore the worldview ascribed to the Bible is confirmed; its protohistory is translated into a heavenly geography. Though the workings of the physical universe are described, the most important message of Enoch is that the unrighteous will be punished and that the suffering of the righteous has a meaning.

The later Enoch material contains descriptions of ascent to which we shall turn after having reviewed the Christian evidence, because they occur in traditions which are under suspicion of having been influenced by Christianity, either directly or polemically.[17] Instead it would be profitable to compare the Enoch legends with the ascent of Levi in the Testament of the Twelve Patriarchs. This document reflects not a minority community under pressure but, probably, as many scholars see it, the

[15] 1 En. 14; Milik, *Books of Enoch*, 196f.

[16] See Milik, introduction to *Books of Enoch*, 15–22.

[17] C. Colpe, "υἱός τοῦ ἄνθρωπου," *TDNT* 8:403–81; Milik, "Problèmes de la littérature hénochique à la lumière des fragments araméens de Qumran," *HTR* 64 (1971): 333–78; idem, "Turfan et Qumran Livre des Géants juifs et manichéens," in *Tradition und Glaube: das frühe Christentum in seiner Umwelt: Festgabe für K. G. Kuhn*, ed. G. Jeremias, H. W. Kuhn, and H. Stegemann (Göttingen: Vandenhoeck & Ruprecht, 1971), 117–27.

Hasmonean Dynasty trying to legitimate its priestly claims.[18] The heavenly journey of Levi confirms the legitimacy of priestly institutions in Israelite culture:

> I, Levi, was born in Haran, and I came with my father to Shechem. And . . . when I was feeding the flocks in Abel Maul, the spirit of the understanding of the Lord came upon me and I saw all men corrupting their way, and that unrighteousness had built for itself walls, and lawlessness sat upon towers. And I was grieving for the race of the sons of men and I prayed to the Lord that I might be saved. Then there fell upon me a sleep and I beheld a high mountain, and I was upon it. And behold the heavens were opened, and an angel of God said to me, Levi, enter. (T. Levi 2:1–6)

Note that the ascent is brought on as an answer to the problem of injustice. The description of heaven in the Testament of Levi is far more developed and organized than in the early Enoch material. Particularly important is the mediator of ascent—the angel of the Lord who serves as the guide of Levi. Levi asks for the name of the angel, in order that he may call upon him in times of trial, but the name of the angel is not stated openly in the text. The angel identifies himself as "he who is appointed over Israel so that they may not be destroyed."[19] Since Levi is the eponymous ancestor of the priestly class, it is the special task of his tribe to speak the secret name of God. So, there can be no doubt that the angel is meant to carry the divine name, YHWH, which he conveys to Levi (and through Levi to the high priests throughout time).

When, in a later vision, Levi is dressed in his priestly splendor by the angels, the result is meant to reinforce the divine favor of the priesthood for his descendants, to legitimate Levi in his priestly duties. The vision

[18] The apocryphal and pseudepigraphical texts are taken from Charles, *Apocrypha and Pseudepigrapha of the Old Testament.* Although the Testament of Levi is not without its Christian interpolations, scholarly opinion is relatively uniform about what can be construed as a Christian addition. However, much doubt still remains about the character of the original text, its date, and its provenance. See H. Slingerland, *The Testament of the Twelve Patriarchs: A History of Research* (Missoula, Mont.: Scholars, 1976) and also Charlesworth, *Pseudepigrapha and Modern Research*; and idem, "Christian and Jewish Self-Definition in Light of the Christian addition to the Apocalyptic Writings," paper for McMaster Project on Normative Self-Definition, published in *Jewish and Christian Self-Definition*, ed. E. P. Sanders (Philadelphia: Fortress, 1981), 2:27–55.

[19] There is a consistent rabbinic polemic against these ideas, saying that God Himself is the guardian of Israel. See pp. 249–50.

may confirm the rights of the Hasmoneans to the priesthood and kingship both, though some scholars feel the statement to be an interpolation.[20]

> And the third shall be called by a new name, because a king shall arise in Judah and shall establish a new priesthood after the fashions of the Gentiles. And His presence is beloved, as a prophet of the most High, the Seed of Abraham our father. (T. Levi 8:14)

Although we cannot be sure of the exact circumstances of the writing, Levi's ascent into heaven, his election to legitimate status, is followed closely by a piece of political propaganda. In this case, the rights of priesthood are eternally sanctioned, the people are promised divine deliverance from enemies, and the role of the kingship as foundation for priesthood is guaranteed. Earthly deliverance for the seed of Levi is dependent on his knowledge of how to call upon his angelic intermediary.

Other functions of ascent, which come to the fore with the downfall of the commonwealth, can be seen in the Apocalypse of Abraham.[21] The book is a reworking of the biblical Abraham story, datable to a time close to the destruction of the second temple on account of the references to the destruction of Judaea, mainly for the sin of idolatry (Apoc. Ab. 29f.). In the first part of the book, Abraham's youth is recounted. Since Abraham opposes the idolatry he finds in his father's house, he is saved from destruction. The first section of the story describes the faithful Abraham as a model for righteous behavior.

The second section of the work begins with chapter 9. As a preparation for the apocalypse, Abraham is told to ready a sacrifice (apparently as in Gen 15:9f.):[22]

> And while I was still lying with my face upon the earth, I heard the voice of the Holy One speaking: "Go Yahoel, and by means of my ineffable name raise me yonder man and strengthen him (so that he will recover) from his trembling." And the angel came, whom He had sent to me, in the likeness of a man, and grasped me by my right hand, set me up upon

[20] See Slingerland, *Testament of the Twelve Patriarchs*, 60–90.

[21] Texts which come down to us in Slavonic versions alone are to be distrusted on account of Bogomil influence. However, there is nothing in the ascension tradition per se that is characteristic of a Bogomil invention. See, e.g., E. Turdeanu, "Le 'Testament d'Abraham' en slave et en roumain," *Oxford Slavonic Papers* 10 (1977): 1–38.

[22] Gen 25:9f. and the covenant of the pieces was supposed by many to be proof that to Abraham was given not only a vision of the sojourn in Egypt but secret knowledge of the end of times. See 4 Ezra 3:14; Bar 4:4.

> my feet, and said to me: ". . . I am called Yahoel by Him who moveth that which existeth with me on the seventh expanse upon the firmament, a power in virtue of the ineffable Name that is dwelling in me. I am the one who hath been given to restrain, according to His commandment, the threatening attack of the living creatures of the cherubim against one another, and teach those who carry Him the song of the seventh hour of the night of man. I am ordained to restrain the Leviathan, for unto me are subject the attack and menace of every single reptile."[23]

This mediator figure, who carries the name of God, whose name is even literally composed of the tetragrammaton YHWH plus the suffix EL (which by now is a standard angelic form), is described as powerful by virtue of the name of God within him. Apparently this is another example of the name of God understood as the personified guide to the ascent. Such an idea was not too hard to detect in Philo's allegory of YHWH as Logos and in the Testament of Levi, but here the name of God is explicitly embodied as an angel. Unlike the Testament of Levi, the privilege of seeing God and using God's name is given to the ancestor of the people as a whole, not specifically to the priesthood. This mediator restrains chaos in the world, becomes the guide for Abraham in his final ascent to heaven, and enigmatically is to teach the "Song of the Seventh Hour of the Night of man to those who carry Him." The function of this passage is quite elusive, but it appears to be related to the mystical hymns which surface again in *merkabah* documents.[24] As in the Testament of Levi there are two lines of mediation—one crossing from above to below in the person of an angel who is virtually God's presence on earth; the other crossing from below upward in the person of Abraham who rises to immortality by means of Yahoel, the psychopomp. While the Testament of Levi stresses earthly deliverance, this document is interested in the heavenly reward of the faithful.

Yahoel relates to Abraham that it was He who intervened for God throughout history. Then the sacrifice is complete and Abraham is addressed by an "unclean bird" (an interpretation of Abraham's chasing away of the birds). But, in this case, the unclean bird is supposed to be

[23] *The Apocalypse of Abraham*, ed. and trans. G. H. Box (New York: Macmillan, 1919), 46f.

[24] See e.g., G. Scholem, "The Merkabah Hymns and The Song of the Kine in a Talmudic Passage," in *Jewish Gnosticism, Merkabah Mysticism and Talmudic Tradition* (New York: Jewish Theological Seminary of America, 1965), 20–30.

Azazel, the fallen angel. While Azazel's lot will be on earth, Abraham's lot is in heaven. Therefore the basic order of the universe is given a moral coding. Those who do not sin may have Abraham as a model and rise. Those who sin, even those who are angels, are condemned to stay on earth in its deepest and most inaccessible parts. Afterwards, the two figures ascend together by means of the undivided birds. Upon reaching heaven Abraham recites the hymn he has been taught, after which he has a vision of the throne chariot of God, the description of which is based on Ezekiel 1. Abraham is treated to a view of the operation of the cosmos, another first-person testimony that the world is as the ancients imagined it, thus confirming their view of the universe. Abraham sees the garden of Eden, Adam and Eve, the origin and spread of sin. Biblical prehistory is again given a geographical verification. The punishment of sinners is next—with a description of the destruction of the temple, followed by the promise of a reconstructed Jerusalem, serving God in righteousness. As in the Enoch material, revelation of the structure of the universe, both its natural order and its history, confirms that the seeming contradictions of life will be resolved. Justice will reign among God's saints and unrighteousness will be punished. Like Enoch, the book does not discuss resurrection. It has, instead, two kinds of restoration. There is an apocalyptic restoration of earth at the end of time and there is the garden of Eden, the heavenly paradise to which the righteous go when they die (Apoc. Ab. 21).

As in the other descriptions then, there are two basic ways in which the contradictions between heaven and earth, mortality and immortality can be resolved. The first is through the descent of an angelic figure, usually God's principal angelic assistant, His earthly manifestation, His name, or some other concept of mediation which functions as the Logos does in Philo. This can be contrasted with the other breach of the opposing zones—an ascent of the hero to understand the secrets, to confirm that God will reward the righteous, to pass on the revelation to those on earth and then to serve as the role model *par excellence* for the saints who will reascend to immortality at the end of earthly life. Therefore, all injustice and death on earth are but ephemeral to the righteous. The problem can be expressed in a number of ways: as a contrast between some concept of immortality and mortality, or as a contrast between immorality and morality. The concepts are usually parallel for the apocalyptic mind.

In the Testament, Abraham is reluctant to die. As reward for his righteousness he is granted a heavenly journey before his demise. As Abraham looks down from the chariot on his way to heaven, he is horrified to see the extent of human sinning—no doubt, the very problem which generated this work. In his rage he calls upon Michael to destroy everything. But God's voice is heard from heaven, explaining that Abraham's virtue has made him too severe a judge. God needs to allow freedom in the world so as to give each man every opportunity to repent before his death.

Abraham is brought to heaven to view hell and paradise from whence he returns to earth where he is shortly to die. Surely, there is no better illustration of the literary relationship between fear of death, the concept of immortality, theodicy, and heavenly journey. The purpose of the story is explicitly to quell the anxieties men feel in the face of death by means of Abraham's verified experience that immortality awaits the righteous.

These themes are also expressed in the Books of Adam and Eve (including The Apocalypse of Moses), which contain a number of related traditions embellished by Christian scribes.[25] In this writing the death and ascent of Adam by a chariot of light (32) is shown to Eve. The angel of the Lord appears—this time as Eve—crying in repentance for all her sins. Instead of interest in celestial geography, Adam's grave is shown to her and the climax of the story comes when God promises resurrection:

> And God called and said "Adam, Adam," and the body answered from the earth and said: "Here I am, Lord." And God said to him: "I told thee (that) earth thou art and to earth shall thou return. Again I promise to thee the Resurrection; I will raise you up in the Resurrection with every man who is of thy seed." (Apoc. Mos. 41:1)

The text occurs only in the Apocalypse of Moses but the Life of Adam and Eve includes this reference: "Man of God, mourn not for thy dead more than six days for on the seventh day is the sign of the resurrection and the rest of the age to come; on the seventh day the Lord rested from all his works" (LAE 51:2). There can be no doubt of the meaning of heavenly ascent here. While it is not a magical process of immortalization,

[25] See Charles, *Apocrypha and Pseudepigrapha of the Old Testament*, 129f.; and Charlesworth, *Pseudepigrapha and Modern Research*, 74.

it serves to confirm that God has made a remedy for the punishment of the fall. Immortality is within grasp for all the true sons of Adam who can repent of their sins.

In all these cases we have sensed that partisan loyalties are at stake, even when they cannot be identified by name. For, according to all reports, the existence of resurrection or immortality was both a controversial and constant issue in sectarian Judaism. Different groups and sects pressed their own perspective on the biblical text to extract a meaning favorable to themselves.[26] Their partisan manifesto was then confirmed, often by means of heavenly ascent.

Third Baruch, or the Greek Apocalypse of Baruch, brings other emphases of the ascent tradition to focus.[27] Though the Baruch literature, like the Enoch literature, is made up of several fragments which circulated independently, it appears that the dramatic situation of the literature is constant. A major aspect of the Baruch literature is the problem of the destruction of the first temple, which is a symbol of the destruction of the second temple. First Baruch raises the issue. It is even more forcefully outlined at the beginning of 2 Baruch. As an answer to Baruch's prayer in 2 Baruch 48, the Lord outlines the final judgment.

> "For this is as follows: he that is corrupted is not at all; he has both wrought iniquity so far as he could do anything, and has not remembered My goodness, nor accepted My longsuffering. Therefore thou shalt surely be taken up, as I before told thee." (2 Bar. 48:29f.)[28]

The sinner dies and is no more. The faithful are taken up. Second-Baruch makes the point that the destruction of the Temple in the time of Nebuchadnezzar was accomplished by angels (i.e., no man could do it). It was not just a matter of military strength, rather it was part of God's plan. So, too, is the resurrection of those who keep faith through the tribulations part of God's plan. These events are read by scholars as attempts to come to terms with the destruction of the temple in 70 C.E. Again, one notes the constant attention to the problem of theodicy, this time brought about by national disaster, accompanied by martyrdom of

[26] H. C. Cavallin, "Leben nach dem Tode im Spätjudentum und im frühen Christentum, I. Spätjudemum," *ANRW* 19.1 (1979): 240–345.

[27] See Charlesworth, *Pseudepigrapha and Modern Research*, 83–88.

[28] See 46:7 for Baruch.

the saints. The havoc demands a first-person verification that God is still vigilant.

The setting brings to the fore the heavenly journey in 3 Baruch.[29] The structure of the heavens confirms not only the order of creation but also the truth of biblical history, since the Tower of Babel and other famous examples of rebellion to God are revealed as actual places in the lower heavens.

The upper heaven, here the fifth one, reveals the reward of the righteous. The narrative concentrates on the mechanism by which the prayers and good deeds of the righteous are turned over to Michael, who holds the keys of the kingdom (3 Bar. 11:2).[30] He takes them in the form of flowers in an "exceedingly great vessel." The angels lament that the vessel is not filled (presumably because of man's unrighteousness and the inability of the righteous), but Michael says it is necessary that the righteous not depart from the wicked until their time is fulfilled. Michael then goes up to discover what the Lord desires. The Lord promises great rewards for those faithful even to a few things (3 Bar. 15:4). Afterwards, Baruch is returned to the place where he began and the ecstatic journey is finished. As in the other Jewish apocalypses, great emphasis of the journey is put on the justification of the Lord's ways to man, which affects even how the physical cosmos is described. The impetus is the seeming injustice and lack of reward to those faithful to the promises of the Lord. It is probable that the texts originated in a Jewish environment but the texts have been transmitted, valued, and edited by a Christian community.

A similar pattern can be seen in the Ezra cycle of material.[31] Again, the issue is the suffering concomitant to the destruction of the temple. Theodicy is revealed through a series of questions and answers. In 4 Ezra 7:75 Ezra asks the Lord:

[29] Charles, *Apocrypha and Pseudepigrapha of the Old Testament*, 528. E.g., 2 En. 2; 15 and 3 Bar. 6–9 have a parallel heavenly cosmology.

[30] In 4 Bar. 9:5 Michael is called the archangel of righteousness who guides the righteous to heaven.

[31] R. A. Kraft, "'Ezra' Materials in Judaism and Christianity," *ANRW* 19.1 (1979): 119–36.

> Whether after death, even now when every one must give back his soul, we shall be kept in rest until those times come in which thou shalt renew the creation, or we suffer torture forthwith?[32]

The answer is that souls are rewarded according to their action on earth. The soul then departs. If it has hearkened to God, it goes to him. If not, it wanders without rest. The seven orders of sinners and their fates after death are shown to Ezra but no specific heavenly journey is mentioned.

One of the most interesting documents for uncovering the thought world of Hellenistic Judaism is The Prayer of Joseph,[33] of whose 1100 lines only sixteen or so survive in the writings of Origen.[34] In what Origen calls "one of the apocrypha popular among the Hebrews," Jacob identifies himself as "Israel, an angel of God (ἄγγελος τοῦ θεοῦ) and a ruling spirit, the first-born of every living thing." Uriel, who is the eighth after Jacob but chief captain among the sons of God, descends to earth and engages in combat with Jacob. Israel either receives angelic status on the basis of the combat or is a preexistent angel incarnated as a man, but the descent-ascent pattern is clear in any case.[35]

The novel Joseph and Aseneth gives us another puzzling attestation of the ascension motif as the mediation of mythical opposites. Whether the book contains Jewish, Christian, or gnostic traditions,[36] most scholars agree that the text is originally Jewish and builds around a key series of oppositions. M. Philonenko expresses the contrast succinctly in these opposing terms:

> *Pain de vie/pain d'étouffement*
> *Coupe d'immortalité/coupe de traitrise*
> *Onction d'incorruptibilité/onction de perdition.*[37]

The structure of positive and negative valences has been incorporated into the plot. Aseneth is raised to new purity by her marriage with Joseph. She seems to represent the same kind of journey from defilement

[32] Charles, *Apocrypha and Pseudepigrapha of the Old Testament*, 587.

[33] See Charlesworth, *Pseudepigrapha and Modern Research*, 140.

[34] Cf. Eusebius, *Praep. ev.* 6.11.

[35] See also the Ladder of Jacob and other works of the Jacob cycle. Charlesworth, *Pseudepigrapha and Modern Research*, 130f.

[36] See Charlesworth, *Pseudepigrapha and Modern Research*, 137.

[37] M. Philonenko, *Joseph et Aseneth: Introduction, texte critique, traduction et notes* (Leiden: Brill, 1968), 90.

to purity to repentance as Sophia makes in Pistis Sophia.[38] Joseph, on the other hand, is viewed as a savior (Jos. Asen. 25:6) both in the national and religious sense of the word. Their marriage, then, represents a kind of ἱερὸς γάμος signifying divine favor. This moral is underscored by Michael's annunciation to Aseneth of what will befall her because of the sincerity of her repentance. Michael is introduced as the "chief captain of the Lord God and commander of all the host of the Most High" (14:7)—in short, as the angel of the Lord (15:3)—but also is the morning star, messenger of the light. After his departure, Aseneth realizes that he is God (17:9). He is described anthropomorphically as the twin of Joseph (ἀνὴρ ὅμοιος κατὰ πάντα τῷ Ἰωσήφ; 14:8) in all things except that his face, eyes, hair, hands, and feet glowed and sparkled as bright as all the earthly incandescences—fire, lightning, torches, molten iron—sure conventions for describing immortal heavenly beings which become central characteristics of the angelic creatures in *merkabah* literature.

Then follows a most mysterious revelation of Aseneth's honeycomb, together with a parable about bees. Those who wish to injure Aseneth die and remain on earth; those who do not can ascend to heaven. Since Aseneth is the converted woman *par excellence*, very probably the parable represents the author's view of the future reward to those who favor conversion. Then, the angel himself ascends to heaven in a fiery chariot. This revelation, with its promise of immortality, is meant to bridge the gap between the opposing forces. In this particular case, the conversion of the gentile women to Judaism is valorized and therefore one should probably assume its popularity to a highly acculturated Hellenistic Jewish community.

The last document to be considered in this section, The Testament of Job, also reflects Alexandrian Judaism, of the first or second century.[39] We are presented with a descending-ascending angelic messenger. The angel comes (ἐλθών; 3:5) and departs (ἀπελθόντες; 5:2) but the ascent-descent pattern is still assumed throughout, as the arrival of Satan[40]

[38] Philonenko, *Joseph et Aseneth*, 85.

[39] See Charlesworth, *Pseudepigrapha and Modern Research*, 134f. See also SBLSP 1 (1974) for a series of articles on the Testament of Job, notably those by Howard Kee, "Satan, Magic, and Salvation in the 'Testament of Job,'" 53–76; and J. J. Collins, "Structure and Meaning in the 'Testament of Job,'" 35–52.

[40] "Came" (8:2) or "came down" (16:1). See J. G. Davies, *He Ascended into Heaven: A Study in the History of Doctrine* (New York: Association Press, 1958), 69f.

shows.[41] After narrating the story of Job's suffering, an angel is revealed to him. The angel that visits Job is also called the "Lord" (T. Job 51:1–2) and probably represents the angel of the Lord, another figuration of the divine presence in human form. He tells Job that his conversion and suffering will be rewarded by resurrection. Indeed, before his first wife dies, she sees her children wearing crowns in heaven. Job's restored wealth on earth is surpassed by the reward he receives on his death—a chariot arrives to bring his soul to heaven, even as his body is buried.

The importance of the descending-ascending pattern for Hellenistic Judaism can be seen in this story. The book of Job is the locus classicus for the problem of theodicy in Hebrew culture. Hellenistic Judaism characteristically relies on the descent-ascent pattern to dramatize its views of justice. The descent of the angel is for revelation of the astral redemption awaiting those who suffer for His name's sake. The ascent of the hero is verification that reward awaits the faithful after death.

It seems clear that the *merkabah* texts, often called Jewish Gnosticism, ought to be seen as offshoots from apocalyptic literature. Though the traditions contained in these texts go back to apocalyptic and Hellenistic mysticism, the texts themselves are late by comparison—most of them are gaonic or later and reflect the level of mysticism practiced in far later times.[42] In spite of the later provenance of this material, the texts still reflect the basic structural system of ascent. The heavenly journey serves to confirm that the world's seeming injustice will be made right by God. The question arises often because of martyrdom or national catastrophe. The texts also help the students to remember their torah training and become filled with the halakah. The documents of *merkabah* mysticism, though they reflect their apocalyptic past and occasionally speculate on the transformation of men into their angelic counterparts,[43] have been fitted to rabbinic society. They show more interest in the rewards of remembered halakah as well as record the important ecstatic hymns and even provide us with a clue to the praxis of the participants. The

[41] See Talbert, "Descending-Ascending Redeemer," 424.

[42] The difficulty, of course, is to separate the Hellenistic core from the later material. In spite of the difficulty in dating, affinity with apocalyptic literature can be assumed. See the new book by Ithamar Gruenwald, *Apocalyptic and Merkabah Literature* (Leiden: Brill, 1979).

[43] See 3 En. or Sefer Hekhalot. A number of interesting medieval Jewish works deserve to be mentioned in passing because of their use or assumption of the heavenly journey motif. See, e.g., Gedulat Moshe, Sefer Harazim.

journey does not promise immortality—in rabbinic society repentance and good works are the basis for future reward. Rather, it confirms that the rabbinic system is true in the face of crisis and transmits a mystical praxis within the community.

THREE

ASCENSION AND MARTYRDOM: ASCENSION IN EARLY CHRISTIANITY

It is therefore no surprise that martyrdom figures strongly in the Jewish use of the ascent-descent structure. Indeed, resurrection and immortality seem to make their appearance in sectarian Israelite thought as an attempt to bridge the problem of the suffering made acute by martyrdom. There is no sure reference to resurrection in the Bible before the book of Daniel, conventionally dated to the time of Antiochus IV Epiphanes (ca. 165 B.C.E.).[1]

> And at that time shall Michael stand up, the great chief angel, who stands for the children of thy people: and there shall be a time of trouble such as never was since there was a nation till that same time: and at that time thy people shall be delivered, everyone who shall be found written in the book. And many of those who sleep in the dust of the earth shall awake, some to everlasting life and some to shame and everlasting contempt. And they who are wise shall shine like the brightness of the firmament; and they who turn many to righteousness like the stars for ever and ever. (Dan 12:1-3, Jerusalem Bible)

At the end of time, justice will be done. Those whose evil was not adequately requited on earth will be resurrected for future damnation. The others, whose righteousness was not fully rewarded, will be resurrected. Those who are still alive among the people and whose names are found in the book will also be delivered. Then comes a most interesting comment: "Those who are wise will then shine as the firmament in heaven" is taken to mean that those who have taught others concerning this doctrine and turned them to righteousness shall be as the stars forever. The interpretation of the passage rests on the meaning of the word "as." Is it purely a metaphor or is there an actuality to the statement—a real

[1] See J. J. Collins, *Apocalyptic and the Book of Daniel* (Missoula, Mont.: Scholars, 1978).

process of transformation? There is no reason to deny the latter, for astral immortality was already well known and the stars already widely associated with the souls of the departed. The most interesting aspect of the legend is that the reward is saved for those most zealous in bringing men over to the truth of sectarian life. It is not a general astral reward. In 2 Maccabees, in the addition to the document of the martyrdom of seven sons, resurrection is again viewed as a reward for the suffering of the martyrs. Here, however, there is no discussion of heavenly journey, showing that the themes of astral journey and life after death are not invariably connected. Note what the second and following sons say to the tyrant in 2 Maccabees 7:

> "You accursed wretch you may release us from our present existence, but the King of the Universe will raise us up to everlasting life because we have died for His laws . . .
>
> "From heaven have I had these, yet because of God's laws I count them as nothing, for from Him I hope to have them back again . . .
>
> "Better is it for people to be done to death by men if they have the hopeful expectation that they will again be raised up by God, but as for you, there will be no resurrection to life . . .
>
> "Do not vainly deceive yourself. We suffer these things because of ourselves, because we sinned against our own God."[2]

The first martyrs die for the honor of their religion but these sons have a more ironic taunt for their torturers. They are sending them to reward, not punishment. Even their seeming power is but a part of God's plan.

Though the belief in resurrection and ascension as the reward for faithfulness is characteristic of sectarian life, it also occurs in nonsectarian documents. As early as 2 Chronicles 3:1, Mount Moriah, the scene of Isaac's sacrifice in Genesis 22, is identified with the Temple Mount. The sacrifice of Isaac is therefore identified in Hellenistic Jewish literature with the temple cult, associating Isaac's patient endurance even unto death[3] with the vicarious atonement of the sacrificial cult.[4] There is

[2] Josippon adds here not just that the death will atone for the individual sin but that the death of the martyrs atones for the sins of people. See *The Second Book of Maccabees*, ed. S. Zeitlin, trans. S. Tedesche (New York: Harper, 1954), 163f.

[3] See 4 Macc 13:12; 16:19-20.

[4] See R. le Déaut, *La Nuit Paschale: Essai sur la signification de la Pâque juive à partir du Targum d' Exode XII 42* (Rome: Pontifical Biblical Institute, 1963); I. Levi, "Le sacrifice d'Isaac et la mort de Jesus," *REJ* 64 (1912): 161–84; H. J. Schoeps, *Paulus: Die Theologie des Apostels im Lichte der jüdischen Religionsgeschichte* (Tübingen: Mohr Siebeck, 1959); H.

no unambiguous evidence that the later midrash of Isaac's actual death, journey to the heavenly Yeshivah, and resurrection already existed at the birth of Christianity, though such a possibility cannot be entirely excluded either. It is clear that suffering, martyrdom, resurrection and ascent have been associated before Christianity. It is only surprising that the New Testament does not make more explicit use of the Isaac tradition.[5] Allusions to it can be found in James 2:21f.; Hebrews 11:17f.; 6:13. It is scarcely more openly mentioned in Romans 8:32. Though Paul's reference is still not explicit, he is apparently making a typological association on the basis of beloved "sonship" in order to further his discussion of atonement.

On the other hand, it is clear that martyrdom, ascension and resurrection are the themes that serve as the cradle for Christology. The combination of the events of Jesus' death as a martyred messianic pretender and the conviction that he was resurrected (justifying the messianic title) is expressed by the use of selected biblical texts reunderstood as prophesies about a crucified messiah.[6] The most often cited and most central text to the New Testament is Psalm 110:1f. which, among other things, is used to maintain that Jesus is raised and enthroned next to God:

> The Lord says to my Lord: Sit at my right hand, till I make your enemies your footstool.[7]

How this came to be associated with the "son of man" prophecy of Daniel 7:13 is not clear but, rather than being a self-designation of Jesus, the "Son of Man" may just as easily have been a title applied to the Christ by the church on the basis of his presumed ascension, seen as a fulfillment of Psalm 110, in turn connected to Psalm 8:4f.[8] However,

---

Riesenfeld, *Jésus Transfiguré: L'arrière-Plan Du Récit Évangélique De La Transfiguration De Notre-Seigneur* (Copenhagen: Munksgaard, 1947), 86–96; E. R. Goodenough, *The Problem of Method*, vol. 4 of *Jewish Symbols in the Greco-Roman Period* (New York: Pantheon, 1954), 172–94; cf. vol. 9, *Symbolism in the Dura Synagogue* (1964), 71–77; vol. 12, *Summary and Conclusions* (1965), 68–71; G. Vermes, *Scripture and Tradition in Judaism* (Leiden: Brill, 1961); and S. Spiegel, *The Last Trial*, trans. J. Goldin (New York: Pantheon, 1967).

[5] See N. A. Dahl, "The Atonement—An Adequate Reward for the Akedah?" in *The Crucified Messiah and Other Essays* (Minneapolis: Augsburg, 1974), 146–60.

[6] See N. A. Dahl, "The Crucified Messiah," in *Crucified Messiah and Other Essays*, 10–36.

[7] See, e.g., Acts 2:34f. and Mark 12:36f.

[8] See, e.g., William O. Walker, "The Origin of the Son of Man Concept as Applied to Jesus," *JBL* 91 (1972): 482–90. Even so, it is likely that Jesus used the term "son of man," in some as yet indefinable way.

the result is clear: the Easter experience of the church was from the earliest time understood and expressed as the fulfillment of Psalm 110 and Daniel 7:13, seen as prophetic Scripture. Jesus is proclaimed as a divine figure on the basis of his ascension to heaven and subsequent identification with the "Lord" (*kyrios* = YHWH) of Psalm 110 and the "son of man" of Daniel 7:13 and Psalm 8:4. Though the divinization of a man certainly risks violating monotheism as the Pharisaic (and later the rabbinic) community understood it, is not entirely foreign to Philo (i.e., Moses' divinization) or the sectarian literature mentioned above. Indeed, it is probable that Jesus' identity was very early associated with the angel of YHWH who is superior to all angels in that he represents God's name on earth.

It is fair to say, however, that the explicit story of Jesus' ascension is not a large topic for the Gospel writers. Of the Gospel writers, only Luke records an independent story of Jesus' ascension into heaven at Luke 24:51 (διέστη = "he withdrew") and Acts 1:9 (ἐπήρθη = "he was taken up").[9] The verses added to the ending of Mark also include such evidence, but they are normally viewed as derivative. An explicit story of an astral journey with the details of the heavens is not characteristic of Christianity until Gnosticism. Rather, resurrection and ascension are normally seen as complementary actions in Christianity, so the basic pre-Christian structural pattern is visible even though the Christian pattern is uniquely ramified. The characteristic Christian exegesis of the pattern is to identify a single mediator—the Messiah who was crucified—thus uniting Jesus' biography with all traditions of mediators (human, divine, or angelic) who announce revelation, mediate the process of creation, or ascend to heaven. It is the Christian community itself that unites all the different Jewish possibilities of mediatorship into one single myth, because it sees Jesus as a unique and definitive mediator. In other words, it is possible to be too heavily influenced by Luke's understanding that *anastasis* (resurrection) and *anabasis* (ascension) are two entirely different

[9] See Westcott and Hort, ad. loc. The added phrase "and was carried up to heaven" is commonly assumed to be an interpolation. For a good description of the research on the problem, see G. Lohfink, *Die Himmelfahrt Jesu—Erfindung oder Erfahrung*, SANT 26 (München: Kösel, 1971), esp. 13–31. There, the New Testament research is reviewed in some detail.

events,[10] without realizing that the other authors in the New Testament canon have conceived of the matter as virtually a single phenomenon. In fact, it seems to be agreed among scholars that the Lukan account of the ascension relies on a conventional view of the previous reports of ascension in Hellenistic Judaism. Prominent among the sources must be the angelophany of Raphael in the book of Tobit (12:14f.), for the situation in Tobit and Luke is quite similar. In both cases the hearers are troubled. Their anxieties are calmed by the intermediary. Eating and drinking is specifically mentioned.[11] In both cases they disappear. The Lukan ascension story appears to be influenced by descriptions of angelophanies after the fulfillment of a special mission, like Raphael's journey to earth, revelation, disclosure of identity, and return to heaven in Tobit.

Another interesting parallel in the Lukan text brings deeper aspects of Luke's purpose into focus. Luke saw some clear similarities between the baptism, the transfiguration, and the ascension. One might expect such a parallel considering the structural parallel between human ascension and angelophanies. But at the transfiguration (which many have misunderstood as a misplaced resurrection appearance), there is little direct development of the resurrection. Instead, Luke stresses the upward movement of men to God. In Luke's account (9:51), Elijah's ascension to heaven and Moses' ascent of Mount Sinai to heaven appears to have controlled the presentation.

The reminiscence of the Sinai theophany is clear: (1) the mountain scene; (2) the six-day interval; (3) the overshadowing cloud; (4) the presence of Moses; (5) the voice from the cloud; (6) the transforming glory. In the Lukan version Moses and Elijah speak of the exodus which Jesus is to accomplish in Jerusalem and the disciples see the glory of the three men. Although the Bible does not speak of a heavenly ascent for Moses at this point, Hellenistic Jewish traditions record that Moses continued to ascend to heaven after Sinai.[12]

[10] See J. G. Davies, *He Ascended into Heaven*; and Lohfink, *Die Himmelfahrt Jesu*, 13–32. Lohfink makes a case for the uniqueness of Luke's account, and the lack of any explicit tradition separating the two events before Luke.

[11] In Tobit the angel does not eat to show he is divine. In Luke Jesus drinks to prove he is really present in bodily form and not merely a spirit or an angelic ambassador.

[12] Scholars note the structural similarities between baptism, the transfiguration, the resurrection, and the ascension. See, e.g., A. Feuillet, "Les perspectives propres à chaque Évangéliste dans les récits de la transfiguration," *Bib* 39 (1958): 281ff; A. Kenny, "The Transfiguration and the Agony in the Garden," *CBQ* 4 (1957): 444ff.; T. Burkill,

However, the Elijah typology is also unmistakable in Luke. When the Samaritans refuse to receive Jesus, James, and John ask him to call fire down upon them. The Western manuscripts make the parallel explicit by adding "as Elias did." What the three figures share is ascent. Rather than disprove of the centrality of the ascent structure in the kerygma, Lukan traditions demonstrate the ascension pattern even more clearly. By using the transfiguration with its (Moses-Elijah) ascent typology as the setting for the revelation of Jesus' necessary suffering and resurrection, Luke is merely underlining the structural relationship between ecstatic ascent, martyrdom, and immortality, which becomes the fundamental aspect of the configuration for Christianity.

In most other places in the New Testament, the ascension is closely associated with resurrection, showing the Lukan separation to be an important but relatively later view. In the Pauline corpus most of the evidence implies that ascension was implicit in resurrection. The interpretation depends on our understanding of the term "exaltation" in Philippians 2:5-11:

> Have this mind among yourselves, which is yours in Christ Jesus, who, though he was in the form of God, did not count equality with God a thing to be grasped, but emptied himself, taking the form of a servant, being born in the likeness of men. And being found in human form he humbled himself and became obedient unto death, even death on a cross. Therefore God has highly exalted him and bestowed on him the name which is above every name, that at the name of Jesus every knee should bow, in heaven and on earth and under the earth, and every tongue confess that Jesus Christ is Lord, to the glory of God the Father.

The term "exalt" (ὑπερυψόω) may mean to increase one's power or wealth (Ps 37:35) or give praise (Dan 4:34), so it would be possible to argue that no ascension is implied by this verb, especially since it is used only here in the New Testament. However, the basic meaning of the term seems to be "to lift up high," as in the enthronement of a king. This can be seen from its use in the LXX to translate Psalm 97:9:

> For thou, Lord, art most high (*hupistos*) above all the earth: Thou art exalted (*huperupsōthes*) far above all gods.

Mysterious Revelation: An Examination of the Philosophy of St. Mark's Gospel (Ithaca, N.Y.: Cornell University Press, 1963).

Luke describes Christ exalted "by the right hand of God." It seems to me, therefore, safe to conclude, as J. G. Davies does,[13] that *upsoō* is virtually a synonym of *anabainō*, except that the latter is intransitive. Furthermore, the Pauline predicates of the exalted Christ in Philippians are divine in character, biblical references referring to God used in Jewish liturgy as doxologies.[14] Finally, the implicit threefold level of the universe entails the belief that Christ has surmounted all the various levels to become its ruler.

Elsewhere in Paul's writings descriptions of resurrection imply a notion of ascension. In his discussion of resurrection in 1 Corinthians 15, Jesus is described as the second Adam, not only man "from" heaven but "of" heaven. In Romans 8:34 Paul says, "It is Christ Jesus that died, yea rather, that was raised from the dead, who is at the right hand of God, who also makes intercession for us." Such evidence leads R. Bultmann[15] to say that for Paul the resurrection of Jesus means his simultaneous exaltation which, as we have seen, implies his ascension as well. For instance, in Paul's description of the end of time Christ will descend from heaven, allowing the saints, already arising, to meet him in the air (1 Thess 4:16-17). Thus, while resurrection and ascension must be viewed as different phenomena in the strict sense, they are so closely associated by Paul that one virtually implies the other. The Philippians hymn (which has all the earmarks of a pre-Pauline liturgical hymn)[16] is to be understood as relating the complete cycle of Jesus' descent, mission, death, resurrection, and ascent. Furthermore, Paul attests that Christians

[13] Davies, *He Ascended into Heaven*, 29; and Lohfink, *Die Himmelfahrt Jesu*, who discusses 1 Thess; 1 Cor 15:3-8; Rom 1:3f.; 8:34; 14:9; Col 3:1; Eph 1:19; 2:5f.; 4:8-10; 1 Tim 3:16; 1 Pet 1:2 f.; 3:21f.; and Heb on pp. 81–92.

[14] M. Smith, *Clement of Alexandria and a Secret Gospel of Mark* (Cambridge, Mass.: Harvard University Press, 1973), 244f. suggests that the Pauline hymn is supposed to refer to Jesus, not the risen Christ. Therefore, it would not be the record of a descending-ascending God, but rather the proof that Jesus' followers attributed heavenly journeys to him during his life. Though this bold hypothesis would emphasize the Pauline letters as primary texts for heavenly ascent, it is fair to say that the church has never read the passage in this way and few scholars have yet agreed with Professor Smith on this point, in spite of his thorough survey of the cultural context for magical ascension.

[15] Bultmann, *Theology of the New Testament*, 2 vols. (New York: Charles Scribner's, 1951/1955), 1:45.

[16] R. P. Martin, *Carmen Christi: Philippians 2:5-11 in Recent Interpretation and the Setting of Early Christian Worship*, SNTSMS 4 (Cambridge: Cambridge University Press, 1967).

were experiencing journeys to heaven in 2 Corinthians 12, where it is possible that he is speaking of his own experience.

The theme of ascension is developed by the deutero-Pauline literature. In Ephesians, for instance, not only is Christ seated at the right hand of God but the believers are enthroned with him (1:20; 2:6; cf. 1:13), which only underlines the importance of the structural mediation between heaven and earth, impermanence and permanence, death and life for the believer. On the basis of Jesus' journey, the reward of those who believe in him is to be guaranteed, for it is the path which awaits them.[17]

The Gospel of John does not speak of the ascension in detail. But it gives us an extremely full articulation of the structure of the *anabasis-katabasis* pattern. It explicitly says that no man has ascended to heaven but he who descended out of heaven—that is, the son of man who is in heaven (John 3:13f.).[18] This may serve as a polemic of the Johannine community against other ascension beliefs. The Gospel of John has explicitly defined Jesus' ability to ascend to heaven on the basis of his assumed prehistory in heaven. It explicitly calls the Logos an aspect of God, and identifies that Logos with the Christ in the prologue, so that from the outset it has postulated a unitary narrative of a single descending and ascending figure. Therefore, any reference to the ascension per se is in a sense secondary—the whole cycle of descent-ascent is the fundamental premise. For instance, when certain of the disciples murmur against Jesus because of the difficulty of his teaching he replies, "What then if you should behold the son of man ascending where he was before?" (6:61-62). Ascension is mentioned but the whole *katabasis-anabasis* pattern is clear. When the risen Christ appears to Mary, he tells her not to touch: "for I am not yet ascended unto the Father. But go unto my brethren and say to them, I ascend unto my Father and your Father, and my God and your God" (20:17). With the exception of the functions of the paraclete, who appears to combine aspects of the Holy Spirit and angelic mediator, the Gospel of John has unified the mediator of mythical contradictions into a single figure. This will be a key step in the development of the gnostic ascent of the soul.

[17] See also Matt 28:18f.

[18] Particularly important for the study of John is W. A. Meeks, "The Man from Heaven in Johannine Sectarianism," *JBL* 91 (1972): 44–72.

This is not the first time that the complete *anabasis-katabasis* pattern has been evidenced. But in the past the complete pattern has been limited either to a presumed descent and ascent of an individual soul or to the announcement of a divine message by means of an angel who ascends after having delivered it. Only one half of the journey had any real significance. Here, for the first time, real unity has been forged in that the same figure is self-consciously viewed as divinity in action—creator, revealer, and redeemer. Furthermore, the cycle only needs happen once. Though it is clear that the pattern is meant to be parallel with the soul of the individual believer, it is not yet true within Johannine literature that there is an identity of substance between the Savior and the soul of the believer, as in the hermetic literature and in Gnosticism.

Two other New Testament locations for ascension motifs are worth noting. In the Letter to the Hebrews, a somewhat similar pattern to the Johannine one is presupposed, except that similar patterns for Moses and Levi are explicitly given subservient roles to the Christ. Christ is viewed as the great high priest who has passed through the heavens (Heb 4:14), to become higher than them (7:26) and entered into highest heaven (9:24). As a consequence of this, he is enthroned on the right hand of God (8:1; 10:12: 12:2) and has become a high priest after the order of Melchizedek.[19]

The Apocalypse of John also presumes a descent-ascent pattern. Through his descent as far as Hades, the redeemer controls the keys of death (Rev 1:18) and, by ascending again, has become ruler of all the earth (1:5). To him the two witnesses ascend in a cloud (11:12) and he is the man-child who was "caught up to God and unto His throne."

At this point it is necessary to stress that we are not dealing with merely the mythical equivalent of the random generation of possible grammatical transformations. Rather the Christian community, like all the groups we have studied, had inherited a set of expectations about the ascension myths—some of which was confirmed by their experience, some of which was disconfirmed. Hence, they reorganized their beliefs on the basis of their understanding of Jesus' death. There is a real interplay between inherited pattern, experience, and expression, followed by

[19] It is clear that Melchizedek was viewed as a principal angelic mediator. See Fred L. Horton Jr., *The Melchizedek Tradition: A Critical Examination of the Sources to the Fifth Century and in the Epistle to the Hebrews*, SNTSMS 30 (Cambridge: Cambridge University Press, 1976).

a period of polemical battle with differing interpretations of the same events and expectations within their community, as well as opposing varieties of the ascension pattern in other communities.

The teaching of the church fathers expanded and deepened the New Testament writers. All the fathers are careful to mention ascension in their summaries of church doctrine. Since the church fathers also record Jesus' important post-resurrection experiences, the interval between resurrection and ascension is usually lengthened.[20] The author of the Epistle of Barnabas (chap. 15), for instance, justifies the hallowing of Sunday, the eighth day, on the basis of Jesus' ascension. Justin, whose theology resembles Philo's so closely, makes ascension an intimate part of the kerygma:

> We say that the Word, who is the first
> offspring of God,
> Was begotten without carnal intercourse
> Jesus Christ our teacher
> and that He was crucified,
> and died,
> and rose again
> and ascended to heaven. (*1 Apol.* 21)

Though he testifies that Jews understand Psalm 110:1-3 as referring to Hezekiah (*Dial.* 33) he sees it as the primary location—together with Psalms 19; 24; 27; and 68—for the prophecy of Christ's ascension.

J. T. Davies points to two church fathers who make independent use of the ascension tradition.[21] Irenaeus links the ascension to his doctrine of ἀνακεφαλαίωσις, Jesus' work of recapitulation in undoing the results of the disobedience of Adam. The ascension is mentioned as that part of the recapitulation which destroys the power of the fallen angels—the theme which occasioned Enoch's heavenly journey. Therefore, the Christ is presented as the new ruler of a renewed creation (*Epid.* 38). It is important to note that for Irenaeus, as for many of the other commentators on heavenly journeys, the journey of the Christ is the pattern for the individual believer.

[20] See Lohfink, *Die Himmelfahrt Jesu*, on the development of the Lukan version of the ascension and the forty-day delay between resurrection and ascent in the church fathers, pp. 98–146.

[21] Davies, *He Ascended to Heaven*, 94.

> So ought we also to await the time of our resurrection prescribed by God, and foretold by the prophets, and so, rising, be taken up, as many as the Lord shall account worthy of this.

Tertullian makes frequent use of the ascension for polemical purposes. The ascension is explicitly mentioned against the docetists to underline the reality of the incarnation.[22] In *Against Praxeus* 30, Tertullian assails modalism by demonstrating that the ascension makes a necessary distinction between Father and Son. Finally, and most interestingly, Tertullian makes use of the ascension to defend the practice of martyrdom against the gnostic contention that it was not necessary. For him, translation is only feasible if there has already been a confession of Christ.

> Heaven lies open to the Christians before the way to it does, because there is no way to heaven but to him to whom heaven lies open; and he who reaches it will enter . . . If you have also heard from Amos, "Who buildeth up to the heavens His way of ascent, and is such as to pour forth His abundance over the earth," know that both that way of ascent was thereafter leveled with the ground, by the footsteps of the Lord, and on entrance thereafter opened up by the might of Christ and that no delay or inquest will meet Christians on the threshold, since they have not to be discriminated from one another, but owned, not put to the question but received in. (*Scorp.* 10)

Here the frequent Jewish convention of ascent as a reward for martyrdom has been maintained but also been turned to exhortation of the value of martyrdom against heretics like the gnostics.[23]

Finally, a writer like Origen can thoroughly individualize the eschatology so that the soul is pictured ascending through the heavenly realms, transcending bodily reality entirely to arrive at the ultimate goal of ascent, the vision of God (*Princ.*).

[22] *De res.* 51. See also 38 and *De anima* 50.

[23] See Elaine Pagels, "Gnostic and Orthodox Views of Christ's Passion: Paradigms for the Christian's Response to Persecution?" in *The Rediscovery of Gnosticism: Proceedings of the International Conference on Gnosticism at Yale, New Haven, Connecticut March 28–31, 1978*, vol. 1, *The School of Valentinus*, ed. B. Layton (Leiden: Brill, 1980), 262–88.

FOUR

SOME ASPECTS OF LATE HELLENISTIC ASCENSION: GNOSTICISM

The Parables of Enoch (1 En. 37–71) were once thought to witness a pre-Christian belief in the coming of a son of man. Now it is possible that they should be seen as a Christian or at least a Jewish, post-Christian document. Therefore, I have waited until this point before mentioning them. On the whole the parables are exegetical expansions of the coming judgment described in Daniel. But there are a number of significant details for the study of heavenly ascents. First of all, in chapter 39 Enoch is carried off to heaven by whirlwind. In chapter 42 a separate fragment traces the ascent of wisdom. After she finds no dwelling place on earth, she takes her seat among the angels.

In the next chapter (43) the fate of the faithful is outlined. The holy are parabolically associated with the stars as in Daniel 8:10; 12:3. The stars have been associated with angelic beings even in Job 38:7 and Deuteronomy 4:19. So here they can be the saints after their demise. In the next chapter the lot of the apostates is outlined. They deny the name of the dwelling of the holy ones and therefore they shall neither ascend to heaven nor come again to earth.

The major contribution of the Parables to the ascension tradition is in the last two chapters (70–71). Here the book takes into its purview the challenge of describing what actually happened to Enoch when he was translated to heaven. When he ascends, he sees the sons of God who appear as angels. His guide in the journey is Michael, who initiates him into the secrets of righteousness and the secrets of the cosmos. Thereafter he ascends to the heaven of heavens where he sees the choirs of angels, the four archangels, and the Ancient of Days. At that point, he is transfigured and becomes the "son of man" who is born into righteousness. Whatever else it presupposes, this passage is the Enoch literature's understanding of the reward promised from Daniel, since the "son of man" is said to represent the saints of the Most High and some of the saints are said to shine as the stars. Whether or not the term "son of man" is yet a title is not clear. Nor is it clear that Enoch is being given a special new identity. All that is clear is that Enoch is associated with the "son of man" or manlike creature to whom judgment of the world has been delegated in the book of Daniel. So, in some fashion, Enoch, who personifies the righteous community, is to participate in the final judgment of the world. It is probable that we shall never know all we would like to know about the ideas portrayed in this puzzling passage.

Second Enoch[1] continues to expand the traditions about Enoch. It is much later and has a vastly more organized discussion of one of Enoch's journeys through the heavens. Its special point seems to be cosmology, though typically the description has soteriological ramifications as well. That someone has actually ascended the heavens and seen the arrangement of the cosmos—both its physical and moral order—confirms that God's plan will soon be evident in the world.

Many of the other apocryphal texts which show significant Christian influence also have notable heavenly journeys. One of the most complex documents is the Ascension of Isaiah, possibly originally a Jewish document, which has received extensive editing by a Christian editor, so as to function mainly as a Christian book. "The Beloved of the Father" descends through the seven heavens assuming the form of the occupants in order not to be recognized. Then, after the events of Jesus' life, his descent to Sheol, and resurrection, the document records his ascension and exaltation in each of the seven heavens.

Some of the ascension stories of the Christian apocrypha and pseudepigrapha should also be noted. The Apocalypse of Peter expands the account of the ascension by means of the Gospels' account of the transfiguration. The Epistle of the Apostles (chap. 51)[2] records Jesus' ascension immediately after his resurrection. The Gospel of Peter and the Letter of Jesus to Abgarus also show the influence of ascension on popular piety. It is also likely that similar Christian pietists were

[1] See J. H. Charlesworth, *The Pseudepigrapha and Modern Research* (Missoula, Mont.: Scholars, 1976), 103f.

[2] *The Apocryphal New Testament: Being the Apocryphal Gospels, Acts, Epistles and Apocalypses with other Narrations and Fragments*, trans. Montague Rhodes James (Oxford: Clarendon, 1924), 503.

responsible for additions to the Jewish material in the Testaments of the Twelve Patriarchs:[3]

> And his star shall arise in heaven as a shedding forth the light of knowledge in the sunshine of the day and he shall be magnified in the world until His ascension (ἀναλήψεως). (T. Levi 18:3)

> He shall arise from Hades and shall pass from earth to heaven and I know how lowly he shall be upon the earth and how glorious in heaven. (T. Benj. 8:5)

In Acts of Andrew and Matthias (chap. 17)[4] the two apostles relate that during their sleep their souls were taken up to heaven by eagles, only to be returned when they awoke.

Besides the continuation of apocalyptic, Jewish-Christian syncretism, and *merkabah* literature there is a significant theosophical syncretism, evincing Jewish, Christian, and Hellenistic philosophical influences. The most prominent member of this category is the first tractate of the Corpus hermeticum, the Poimandres. The Poimandres begins as a revelation text (in ecstasy) and ends with the description of the ascent of the soul. In this famous writing the identity of mediator figure with the immortal essence of man is stressed at the beginning.

> Learn my meaning from looking at what you yourself have in you, for in you too the word (λόγος) is son and the mind is father of the word. They are not separate one from the other.[5]

C. H. Dodd[6] has pointed out the use of biblical text in this document. It is fair to note that within this treatise the descent of the mediating and the ascent of the soul have a new and more thoroughly Greek context. There is no attempt to find a biblical pretext of history for the text. Unlike the apocalyptic and *merkabah* material, it is psychology and not theodicy which is the primary locus of the discussion. Creation by

[3] See above p. 215.

[4] *Acta Apostolorum Apocrypha*, ed. R. Lipsius and M. Bonnet (Leipzig: Mendelssohn, 1891–1903) 2.1:85f.

[5] Corp. herm. 1.6, according to W. Scott, ed. and trans., *Hermetica*, vol. 1 (Oxford: Clarendon, 1924).

[6] C. H. Dodd, *The Bible and the Greeks* (London: Hodder & Stoughton 1935; 3rd ed. 1964). The dissertation of Robert Alan Segal, Princeton (published as *The Poimandres as Myth: Scholarly Theory and Gnostic Meaning*, Religion and Reason 33 [Berlin: de Gruyter, 1986]) deals with the Poimandres within the context of the study of myth.

means of *logos*, the original unity of the sexes, and the identity of the *logos* with the mind are other important points to note along the way, nor is morality entirely forgotten. The author of the Poimandres believes only the good will find God and hence only the good will ascend.

> "But from men that are foolish and evil and wicked and envious and covetous and murderous and impious I keep far aloof, and give place to the avenging daemon. And he brings to bear on such a man the fierce heat of fire, and tortures him, tossing him about in the tumult of the senses; and he equips the man more fully for his lawless deeds, that so he may incur the greater punishment.
>
> "And that man ceases not to struggle blindly; he gives way to boundless appetites, his desire being insatiable; and so by his own doing he makes the fire yet hotter for his torment."
>
> "Full well have you taught me all, O Mind," said I, "even as I wished. But tell me furthermore of the ascent by which men mount; tell me how I shall enter into Life." Poimandres answered, "At the dissolution of your material body, you first yield up the body itself to be changed, and the visible form you bore is no longer seen. And your . . . you yield up to the . . . , so that it no longer works in you; and the bodily senses go back to their own sources, becoming parts of the universe, and entering into fresh combinations to do other work. And thereupon the man mounts upward through the structure of the heavens. And to the first zone of heaven he gives up the force which works increase and that which works decrease; to the second zone, the machinations of evil cunning; to the third zone, the lust whereby men are deceived; to the fourth zone, domineering arrogance; to the fifth zone, unholy daring and rash audacity; to the sixth zone, evil strivings after wealth; and to the seventh zone, the falsehood which lies in wait to work harm. And thereupon, having been stripped of all that was wrought upon him by the structure of the heavens, he ascends to the substance of the eighth sphere, being now possessed of his own proper power; and he sings, together with those who dwell there, hymning the Father; and they that are there rejoice with him at his coming. And being made like to those with whom he dwells, he hears the Powers, who are above the substance of the eighth sphere, singing praise to God with a voice that is theirs alone. And thereafter, each in his turn, they mount upward to the Father; they give themselves up to the Powers, and becoming Powers themselves, they enter into God. This is the God; this is the consummation, for those who have got gnosis.
>
> "And now, why do you delay? Seeing that you have received all, why do you not make yourself a guide to those who are worthy of the boon, that so mankind may through you be saved by God?" And when

> Poimandres had thus spoken to me, he mingled with the Powers. (Corp. herm. 1.23–26)

The knowledge of the structure of the universe and the identity of the soul with the *logos*, the plan of the universe, leads naturally to the ascent and guarantee of immortality. The immortalizing ascent is not precisely an innate opportunity to every soul. The soul needs instruction (gnosis) to discover its full capacities; without instruction it fails to rise to its proper place. The speaker (Hermes), after his revelation, goes into the world and spreads the gnosis which he has been taught. Therefore in book 13, the divinity of the believer can be maintained: "The physical body, which is an object of sense, differs widely from the other body, which is of the nature of true Being. The one is dissoluble, the other is indissoluble. The one is mortal, the other is immortal. Do you not know that you have become a god, and the son of one, even as I have?" (Corp. herm. 13.14) Thus, we have a strong statement of the *katabasis-anabasis* pattern which goes beyond even the Johannine Christianity's interpretation of ascent. The divine in man is identified with God. Indeed, the entire cosmogony at the beginning seems to mirror and prepare the scene for the eschatology at the end. It appears as though the expected heavenly journey at the end and the divine nature of man has made a new mythic structure of the cosmos necessary. Though this seems logically backwards it gives the right emphasis to discovery of the immortality of the soul which is the central topic of the document.

The so-called Mithras Liturgy, the Paris magical papyrus (*PGM* IV), evinces another ascent narrative. The adept is immortalized by means of the ecstatic ascent. He breathes in the divine and, according to one version, prays to become one with the God:

> And at once produce a long bellowing sound, straining your belly, that you may excite the five senses: Bellow long until the conclusion, and again kiss the amulets, and say: ". . . life of me . . . : Stay! Dwell in my soul! Do not abandon me."[7]

The divinity invoked is not God himself, because he is described as having been exalted and praised by God. He is rather a kind of intermediate or mediating god here called Helios. But the structure of the magical praxis ought to be familiar by now. These texts appear to presuppose

[7] *The Mithras Liturgy*, ed. M. Meyer, Texts and Translations 10 = Greco-Roman Religion Series, 2 (Missoula, Mont.: Scholars, 1976), line 705.

the mythical structure of an ascending and descending figure. He grants immortality, and because the praxis is a ritual rebirth, also a new horoscope:

> O Lord, while being born again, I am passing away; while growing and having grown, I am dying; while being born from a life-generating birth, I am passing on, released to death—as you have founded, as you have decreed, and have established the mystery. I am. . . .[8]

The expected result of the long ceremony is not merely to understand the future, though that was involved as well. The expected result is to gain an immortal rebirth[9] or immortalization.[10] The rebirth is described often as a mystery. Furthermore, the adept is described as an *epoptēs*,[11] the technical term for a participant in the mystery cults. The adept appears to gain his immortality through what he sees and experiences. He rises in an ecstatic heavenly journey by appeasing the various tutelary divinities. His soul is restored through breathing in the divine.[12] At the end he appears to be vouchsafed a vision of the great god Helios Mithras, of whom the magician is the archangel. Thus we have a body of material which is nominally magical, yet has significant religious characteristics.

In the magical papyrus there is absolutely no mention of ethical behavior. The immortalization process is acquired through the proper performance of the rite. Although we have no consensus as to whether this document is a liturgy from an actual mystery cult or only a magical procedure, it represents the structural ascent pattern and strongly emphasizes the immortalization process which the entire Hellenistic world came to understand as inherent in crossing the boundary between earth and heaven. As opposed to the apocalyptic and mystical understanding of the ascent pattern, there is no evident communal aspect in the magical papyri and no discussion of man's necessary behavior.[13]

[8] See *Mithras Liturgy*, ed. Meyer, 21. This was the end of the liturgy according to Dieterich.

[9] *Metagenethentos*, line 645/650.

[10] *Apathanatistheis*, line 645/650.

[11] Line 505.

[12] Line 630.

[13] In 1903 Albrecht Dieterich (*Eine Mithrasliturgie* [Leipzig: Teubner, 1903]) proposed that lines 475–834 of the Paris magical papyrus were part of the official liturgy of the Mithras cult, hence religion. However, since the publication of Dieterich's book many scholars, notably Cumont and Riltzenstein, have criticized the theory (see *Nachträge* to the 3rd ed.). Dieterich was forced to moderate his claims by suggesting that Egyptian

But that is not to say that the actions of the so-called magicians were devoid of religious connotations. The term *magus* was open to various interpretations,[14] frequently being the unfriendly term applied to Hellenistic "divine men."[15] The clearest example of this kind of figure is Apollonius of Tyana, as he is described in Philostratus' biography. Ever sensitive to the charge of magic leveled against his subject, Philostratus takes great pains to show that conversing with magicians and speaking of the demonic realm is not the same thing as practicing evil acts (*Vit. Apoll.* 1.2). Yet, he understands doing miracles as signs that Apollonius was a great philosopher, indeed a god on earth. Furthermore, Apollonius' supposed ascent after his death is taken as the proof of his divinity and the immortality of his soul (*Vit. Apoll.* 8.30).

Morton Smith, in two of his latest publications,[16] has argued strongly that Jesus himself can be described in magical terms and that heavenly ascent constituted a secret doctrine in Christianity from the very beginning. Though the evidence does not entirely warrant such a radical conclusion, Dr. Smith has shown in detail the phenomenological similarity of holy men and magicians in the Hellenistic world. Theurgy, more than anything else, represents the force that transformed many naive magical acts into an acceptable religion in the Roman Empire. As far as we know, the earliest person claiming to practice the art was Julianus, a contemporary of Marcus Aurelius. He, in turn, claimed an association with an earlier Julianus who gave him the secrets of the Chaldean Oracles.[17] The technique of theurgy became so associated with the late Neoplatonic

---

magicians changed the text substantially. Hence, though Dieterich's evidence that the document represents a religious mystery is sound, important aspects of his argument for its Mithraic origin must be dismissed.

[14] See, e.g., Apuleius, *Apol.*

[15] For summaries of the research, see D. L. Tiede, *The Charismatic Figure as Miracle Worker*, SBLDS (Missoula, Mont.: Scholars, 1972); and C. R. Holladay, Theios Aner *in Hellenistic Judaism* (Missoula, Mont.: Scholars, 1977).

[16] *Clement of Alexandria and a Secret Gospel of Mark* (Cambridge, Mass.: Harvard University Press, 1973); *Jesus the Magician* (New York: Harper & Row, 1978).

[17] See M. Smith, "Observations on Hekhaloth Rabbati," in *Biblical and Other Studies*, ed. A. Altmann, Studies and Texts 1 (Cambridge, Mass.: Harvard University Press, 1963). See also *Jamblique, Les Mysteres d'Egypte*, ed. É. des Places (Paris: Les Belles Lettres, 1966); *Oracles Chaldaïques*, ed. É. des Places (Paris: Les Belles Lettres, 1971); Hans Lewy, *The Chaldaean Oracles and Theurgy: Mysticism, Magic and Platonism in the Later Roman Empire*, vol. 13 of *Recherches d'archeologie, de philologie et d'histoire* (Cairo: Imprimerie de l'Institut Français d'Archéologie Orientale, 1959).

school that Proclus could define theurgy grandly as "a power higher than all human wisdom, embracing powers of divination, the purifying powers of initiation, and, in short, all the operation of divine possession" (*Theol. Plat.* 63). Theurgy allowed that rituals could be employed to summon gods to earth. But it also, according to Lewy, maintained that ecstatic ascent was possible, thus uniting the mythical pattern of Hellenistic religion with the system of emanations characteristic of Neoplatonism. The techniques of theurgy probably appealed to philosophers because it allowed them, as it were, to put their theories into practice while at the same time keeping their independence from other organized cults. This explains why the practices of magic became so acceptable in some aristocratic circles. Under the influence of philosophical systematization, it became a sophisticated and consistent religion.

A number of works similar to Poimandres and the Chaldean Oracles are described as "gnostic" by the church fathers, though the works themselves do not always show all the characteristics of gnostic thought. For instance, The *Apophasis Megale*, which is used by Schmithals as evidence of the pre-Christian gnostic salvation myth,[18] has neither a redeemer nor an ignorant demiurge. The *logos*, however, figures prominently in it and as "the seventh power" is present within all men as a potentiality. According to Irenaeus, however (*Haer.* 1.30.4), it is characteristic of Christian Gnosticism that the ascended Christ is a mediator. He receives the souls of the true gnostic until all the divine light is again gathered above.

In the so-called Na'asene Sermon (Hippolytus, *Haer.* 5.6.3–11.1) there is an enormous interest in the structure of the universe, which, for the Na'asenes was triune—the preexistent, the self-originate, and the outpoured chaos. It is the mediator figure Adamas, however, that occupies the attention of the Na'asenes. The mediator can be identified with Hermes who is the guide of souls. The document mentions several Near Eastern gods and tries to synthesize a single understanding. The soul of the believer is supposed to awaken and reattain its spiritual place by rebirth and ascent (8.28.32). Hence, proof of this can be brought from everywhere—the Hebrew Bible, the New Testament, the Phrygian and Greek mysteries:

> And the mystery aforesaid is called Eleusis and Anactoreum; Eleusis he says because we have come, we who are spiritual flowing down from

[18] W. Schmithals, *Gnosticism in Corinth* (Nasvhille: Abingdon, 1971), 36f.

above—from Adamas—for *eleusesthai* he says, means "to come"—and Anactoreum because of our ascent on high (*ano*).

This, he says, is what the devotees of the Eleusinian cult call the great mysteries; for it is the custom that those who have been initiated in the lesser should again be initiated into the great ones . . . (Hippolytus, *Haer.* 8.41.42)

In the Gnostic Book of Baruch (Hippolytus, *Haer.* 5.26.1–27.5) there is another description of the ascension, like the Na'asene Sermon, linking baptism and ascension together. Elohim, who functions both as man's father and author of his spiritual salvation, ascends beyond earth to the lofty parts of heaven and is enthroned next to the god.[19] This story can be seen as parallel to the story of the savior of the Jews—Jesus (5.29f.)—and the savior of the Greeks—Hercules (5.27f.). It mentions an oath, mystery, and baptism (5.27.1) as ritual means for ascent. Since the cosmos is populated by evil powers (notably Eden and Na'as), the work uses the ascent structure to reinforce the idea that we live in a world dominated by evil powers and must ascend to the kingdom of light above.

In the Nag Hammadi material itself[20] many tractates mention heavenly ascent. Second only to the overriding theme of asceticism, ascent is the major theme of the collection. The experience of human believers in heavenly journey and the ascent of a savior) returning to heaven after completing his mission, are related in great detail. Some of the most important documents are: The Apocryphon of John, the Exegesis of the Soul, and the Apocalypse of the Soul. Though the tractates constitute a library, hence represent a spectrum of belief, it is fair to say that normally ascent refers to an anticipated real journey of the soul, usually as an explicit reward of accepting gnosis. However, ascension may be exegeted in many different ways in different documents because, being a dominant religious structure, all the ramifications of ascent are important.

The transition from Jewish and Christian sectarianism to Gnosticism is marked by several features. First, all commentators of Gnosticism note dualism, both ethical and cosmological, as a prominent characteristic. Hence, the single mediator figure is sometimes divided into two distinct

[19] Using Ps 110:1.

[20] *The Nag Hammadi Library in English*, ed. J. M. Robinson (New York: Harper & Row, 1977).

types—at least one good savior figure and at least one ignorant demiurge. This can be simply understood as a transformation of the basic pattern in line with the dualist worldview. Normally, there are a number of evil archons who assist the demiurge. Hence, the second feature of the gnostic mediation is increasing complexity in the single pattern. No single mediator is sufficient; rather, a group of archons assist the demiurge and have dominion over a part of creation. The result is to dramatize the contrast already discussed as the most common exegesis of the structure—permanence and impermanence, life and death, perfection and imperfection. In the gnostic system, there is normally at least one figure who represents the world in its impermanent or evil manifestation, another representing the perfection at the goal beyond. The radically gnostic intuition is that the world in which we live is totally devoid of salvation and must be transcended entirely. The gnosis, which is simply the knowledge that the world is so cursed, together with the technique for transcending the cosmos, is what provides escape.

In Gnosticism we have entered a new stage in the enterprise—a creative use of myth to synthesize a single understanding of reality from all the ancient cults that comprised Hellenistic culture. Though Gnosticism remains one of the more free and chaotic attempts at a synthesis, because it treated all myths as meaningful once repatterned to gnostic intuitions, it is evident that a synthesis was meant to come about. Unlike *theokrasis*, the identifying of one nation's god with another, which was a kind of primitive, structural universalism of the earlier Hellenistic world, Gnosticism was partly and sometimes an attempt to recognize all religions of the Hellenistic world as fitting and revealing the same structural pattern: a cosmological descent explaining an evil and inhospitable world followed by an ascent of the savior to his original home which serves as the pattern for the soul of the believer.

It is a mistake to believe that all the religions naturally and originally fit into this structural mold. The material from Judaism and early Christianity has pointed out that each myth was adapted and evolved according to unique cultural conditions. However, the frequent link between the soul of the individual and the descent and ascent of a mediator points out significant underlying commonalities which can be described as the late Hellenistic world picture. On the other hand, powerful ideological, political, economic, and social forces continued to make the existence of separate religions necessary, however similar the structural assumptions may have been. Gnosticism may be seen as a first attempt to unite all the perceptions under a kind of cultural *anomie*.

I cannot help noting that this situation is rather similar to the one which Lévi-Strauss described in his studies of South American Indian mythology. He showed that the mythology of several neighboring Indian cultures amounted to regular transformations of the same structure, though he asserted that an underlying single feature of the mind produced the similarity. It is possible that the same mosaic can be perceived in late Hellenistic culture—only on an ethnic and national level instead of a tribal one, with the added proviso that several religious movements had enough overview of the situation to note the similarities and to attempt consciously to conform their tradition to the *interpretatio Graeca* or to defend their tradition from being confused with a less complete truth. As well, we have more historical data in the Hellenistic period than was available to Lévi-Strauss. Therefore, we have more evidence to show how some transformations actually took place. Christianity developed a new transformation by applying all mediation stories to Christ, thus coming up with a preexistent cosmic mediator who was also Messiah—both a descending and ascending mediator who was both demiurge and Savior. This can be related to their sectarian history and to their ideology which involved a single figure who was associated with both a messianic deliverance and an ascension after a revelation.

The reasons for some other kinds of transformations can be understood polemically. For instance, it seems evident that the rabbinic movement, as distinct from other Hellenistic Judaism, was deeply skeptical about the relevance and importance of ascension traditions. Though they sometimes developed traditions about heavenly journey—in *merkabah* mysticism and some midrash about biblical heroes—they also vociferously denied that these journeys had the power to confer immortality or divinity, warning against those who thought otherwise. For instance, there is the well-known passage attributed to R. Hiyya:

> If a man says "I am God," he lies. "I am the son of man," he will regret it. "I ascend to heaven," he will not achieve it. (y. Ta'an. 2:1)[21]

[21] Also see J. Goldin, "Not by Means of an Angel and Not by Means of a Messenger," in *Religions in Antiquity: Essays in Memory of Erwin Ramsdell Goodenough*, ed. J. Neusner, Studies in the History of Religions 14 (Leiden: Brill, 1968). However, there are some places where the ascension pattern comes through, especially where the danger of blasphemy is

Such derision is designed to counter Christian, gnostic, and other ascension traditions. The rabbis warned explicitly that no mediator figure should be mistaken for God.[22] They reminded their listeners of the sins of the Prince of Tyre and King of Babylon, both of whom tried to ascend to heaven and claimed to be gods. In defense they stressed traditional Scripture where YHWH maintains His uniqueness—Deuteronomy 32 and Isaiah 44–46, for instance—thus showing there is but one God. These Scriptures figure prominently in Christian and gnostic exegesis as well. The Christians usually tried to show that their theology allows two or three hypostases while monarchians and modalists stressed the unity of God against orthodoxy by using the same passages that the rabbis did. In the gnostic case, the history of exegesis is more interesting still. The Old Testament God's claim to unity and uniqueness is always spoken by the gnostic demiurge, who is always shown to be ignorant and mistaken. Thus, the gnostic answer to the Jewish denial of the value of heavenly ascension was to turn the Hebrew high god into a mediator figure instead of a high god and to associate His teaching with the fallen state of man. This strategy had clear polemical value and probably corresponds to the gnostics' outcast status from Judaism and Christianity. The gnostics were being criticized and persecuted by both Jews and Christians, so they took the God of their persecutors and figured him as an ignorant deity. But it appears that there were at least two stages in the polemic. In the first stage the Jewish community oppose ascension stories, mainly of the Christian variety. In the second, the Christian and gnostic communities used and developed their own answers to the questions posed by the opposition of the other. By the time of the gnostic documents, the gnostic argument against the Old Testament God may be aimed not directly at the Jews themselves but against orthodox Christians who are using the

---

not perceived as great. See, e.g., Sifre Deut. 34:5 and Midrash Hagadol to Deuteronomy, where the ascensions of Enoch, Elijah, and Moses are cited.

[22] See my *Two Powers in Heaven: Early Rabbinic Reports about Christianity and Gnosticism*, Studies in Judaism in Late Antiquity 25 (Leiden: Brill, 1977; repr. Waco, Tex.: Baylor University Press, 2012). Also see N. A. Dahl, "The Arrogant Archon and the Lewd Sophia," in *The Rediscovery of Gnosticism*, vol. 2, *Sethian Gnosticism*, ed. B. Layton (Leiden: Brill, 1980), 689–712; and my articles "The Ruler of This World: Attitudes about Mediator Figures and the Importance of Sociology for Self-Definition," in Sanders, ed., *Jewish and Christian Self-Definition*, 2:245–68, and "Rabbinic Polemic and the Radicalization of Gnosticism," *ANRW* 22 (1981).

Old Testament references against the gnostics.[23] In other words, the reference to Jews and the Old Testament God is partially a cipher for the relatively more Judaized position of the orthodox church. The very polemical argument against rabbinic sages appears to have started earlier, as early as the Jewish opposition to Christianity mirrored in the Gospel of John.[24] By the fourth century, rabbinic literature records the arguments mainly as advice and paraenesis for the faithful.

Though the history of religions school was mistaken in positing a particular myth born in Persia or India and transformed into Christianity, they had a remarkable intuition in stressing the mythical aspect of Hellenistic religion. I have tried to show that what preceded Christianity was not a single myth but a mythical structure of *katabasis* and *anabasis*, which was shared by most cultures of their time. However, the mythical structure was developed in specific ways according to individual cultural traditions. In Jewish Hellenistic circles, it was most often allied with questions of theodicy and became closely associated with stories of martyrdom. On the other hand, the *katabasis* pattern could be seen frequently in cosmogony and in angelic revelation texts. Christianity applied all the traditions to their crucified Messiah, creating a new unity and, at the same time, what amounts to a new transformation of the pattern by promulgating a single cycle with salvific consequences for everyone. This, in turn, was one very important influence on the radically gnostic version of the story in later centuries. The ignorant demiurge was at least partially the result of orthodox Christian and rabbinic opposition to speculation in protognostic communities. The God in whose name Jewish Christians were ostracized from the synagogue and in whose name gnostics were purged from the church, was believed by the gnostics to be ignorant when He claimed to be unique. However, Christianity, the mystery cults, emperor cult, magic, theosophy, late classical philosophy, and even rabbinic Judaism, to a lesser extent, were committed to the ascension pattern, tailored to their own needs. Such was the power of the ascension pattern to express the late classical world's desire for immortality. To see this pattern as the inevitable result of the structure of the mind is perhaps too grandiose, but it is possible to see the heavenly

[23] K. Koschorke, *Die Polemik der Gnostiker gegen das kirchliche Christentum* (Leiden: Brill, 1978).

[24] See J. Louis Martyn, *Theology and History in the Fourth Gospel* (Nashville: Abingdon, 1968; rev. ed., 1979).

journey of the soul, its consequent promise of immortality, and the corollary necessity of periodic ecstatic journeys to heaven as the dominant mythical constellation of late classical antiquity.

BIBLIOGRAPHY

Abt, Adam. *Die Apologie des Apuleius von Madaura und die antike Zauberei: Beiträge zur Erläuterung der Schrift der Mageia*. Giessen: Töpelmann, 1908.

Adam, James, ed. *The Republic of Plato*. 2nd rev. ed. by D. A. Rees. 2 vols. Cambridge: Cambridge University Press, 1963.

Althaus, P. *Der Brief an die Römer*. NTD 6. Göttingen: Vandenhoeck & Ruprecht, 1953.

Altmann, Alexander. *Biblical Motifs: Origins and Transformations*. Cambridge: Cambridge University Press, 1966.

———. "The Ladder of Ascension." Pages 1–32 in *Studies in Mysticism and Religion Presented to G. G. Sholem*. Edited by E. E. Urbach, R. J. Werblowsky, and C. Wirzubski. Jerusalem: Magnes, 1967.

Anz, Wilhelm. *Zur Frage nach dem Ursprung des Gnosticismus: Ein religionsgeschichtlicher versuch*. Leipzig: 1897.

Argyle, A. W. "The Ascension." *Expository Times* 66 (1954/1955): 240–42.

Athanassakis, Apostolos N., ed. and trans. *The Orphic Hymns: Texts, Translation and Notes*. Missoula, Mont.: Scholars, 1977.

Bacon, B. W. "The Ascension in Luke and Acts." *Expositor* 7 (1909): 254–61.

Barbour, Ian. *Myths, Models, and Paradigms*. New York: Harper & Row, 1974.

Barrett, C. K. "Things Sacrificed to Idols." Pages 40–59 in *Essays on Paul*. Philadelphia: Westminster, 1982.

Bartsch, H. W., ed. *Kerygma and Myth*. London: SPCK, 1953.

Bauckham, Richard. "The Martyrdom of Enoch and Elijah." *JBL* 95 (1976): 447–58.

Behm, J., and G. Quell. "διαθηκη." *TDNT* 2:124.

Beker, J. Christiaan. *Paul the Apostle: The Triumph of God in Life and Thought*. Philadelphia: Fortress, 1980.

Belkin, Samuel. *Philo and the Oral Law*. Cambridge, Mass.: Harvard University Press, 1940.

Benedict, Ruth. "Magic." Pages 10:39–44 in the *Encyclopedia of the Social Sciences*. New York: Macmillan, 1933.

Benko, Stephen. "Vergil's Fourth Eclogue in Christian Interpretation." *ANRW* 31.1 (1980): 646–705.

van den Berghe, Pierre. "Dialectic and Functionalism: Toward a Theoretical Synthesis." *American Sociological Review* 28 (1963): 695–705.

Bernard, J. H. "Assumption and Ascension." Pages 2:151–57 in *Encyclopedia of Religion and Ethics*. Edited by James Hastings. Edinburgh: 1909.

Bertram, G. "Die Himmelfahrt Jesu yom Kreuz aus und der Glaube an seine Auferstehung." Pages 187–217 in *Festgabe fur Adolf Deissmann zum 60*. Tübingen: J.C.B. Mohr (Paul Siebeck), 1927.

Betz, Hans Dieter, ed. *Greek Magical Papyri in Translation: Including the Demotic Spells*. Chicago: University of Chicago Press, 1986.

Betz, Otto. *Der Paraklet: Fürsprecher im häretischen Spätjüdentum im Johannes-Evangelium und in neugefundenen gnostischen Schriften*. Leiden: Brill, 1963.

Bickermann, Elias. "The Date of 4 Maccabees." Pages 105–12 in *Louis Ginzberg: Jubilee Volume on the Occasion of His Seventieth Birthday*. New York: American Academy for Jewish Research, 1945.

———. "Die römische Kaiserapotheose." *AR* 27 (1929): 1–34.

Bidez, Joseph, and Franz Cumont. *Les mages héllenisés: Zoroastre, Ostanès, and Hystaspe d'après la tradition grecque*. 2 vols. Paris: Les Belles Lettres, 1938.

Bietenhard, H. *Die himmlische Welt im Urchristentum und Spätjudentum*. Tübingen: Mohr Siebeck, 1951.

Black, Matthew. "The Throne-Theophany Prophetic Commission and the 'Son of Man': A Study in Tradition-History." Pages 57–73 in *Jews, Greeks and Christians: Essays in Honor of W. D. Davies*. Edited by R. Hamerton-Kelly and R. Scroggs. Leiden: Brill, 1976.

Bloch, Herbert. "A New Document of the Last Pagan Revival in the West, 393–394 A.D." *HTR* 38 (1945): 199–244.

Böhlig, Alexander. *Mysterion und Wahrheit: Gesammelte Beiträge zur spätantiken Religionsgeschichte*. Leiden: Brill, 1968.

Böhlig, Alexander, and Pahor Labib, eds. *Die Koptisch-gnostische Schrift ohne Titel aus Codex II von Nag Hammadi im koptischen Museum zu Alt-Kairo*. Berlin: Deutsch Akademie, 1962.

Bokser, Baruch M. "Recent Developments in the Study of Judaism, 70-200 C.E." *The Second Century: A Journal of Early Christian Studies* 3 (1983): 1–69.

Bonwetsch, Gottlieb Nathanael, ed. and trans. *Die Apokalypse Abrahams und Das Testament der vierzig Märtyrer*. Aalen: 1972.

Borgen, Peder. "God's Agent in the Fourth Gospel." Pages 137–48 in Neusner, ed., *Religions in Antiquity*.

Bousset, Wilhelm. "Die Himmelsreise der Seele." *AR* 4 (1901): 136–69; 228–73. Repr., Darmstadt: 1960.

———. *Kyrios Christos: A History of the Belief in Christ from the Beginnings of Christianity to Irenaeus*. Translated by J. E. Steely. Nashville: Abingdon, 1970. Repr., Waco: Baylor University Press, 2013.

Boyancé, Pierre. *Études sur le "Songe de Scipion."* Bibliothèque des Universités du Midi 20. Bordeaux: 1936.

———. "La religion astrale de Platon à Ciceron." *Revue des Études Grecques* 65 (1952): 312–51.

Brandenberger, E., U. B. Müller, and A. F. J. Klijn. *Apokalypsen: Himmelfahrt Moses, Die griechische Esra-Apokalypse, Die syrische Baruch-Apokalypse*. Gütersloh: 1976.

Brandt, W. "Das Schicksal der Seele naell clem Tode nach mandäischen und persischen Vorstellungen." *Jahrbücher für protestantische Theologie* 18 (1892): 405–38, 575–603.

Braude, William, trans. *Pesikta Rabbati: Discourses for Feasts, Fasts, and Special Sabbaths*. New Haven, Conn.: Yale University Press, 1968.

Brehier, Émile. *The Hellenistic and Roman Age*. Translated by Wade Baskin. Chicago: University of Chicago Press, 1965.

Breitenstein, U. *Beachtungen an Sprache, Stil und Gedankgut des vierten Maccabärbuches*. Basel: Swabe, 1976.

van den Broek, R. "The Present State of Gnostic Studies." *VC* 37 (1983): 41–71.

———. "The Serapis Oracle in Macrobius Sat. 1, 20, 16-17." Pages 1:123–41 in *Hommages à Maarten J. Vermaseren*. Edited by T. A. Edridge and M. Boer. 2 vols. Leiden: Brill, 1978.

van den Broek, R., and Maartin J. Vermaseren, eds. *Studies in Gnosticism and Hellenistic Religions: Presented to Gilles Quispel on the Occasion of his Sixty-Fifth Birthday*. Leiden: Brill, 1981.

Brown, Peter. "Sorcery, Demons and the Rise of Christianity from Late Antiquity into the Middle Ages." Pages 17–46 in Douglas, ed., *Witchcraft: Confessions and Accusations*.

Brown, Raymond E. *The Gospel according to St. John*. AB 29–29A. New York: Doubleday, 1966.

Brown, Raymond E., and John P. Meier. *Antioch and Rome: New Testament Cradles of Catholic Christianity*. Ramsey, N.J.: Paulist, 1983.

Büchler, Adolf. "The Minim of Sepphoris and Tiberius in the Second and Third Centuries." Pages 245–74 in *Studies in Jewish History*. Edited by I. Brodie and J. Rabinowitz. Oxford: Oxford University Press, 1956.

Bullard, Roger A. *The Hypostasis of the Archons: The Coptic Text with Translation and Commentary*. With contribution by Martin Krause. Berlin: de Gruyter, 1970.

Bulter, H. E., trans. *The Apologia and Florida of Apuleius of Madaura*. Oxford: Clarendon, 1909.

Bultmann, Rudolf. *Das Evangelium des Johannes*. Meyer's Commentary. Abteilung. Göttingen: Vandenhoeck & Ruprecht, 1941.

———. *The Gospel of John*. Louisville, Ky.: Westminster, 1971.

Burkill, Tom. *Mysterious Revelation: An Examination of the Philosophy of St. Mark's Gospel*. Ithaca, N.Y.: Cornell University Press, 1963.

Cagnat, R., ed. *Inscriptiones Graecae ad Res Romanas Pertinentes*. Vol. 1. Paris: Leroux, 1906.

Carr, A. W. "The Rulers of this Age—1 Corinthians 2:6-8." *NTS* 23 (1976): 20–35.

Carroll, Michael. "Leach, Genesis and Structural Analysis." *American Ethnologist* 4 (1977): 663–77.

———. "Lévi-Strauss on the Oedipus Myth: A Reconsideration." *American Anthropologist* 80 (1978): 805–14.

———. "One More Time: Leviticus Revisited." Pages 117–26 in *Anthropological Approaches to the Old Testament*. Edited by B. Lang. Philadelphia: Fortess, 1985.

Cavallin, H. C. "Leben nach dem Tode im Spätjudentum und im frühen Christentum, 1. Spätjudentum." *ANRW* 19.1 (1979): 240–345.

———. *Life After Death: Paul's Argument for the Resurrection of the Dead in I Corinthians 15*. Part 1: *An Inquiry into the Jewish Background*. Lund: CWK Gleerup, 1974.

Charles, R. H. *The Apocrypha and Pseudepigrapha of the Old Testament*. Oxford: Clarendon, 1912.

Charlesworth, J. H. "A Critical Comparison of the Dualism in 1QS 3.1–4.26 and the 'Dualism' Contained in the Gospel of John." *NTS* 15 (1968–1969): 389–418.

———. "Christian and Jewish Self-Definition in Light of the Christian Additions to the Apocryphal Writings." Pages 2:27–55 in Sanders, ed., *Jewish and Christian Self-Definition*.

———, ed. *John and Qumran*. London: Geoffrey Chapman, 1972.

———. *The Pseudepigrapha and Modern Research*. Missoula, Mont.: Scholars, 1976.

———. "The SNTS Pseudepigrapha Seminar at Tübingen and Paris on the Books of Enoch." *NTS* 25 (1979): 315–29.

Cohen, S. Review of *Two Powers in Heaven*. *AJS Review* 10, no. 1 (1985): 114–17.

Collins, John. J. *Apocalyptic and the Book of Daniel*. Missoula, Mont.: Scholars, 1978.

———. "Structure and Meaning in the 'Testament of Job.'" Pages 35–52 in *SBL Seminar Papers 1974*. Edited by G. W. MacRae. SBLPS 1. Missoula, Mont.: Scholars, 1975.

Collins, John J., and G. W. E. Nickelsburg Jr., eds. *Ideal Figures in Ancient Judaism: Profiles and Paradigms*. Chico, Calif.: Scholars, 1980.

Colpe, Carston. *Die Religionsgeschichtliche Schule: Darstellung und Kritik ihres Eildes vom gnostischen Erloscrmythus*. FRLANT 78. Göttingen: Vandenhoeck & Ruprecht, 1961.

———. "ὑιος του ανθροπου." *TDNT* 8:403–81.

Cooke, G. A. *A Text-Book of North-Semitic Inscriptions*. Oxford: Clarendon, 1903.

Cooper, Alan. "Divine Names and Epithets in the Ugaritic Texts." Pages 3:431–41 in *Ras Shamra Parallels: The Texts from Ugaritic and the Hebrew Bible*. Edited by Stan Rummel. Analecta Orientalia 51. Rome: Pontifical Biblical Institute, 1981.

Cozer, Lewis. *The Functions of Social Conflict*. New York: Simon & Schuster, 1956.

Craig, J. A. *Assyrian and Babylonian Religious Texts*. Vol. 1, *Prayers, Oracles, Hymns*. Leipzig: Hinrichs, 1895.

Cruvellier, J. M. E. *L'Exégèse de Romains 7 et le mouvement de Keswick*. Amsterdam: Academisch Proefschrift, Universiteit te Amsterdam, 1961.

Culianu, I. P. "The Angels of the Nations and the Origins of Gnostic Dualism." Pages 78–91 in van den Broek and Vermaseren, eds., *Studies in Gnosticism*.

———. *L'expériences de l'extase*. Paris: Payot, 1984.

———. *Psychanodia I: A Survey of the Evidence Concerning the Ascension of the Soul and Its Relevance*. Leiden: Brill, 1983.

Cullmann, Oscar. *Immortality of the Soul or Resurrection of the Dead?* London: Epworth Press, 1958.

Cumont, Franz. *Afterlife in Roman Paganism*. New Haven, Conn.: Yale University Press, 1922.

———. *Astrology and Religion among the Greeks and Romans*. New York: G. P. Putnam's Sons, 1912. Repr.: 1960.

———. *Lux Perpetua*. Paris: P. Geuthner, 1949.

———. *The Mysteries of Mithra*. Chicago: Open Court, 1903. Repr., New York: Dover, 1956.

———. "Le mysticisme astrale dans l'antiquite." *Bulletin de l'Académie Royale de Belgique* 1909: 256–86.

———. "La théologie solaire du paganisme romain." *Memoires, Academie des Inscriptions et Belles-Lettres* 12 (1913): 448–81.

———. *Textes et monuments figurés relatifs aux mystères de Mithra*. 2 vols. Brussels: Lamertin, 1899.

Cumont, Franz. *The Oriental Religions in Roman Paganism*. Chicago: Open Court, 1911.

Cuss, Dominique. "Der Erstgeborene Satans und der Vater des Tüfels (Polyk. 7:1 und Joh. 8:44)." Pages 70–84 in *Apophoreta: Festschrift fur Ernst Hänchen*. Edited by W. Eltester. BZNW 30. Berlin: Töpelmann, 1964.

———. *Imperial Cults and Honorary Terms in the New Testament*. Fribourg: Fribourg University Press, 1974.

Dahl, N. A. "The Arrogant Archon and the Lewd Sophia: Jewish Traditions in Gnostic Revolt." Pages 2:689–712 in Layton, ed., *The Rediscovery of Gnosticism*.

———. *The Crucified Messiah and Other Essays*. Minneapolis: Augsburg, 1974.

———. "The Johannine Church and History." Pages 124–42 in *Current Issues in New Testament Interpretation*. Edited by W. Klassen and G. Snyder. London: SCM Press, 1962.

———. *Das Volk Gottes: Eine Untersuchung zum Kirchenbewusstsein des Urchristentums*. Darmstadt: Wissenschaftliche Buchgesellschaft, 1963.

———. "Widersprüche in der Bibel." *ST* 25 (1971): 9–11.

Dahl, N. A., and Alan F. Segal. "Philo and the Rabbis on the Name of God." *JSJ* 10 (1979): 1–28.

Dalton, O. M. *Catalogue of Ivory Carvings of the Christian Era*. London: Trustees of the British Museum, 1909.

Darmesteter, J., trans. *The Zend-Avesta*. 2 vols. Oxford: Clarendon, 1880–1883.

Davies, P. R., and B. D. Chilton. "The Akedah: A Revised Tradition History." *CBQ* 40 (1978): 514–46.

Davies, W. D. *Paul and Rabbinic Judaism*. London: SPCK, 1948.

Dean-Otting, Mary. *Heavenly Journeys: A Study of the Motif in Hellenistic Jewish Literature*. New York: Peter Lang, 1984.

Dekker, W. "De Geliefde Zoon in de synoptische Evangelien." *NedTT* 16 (1961–1962): 94–106.

Delling, Gerhard. *Bibliographie zur jüdisch-hellenistischen und intertestamentarischen Literatur 1900–1965*. Berlin: Akademie, 1969.

des Places, Édouard, ed. and trans. *Jamblique, Les Mysteres d'Egypte*. Paris: Les Belles Lettres, 1966.

———, ed. and trans. *Numénius Fragments*. Paris: Les Belles Lettres, 1975.

———, ed. and trans. *Oracles Chaldaïques*. Paris: Les Belles Lettres, 1971.

Detweiler, Robert. *Story, Sign, and Self*. Missoula, Mont.: Scholars, 1978.

Dey, L. K. K. *The Intermediary World and Patterns of Perfection in Philo and Hebrews*. Missoula, Mont.: Scholars, 1975.

Dhorme, Edouard. *Choix de textes religieux assyro-babyloniens*. Études bibliques 7. Paris: J. Gabalda, 1907.

Dieterich, Allbrecht. *Eine Mithrasliturgie*. Leipzig: Teubner, 1903. 3rd ed.: 1903.

Doane, T. W. *Bible Myths and their Parallels in Other Religions*. 7th ed. New York: Truth Seeker, 1948.

Dobschütz, Ernst. "Wir und Ich bei Paulus." *Zeitschrift für systematische Theologie* 10 (1933): 251–77.

Dodd, C. H. *The Bible and the Greeks*. London: Hodder & Stoughton 1935. 3rd ed.: 1964.

Dodds, E. R. *The Greeks and the Irrational*. Berkeley: University of California Press, 1968.

———, ed. and trans. *Proclus: The Elements of Theology*. 2nd ed. Oxford: Clarendon, 1963.

Donin, H. H. *To Pray as a Jew: A Guide to the Prayer Book and the Synagogue Service*. New York: Basic Books, 1991.

Doresse, Jean. *The Secret Book of the Egyptian Gnostics*. New York: Viking, 1960.

Douglas, Mary. *Implicit Meanings: Essays in Anthropology*. London: Routledge, 1975.

———. *Natural Symbols: Explorations in Cosmology*. 2nd ed. London: Barrie and Jenkins, 1973.

———. *Purity and Danger*. London: Routledge & Kegan Paul, 1966.

———. "Thirty Years after *Witchcraft, Oracles, and Magic*." Pages xiii–xxxvi in Douglas, ed., *Witchcraft: Confessions and Accusations*.

———, ed. *Witchcraft: Confessions and Accusations*. London: Tavistock, 1970.

Dunn, J. D. G. *Christology in the Making: A New Testament Inquiry into the Origins of the Doctrine of the Incarnation*. Philadelphia: Westminster, 1980.

Elbogen, I. *Der jüdische Gottesdients in seiner geschichtlichen Entwicklung*. Frankfurt am Main: 1931. Repr., Hildesheim: 1962.

Elferink, M. A. *La descente de l'ame d'après Macrobe*. Leiden: Brill, 1968.

Eliade, Mircea. *Shamanism: Archaic Techniques of Ecstasy*. Princeton: Princeton University Press, 1964.

———. *Zalmoxis, the Vanishing God: Comparative Studies in the Religions and Folklore of Dacia and Eastern Europe*. Chicago: University of Chicago Press, 1972.

Enslin, M. S. "The Ascension Story." *JBL* 47 (1928): 60–73.

Farnell, Lewis Richard. *Greek Hero Cults and Ideas of Immortality*. Oxford: Clarendon, 1921.

Fascher, Erich. "Anastasis-Resurrectio-Auferstehung." *ZNW* 40 (1941): 166–229.

Festugière, Andre-Jean. *Personal Religion Among the Greeks*. Berkeley: University of California Press, 1960.

———. *La révélation d'Hermès Trismégiste*. 4 vols. Paris: Gabalda, 1950–1954.

Feuillet, A. "Les perspectives propres à chaque Évangéliste dans les récits de la transfiguration." *Bib* 39 (1958): 281–301.

Fisher, Humprey. "Conversion Reconsidered: Some Historical Aspects of Religious Conversion in Black Africa." *Africa* 43 (1973): 27–40.

Flusser, David. "Not by Means of an Angel . . ." *Toray Yeshurun* 29 (1971–1972): 18–20. Hebrew.

Forkman, Göran. *The Limits of the Religious Community: Expulsion from the Religious Community within the Qumran Sect, within Rabbinic Judaism, and within Primitive Christianity*. Lund: Gleerup, 1972.

Förster, Werner, ed. *Gnosis: A Selection of Gnostic Texts*. Vol. 2, *Coptic and Mandaean Sources*. Translated by R. McL. Wilson. Oxford: Oxford University Press, 1972.

Fossing, Poul. *Catalogue of the Antique Engraved Gems and Cameos*. Copenhagen: G. E. C. Gad, 1929.

Fossum, Jarl E. "Gen. 1,26 and 2,7 in Judaism, Samaritanism and Gnosticism." *JSJ* 16, no. 2 (1985): 202–39.

———. "Kyrios Jesus as the Angel of the Lord in Jude 5-7." *NTS* 33 (1987): 226–43.

———. *The Name of God and the Angel of the Lord: Samaritan and Jewish Concepts of Intermediation and the Origin of Gnosticism*. WUNT 36. Tübingen: Mohr Siebeck, 1985.

———. "The Origin of the Gnostic Concept of the Demiurge." *Ephemerides Theologicae Lovanienses* 61 (1985): 142–52.

———. "The Samaritan Origin of the Concept of the Demiurge." Paper delivered at the Yale International Conference on Gnosticism, April 1978.

Friedländer, Moriz. *Der vorchristliche jüdische Gnosticismus*. Göttingen: Vandenhoeck & Ruprecht, 1898.

Friedrich, H., ed. and trans. *Thessalos von Tralles*. Meisenheim am Glan: Hain, 1968.

Gager, John. *The Origins of Anti-Semitism: Attitudes toward Judaism in Pagan and Christian Antiquity*. New York: Oxford University Press, 1983.

Gaston, Lloyd. "Paul and the Law in Galatians Two and Three." Pages 37–58 in *Anti-Judaism in Early Christianity*. Vol. 1, *Paul and the Gospels*. Edited by Peter Richardson and D. Granskou. Waterloo, Ont.: Wilfred Laurier University Press, 1986

Gaugler, E. *Der Brief an die Römer*. Zurich: Zwingli, 1945.

Gawlikowski, Michel. *Recueil d'inscriptions palmyréniennes provenant des fouilles syriennes et polonaises récentes à Palmyre*. Paris: Imprimerie National, 1974.

Gershenzon, Rosalie, and Elieser Slomovic. "A Second-Century Jewish-Gnostic Debate: Rabbi Jose ben Halafta and the Matrona." *JSJ* 16 (1985): 1–41.

Gerstenberger, Erhard. "Jeremiah's Complaints: Observations on Jer 15.10-21." *JBL* 82 (1963): 393–408.

Ginzberg, Louis. *Die Haggada bei den Kirchenvätern*. Amsterdam: 1899.

———. *The Legends of the Jews*. Philadelphia: Jewish Publication Society, 1900.

Goldin, Judah. "Not by Means of an Angel and Not by Means of a Messenger." Pages 412–24 in Neusner, ed., *Religions in Antiquity*.

———. *The Song at the Sea: Being a Commentary on a Commentary in Two Parts*. New Haven, Conn.: Yale University Press, 1971.

Goodenough, Erwin R. *By Light, Light: The Mystic Gospel of Hellenistic Judaism*. New Haven, Conn.: Yale University Press, 1935.

———. *Jewish Symbols in the Greco-Roman Period.* 13 vols. New York: Pantheon, 1953–1968.

———. *The Theology of Justin Martyr: An Investigation into the Conceptions of the Earliest Christian Literature and Its Hellenistic and Judaistic Influences.* Jena: Frommannsche Buchhandlung, 1923.

Graves, Robert, and Raphael Patai. *Hebrew Myths: The Book of Genesis.* Garden City: Doubleday, 1964.

Green, Henry. *The Economic and Social Origins of Gnosticism.* Atlanta: Scholars, 1985.

———. "Gnosis and Gnosticism: A Study in Methodology." *Numen* 24 (1977): 95–134.

———. "Suggested Sociological Themes in the Study of Gnosticism." *VC* 31 (1977): 169–80.

Greene, Thomas. *Descent from Heaven.* New Haven, Conn.: Yale University Press, 1963.

Griffiths, J. Gwyn, ed. *Apuleius of Madauros: The Isis-Book.* EPRO 39. Leiden: Brill, 1975.

Gruenwald, Ithamar. *Apocalyptic and Merkabah Literature.* Leiden: Brill, 1979.

———. "Aspects of the Jewish-Gnostic Controversy." Pages 2:713–23 in Layton, *The Rediscovery of Gnosticism.*

———. "Jewish Sources for the Gnostic Texts from Nag Hammadi?" Pages 45–56 in *Proceedings of the Sixth World Congress of Jewish Studies.* Jerusalem: World Congress of Jewish Studies, 1977.

———. "The Problem of Anti-Gnostic Polemic in Rabbinic Literature." Pages 171–89 in van den Broek and Vermaseren, eds., *Studies in Gnosticism.*

Guthrie, Kenneth S. *Numenius of Apamea: The Father of Neo-Platonism.* London: George Bell & Sons, 1917.

Guthrie, W. F. C. *Orpheus and Greek Religion.* Princeton: Princeton University Press, 1935.

Haardt, Robert. "Zur Methodologie der Gnosisforschung." Pages 77–88 in Tröger, ed., *Gnosis un Neues Testament.*

Hadas, Moses, ed. and trans. *The Third and Fourth Books of Maccabees.* New York: Harper & Brothers, 1953.

Hadas, Moses, and Morton Smith. *Heroes and Gods: Spiritual Biographies in Antiquity.* New York: Harper & Row 1965.

Hage, W., and K. G. Eckart, eds. *Apokalypsen: Die griechische Baruch-Apokalypse. Das Apokryphon Ezekiel.* Gütersloh: Gütersloher Verlagshaus, 1974.

Hallo, William. *Early Mesopotamian Royal Titles.* New Haven, Conn.: American Oriental Society, 1957.

Hänchen, Ernst. *Die Apostelgeschichte.* Göttingen: Vandenhoeck & Ruprecht, 1955.

Haug, M., and E. W. West, eds. and trans. *The Book of Arda Viraf.* London: Trübner, 1872. Repr., 1971.

Hegermann, Harald. *Die Vorstellung vom Schöpfungsmittler im hellenistischen Judentum und Urchristentum*, TUGAL 82. Berlin: Akademie, 1961.

Heinemann, Isaac. *Darkhe ha-Agadah.* Jerusalem: Magnes, 1954.

Heinemann, Joseph. "Once More *Melekh Ha-'Olam.*" *JJS* 15 (1964): 149–54.

———. *Prayer in the Talmud: Forms and Patterns.* Translated by Richard S. Sarason. Berlin: de Gruyter, 1977. From the 2nd Heb. ed. Jerusalem: Hebrew University Press, 1966.

Hengel, Martin. *The Atonement: The Origins of the Doctrine in the New Testament.* Translated by John Bowden. Philadelphia: Fortress, 1981.

Herford, R. Travers. *Christianity in Talmud and Midrash.* London: Williams & Norgate, 1903.

Himes, Joseph. "The Function of Racial Conflict," *Social Forces* 45 (1966): 1–10.

Himmelfarb, Martha. "From Prophecy to Apocalypse: The *Book of the Watchers* and Tours of Heaven." Pages 145–65 in *Jewish Spirituality: From the Bible Through the Middle Ages.* Edited by Arthur Green. New York: Crossroads, 1986.

———. *Tours of Hell: The Development and Transmission of an Apocalyptic Form in Jewish and Christian Literature.* Philadelphia: University of Pennsylvania Press, 1983.

Hinnels, John, ed. *Mithraic Studies: Proceedings of the First International Congress of Mithraic Studies.* 2 vols. Manchester: Manchester University Press, 1975.

Holladay, Carl R. Theios Aner *in Hellenistic Judaism.* SBLDS. Missoula, Mont.: Scholars, 1977.

Holland, R. "Zur Typik der Himmelfahrt." *AR* 23 (1925): 207–20.

Hoenn, C. *Studien zur Geschichte dei Himmelfahrt.* Mannheim: Mannheimer Vereinsdr., 1910.

Hooker, M. D. *Jesus and the Servant.* London: SPCK, 1959.

Horbury, William. "The Benediction of the Minim and the Early Jewish Christian Controversy." *JTS* 33 (1982): 19–61.

Horowitz, H., and A. Rabin, ed. *Mechilta d' Rabbi Ismael.* Frankfort: J. Kaufman, 1931.

van der Horst, P. W. "De joodse toneelschrijver Ezechiel," *Nederlands Theologisch Tijdschrift* 36, no. 2 (1982): 97–112.

Horton Jr., Fred. L. *The Melchizedek Tradition: A Critical Examination of the Sources to the Fifth Century A.D. and in the Epistle to the Hebrews*. SNTSMS 30. Cambridge: Cambridge University Press, 1976.

Horton, John. "Order and Conflict: Theories of Social Problems as Competing Ideologies." *American Journal of Sociology* 71 (1966): 701–13.

Horton, Robin. "African Conversion." *Africa* 41 (1971): 85–107.

———. "On the Rationality of Conversion." *Africa* 45 (1975): 219–35; 373–99.

Hull, John M. *Hellenistic Magic and the Synoptic Tradition*. SBT. London: SCM Press, 1974.

Hunzinger, C. H. "Die jüdische Bannpraxis im neutestamentlichen Zeitalter." Ph.D. diss., University of Göttingen, 1954.

Hurd, John C. *The Origin of 1 Corinthians*. London: SPCK, 1965. New ed., Macon, Ga.: Mercer University Press, 1985.

Hurtado, Larry. *One God, One Lord*. Philadelphia: Fortress, 1988.

Isbell, Charles D. *Corpus of the Aramaic Incantation Bowls*. Missoula, Mont.: SBL, 1975.

Isenberg, Sheldon. "Mary Douglas and Hellenistic Religions: The Case of Qumran." Pages 1:179–85 in *SBL 1975 Seminary Papers*. 2 vols. SBLSP 12. Missoula, Mont.: Scholars, 1975.

Isenberg, Sheldon, and Dennis F. Owen. "Bodies, Natural and Contrived: The Work of Mary Douglas." *Religious Studies Review* 3 (1977): 1–17.

Jacobsen, Thorkild. *The Treasures of Darkness: A History of Mesopotamian Religion*. New Haven, Conn.: Yale University Press, 1976.

James, E. O. *Sacrifice and Sacrament*. London: Thames & Hudson, 1962.

Jaubert, Annie. *La notion d'alliance dans le Judaïsme aux abords de l'ère Chrétienne*. Patristica Sorbonensis 6. Paris: Editions du Seuil, 1963.

Jaussen, A. J., and R. Savignac, *Mission archéologique en Arabie*. Vol. 1, *De Jérusalem au Hedjaz Médaine-Saleh*. Paris: Paul Geuthner, 1909.

Jewett, Robert, ed. *Christology and Exegesis*. Chico, Calif.: Scholars, 1985.

———. *A Chronology of Paul's Life*. Philadelphia: Fortress, 1979.

Joël, Manuel. *Blicke in die Religionsgeschichte zu Anfang des zweiten christlichen Jahrhunderts*. Breslau: Schottlaender, 1883.

Johnston, George. *The Spirit-Paraclete in the Gospel of John*. Cambridge: Cambridge University Press, 1970.

Juel, Donald. "The Image of the Servant Christ in the New Testament." *SwJT* 21 (1979): 7–22.

———. *Messianic Exegesis*. Philadelphia: Fortress, 1987.

Kee, Howard. *Miracle in the Early Christian World: A Study in Sociohistorical Method*. New Haven, Conn.: Yale University Press, 1983.

———. "Satan, Magic, and Salvation in the 'Testament of Job.'" Pages 53–76 in *SBL Seminar Papers 1974*. Edited by G. W. MacRae. SBLSP 1. Missoula, Mont.: Scholars, 1975.

Kelly, J. N. D. *Early Christian Doctrines*. New York: Harper & Row, 1958.

Kenny, A. C. "The Transfiguration and the Agony in the Garden." *CBQ* 4 (1957): 444–52.

Kimelman, Reuben. "*Birkat Ha-Minim* and the Lack of Evidence for an Anti-Christian Prayer in Late Antiquity." Pages 2:226–44 in Sanders, ed., *Jewish and Christian Self-Definition*.

Kippenberg, Hans. "Versuch einer soziologischen Verortung des antiken Gnostizismus." *Numen* 17 (1950): 211–31.

Klein, Charlotte. *Anti-Judaism in Christian Theology*. Translated by Edward Quinn. Philadelphia: Fortress, 1975.

Kleinknecht, H., and W. Gutbrod. "νομος." *TDNT* 4:1036–91.

Kluckhohn, Clyde. *Navajo Witchcraft*. Cambridge: Cambridge University Press, 1944.

Knibb, M. A., and E. Ullendorff, eds. *The Ethiopic Book of Enoch: A New Edition in the Light of the Aramaic Dead Sea Fragments*. Oxford: Clarendon, 1978.

Koester, Helmut. "*Nomos Phuseos*: The Concept of Natural Law in Greek Thought." Pages 521–41 in Neusner, ed., *Religions in Antiquity*.

Kolenkow, Anitra B. "A Problem of Power: How Miracle Workers Counter Charges of Magic in the Hellenistic World." Pages 105–10 in *SBL 1976 Seminar Papers*. Edited by G. MacRae. SBLSP 10. Missoula, Mont.: Scholars, 1976.

Koschorke, Klaus. *Die Polemik der Gnostiker gegen das kirchliche Christentum*. Leiden: Brill, 1978.

Kragerud, A. *Die Hymnen der Pistis Sophia*. Oslo: Universitetsforlagets, 1967.

Kraft, R. A. "'Ezra' Materials in Judaism and Christianity." *ANRW* 19.1 (1979): 119–36.

Kraus, W. W. "Vergils vierte Ekloge: Ein kritisches Hypomnema." *ANRW* 31.1 (1980): 604–45.

Kroll, J. *Die Himmelfahrt der Seele in der Antike*. Koin: 1931.

Kummel, W. G. *Römer 7 und die Bekehrung des Paulus*. Leipzig: Hinrichs, 1929.

Kuss, Otto. *Der Römerbrief*. 2nd ed. Regensburg: F. Pustet, 1963.

Laeyendecker, L. *Religie en Conflict*. Meppel: J. A. Boom en Zoon, 1968.

Larrañaga, V. *L'Ascension de Notre Seigneur dans le Nouveau Testament*. Rome: Pontifical Biblical Institute, 1938.

Lauterbach, Jacob, trans. *Mekilta de-Rabbi Ishmael*. Philadelphia: Jewish Publication Society, 1961.

———. "Some Clarifications of the Mekhilta." Pages 181–88 in *Sefer Klausner: A Collection of Science and Belle-lettres Gathered for Professor Klausner on his Sixtieth Birthday Celebration*. Edited by Torchyner, Tcherikover, Kubeck, and Shortrnan. Tel Aviv: 1937.

Layton, Bentley. "The Hypostasis of the Archons." *HTR* 67 (1974): 351–25; 69 (1976): 31–101.

———, ed. *The Rediscovery of Gnosticism: Proceedings of the International Conference in Gnosticism at Yale University March 28–31, 1978*. Vol. 1, *The School of Valentinus*. Vol. 2, *Sethian Gnosticism*. Leiden: Brill, 1981.

Le Déaut, R. "Aspects de l'intercession dans le Judaisme ancien." *JSJ* 1 (1970): 35–57.

———. *La Nuit Paschale: Essai sur la signification de la Pâque juive à partir du Targum d' Exode XII 42*. Rome: Pontifical Biblical Institute, 1963.

Leach, Edmund. *Culture and Communication*. Cambridge: Cambridge University Press, 1966.

———. "Myth as a Justification for Faction and Social Change." Pages 264–78 in *Political Systems of Highland Burma*. London: Athlone, 1954.

Leaney, A. R. C. "The Johannine Paraclete and the Qumran Scrolls." Pages 38–61 in Charlesworth, ed., *John and Qumran*.

Leenhardt, F. J. *L'Épître de St. Paul aux Romains*. Paris: Delachaux et Niestle, 1957.

Lerch, David. *Isaaks Opferung, christlich gedeutet*. Tübingen: Mohr Siebeck, 1950.

Lévi, Israel. "Le sacrifice d'Isaac et la mort de Jesus." *REJ* 64 (1912): 161–84.

Lévi-Strauss, Claude. *From Honey to Ashes*. New York: Harper & Row, 1966.

———. *Myth and Meaning*. Toronto: University of Toronto Press, 1978.

———. *The Raw and the Cooked*. Translated by John Weightman and Doreen Weightman. New York: Harper & Row, 1969.

———. *The Savage Mind*. Chicago: University of Chicago Press, 1962.

———. *Structural Anthropology*, Translated by C. Jacobson and Brooke Grundfest Schoepf. New York: Basic Books, 1963.

Lewy, Hans. *The Chaldaean Oracles and Theurgy: Mysticism, Magic and Platonism in the Later Roman Empire*. Vol. 13 of *Recherches d'archeologie, de philologie et d'histoire*. Cairo: Imprimerie de l'Institut Français d'Archéologie Orientale, 1959.

———. *Sobria Ebrietas: Untersuchungen zur Geschichte der antiken Mystik*. Giessen: Töpelmann, 1929.

Lieberman, Saul. *Greek in Jewish Palestine: Studies in the Life and Manners of Jewish Palestine in the II–IV Centuries C.E.* New York: Feldheim, 1965.

———. *Hellenism in Jewish Palestine: Studies in the Literary Transmission, Beliefs, and Manners of Palestine in the I Century B.C.E.–IV Century B.C.E.* New York: Jewish Theological Seminary of America, 1962.

Lietzmann, Hans. *The Beginnings of the Christian Church*. Translated by L. B. Woolf. London: Lutterworth, 1937.

Linforth, I. M. *The Arts of Orpheus*. Berkeley: University of California Press, 1941.

Lipsius, R., and M. Bonnet, eds. *Acta Apostolorum Apocrypha*. Leipzig: Mendelssohn, 1891–1903.

Loew, Cornelius. *Myth, Sacred History and Philosophy*. New York: Harcourt, Brace & World, 1967.

Lohfink, Gerhard. *Die Himmelfahrt Jesu—Erfindung oder Erfahrung*. SANT 26. München: Kösel, 1971.

Lohse, Edouard. *Märtyrer und Gottesknecht*. Göttingen: Vandenhoeck & Ruprecht, 1963.

van der Loos, Hendrik. *The Miracles of Jesus*. NovTSup. Leiden: Brill, 1965.

Lowe, J. E. *Magic in Greek and Latin Literature*. Oxford: Basil Blackwell, 1929.

Lüdemann, Gerd. *Untersuchungen zur simonianischen Gnosis*. Göttinger theologische Arbeiten 1. Göttingen: Vandenhoeck & Ruprecht, 1975.

Machinist, Peter. "Literature as Politics: The Tikulti-Ninurta Epic and the Bible." *CBQ* 38 (1976): 455–82.

Mack, B. L. *Logos und Sophia: Untersuchungen zur Weisheitstheologie im hellenistischen Judentum*, SUNT 10. Göttingen: Vandenhoeck & Ruprecht, 1973.

———. "Wisdom, Myth and Mythology." *Int* 24 (1970): 46–60.

MacKenna, Stephen, trans. *The Enneads of Plotinus*. 3rd rev. ed. by B. S. Page. London: Faber, 1965.

MacMullen, Ramsay. *Enemies of the Roman Order: Treason, Unrest, and Alienation in the Empire*. Cambridge, Mass.: Harvard University Press, 1967.

Maier, Johann. "Das Gefährdungsmotiv bei der Himmelsreise in der jüdischen Apokalyptik und Gnosis." *Kairos* 5 (1963): 18-40.

Mair, Lucy. *Witchcraft*. New York: McGraw-Hill, 1969.

Malinowski, Bronislaw. *Myth in Primitive Psychology*. New York: W.W. Norton, 1926.

———. *A Scientific Theory of Culture and Other Essays*. Chapel Hill: University of North Carolina Press, 1944.

Marmorstein, Arthur. *The Old Rabbinic Doctrine of God*. Vol. 1, *The Names and Attributes of God*. Oxford: Oxford University Press, 1927.

———. *Religionsgeschichtliche Studien: Die Bezeichnungen für Christen und Gnostischen im Talmud und Midras*. Schotschau: Selbst Verlag des Verfasser, 1910.

Martin, R. P. *Carmen Christi: Philippians 2:5-11 in Recent Interpretation and the Setting of Early Christian Worship*. SNTSMS 4. Cambridge: Cambridge University Press, 1967.

Martroye, F. "La répression de la magie et les cultes des gentils au IVe siècle." *Revue historique du droit français et étranger*, 4th series, 18 (1930): 669–701.

Martyn, J. Louis. *History and Theology in the Fourth Gospel*. 2nd ed. Nashville: Abingdon, 1979.

———. *Theology and History in the Fourth Gospel*. Nashville: Abingdon, 1968. Rev. ed.: 1979.

———. "We Have Found Elijah." Pages 181–219 in *Jews, Greeks and Christians: Essays in Honor of W. D. Davies*. Edited by R. Hamerton-Kelly and R. Scroggs. Leiden: Brill, 1976.

Massonneau, Eliane. *Le crime de magie et le droit romain*. Paris: Recueil Sirey, 1933.

Mead, G. R. S. *The Doctrine of the Subtle Body in Western Tradition*. London: J.M. Watkins, 1919.

Meeks, Wayne A. "'Am I a Jew?' Johannine Christianity and Judaism." Pages 163–86 in Neusner, ed., *Christianity, Judaism, and other Greco-Roman Cults*. Part 1: *New Testament*.

———. "The Divine Agent and His Counterfeit in Philo and the Fourth Gospel." Pages 45–49 in *Aspects of Religious Propaganda in Judaism and Early Christianity*. Edited by E. Schüssler Fiorenza. Notre Dame, Ind.: University of Notre Dame Press, 1976.

———. "The Man from Heaven in Johannine Sectarianism." *JBL* 91 (1972): 44–72.

———. *The Prophet-King: Moses Traditions and the Johannine Christology*. Leiden: Brill, 1967.

Meiser, A. B. *Pyramid Texts*. New York: Longmans & Green, 1952.

Mendelson, E. M. "Some Notes on a Sociological Approach to Gnosticism." Pages 668–76 in *Le origini dello gnosticismo*. Edited by Ugo Bianchi. Numen Supplement 12. Leiden: Brill, 1967.

Metzger, B. M. "The Meaning of Christ's Ascension." Pages 118–28 in *Search the Scriptures: New Testament Studies in Honor of R. T. Stamm*. Leiden: Brill, 1969.

Meyer, Marvin, ed. and trans. *The Mithras Liturgy*. Texts and Translations 10 = Greco-Roman Religion Series, 2. Missoula, Mont.: Scholars, 1976.

Meyer, Paul. "Romans 10:4 and the End of the Law." Pages 59–78 in *The Divine Helmsman: Studies on God's Control of Human Events, Presented to Lou H. Silberman*. Edited by James L. Crenshaw and Samuel Sandmel. New York: Ktav, 1980.

Michel, Otto. *Römerbrief*. 14th ed. Meyer Commentary. Göttingen: Vandenhoeck & Ruprecht, 1977.

Mignard, J. E. "Jewish and Christian Cultic Discipline to the Middle of the Second Century." Ph.D. diss., Boston University, 1966.

Milik, J. T. "Milki-sedeq et Milki-rasha dan les anciens écrits Juifs et Chrétiens." *JJS* 4 (1972): 95–144; *RB* 79 (1972): 77–97.

———. "Problèmes de la littérature hénochique à la lumière des fragments araméens de Qumran." *HTR* 64 (1971): 333–78.

———. "Turfan et Qumran Livre des Géants juifs et manichéens." Pages 117–27 in *Tradition und Glaube: das frühe Christentum in seiner Umwelt: Festgabe für K. G. Kuhn*. Edited by G. Jeremias, H.-W. Kuhn, and H. Stegmann. Göttingen: Vandenhoeck & Ruprecht, 1971.

Milik, J. T., with Matthew Black, eds. *The Books of Enoch: Aramaic Fragments of Qumran Cave 4*. Oxford: Clarendon, 1976.

Millgrom, Abraham. *Jewish Worship: A Guide to the Prayer Book and the Synagogue Service*. Philadelphia: Jewish Publication Society, 1971.

Minear, Paul. *The Obedience of Faith: The Purposes of Paul in the Epistle to the Romans*. Napierville, Ill.: Alec Allenson, 1971.

Momigliano, Arnaldo. *Alien Wisdom: The Limits of Hellenization*. Cambridge: Cambridge University Press, 1975.

Montefiore, Claude G. *Judaism and St. Paul*. London: Max Goschen, 1914.

———. “Rabbinic Judaism and the Epistles of St. Paul.” *JQR* 13 (1900): 161–217.

Moule, C. F. D. “The Ascension—Acts 1:9.” *ExpT* 69 (1956/1957): 205–9.

Moxnes, Halvor. “God and His Angel in the Shepherd of Hermas.” *ST* 28 (1974): 49–56.

Mras, K., ed. *Praeparatio evangelica. Eusebius Werke*, bd. 8. 2 vols. GCS 43. Berlin: Akademie, 1954.

Munz, Peter. “The Problem of ‘Die soziologische Verortung des antiken Gnostizismus.”’ *Numen* 19 (1972): 41–51.

Neusner, Jacob. *Christianity, Judaism, and other Greco-Roman Cults: Studies for Morton Smith at Sixty*. Part 1: *New Testament*. Leiden: Brill, 1975.

———, ed. *Eliezer ben Hyrcanus: The Man and The Legend*. Leiden: Brill, 1973.

———. *From Politics to Piety: The Emergence of Pharisaic Judaism*. Englewood Cliffs: Prentice Hall, 1973.

———. *The Rabbinic Traditions about the Pharisees Before 70*. Leiden: Brill, 1971.

———. “The Rabbinic Traditions about the Pharisees Before 70 CE: The Problem of Oral Transmission.” *JJS* 22 (1971): 1–18.

———, ed. *Religions in Antiquity: Essays in Memory of Erwin Ramsdell Goodenough*. Numen Supplement 14. Leiden: Brill, 1968.

Neyrey, Jerome. “‘My Lord and My God’: The Divinity of Jesus in John’s Gospel.” Pages 152–82 in *Society of Biblical Literature 1986 Seminar Papers*. Edited by David J. Lull. SBLSP 25. Atlanta: Scholars Press, 1986.

Nickelsburg, G. W. E. Jr. *Resurrection, Immortality, and Eternal Life in Intertestamental Judaism*. Missoula, Mont.: Scholars, 1972.

Nilsson, Martin P. *Geschichte der griechischen Religion*. Vol. 2, *Die hellenistische und römische Zeit*. München: Beck, 1961.

———. “Greek Magical Papyri.” *Journal of Egyptian Archaeology* 15 (1929): 219–35.

———. “The Origin of the Belief among the Greeks in the Divinity of the Heavenly Bodies.” *HTR* 33 (1940): 1–8.

———. “Die Religion in den griechischen Zaubetpapyri.” Pages 3:129–66 in *Opuscula Selecta*. Lund: Gleerup, 1951–1960.

Nock, A. D. *Conversion: The Old and the New in Religion from Alexander the Great to Augustine of Hippo*. Oxford: Oxford University Press, 1969.

———. “The Emperor’s Divine Comes.” *JRS* 37 (1947): 102–16.

———. *Essays on Religion and the Ancient World*. Edited by Zeph Steward. Oxford: Oxford University Press, 1972.

———. "Paul and the Magus." Pages 5:164–88 in *The Beginnings of Christianity: The Acts of the Apostles*, ed. F. J. Foakes-Jackson and K. Lake, 5 vols. London: Macmillan, 1920–1933. Repr., Grand Rapids: Baker, 1966.

Norman, A. F., ed. and trans. *Libanius' Autobiography (Oration 1)*. London: Oxford University Press, 1965.

Nygren, Anders. *Commentary on Romans*. Philadelphia: Fortress, 1949.

Odeberg, H., trans. and ed. *3 Enoch or the Hebrew Book of Enoch*. New York: KTAV, 1973.

Oepke, Albrecht. "Μεσιτης." *TDNT* 4:598–624.

Oppenheim, A. Leo. *Ancient Mesopotamia: Portrait of a Dead Civilization*. Rev. ed. Chicago: University of Chicago Press, 1977.

Pagels, Elaine. "The Demiurge and his Archons—Gnostic Views on the Bishop and Presbyters?" *HTR* 69 (1976): 301–24.

———. "Gnostic and Orthodox Views of Christ's Passion: Paradigms for the Christian's Response to Persecution?" Pages 1:262–88 in Layton, ed., *Rediscovery of Gnosticism*.

———. *The Gnostic Gospels*. New York: Random House, 1979.

———. "Origen and the Prophets of Israel." *JANES* 5 (1973): 335–44.

Parkes, James W. *Jesus, Paul, and the Jews*. London: SCM Press, 1934.

Patte, Daniel. *What Is Structural Exegesis?* Philadelphia: Fortress, 1976.

Parrinder, Geoffrey. *Witchcraft: European and African*. London: Faber & Faber, 1963.

Pearson, Birger. "Friedlaender Revisited: Alexandrian Judaism and Gnosticism." *Studia Philonica* 2 (1973): 23–39.

Pelikan, Jaroslav. *The Christian Tradition: A History of the Development of Doctrine*. Vol. 1, *The Emergence of the Catholic Tradition (100–600)*. Chicago: University of Chicago Press, 1971.

Pemberton III, John. "A Cluster of Sacred Symbols: Orisha Worship Among the Ibgomina Yomba of Ila-Orangun." *History of Religions* 17 (1977): 1–28.

Peterson, Erik. "Die Befreiung Adams aus der Αναγκη." Pages 107–28 in *Frühkirche, Judentum, und Gnosis*. Freiburg: Herder, 1959.

———. "Herkunft und Bedeutung der *Monos pros Monon*-Formel bei Platon." *Philologus* 88 (1933): 30–41.

———. "La liberation d'Adam de l'Αναγκη." *RB* 55 (1948): 199–214.

Philonenko, Marc. *Joseph et Aseneth: Introduction, texte critique, traduction et notes*. Leiden: Brill, 1968.

Pokorny, Petr. "Der soziale Hintergrund der Gnosis." Pages 77–88 in Tröger, ed., *Gnosis und Neues Testament.*

Puech, H. C., Gilles Quispel, and W. C. van Unnik. *The Jung Codex: A Newly Recovered Gnostic Papyrus*. Translated by F. L. Cross. London: A. R. Mowbray, 1955.

Quispel, Gilles. "The Demiurge in the Apocryphon of John." Pages 1–33 in *Nag Hammadi and Gnosis*. Edited by R. McL. Wilson. Leiden: Brill, 1978.

———. "Gnosis." Pages 413–35 in *Die orientalischen Religionen im Römerreich*, edited by M. J. Vermaseren. Leiden: Brill, 1981.

———. *Gnosis als Weltreligion*. Zurich: Origo, 1951.

———. *Gnostic Studies*. 2 vols. Istanbul: Nederlands Historisch-Archaeologisch Instituut te Istanbul, 1975.

———. "The Origins of the Gnostic Demiurge." Pages 1:271–76 in *Kyriakon: Festschrift for Johannes Quasten*. 2 vols. Leiden: Brill, 1970.

———. "Qumran, John and Jewish Christianity." Pages 137–55 in Charlesworth, ed. *John and Qumran*. Edited by J. H. Charlesworth. London: Geoffrey Chapman, 1972.

———. "Review of J. Frickel, *Hellenistische Erloesung in christlicher Deutung*." *VC* 39 (1985): 186–88.

von Rad, Gerhard. *Old Testament Theology*. New York: Harper, 1962.

Reichers, P. Athanas. *Engel, Tod und Seelenreise: Das Wirken der Geister beim Heimgang des Menschen in der Lehre der alexandrinischen und kappadokischen Väter*. Rome: Edizioni di storia e letteratura, 1955.

Reisenfeld, Harald. *Jésus Transfiguré: L'arrière-Plan Du Récit Évangélique De La Transfiguration De Notre-Seigneur*. Copenhagen: Munksgaard, 1947.

Reitzenstein, Richard. *Hellenistic Mystery Religions: Their Basic Ideas and Significance*. Translated by J. E. Steely. PTS Monographs 15. Pittsburgh: Pickwick, 1978.

———. *Die hellenistischen Mysterienreligionen nach ihren Grundgedanken und Wirkungen*. Leipzig: Teubner, 1910.

———. *Das Iranische Erlösungsmysterium*. Bonn: Marcus & Weber, 1921.

———. *Poimandres: Studien zur Griechischägyptischen und frühchristlichen Literatur*. Leipzig: Teubner, 1904.

———. "Religionsgeschichte und Eschatologie." *ZNW* 13 (1912): 1–28.

Remus, Harold. *Pagan-Christian Conflict over Miracle in the Second Century*. Patristic Monograph Series. Cambridge, Mass.: Philadelphia Patristic Foundation, 1983.

Richardson, Peter. "On the Absence of 'Anti-Judaism' in 1 Corinthians." Pages 59–74 in *Anti-Judaism in Early Christianity*. Vol. 1, *Paul and the Gospels*. Edited by Peter Richardson and D. Granskou. Waterloo, Ont.: Wilfred Laurier University Press, 1986.

Riesenfeld, H. *Jésus Transfiguré: L'arrière-Plan Du Récit Évangélique De La Transfiguration De Notre-Seigneur*. Copenhagen: Munksgaard, 1947.

Robinson, J. M. "Ascension." Pages 1:245–47 in *The Interpreter's Dictionary of the Bible*. Nashville: Abingdon, 1962.

———. *The Nag Hammadi Library in English*. New York: Harper & Row, 1977.

Robinson, J. M., and Helmut Koester. *Trajectories Through Early Christianity*. Philadelphia: Fortress, 1971.

Rohde, Erwin. *Psyche: The Cult of Souls and Belief in Immortality among the Greeks*. Translated by W. B. Willis. London: K. Paul, Trench, Trubner, 1925. Orig. German ed.: 1903.

Rössler, Dietrich. *Gesetz und Geschichte: Untersuchungen zur Theologie der jüdischen Apokalyptik und der pharisäischen Orthodoxie*. WMANT 3. Neukirchen: Neukirchener, 1960.

Rougier, Louis. *L'origine astronomique de la croyance Pythagoricienne en l'immortalité céleste de l'âme*. Le Caire: 1933.

Rowland, Christopher. *The Open Heaven: A Study of Apocalyptic in Judaism and Early Christianity*. London: SPCK, 1982.

Rudolf, Kurt. "Das Problem einer Soziologie und sozialen Verortung der Gnosis." *Kairos* 19 (1977): 35–54.

———. "Stand und Aufgaben in der Erforschung des Gnostizismus." Pages 510–53 in *Gnosis und Gnostizismus*. Edited by K. Rudolf. Darmstadt: Wissenschaftliche Buchgesellschaft, 1975. Orig. pub. Jena: 1963.

Saffrey, Henri, and Lendeert Westerink. *Proclus: Théologie platonicienne*. Vol. 1. Paris: Les Belles Lettres, 1968.

Sanders, E. P. *Jesus and Judaism*. Philadelphia: Fortress, 1985.

———. *Paul, the Law and the Jewish People*. Philadelphia: Fortress, 1983.

———. *Paul and Palestinian Judaism: A Comparison of Patterns of Religion*. Philadelphia: Fortress, 1977.

Sanders, E. P., A. I. Baumgarten, and Alan Mendelson, eds. *Jewish and Christian Self-Definition*. Vol. 2, *Aspects of Judaism in the Greco-Roman Period*. Philadelphia: Fortress, 1981.

Sanders, James. "Torah." Pages 909–11 in *The Interpreter's Dictionary of the Bible: Supplementary Volume*. Edited by V. P. Furnish, K. R. Crim, and L. R. Bailey. Nashville: Abingdon, 1976.

Sandmel, Samuel. *The Genius of Paul*. New York: Farrar, Straus, & Cudahy, 1958.

———. *Judaism and Christian Beginnings*. New York: Oxford University Press, 1978.

———. *Philo of Alexandria: An Introduction*. New York: Oxford University Press, 1979.

Schaeffer, P. *Rivalität zwischen Engeln und Menschen*. Berlin: de Gruyter, 1975.

Schechter, Solomon. *Aspects of Rabbinic Theology*. New York: Schocken, 1961. Orig. pub. 1909.

Schenke, H. M. *Der Gott "Mensch" in der Gnosis: Ein religionsgeschichtlicher Beitrag zur Diskussion über die paulinische Anschauung von der Kirche als Lieb Christ*. Göttingen: Vandenhoeck & Ruprecht, 1962.

Schmiedel, P. W. "Resurrection and Ascension Narratives." Pages 4039–87 in *Encyclopaedia Biblica* 4. London: 1903.

Schoeps, H. J. *Paulus: Die Theologie des Apostels im Lichte der jüdischen Religionsgeschichte*. Tübingen: Mohr Siebeck, 1959.

Scholem, Gershom. "Jaldabaoth Reconsidered." Pages 405–21 in *Mélanges d'Histoire Religions*: *Festschrift H-Ch. Peuch*. Paris: Presses Universitaires, 1974.

———. *Jewish Gnosticism, Merkabah Mysticism, and Talmudic Tradition*. New York: Jewish Theological Seminary of America, 1965.

———. *Major Trends in Jewish Mysticism*. New York: Schocken Books, 1961.

———. "The Merkabah Hymns and The Song of the Kine in a Talmudic Passage." Pages 20–30 in *Jewish Gnosticism, Merkabah Mysticism and Talmudic Tradition*. New York: Jewish Theological Seminary of America, 1965.

———. "Über eine Formel in den koptischgnostischen Schriften." *ZNW* 111 (1931): 170–76.

Schmithals, Walter. *Gnosticism in Corinth: An Investigation of the Letters to the Corinthians*. Translated by John E. Steely. Nashville: Abingdon, 1971.

Schneemelcher, Wilhelm. *New Testament Apocrypha*. Vol. 2, *Writings Relating to the Apostles; Apocalypses and Related Topics*. Translated by R. McL. Wilson. Louisville, Ky.: Westminster, 1965.

Schultz, J. "Angelic Opposition to the Ascension of Moses and the Revelation of the Law." *JQR* 61 (1970/1971): 282–307.

Segal, Alan F. *Paul the Convert: The Apostolate and Apostasy of Saul the Pharisee*. New Haven, Conn.: Yale University Press, 1990.

———. "Rabbinic Polemic and the Radicalization of Gnosticism." *ANRW* 22 (1981).

———. *Rebecca's Children: Judaism and Christianity in the Roman World*. Cambridge, Mass.: Harvard University Press, 1986.

———. *Two Powers in Heaven: Early Rabbinic Reports about Christianity and Gnosticism*. Leiden: Brill, 1977. Repr., Waco, Tex.: Baylor University Press, 2012.

Segal, Robert Alan. *The Poimandres as Myth: Scholarly Theory and Gnostic Meaning*. Religion and Reason 33. Berlin: de Gruyter, 1986.

Simmel, Georg. *Conflict and the Web of Group-Affiliations*. Translated by Kurt Wolff and Reinhard Bendix. New York: Free Press, 1955.

Simon, Marcel. *Verus Israel: Étude sur les relations entre Chrétiens et Juifs dans L'Empire Romain (135–425)*. Paris: de Boccard, 1964.

Skorupski, John. *Symbol and Theory: A Philosophical Study of Theories of Religion in Social Anthropology*. Berkeley: University of California Press, 1976.

Slingerland, H. D. *The Testament of the Twelve Patriarchs: A History of Research*. Missoula, Mont.: Scholars, 1976.

Smith, Jonathan Z. "Good News is No News: Aretalogy and Gospel." Pages 21–38 in Neusner, ed., *Christianity, Judaism, and Other Greco-Roman Cults*. Part 1: *New Testament*.

———. "The Prayer of Joseph." Pages 251–94 in Neusner, ed., *Religions in Antiquity*.

———. "The Temple and the Magician." Pages 233–47 in *God's Christ and His People: Studies in Honor of N. A. Dahl*. Edited by J. Jervell and Wayne A. Meeks. Oslo: Universitetsforlaget, 1977.

Smith, Morton. *Clement of Alexandria and a Secret Gospel of Mark*. Cambridge, Mass.: Harvard University Press, 1973.

———. *Jesus the Magician*. New York: Harper & Row, 1978.

———. "Observations on Hekhaloth Rabbati." Pages 142–60 in *Studies and Texts*. Vol. 1 of *Biblical and Other Studies*. Edited by Alexander Altmann. 2 vols. Cambridge, Mass.: Harvard University Press, 1963.

———. "On the Differences Between the Culture of Israel and the Major Cultures of the Ancient Near East." *JANES* 5 (1973): 389–96.

Sommer, A. Dupont. *Le quatrième livre des Maccabées*. Paris: H. Champion, 1939.

Sperber, Dan. *Rethinking Symbolism*. Translated by A. L. Morton. Cambridge: Cambridge University Press, 1975. Repr., 1975. Orig. French ed., 1974.

Spiegel, Shalom. *The Last Trial: On the Legends and Lore of the Command to Abraham to Offer Isaac As a Sacrifice*. Translated by Judah Goldin. New York: Random House, 1976. Orig. pub. 1950.

———. "Me-Aggadot ha-Akedah: Piyyut 'al shehitat Yizhaq u-tehiyato le-Efrayim mi-Buna." Pages 471–574 in *Alexander Marks: Jubilee Volume on the Occasion of His Seventieth Birthday* (*Sefer Ha-yovel Icvod Alexander Marx*). New York: Jewish Theological Seminary, 1950.

Spiro, Abram. "The Ascension of Phinehas." *PAAJR* 22 (1955): 91–114.

Stauffer, E. "εγω." *TDNT* 2:356–62.

Steindorff, Georg, ed. and trans. *Die Apokalypse des Elias: Eine unbekannte Apokalypse und Bruchstücke der Sophonias-Apokalypse*. Leipzig: 1899.

Stendahl, Krister. "Paul and the Introspective Conscience of the West." *HTR* 56 (1963): 199–215.

———. *Paul among Jews and Gentiles and Other Essays*. Philadelphia: Fortress, 1976.

Swetnam, James. *Jesus and Isaac: A Study of the Epistle to the Hebrews in the Light of the Akedah*. Rome: Pontifical Biblical Institute, 1981.

Talbert, Charles. "The Myth of a Descending-Ascending Redeemer in Mediterranean Antiquity." *NTS* 22 (1977): 418–39.

Taran, Leonardo, ed. and trans. *Parmenides: A Text with Translation, Commentary, and Critical Essay*. Princeton: Princeton University Press, 1965.

Tardieu, Michel. *Trois Mythes Gnostiques. Adam, Éros et les animaux d'Égypte dans un écrit de Nag Hammadi (II, 5)*. Paris: Études augustiniennes, 1974.

Tavenner, Eugene. *Studies in Magic from Latin Literature*. New York: Columbia University Press, 1916.

Teixidor, Javier. *The Pagan God: Popular Religion in the Greco-Roman Near East*. Princeton: Princeton University Press, 1977.

Temporini, Hildegard. *Die Frauen am Hofe Trajans: Ein Beitrag zur Stellung der Augustae im Principat*. Berlin: de Gruyter, 1979.

Theissen, Gerd. "The Strong and the Weak in Corinth." Pages 121–43 in *The Social Setting of Pauline Christianity: Essays on Corinth*. Edited and translated by J. H. Shütz. Philadelphia: Fortress, 1982. Orig. pub. 1974.

———. *Urchristliche Wundergeschichten: Ein Beitrag zur formgeschichtlichen Erforschung der synoptischen Evangelien*. Gütersloh: Mohn, 1974.

Tiede, David L. *The Charismatic Figure as Miracle Worker*. SBLDS. Missoula, Mont.: Scholars, 1972.

Tisserant, E., trans. *Ascension d'Isaie: Traduction de la version Éthiopienne*. Paris: Letouzey et Ané, 1909.

Tröger, K., ed. *Gnosis und Neues testament: Studien aus Religionswissenschaft und Theologie*. Berlin: Evangelische Verlagsanstalt, 1973.

Turdeanu, E. "Le 'Testament d'Abraham' en slave et en roumain." *Oxford Slavonic Papers* 10 (1977): 1–38.

Turner, C. H. "ὁ ὑιος μου ὁ ἀγαπητός." *JTS* 27 (1926): 113–29.

Turner, Victor. *Drama, Fields and Metaphors*. Ithaca, N.Y.: Cornell University Press, 1974.

Urbach, Ephraim E. *The Sages: Their Concepts and Beliefs*. Jerusalem: Magnes, 1975.

———. "Teshubat Anshe Ninevah ve-Havikuah Ha-Yehudi-Nozri." *Tarbiz* 20 (1950): 118–22.

Vermaseren, M. J. *Études préliminaires aux religions orientales dans l'Empire Romaín*. Leiden: Brill, 1961–

———. *Mithras: The Secret God*. New York: Barnes & Noble, 1963.

Vermes, Geza. *Scripture and Tradition in Judaism*. Leiden: Brill, 1961.

Wagner, S. M. "Religious Nonconformity in Ancient Jewish Life." Ph.D. diss., Yeshiva University, 1964.

Walker, William O. "The Origin of the Son of Man Concept as Applied to Jesus." *JBL* 91 (1972): 482–90.

Wax, Rosalie, and Murray Wax. "The Magical World View." *JSSR* 1 (1962): 179–88.

———. "The Notion of Magic." *Current Anthropology* 4 (1963): 495–503.

Weisenberg, E. J. "The Liturgical term *Melekh Ha-'Olam*." *JJS* 15 (1964): 1–56.

Weiss, H. F. *Untersuchungen zur Kosmologie des hellenistischen und palästinischen Judentums*. TUGAL 97. Berlin: Akademie, 1966.

Weiss, J. G. "On the Formula *Melekh Ha-'Olam* as Anti-Gnostic Protest." *JJS* 10 (1959): 169–71.

Weiss-Halivni, David. "On the Supposed Anti-Asceticism or Anti-Naziritism of Simon the Just." *JQR* 58 (1968): 243–52.

Weizsäcker, C. "Die Theologie des Märtyrers Justinus." *Jahrbücher für deutsche Theologie* 13 (1867): 63.

Werblowsky, R. J. Z. "Structure and Archetype." Pages 435–42 in *Festschrift for T. Gaster = Journal of the Ancient Near Eastern Society of Columbia* 5 (1973).

West, E. W., ed. *Pahlavi Texts*. Part 1: *The Bundahis, Bahman Yast, and Shayast La-Shayast*. Sacred Books of the East 5. Oxford: Clarendon, 1880.

———, ed. *Pahlavi Texts*. Part 3: *Dina-I Mainog-i Khirad, Sikand-gumanik Vigar, and the Sad Dar*. Sacred Books of the East 24. Oxford: Clarendon, 1885.

Westerholm, Stephen. "Torah, Nomos, and Law: A Question of 'Meaning.'" *Studies in Religion/Sciences Religieuses* 15, no. 3 (1986): 327–36.

Widengren, Geo. *The Ascension of the Apostle and the Heavenly Book*. Vol. 3 of *King and Saviour: Studies in Manichaen, Mandaean, and Syrian-gnostic Religion*. Uppsala: Uppsala Universitets Årsskrift, 1950, 1957.

Wilson, Reid. *Genealogy and History in the Biblical World*. New Haven, Conn.: Yale University Press, 1976.

Wilson, S. G. "The Ascension: A Critique and an Interpretation." *ZNW* 59 (1968): 269–81.

Windisch, Hans. *The Spirit-Paraclete in the Fourth Gospel*. Translated by J. Cox. Philadelphia: Fortress, 1968.

Wisse, Frederik. "The Redeemer Figure in the Paraphrase of Shem." *NovT* 12 (1970): 130–40.

Wolfson, Harry. *Philo: Foundations of Religious Philosophy in Judaism, Christianity, and Islam*. 2 vols. Cambridge: Cambridge University Press, 1947.

———. "The Pre-existent Angel of the Magharians and Al-Nahawandi." *JQR* 11 (1960): 89–106.

Wrede, William. "Paulus." Pages 1–97 in *Das Paulusbild*. Edited by R. Rengstorf. Darmstadt: Wissenschaftliche Buchsgesellschaft, 1907.

Yamauchi, E. M. "Jewish Gnosticism? The Prologue of John, Mandaean Parallels, and the Trimorphic Protennoia." Pages 467–97 in van den Broek and Vermaseren, eds., *Studies in Gnosticism*.

———. *Pre-Christian Gnosticism: A Survey of the Proposed Evidence*. Grand Rapids: Eerdmans, 1973.

Yassif, Eli, ed. *The Sacrifice of Isaac: Studies in the Development of a Literary Tradition*. Jerusalem: Makor, 1978.

Zeron, Alexander. "The Martyrdom of Phineas-Elijah." *JBL* 98 (1979): 99–100.

Zimmerli, Walther, and Joachim Jeremias. *The Servant of God*. Translated by Harold Knight. London: SCM Press, 1957.

INDEX OF PRIMARY SOURCES

Apocrypha/Pseudepigrapha

Dead Sea Scrolls

Rabbinic Writings

Nag Hammadi Codices

Other Ancient Sources

MODERN AUTHOR INDEX